HOW TO WIN *ANY* SLOGAN COMPETITION

ANGELINA KAYE

DEDICATION

'Knowledge itself is power'
Francis Bacon 1561–1626

I wish to dedicate this book to my parents Rosa and Zenon, without whom I would never have known the joy of the congratulatory letter or L.W.E. (long white envelope) as it is known amongst fellow 'compers'. Also, I will never forget my dear and trusted friends whose support and enthusiasm will always be invaluable throughout my life.

Editor: Beatrice Frei
Design and Layout: Stonecastle Graphics Ltd.

The Work Copyright © Angelina Kaye, 1994

The right of Angelina Kaye to be identified as the Author of this Work has been asserted in accordance with the Copyright, Design & Patents Act 1988.

First published in 1994 by
Guinness Publishing Ltd.
This Publication Copyright ©
Guinness Publishing Ltd., 1994
33 London Road, Enfield, Middlesex.

'GUINNESS' is a registered trade mark of Guinness Publishing Ltd.

Typeset in Great Britain by
Ace Filmsetting Ltd, Frome, Somerset
Printed and bound in Great Britain by
Cox & Wyman Ltd.

A catalogue record for this book is available from the British Library

ISBN 0–85112–751–7

CONTENTS

(**KEY WORD** and CATEGORY)

ACCESSORIES **ACCOMPANIMENT** ACCOUNT **ACTING ADVANTAGE AHEAD** ANIMALS **ANYWHERE AUTOMATIC AWAY**

BAGSFUL BANK BARE BARGAIN BEAT BENEFITS BEST & BETTER BIRTHDAY BISCUITS, CAKES & CRACKERS BREAD & CEREALS **BREAK BREAKTHROUGH BRIGHTEN BRILLIANT** BRITISH **BUY**

CALENDAR **CALL CAPITAL** CAPTION CAR, ENGINES & TRANSPORT **CARE CARNIVAL & PARTY CHALLENGE** CHAMPAGNE **CHAMPION** CHARACTER **CHOICE CHOOSE** CHRISTMAS **CLEAN** CLEANERS COFFEE **COMBINATION** COMMUNITY COMPUTER COSMETICS COSTS COUNTRIES, CITIES & TOWNS **CRACKERS** CREDIT CARD **CUT**

DAIRY **DANCING DELIGHTFUL** DIAMOND **DIFFERENCE DIFFERENT** DISH DISNEY **DISTINCTION** DO-IT-YOURSELF **DOUBLE DREAM**

EASY ENJOY EXCELLENT EXCITING EXHILARATING

FAMILY FAMOUS PEOPLE FARM FRESH **FAVOURITE FIESTA FINISH FIRST** FISH **FIXED FLAVOUR FLOCK FLYING FORTUNE** FREEZERS **FRESHNESS FRIEND FUTURE**

GASTRONOMY **GET ON DOWN GOLD & TREASURE GOOD LIFE GREAT**

HAPPY & FUN HARVEST & FRUIT HEALTH & FITNESS **HELPS HIT** HOLIDAY HORTICULTURE

I COULD . . . IDEA IDEAL IMAGINATION **IMPORTANT IN . . . INSIST** INVENT **IS . . . ITEM**

JUICES

KEY

LANDMARK LEADERS LIKE LIMERICKS & RHYMES **LIMIT LINK LOOK & LOOK GOOD LORD, KING & QUEEN LOVE LUXURY**

MACHINERY **MAGIC** MAN **MEANS** MEAT MEET **MILES MILLION** MISCELLANEOUS **MIX IT MORE MUSIC**

NAME **NATURAL NEED NUMBER ONE NUTS**

OCCASION **OUTDOOR**

PARADISE PARTNERS PASSPORT PERFECT PERFORMANCE PERFORMERS PERSONALITY **PICTURE &** **FILM PLAY PLEASURE PLUS** POCKET GUIDE **POPULAR** POWER **PREFER PREMIUM**

QUALITY QUICK

RACE ON RECOMMEND REFRESHING REGULAR REMEMBER REMINDS RESULTS RIDING & CYCLING RIGHT ROAD ROBBERY & CRIME ROCK **ROMANCE**

SAFE SAILING SATELLITE SAUCES SAVING & INVESTING SCHOOL SHEEP **SHINES** SHOES **SHOP & SHOPPING SHOWER** SIGN & SIGHT **SIMPLE SING SIZZLING** SLIMMING **SMILE** SNACKS **SNOOKERED SOPHISTICATION SOUNDS SPECIAL SPICE** SPIRITS & DRINKS SPORT SPREADS **STANDARD STAR START STAYING STICK & STUCK** STORES **STYLE, LIFESTYLE & IMAGE SUITS** SUN & SUNSHINE SWEETS **SWITCHED ON**

TASTE TEA **TEAM TEMPTED** TENNIS **TERROR THINK TICKET** TIGHTS & STOCKINGS **TIME & DATES TO ...** TOBACCO **TOGETHER** TOILETRIES **TOP TOP SCORE TRADITION** TRAIL & TRACK **TRAVEL** TREASURE **TUNED**

UNBEATABLE UNDERWEAR **USE**

VALUE VEGETABLES **VIEW VISIT**

WATCH WEAR WEIGHT **WICKED** WILD WEST **WIN WINNER WINNING** WINTER **WITHOUT** WOMAN **WONDERLAND WORLD**

ZEALOUS

COMPETITION
(Your chance to win a copy of every book published by Guinness in 1994 – worth over £600.)

INTRODUCTION

The art of winning a prize by entering a consumer competition has, and always will be, a skill and as with any skill, practice makes perfect. Anyone can learn the skill of winning prizes in competitions and over the last 23 years the author, who is completely self-taught, has done exactly that. Every year there are many thousands (if not millions) of poundsworth of prizes just waiting to be won by the average consumer and it is no wonder that this hobby continues to become more and more popular each year.

Of course, there are literally thousands of products available to consumers and at various times most major manufacturers and stores have held promotions, mainly aimed at introducing the consumer to a product with the quite deliberate aim of increasing sales.

There are, of course, various other types of consumer competitions such as lotteries, raffles and draws but this book concentrates on those requiring the entrant to compose a slogan, often as a tie-break.

The author has never met anyone who does not enjoy the thrill of being a winner and this book merely highlights the fact that such an achievement is certainly not beyond anyone's reach.

The purpose of the book is both to provide further help for those who consider themselves well seasoned competitors, and to encourage new competitors to improve their initially primitive slogans. The many slogans featured should encourage everyone to use their own imagination when completing a slogan. There is no more satisfying feeling than to create a new and original slogan of one's very own, one which has not appeared before, and which, even if it does not prove successful initially, might be modified for use in another competition. Originality stands out a mile.

The first time you receive the letter informing you that you have won a prize is always memorable. Luck does play a part in consumer competitions but in general the more knowledge and experience you collect the less you will rely solely on luck. Willingness to learn and tenacity are some of the most essential ingredients of any competitor. No competitor can guarantee to be a consistent winner because every competition is to some extent a gamble, dependent on the quality, originality and number of entries in any promoter's postbag. Whether the gamble pays off for you is indeed one of the most exciting and baffling mysteries you will ever encounter.

If you have never attempted to make up a slogan, now is the time to begin. The author wishes you good luck, urges you to be persistent and hopes your efforts will be rewarded.

NOTES AND COMMENTS

1   Words appearing in round brackets within a slogan are the author's comments. The author has not sought to be judgmental of any slogan although in some cases felt that special praise had to be given to those which were obviously truly inspired.

2   Some words appear in brackets in capital letters at the end of a slogan e.g. *(BORDEAUX SUPERIOR = ACROSTIC)* [page 249]. An ACROSTIC is made up by using the first letter from all the words in a tiebreaker sentence, or sometimes just part of it to form a phrase or a well known brand name. This is the slogan from which the acrostic BORDEAUX SUPERIOR comes: 'They are Beautiful, Original, Robust yet Delicate, Exceptionally Aromatic, Usually Xceptional, Sometimes Unusual but Perfectly Elegant, Rarely Improvable, Otherwise Remarkable'. Acrostics do not necessarily have to be in proper sequence either, as in the acrostic (IBSTO) in the section of Sauces [page 171] which spells out an anagram of the product name i.e. Bisto. To help you recognise an acrostic made up by a competition entrant, all words making an acrostic sentence, phrase or jumbled brand name throughout this book begin with a capital letter. Acrostics are simply a clever way of adding something extra to a slogan, other than just quoting one sentence to praise a brand name, shop or product.

3   Some slogans appear on more than one page of this book, under different headings. This is because the tiebreaker might use a key word but the general subject matter is also part of a much broader category, e.g. BREAD and BEST as mentioned in the lead-in sentence 'Countryman bread is best because . . .' [page 27]. The same group of slogans appear in the key word BEST and also in the BREAD & CEREALS category [pages 34]. This is to help you appreciate that more help can be gained by looking in different sections, rather than just considering one key word or category. This can be especially useful when you have recognised the product slot but may need help from more than one section in the book.

4   When trying to find inspiration for a slogan, it can be helpful to take into account the type of prize on offer. For instance the lead-in sentence 'Moët & Chandon, Britain's best selling champagne is a WINNER because . . .' superbly justifies the slogan 'It's the thoroughbred that leads the field' [page 367] (Prizes – Day at the Races with a Champagne Lunch). The slogan not only uses the word thoroughbred, i.e. something that implies a first class or winning commodity, but also takes into account the subject of the prize, i.e. horse racing.

5   It is always worth remembering that no matter how clever or ordinary some of these published slogans appear to be, they all have one thing in common: they have all won a prize for the entrant who has sent it in.

Please note: Slogans have been reproduced as submitted by entrants; some may be grammatically incorrect.

SEVEN EASY STEPS TO COMPLETING A SLOGAN COMPETITION

If you have ever been put off entering a consumer competition because you think you don't have a chance of making up a winning slogan, just remember this: you have as much chance as anyone else entering the same competition – and here's how it's done!

One day I saw a competition on the back of a box of cereal at a supermarket. The prizes offered were really attractive: there were 100 portable CD players and 200 cassette recorders, making a total of 300 prizes in all (the cereal was Kellogg's Frosties). The competition was to be held in four separate judging stages and the prizes were divided accordingly. It was an opportunity not to be missed. Already in my mind I could imagine receiving the parcel from the postman and playing my favourite music on the prize I had won in this competition (you need a good imagination to do competitions!).

Reading the rules on the entry form, I saw that I first had to answer three music questions and then make up an appropriate slogan – I couldn't wait to have a go.

STEP 1   Read the competition rules on the packet and make sure you understand them all. Remember that if you break any of the rules then no prize will reach your door.

STEP 2   The most essential factor you will have to take into account in any lead-in sentence is to find the KEY WORD. This is the word on which your slogan must be based. Here the lead-in sentence from which you were expected to make a slogan read: 'Tony the Tiger and I love the gr-r-reat taste of Frosties because . . .' The key word is LOVE: you are asked to explain why Tony and yourself LOVE the great taste of Kellogg's Frosties. In any competition your biggest difficulty is to recognise the key word in a lead-in sentence. Sometimes it can be a verb and other times it can be a noun. When you have mastered this skill, you will be thinking along the right lines when completing your slogan. If you read through the rest of this book, you will find many examples to help you develop the skill of recognising a key word.

So, for competitions connected with music and love, look at the key word section of LOVE in this book and also the various other sections connected with music in some way.

STEP 3   After reading the rules properly, I found I was expected to complete the lead-in sentence (or tie-breaker) in NOT MORE THAN 12 WORDS in an APT way. The word apt here means APPROPRIATE. You are therefore asked to give an appropriate slogan of 12 words – less than 12 words if possible but most definitely not more than 12 words under any circumstances. This is known as taking into account the CRITERIA of the lead-in sentence. Every good set of rules will always give criteria to help you stick to what is required, so that you do not work along the wrong lines. You can never be sure whether judges will count contractions (can't, won't, it's, etc.) as two words or one word, so to be on the safe side, always count each contraction you use as two words. It is perfectly acceptable for you to use contractions in your slogans and there are some good examples throughout this book.

STEP 4   Write down the lead-in sentence on a big sheet of paper. This is where you will write all your immediate thoughts and ideas which you think are relevant to the slogan and which should eventually come together to form some sort of sensible slogan.

Therefore, after considering these first few points it was fairly logical for me to assume that the key word LOVE could in some way be connected to music, although this was just one of a number of ideas relevant to what was required. A good lead-in sentence should give you many different ideas of how a slogan can be tackled, although the key word should never be ignored. Therefore, in this instance, I chose to connect the LOVE theme with the music theme, using popular love songs which could be altered slightly in meaning and which would also refer to Kellogg's Frosties in some way. Not having such a good memory of the many popular love songs available, I knew I needed help, so I made straight for my copy of *British Hit Singles* from Guinness which gave me plenty of inspiration. On a regular basis, I jotted down ideas straight out of my head on to my work sheet which soon began to look something like this:

love   Eros (Cupid)   song   attractive   infatuation

'bow'-ls   CD-uctive   dip into bowl   milli-ki vanilli

sugar frosting   crunchy   creamy   dreamy   Bananarama

Right Said Fred   Valentine   lips   music   beat

Venus Goddess of Love   mouth   smacker

No matter how silly you think your first ideas are, the more of them you jot down, the more probable it will be that you finally reach some really clever and appropriate ones. A point to bear in mind, however, is that your first ideas might well also be the first ideas of many other people. Good slogan-making is about originality; a judge doesn't want to read the same slogan many times. In order to get your slogan noticed, the thing to remember is that you must produce something just a bit different from all the other entrants – who hope to win the prize as much as you do!

STEP 5   It is also quite a good idea to look at the general theme of the competition and take into account the prizes on offer as these can often help you to understand what might be wanted in your slogan. Also, if you can, take a good look at the packaging of the brand or advertisements on TV showing the same product. If the competition is printed on a separate entry form, then look closely at the entry form for further clues. All these avenues can help to give you a wider range of ideas.

In this particular instance, the packet showed a picture of Tony the Tiger with a big bowl of Kellogg's Frosties. It also showed a CD player and a cassette recorder. Other places to look for inspiration might have been Kellogg's advertisements on TV and other slogans in this book connected to love and music.

STEP 6   After the hard work of sorting out my ideas and putting them into proper sentences by way of what I thought were apt slogans, I decided to submit each of the following:

1. So CD-uctive, they're deeply dippy and too crunchy for their packets.

2. Tony, Me and Venus like ours with Banana-rama.

3. They have an itsy, bitsy, teeny, weeny, sugar frosting, really dreamy.

I then neatly filled in my entry forms which had been carefully cut from the Frosties packets.

STEP 7   When I had done all the above steps, I posted my forms in good time for the first judging session. I had noted that it also said on the packet that any entries not winning in the first judging session would be carried forward to subsequent judging sessions, which was obviously an advantage. It was not too long before I received news of the following prizes in the competition.

Slogan number **1.** won a cassette recorder in the first judging session

Slogan number **2.** won a CD player in the first judging session

Slogan number **3.** won a CD player in the second judging session

I am sure you will agree that the above slogans were apt to what was required in relation to the lead-in sentence and did interpret what the key word was. Each slogan used love songs together with a positive description of Kellogg's Frosties. Because I had followed the rules properly and had understood what was wanted from the competition, my efforts were fully rewarded.

So, the next time you are in a supermarket, or see a competition leaflet in a shop, garage or in the many other places where forms can be found, the above steps will perhaps give you enough confidence to have a go. Once you have tackled these seven easy steps, then further inspiration and understanding should come from reading the rest of the book. Let me assure you that if I can do it, you can do it too. All it takes is a little practice and a lot of dedication but the rewards can be very high. If this hobby is new to you, my advice is to treat every competition as a new challenge, with the exciting prospect of a prize coming your way, and you should always have a lot of fun with the hobby.

Quick Summary

1. Read the rules.
2. Find the Key Word.
3. Understand the criteria of your slogan.
4. Jot down ideas and thoughts.
5. Take into account prizes offered, consult brand packaging, adverts, the competition form itself, and other slogans for inspiration.
6. When happy with slogan and answers to questions, fill in form.
7. Post off entries in good time before closing date.

ACCESSORIES

▶ **Unipart accessories make great gifts because...**

PRODUCT: *Car parts*

They keep motorists in gear

ACCOMPANIMENT

▶ **Cranberry sauce is the perfect ACCOMPANIMENT to my Christmas turkey because...**

PRODUCT: *Cranberry sauce*
COMPETITION: *Ocean Spray cranberry sauce*
PRIZES: *Christmas hampers*

Fruity, juicy, sharp yet sweet, makes any turkey taste unique
The rich fruit, the bright berry, Ocean Spray makes Christmas merry
Its fruity flavour enhances the day, but only if it's Ocean Spray
The best part of tradition is Ocean Spray's addition
No doubt about it – can't eat my turkey without it!
Cranberry sauce by Ocean Spray compliments turkey in every way
The perfect partners for Christmas Day, turkey served with Ocean Spray
The cost is nominal, the taste phenomenal
The cranberries in Ocean Spray keep the taste buds popping on Christmas Day
Ocean Spray is 'jolly' fruity - turns our bird into a festive beauty
All the trimmings I can boast, if Ocean Spray completes my roast
Christmas turkey isn't dressed, unless it wears the 'berry' best
My dish of the day is 'made' with Ocean Spray
Always fresh, always sound, always a joy to pass around
Our Christmas wouldn't be Merry, without this little red berry
Ocean Spray on Christmas Day, delicious in its 'saucy' way

▶ **My perfect ACCOMPANIMENT to Safeway wine is...**

PRODUCT: *Wine*
COMPETITION: *Safeway/Holidays in Cotswolds/Wine*
PRIZES: *Weekends in Cotswolds/Year's supply of wine*

A few good friends, simple fare, highlighting quality that's beyond compare
Congenial company, first class meal, with Safeway's selection setting the seal
A simple meal prepared with flair, enhancing a vin never ordinaire
Lively music, a Safeway's platter, lots of friends and lots of chatter

ACCOUNT

▶ **The Co-operative Bank/Top Tier High Interest Access Savings Account is ideal for my savings because...**

PRODUCT: *Savings Account*
PRIZES: *Weekends for two in New York to see Pavarotti*

It puts my 'notes' into the right 'band'
They credit me with more than intelligence

▶ **I have an Abbey National Instant Saver Account because...**

PRODUCT: *Savings Account*
FIRST PRIZE: *Rover 216 GSi car*

Be it mattress, floorboards, any little nook, there's nothing to beat my little red book

SECOND PRIZE: *Caribbean cruise*

It suits my favour, to be a classic Instant Saver

THIRD PRIZES: *Roman holidays*

Being a money saving kind of fella, I'll always choose the Abbey National umbrella
Its flexibility, its accessibility, its apparent profitability, to me add up to super suitability
While I make my dough, your vital ingredients ensure my bread rises
For easy access, it's just the ticket, for investors' rates you just can't lick it
Abbey National Instant Savers, can do themselves financial favours

FOURTH PRIZES: *Television and video sets*

It's an easy instant way, to draw on your funds without delay
The nest egg there, will with care, expand to that 'bird in the hand'
When I invest, I want the best and being rational – I choose Abbey National
The money has got to last, but when I want it, I want it fast
I know my best interests are served by your better interests
To every saver, large or small, Instant Saver is fair for all
Home or away – coast to coast, your savings are there when you need them most
It's interesting on every level!
In a nutshell, saving is tremendous with the Abbey National tree – branches everywhere
Unlike the pound and ERM, I'm locked into a rate that's more competitive!

FIFTH PRIZES: *£500 store vouchers*

I get fast transactions, plus high interest rates of exchange, guaranteed satisfaction from staff expertly trained

For once I don't mind getting six of the best
A visit to town is not complete, without the friendly smiles and conversations
    with staff
Its 'one for all' means more for me, Instant Saver is my cup of tea
I have no need to speculate, just appreciate
It's like joining a club – at least all my friends talk Abbey, a nice language
If in the Abbey you place your trust, the Instant Saver is a must
It has always been my treasure chest, it's safe, secure and pays the best
Nothing's lost, only gained, when money's withdrawn, the interest's retained
With my hard-earned pence, cared for with Abbey's sense, the lifetime benefits
    are immense
Even the pyramids began with one brick, with Abbey's help, I'll get there quick
You can become a Big Saver in an instant
Abbey's big hit for six, means endless boundaries for Instant Savers
In this galaxy they are the best, their interest rates eclipse the rest
I'm rational, I go national – Abbey National
It achieves a place in the race against inflation and deserves a 'National Medal'
It's quick and up-to-date, the more you save, the better the rate
Old Abbey habits die hard
I like to see my savings swell, I like the extra interest as well
My money's always handy and that's just dandy
Home or away, work or play, Abbey National do it my way
I see my money mount, and the more it mounts, the more I count
You can draw up to £250 per day – no notice and penalties to pay
It's discerning, keeping my money earning, knowing the more I'm saving the
    more I'm gaining
Choice is up to us; banking we do trust; an Instant Saver is a must

SIXTH PRIZES: Weekend breaks

Money is safe, it will grow, if I want it, you won't say no!
It is nifty, thrifty and absolute simplicity for anyone over fifty
Money is so hard to get, I need it safe, I never bet
It's a wonderful way to look after my pay
A little saved each day, keeps the bailiff away
As a young saver, Abbey National will help to make me wealthy one day
The Abbey's great, it's bang up to date, no need to fret about the rate
Lots of branches, nice and bright, open most days, that's just right
Saving my pennies, also pounds, in Instant Saver, they grow in leaps and
    bounds
My capital's at hand as I climb from band to band
If saver or spender be, Abbey helps you instantly
Whichever division you're in, you still can't fail to score without any penalties
Instant Saver, instant cash, come and join the Abbey Nash!
Daddie says wun day it will help pay four mi educashun
With all the benefits coming my way, with the Abbey National I shall stay
I am young, maybe a little bit foolish, but sensible enough to be Abbey
By all accounts this is the one for interested parties

My money must work hard to be ready to play
Without the competition, I'm on a winner anyway
A pound in my account lasts longer than two in my purse!
I can bank on this account and take all the credit
Demands to meet, bills to pay, relax, just have an Abbey day
Start low, aim high, saving with Abbey to reach the sky
It's six steps to heaven and heaven's what I'm saving for – a car!
For the rewards that I seek, it allows me to reap!
To be young and to have some fun, Abbey National is the one!
Saving the Abbey National way keeps unexpected money troubles at bay
It's a definite saviour, for my impulsive behaviour
Money needed, no need to wait, balance left at an excellent rate
I like to have Abbey Christmases, Abbey birthdays, Abbey holidays and one big
    Abbey family
The money grows so I can play, or keep it safe for a rainy day
I prefer yourselves and work in a bank – now that could cost me my job!
Save or spend, Abbey National is my flexible friend
My mattress is too high already
It grows as you feed it, but there if you need it
It's so simple to use, with nothing to lose
It is another basket for my eggs
I like to stash my cash with the Abbey Nash!
Be you shy or a raver, you're treated best as an Abbey National Saver
It reminds me of a good husband, easy to understand, versatile and earns
    increasingly more
With very great ease, I save and withdraw just as I please
It's all gain and no pain!
Of all my habits, Abbey National is the best
Its flexibility is the key, to even greater wealth for me
It makes my money grow, and keeps me in the know
This habit's no dead loss, the interest's in increasing dosh
It is the friend of my cheque account which gets hungry and needs feeding
I am a senior citizen and say it is first class for us golden oldies
With the Abbey habit, a burglar cannot grab it
TV's broken – who cares? Video's kaput – not impressed? Thank goodness the
    Abbey shows more interest

SEVENTH PRIZES: Portable CD players

It may not have much in at the moment but it's got a great future
It has six 'tiers' so I'm all smiles, whatever the balance
Saving the Abbey National way, makes every day bright and gay
If you spend your money when you get it, growing older you'll regret it
Of instant awareness, of everyday needs, pyramid saving at interesting speeds
Instant cash is always at hand, in places I visit throughout the land
Any sum, big or small, Instant Saver saves them all
I need reliable financial growth in an unreliable world
From cradle to the grave, there's always money I have saved

Instant Saver and me – we're a fabulous mix, together one day, we'll reach level six!

You can't help but rejoice, with such an excellent choice

They make saving a pleasure and reward you with treasure

I invest with the best and stay impressed

The money they pay can't be beat, anywhere on the High Street

Of the friendly staff with jolly smiles, you find no hidden charges – not for miles

Putting money in my Abbey account, I like to watch the figures mount

I want a new car, so when I am seventeen I can travel far

Courteous care with every transaction, forty years' saving with complete satisfaction

It annually gives me many Abbey returns

For atmosphere beyond compare, the staff involved make you welcome there

With quick deposits, large or small, Abbey National suits us all

Whether mother, father, teenager, tot, this account is for the lot

It's an 'abit I'm 'Abbey' to 'ave

Wherever I am across the land, I know my money is always at hand

I would have to go a mile, to find a better account for my lifestyle

Having my money around me, to protect and surround me, really is important

I always copy the habits of my mum and dad

It lets me dip in when I want to splash out

INstant Savers Trust Abbey National Terms *(INSTANT = ACROSTIC)*

It's quick, easy, no need to think, with a piece of plastic called the Abbeylink

When the money's in, you're in the money

Heads or tails, I'm a winner, it really is a money spinner

Some people's peaks are the highest mountains, mine is the £25,000

Abbey National Plc, have the best commercial on TV

The Abbey National way, helps my money work, invest and pay

I've put Instant Saver to the test and I find it comes out best

It's like having a gold mine in your High Street

It's there when I need it and when I need it, it's there

An Abbey customer is a happy customer

I am a saver now I am seven, I'll be rich when I'm eleven

It's logical, it's rational, it's Abbey National

I Need To Enjoy Realistic, Exciting, Saving Targets *(INTEREST = ACROSTIC)*

I was fed up with finding IOUs in my money box

By paying into my Instant Saver, I'm doing my future a big favour

Pounds count in rising amounts and I'll never sink with my Abbeylink

I like to watch my money grow, so Abbey National is the place to go

They'd keep my money I did fear, mummy says it's a good idea

I'm saving enough for future years, if I don't win I'd be in tears

Instant Saver is an anagram of 'an invest star' (*now that's clever!)

It's high powered and geared to ride the recession!

In for a penny, in for a pound, Abbey rates still amongst the best around

Next year we are getting married and that is for life, so is Abbey National

I'm a reformed saver, not a raver, who wants a better life saver?

Whilst the seeds are growing into a garden, I can still enjoy picking the flowers

Alas, on trees money doesn't grow, I need a safe haven for my dough

I get good honest banking, no fuss, my money cared for by people I trust

It copes with my wealth's ups and downs better than I do

With as little as a pound, I had nothing to lose and everything to gain

You don't get withdrawal symptoms

Although I have a little, it could become a lot

My grandparents being so very wise, secured for me a growing 18th birthday surprise

With many levels of interest payable; easily accessible; instantly available; can't be bettered – that's unassailable

I want a pyramid as big as Tutankhamen's, I'm with the best builders

I can pay my money in with ease and getting it out is a breeze

My parents got to the top with Abbey and I would like to follow them

It's my passbook to success

On balance, it's clearly better

This outlay on payday is brainy, with no panic on days that are rainy

It makes my money grow, more than any other bank I know

When I put in the dough, it soon starts to grow

For investors, it stacks up to a great deal

It's the convenient way for living today

Large or small, all savings count, it offers good interest on any amount

I know my money's secure and will surely grow, friendly service and easy cash flow

It lets me save all my pounds and pennies, and helps my dreams become realities

Although I'm a hard-up student, this account helps me to be prudent

It's the place for my cash, no-one else can match

I only have a small amount of money, so every little helps

I wanted my cash safe and sound, and the Abbey sounded the best all round

It suits me just fine, when I can withdraw at any time

I take upward steps to make my money work for me

Life doesn't bring instant rewards but my Instant Saver account does

No matter how my savings go up or down, there will always be extra pounds

I always feel steady with some cash at the ready

I Sphinx honestly, it's the best policy!

It is Absolutely Brilliant Bringing Earnings Yearly *(ABBEY = ACROSTIC)*

It's tailored to suit your pocket and fits comfortably

It makes my life a little Abbier

With interest rates high and service fast, the Abbey National is unsurpassed

It builds my future, while I build my present

Abbey a fool not to have one

ACTING

▶ **Men just can't help ACTING on Impulse because…**

PRODUCT: Perfumed body spray

They ignore common scents
It's a fragrance they cannot resist this warm, feminine sensuous mist
Whilst blended to freshen, it excites indiscretion
Its sure allure has no known cure
The fragrant persistence lowers their resistance
The perfume's terrific, the effect stunning, a welcome addition to feminine
cunning

ADVANTAGE

▶ **Add a sixth ADVANTAGE of Anchor Half Fat…**

PRODUCT: Low fat butter
COMPETITION: Half Fat Anchor
FIRST PRIZES: Sony Camcorders

The spread's in the taste – not in the waist
Convenience, taste and price, make 'Half Fat Anchor' really nice
Half the fat, all the action, full of Anchor satisfaction
Don't look like a tanker, go for Half Fat Anchor
Tasty, tempting and delicious, better for you and really nutritious

SECOND PRIZES: Sony Watchman TVs

Its popularity is spreading
Healthy, tasty, full of 'vits', helps smooth out the bumpy bits!
Cholesterol's aweigh with Half Fat each day
It anchors you to a healthier lifestyle
Be healthy, wealthy, happy too, Anchor butter's best for you
Lots and lots of lovely taste, very very little waist
A low fat start for a healthier heart
Natural goodness oozing through, only Anchor cows will do
With the Anchor tradition, you're spreading nutrition

RUNNERS-UP: Three Sony video tapes

Anchors aweigh, Half Fat rules the day
50% less fat but still 100% Anchor quality
Buttery taste passing my lips, eternally slim, pat-able hips
Helps reduce your size and stops spread on your thighs
Let's spread the moo's, it's Anchor you should choose
When trying to slim, Half Fat Anchor helps you win

Half Fat Anchor – it won't weigh you down
It helps breed healthier heifers – and that's no bull!
In its 'field' it's an outright winner
This palatable treasure, gives me twice as much pleasure
Spreads on the bread, not on the hips
The taste of butter without the bulge
Anchor onto Half Fat, your pounds will sail away
With toast, bun and bread, there's less cholesterol spread
Not a butter substitute but a slimmer's treat without dispute
Its heavenly flavour doesn't cost the earth
Smooth texture, smooth taste, less fat, less waist
For an all-action life, Anchor's better by half
This popular pack helps prevent a heart attack
It's butter by half
A keep-you-slimmer knife edge thriller
It's no secret, Anchor has healthy goodness under wraps
Half Fat, but not half-hearted
An unrivalled favourite with parents and kids alike
It's got everything except an equal
Once hooked on Half Fat you swallow the Anchor
Holds its own against a tide of opposition
Crump-it, Jack-it! Half Fat's the tick-et!
The Anchor I've chosen can also be frozen

AHEAD

▶ **Thomas Cook travellers' cheques and Girobank are streaks AHEAD at the Post Office because...**

PRODUCT: Travellers' cheques
COMPETITION: Thomas Cook/Girobank

Their track record leaves other competitors behind in the starting grid
There's no racing about to put you in a spin
They get your holiday off to a racing start
They're twinned for speed and reliability
No queues, no wait, first to the airport gate
They are today's financial facilities for tomorrow's travellers
They have the number one formula to beat their rivals by hours
Their high-speed trouble-free performance covers any distance with ease
Banking on this recipe steers you through – trouble-free
Monies safe when ready to spend, won't be driven round the bend
Going abroad, gotta hurry, this winning team saves me worry
Down the straight, through the chicane, Thomas Cook and Girobank win again
Faster service close at hand is formula one for travel planned
Countrywide, coast to coast, you're always near the winning post

ANIMALS

▶ **I would have my safari holiday photos developed where I see the Kodak colour check sign because...**

PRODUCT: *Photographic processing service*

It's a sign of safety in the processing jungle
Why hunt for quality when it can be assured
Without Kodak, Kenya's colours become a 'pigment' of my imagination
If I want my prints up to spec I get them Kodak colour checked
Neither splash nor fleck escapes the Kodak colour check
Kodak ensures my prints are never endangered species
Kodak checked prints mean better wild life tints
Big game treks deserve big name checks
Lichfield, Snowdon or mere beginners, Kodak colour check – outright winners
It protects photographers from the predators of the developing world
Kodak knocks spots of the cheatahs in the game
Kenyan sunset? Dusty track? Perfect portrayal on the Kodak snap
This Kodak symbol stands supreme, setting standards seldom seen
Kodak's inspection is my protection
Steady hands, nerves of steel, perfect photos with Kodak seal
Colours bright, day or night, Kodak colour check is right
I want the hue without the sty
They'd never bungle my snaps from the jungle

▶ **I would like to win the wonderful wildlife weekend because...**

PRODUCT: *Cleaners*
COMPETITION: *Asda/Ajax wildlife*

It would be twiffick to wander awound in a wange wover
We could enjoy the goodlife watching the wildlife
Adventure reaches the parts everyday life cannot reach
It will make a change from hunting bargains and snapping them up
It's a gnu-dimension in family entertainment
I'm sure I could adapt to my husband's natural habitat
'Jungle Book' was terrific, I'd love to see a live performance
Then the children would not complain I was 'beastly' to them again
Without liquid assets I could clean up a cream of a dream
It panda's my need to monkey around and if fine, toucan play
My 'tribe' would love it
On safari without financial care, cos Ajax paid the lion's share
It would stop my lazy monkey 'lion' in bed all weekend
With my 'kids' I have no 'bucks' and only a little 'doe'
My weekends are always the same, really 'tame'
Workaholic Tarzan and housewife Jane need to learn to 'swing' again

Pet food products

He's a boxer who gets 'knockout' meals at a 'knockdown' price
There's no bone of contention just a tail of contentment
One good tin leads to another
There's a lot of wag in an Armitage bag
An extra bounce in every ounce
It says 'Auf Wiedersehen' to odour, pet
It perfumes purr fumes
Hearing her purr, watching her play, who could resist the KiteKat way
His master's choice is his best friend's chum
Trill-fed budgies are healthy perch-aces
Chum is the four letter word dog lovers swear by
My dog is a Pedigree 'Chum'pion

ANYWHERE

▶ **Marmite yeast extract is tasty ANYWHERE in the world because...**

PRODUCT: *Savoury spread*

There isn't a more delicious spread, within the four corners of my bread
When the menu's exotic, Marmite's patriotic
A familiar treat in an exotic location, sets the seal on a perfect vacation
Sushi's tasty, squid's alright, when in Rome make mine Marmite
The flavour that delighted gran, still tastes great to a globe-trotting man
It can be enjoyed anywhere on the earth's crust
Capricorn to Cancer, wherever I roam, Marmite reminds me of tea and toast at
      home
World scenes and climates alter, but Marmite's quality doesn't falter
It's the message in a bottle understood by every tongue
Wherever you are, whatever you do, one little jar will fortify you
It's available, it's instant and its taste is out of this world
That rich wholesome flavour for gravy or spread, a true family favourite
      wherever you tread
The earth's crust never goes to waste, spread with Marmite's tempting taste
Buttered bread, wherever eaten, spread with Marmite can't be beaten
Frogs legs? Birds nest? Do me a favour, Marmite's flavour is the one to savour
Its flavour spreads from coast to coast, to every corner of my toast
Over the Channel, Atlantic or Med., Marmite's the healthiest tastiest spread
A loaf of bread, a Marmite jar, brings instant happiness near or far
From Blackpool beach to Ivory Coast, Marmite goodness gets my toast
Jars of Marmite small and large, make every trip a 'Bon Voyage'
Wherever I suffer a hunger attack, it's a healthy convenient any time snack
Rio or Sydney, wherever you are, home is in the Marmite jar

Flavour from the little brown jar, appeals to folk both near and far
Going through customs I must declare, it's a seasoned traveller welcomed
    everywhere
When battle's over, meals begin, Marmite soldiers always win
It spreads a smile on your soldier's face, so spread the word, spread the taste

AUTOMATIC

▶ **New improved Ariel AUTOMATIC and the new Hoover Logic
1200 are the best cleaning partners because...**

PRODUCT: Washing powder
PRIZES: Hoover washing machines

They love to take stains out for a spin
Partners should go around together, hope these two go on forever
Without phantom boast or masking fact, nothing equals their soap opera act
They are 'clothes companions'
When Hoover needs a fill, Ariel automatically fits the bill
They bring tomorrow's world to today's wash
Washing lined up for inspection, salutes these partners to perfection
Faced with such almighty foe, stubborn stains give up and go
Nice and cool and quickly spun, the partnership that gets it done
All housewives can profit from their merger
In their field they're no beginners, both clean favourites and clear winners
Their spin and tonic makes mums seem bionic
They're designed and refined for a performance stream-lined
Both take pride in the care they provide
Now I'm Krystal in suspenders, instead of Pauline in Eastenders
Ariel provides the biology and Hoover 'chips' in with technology
This packet and model make washday a doddle
Clothes are no longer 'Les Misérables' since this brand-new revolution

▶ **Asda biological AUTOMATIC powder is a must for my trolley
because...**

PRODUCT: Washing powder

I'm tickled pink with my dazzling whites
It does the job at half the price
I'd be off my trolley to wash without it
I can't get into gear without it
Their cool clean act follows every drum roll
I'll give it a whirl to lighten the load
It's a load cheaper for a load cleaner
My spending needs to curb but results are quite superb
Without it I would be in a proper lather

Value and performance is second to none
It dispels washday blues, gives my washing brighter hues
My automatic choice is biological and Asda is 'buyer logical'

▶ **Heinz and Budgens are my AUTOMATIC choice because...**

PRODUCT: Supermarket foods

These great 'distributors' offer a 'bumper' range and 'manifold' savings to 'boot'

AWAY

▶ **I get carried AWAY with Quorum because...**

PRODUCT: Aftershave
PRIZES: Trips for two to the Olympic Games

Born in Barcelona, worn all over the world
The unique fragrance created to capture the vibrance and beauty of Barcelona
It's the international fragrance that knows no frontiers

▶ **I dance AWAY with KP crisps because...**

PRODUCT: Crisps

When it comes to the crunch you cannot 'beat' them for lunch
Without their attraction I can't get no satisfaction
Partners buzz round me like bees – cupboard love for my crispy KP's
Jazz or punk, soul or funk, KP keeps the blues at bay
I forget about my bunion with a bag of cheese and onion
They're chart topping, crisp whopping, and ring-a-ding flavour popping
Father Abbot's disco beneath the Friary, is truly a 'Crypt' amongst 'Crypts'
(*Note – logo on packet depicted cartoons of monks)
They keep a smile on my dial, while rocking around the clock
It's great rompin' as feet are stompin' to the beat of chompin'

BAGSFUL

▶ **Wherever I travel in Britain I'm always BAGSFUL better off in Gateway, Carrefour or Fine Fare because...**

PRODUCT: Supermarket foods

They 'holdall' to suit one's will when you 'haversack' to fill
Local knowledge, regional trends, come bagged to perfection at journey's end
I love the route to checkout hill, through Valuetown and Bargainsville
Whilst I broaden my horizons they keep things in 'pursepective'
They're 'places of interest' for lovers of traditional value

BANK

▶ **Associated Biscuits don't break the BANK because...**

PRODUCT: Biscuits

Their biscuits create so much interest, they're a positive credit

BARE

▶ **The cupboards are never BARE at the Co-op because...**

PRODUCT: Supermarket foods

Service is slick and turnover quick, with guaranteed value whatever I pick

BARGAIN

▶ **Biscuits are always a BARGAIN because...**

PRODUCT: Biscuits

Round, square, chocolate or bare, there's a kind with everyone in mind

BEAT

▶ **I can BEAT the winter with Unichem...**

PRODUCT: Chemist goods
COMPETITION: Unichem Healthy Times
PRIZES: Holiday vouchers: £2,000, £1,000 & £500

Cold gone, feeling fab, now needing a visa and jab
Autumn, winter, all year through, Unichem products look after you
Accessibility – no sweat, affordability – no debt, reliability – best yet

▶ **Asda shopping BEATS the rest because...**

PRODUCT: Supermarket foods

Each receipt defies defeat
Their selection is expansive without being expensive
Asda sells more, conveniently at one store
Their prices stay cheaper while others stay steeper
In spite of inflation, they're still a sensation
Prices are born at Asda, they're raised elsewhere
They cater more for those with less
It gives larger dimensions to the smallest of pensions

BENEFITS

▶ **The BENEFITS of Sudmilch long life yoghurts and desserts are...**

PRODUCT: Desserts

They're great for packed lunches, wholesome and nutritious, and kept for a
    month, they still taste delicious
Long life, fresh taste, cool price, no waste
They are tasty, tempting and nutritious, longer lasting and quite delicious

BEST & BETTER

▶ **I get the BEST of both worlds when I shop at Woolworths because...**

PRODUCT: Chain store goods
COMPETITION: Woolworths 'Best of both Worlds'

Crackdown prices, competitions galore, no wonder Woolworth's my kind of
    store

▶ **I think Knorr casserole sauces are the BEST because...**

PRODUCT: Sauces in packets

When it's dash, dash, dash, Knorr's code spells panache

▶ **Ronseal quick drying woodstain is the BEST woodstain because...**

PRODUCT: Stains and varnishes

While rival stains fail and fade, Ronseal lasts another decade
What used to take hours can be done between showers

▶ **Tesco's British beef pies are the BEST because...**

PRODUCT: Meat pies
PRIZE: Flight on Concorde

Tender beef, crispy crust, perfectly concorded, delicious, nutritious and easily
    afforded

▶ **Quality approved Scottish salmon is simply the BEST
because...**

PRODUCT: Fish

Tartan on the label means perfection on the table

▶ **Countryman bread is BEST because...**

PRODUCT: Bread

Natural goodness makes it the natural choice
Soft grains of rye and wheat make sandwiches a special treat
One part vigour, one part health, it's a 'whole-meal' in itself
If you want quality and wholesome goodness, it's in the bag
It naturally contains a wealth of health
Full of goodness through and through, it's wholesome, fresh and delicious too
It surpasses the rest in the tastebud test
It can be buttered – but not bettered
Its variety is the slice of life
Those who try it enjoy a healthy diet

▶ **Spanish wines are the BEST because...**

PRODUCT: Wine

They are chosen by experts for perfection
They qualify for thirst class honours
For value they're the best cellars
There is sunshine in every glass

▶ **The RAC is BEST for car ferry bookings because...**

PRODUCT: Royal Automobile Club

Eager to please, they make crossing the seas – a breeze
RAC means C.A.R. care both ways
Expert advice is provided when opinion is divided
It's the one stop shop for the touring driver
RAC's expertise smoothes the way to a carefree car free holiday

▶ **I think Thorntons special toffee is the BEST in the world because...**

PRODUCT: *Confectionery*

With quality and value tipping the scales, Thorntons special recipe never fails

▶ **Sony tape is the BEST for sports because...**

PRODUCT: *Video tapes*

It's action backtrack plays the thrills of the track back
Sportsmen should be seen and not blurred
I can watch yesterday's games in today's frames
It is the winner in its field
It's the Grand National favourite

▶ **Marigold gloves are the BEST hand beauty care because...**

PRODUCT: *Household gloves*
COMPETITION: *Marigold/Tesco*

Marigold hands are like ladies of leisure – Tesco savings double the pleasure

▶ **Trex helps produce the BEST of British cuisine because...**

PRODUCT: *Solid white cooking fat*
PRIZES: *Hostess trolleys*

The great Trex tradition gives nouvelle cuisine the guillotine
Perfect pastry, better batter, Trex improves our favourite platter
Quality that delighted gran has been improved for modern man
Foreign sauces aren't required when British food is Trex inspired
Its reputation's sure to rise with the Star Trex Enterprise
By royal command they're changing the lard at Buckingham Palace
The kitchen runs smoother when it's well oiled
British food and Trex make the perfect union, Jack

▶ **Porkinson's sausages are the BEST because...**

PRODUCT: *Sausages*

They make bangers and mash incredibly flash
Porkinson's sausages sizzled to fame by placing taste behind the name
Porkinson's sausages are a beautiful sight, pork filled perfection in every bite

▶ **Bernard Matthews products are BEST for barbecues because...**

PRODUCT: *Meat*
PRIZES: *Barbecues*

You get succulent slices at sizzling prices
With standards so high they're an excellent buy

They're the money savers with the 'bootiful' flavours
There's no wasting, no basting, just wonderful tasting
Always tasty, always lean, they never ruin Dad's big scene
Norfolk flavour beyond compare, tastes even better in open air
They're handy, delicious, always tender and nutritious
No fuss, no waste, our Bernard's got taste
They are quick and delicious, lean and nutritious
The waste is removed and the taste improved – bootiful

► **Shopping at Kwik Save is BETTER because...**

PRODUCT: Stock cubes
COMPETITION: Kwik Save/Oxo stock cubes
PRIZES: Casio pocket TVs

There's a satisfying choice at a gratifying price
You can save more lolly with a Kwik Save trolley
Bargains are always in stock without giving your purse a shock
They offer high-class goods at down-to-earth prices
When the house keeping's dickie, you can't beat a kwikie
Visited the others, results were tragic, went to Kwik Save, shopping was magic
Their variety and smaller bills, get shoppers smiling at the tills
Quality's high, prices low, Kwik Save is the place to go
When I reach the till, I'm pleased with the bill
You get most for least, yet fit for a feast
Soaps, serials or ices, you're never 'cheesed' off with Kwik Save prices
When the chips are down, so are all their other prices
What turns me on, makes me glow, Kwik Save's prices turned down low
You get pocket TVs with your cheeses
Quality and economy are topmost, supreme as any jury host
Service is slick, turnover quick, guaranteed value whatever I pick
An itsy, bitsy, teeny, weeny, bill rings from the till machinery
Top name brands, bargain shopping, Kwik Save keeps the opposition hopping
Nothing fussy, nothing frilly, but paying more would be quite silly
It's the store where opportunity knocks to save a few bob
It's a trolley good place to make a Kwik Saving cheesally
Turn-on products, 'tuned-in' price, makes Kwik Save selection doubly nice
Quality food, everything's jolly – if you shop elsewhere, you're off your trolley
When viewing Kwik Save's bargain buys, Cilla could shout 'surprise surprise'
Kwik Save's super low prices (like Casio TVs) need no 'plug'
Logical prices have customers beaming all over the trek out

► **International gives a world of BETTER shopping because...**

PRODUCT: Supermarket foods

The best all round service brings down-to-earth prices

▶ **Colman's make cooking a touch BETTER because...**

PRODUCT: *Sauces in boxes*

With Colman's I can ring the changes without circling the world
They've put a world of new ideas at my fingertips
Everyone will spot the difference at my next Home Style meal
You'll find a welcome home to Colman's
What's sauce for the goose is always worth a gander
The only additive is pure genius
Colman's are a cook's best blend
With simple instructions from packet to pot, this galloping gourmet can slow to a trot
Added to my favourite dinner, it makes the dish an instant winner
It turns boring dinners into tasty winners
Behind suburban kitchen doors, mums simmer with pride when Colman's pours
Tasty tricks are worked by each magic mix
Quick, efficient and tasty and the family spot the difference

BIRTHDAY

▶ **The Mars Bar has given 50 years of big bar value because...**

PRODUCT: *Confectionery*

Memories are made by Mars, three generations favourite chocolate bars
No generation can resist Mars temptation
Goodness and taste are beyond price, but the price is beyond nobody
Times may change but a Mars remains marvellous
It's kept the pace in the race for the perfect taste
Once tasted always eaten, as for value, never beaten
The goodness and taste never fades, even after five decades
Its flavour and price have always been nice
Fifty years it's stood the test, with bigger value than the rest
Mars have always proved their worth and do not cost the earth
It makes life sweeter, being a Mars eater
Mars has an ageless quality with a down-to-earth price
It's the golden bite that brings delight
Anything well made will last, but take Mars home, they vanish fast
Grandpa loved them, so did dad, now they're favourite with the lad
Quality tells and economy sells
For grandad, dad and son, Mars has been the golden one
Since '32 still going strong, generations can't be wrong
That longer lasting energy store, has kept us coming back for more
Families have thrived on the benefits derived

▶ **I would like to wish Norwest Co-op a happy birthday...**

PRODUCT: *Supermarket foods*

For a decade of transforming hot cross shoppers into real cool customers

BISCUITS, CAKES & CRACKERS

▶ **The Co-op leaves other biscuits snookered because...**

PRODUCT: *Biscuits*
COMPETITION: *Co-op '99' Tea/Tennent's lager*

Co-op's atTENNENTion to biscuit cravings, crumble inflation with
    CHAMPION savings
They're the best TENNENT'S in my LADA
For the perfect break they DAVIState the opposition
They have the biscuit to suit every type of break
Every bicky they bake is my lucky break
'99' pots and Co-op bakes are incomparable super breaks
Even hurricane slows to savour Co-op's century breaking flavour
You don't need Dennis Taylor glasses to see quality
Their biscuit mix knocks them for six
You can improve any break with biscuits the Co-op make
The Co-op give the break the rest cannot make
They make champion breaks while the opposition crumbles
Co-op cushion prices and leave you in the pink
During a break they disappear at hurricane speed
They're the RAY of sunshine I've been REARDON
From packet to pocket there's safety assured and members applaud
For good value eatin' they just can't be beaten
Their six winning hot shots have cornered the angles
One crisp break and I am ready for a clearance
Their CUEnique taste is worthy of any break
For a nominal stake – the perfect winning break
They're so good everybody is going potty over them
Co-op scrumptious bakes makes many maxi-mmm breaks

▶ **Co-op stores take the biscuit because...**

PRODUCT: *Biscuits*

They are inviting, exciting and crumbs – they're nice
Caring sharing they are the champs, top quality value and dividend stamps
They crunch inflation by giving the customer a nibble at the profits
When I'm fishing for bargains, their Jacob's lines mean fine catches

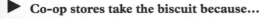

Co-op racks have the choicest packs that make the most economical snacks
By shopping there one can have one's shortcake and eat it
Nabisco is a treat in store, with Co-op prices I buy more
They butter me up with their half-baked prices
I can buy 'Nabisco' for 'Tea-Time' at Co-op prices
Nabisco never bakes mistakes
With Nabisco on the label, the Co-op puts perfection on the table

▶ **McVities biscuits are wise buys at Woolworths because...**

PRODUCT: Biscuits

When you need a snack, they give you a wholemeal

▶ **I give Jacob's and Hovis cream crackers more than a sporting chance because...**

PRODUCT: Crackers

Whatever the venue, they appear on my menu
Their track record is second to none, always be my number one
Eaten plain or with topping, once started there's no stopping
They consistently make first class 'breaks'
For me they're just the ticket to enjoy whilst watching the cricket
Snap! They're a dead eat at the winning post
When packing school dinners, they're cracking good winners
They're more than a match for any biscuit
They make 'grandstand' thrillers for 'home in tum' fillers
Every sportsman worth his salt savours their taste for a hunger assault

▶ **With Jacob's I get a super snap because...**

PRODUCT: Crackers

I never supper from over-exposure
I get 35mms to every packet
This winning line is so compact
Once exposed for tasting, a likeness soon develops
When I unwrap the film, good results always develop
Since 1885 Jacob's have always won in the photo finish
These delicious biscuits I just F.2.8. (*have to eat)
Like the camera, the taste never lies
They're always a delight, 35mms per bite
Say cheese and this cracker wins by a smile
They're the best biscuit since the boxed brownie
Just Anyone Can Obtain Brilliant Snaps (*JACOBS = ACROSTIC*)
Each pack oPEN TAX's my purse so little (*Pentax camera)
They focus attention on never baking mistakes
I zoom in on the plate before it's too late
I like-a-da crackers so shutter your face

My husband's the photographer so I NAB 'IS COmpact camera *(NABISCO =
  ACROSTIC)*
Each bite means snappy days are here again

▶ **Jacob's crackers are like Concorde because...**

PRODUCT: *Crackers*

They came, they saw, they 'Concorde' the market – the cream of crackers
One excites the palate – the other unites the planet
Home is 'Teethrow'
Concorde flies the flag, Jacob's raise the standard
Outstanding qualities they combine, are 'original and best' – by *sound* design
For top flight taste I'mach two (*Mach 2) with cheese and get cracking

▶ **Ginger loaf adds spices to life because...**

PRODUCT: *Cake*

This hot favourite is a certain tea-time winner

Baking products

My pastry is light and my cakes are just right
Both are examples of using dough wisely
Quality and value when you bake puts the cherry on the cake
I never bake mistakes using McDougalls to make my cakes
McDougalls baking, sure to please, superb results achieved with ease
Perfection from pie to flan, is McDougalls master plan

BREAD & CEREALS

▶ **Hovis bread is good news at breakfast because...**

PRODUCT: *Bread*

The sun rises in the yeast
Once bitten that's why
It boosts the vigour but not the figure
For my tummy it's the perfect space invader
Nothing can top it, except butter, marmalade, cheese, beans, eggs, jam, pâté
Hovis offers value in slices
At 6 a.m. it is the only thing we all agree upon
It starts you off with a bright inside story
It is Anna-Ford-able source of wheatgerm every day
It is the thread of gold in the fabric of life
It would be bad news without it
It's as fresh as the latest bulletin

▶ **I Think Vitbe bread makes super sandwiches because...**

PRODUCT: Bread

It's filled with goodness, to put new life into a loafing breadwinner

▶ **Countryman bread is best because...**

PRODUCT: Bread

Natural goodness makes it the natural choice
Soft grains of rye and wheat make sandwiches a special treat
One part vigour, one part health, it's a 'whole-meal' in itself
If you want quality and wholesome goodness, it's in the bag
It naturally contains a wealth of health
Full of goodness through and through, it's wholesome, fresh and delicious too
It surpasses the rest in the tastebud test
It can be buttered – but not bettered
Its variety is the slice of life
Those who try it enjoy a healthy diet

▶ **I buy Kellogg's corn flakes at Asda because...**

PRODUCT: Breakfast cereal

Prices and cereals are unsurpassed, for this Asda/Kellogg's enthusiast
Kellogg's Cornflakes, krispy rice, are twice as nice at Asda price
Packeted sunshine, such variety, at Asda price there's no anxiety
The breakfast programme mothers learn is enter Asda, save, return
Asda value, toasted bran, reduce the price of fibre plan
Asda lightens the tab while toasted brans fight the flab

Cereals with a computer theme

PRODUCT: Breakfast cereals

It's the key to programs for health and energy
Those energising little chips aren't bugged with additives
I can feel the answer on the tip of my tongue
It's the logical solution to the basic breakfast program

Nabisco Weetabix at Asda

PRODUCT: Breakfast cereal

Shreds of evidence are never left on the plate
Weetabix are great shakes judging by the number it takes
Weetabix's long history of value is well cerealised at Asda
They're worth their wheat in gold
These threads of gold bring joy untold
It's the double feature the whole family can enjoy

Quaker Harvest Crunch

PRODUCT: Breakfast cereal

Fancy a nutty fruity munch, have some Harvest Crunch
Even a 'nut' would enjoy this crunch
What a honey of a way to start the day
Harvest Crunch – the everyday 'serial' for country folk

Quaker Oats porridge

PRODUCT: Breakfast cereal

A wee fling around the aisles buys bonny breakfast smiles
They are mixers and hot stuff on cold mornings
Their hot oat filling gives them red star billing
This internal heater makes them a world beater
A warm start makes a glowing finish
Input inner glow, output extra go

Ready Brek porridge

PRODUCT: Breakfast cereal

Seeing hunger disappear puts mind and body in top gear
Input inner glow – output extra go
They get more mileage per day the Ready Brek way
Ready Brek is top of the pops on tabletops
Anything goes when Ready Brek glows
With Ready Brek satisfaction they glow into action

Ready Brek with a BMX bike theme

PRODUCT: Breakfast cereal

They eat Ready Brek which makes them BMX-perts
Ready rider is their name – BMXing is their game
Daily Ready Brek is ace, ready riders set the pace
With the Ready Brek glow, your stunts steal the show
They've the strongest 'frames' to enjoy fun and games
They're always 'frame-ing' tasty
Their trak (B) rekord is glowing
They get more mileage per day the Ready Brek way
They can BMX-tra smart glowing with a Ready Brek start
Their 'ce-real' action, ready with skills and Brek-neck speeds
Ready Brek warms and fills ready for skills and thrills
Make no mistake Ready Brek helps overtake
Ready Brek gives them amazing blazing pedal pushing power
They can perform to spec. on the high tec. brek
Ready Brek riders keep on glowing while the rest are slowing
With the Ready Brek glow your stunts steal the show

Ready Brek prevents stunt-ed glow-th
Ready Brek's energy 'chain' reaction means powerful traction, resilient action
With a rollback or bunnyhop, Ready Brek riders never flop
They get a kick out of life that's wheelie great
They've got extra whoops swooping, bump jumping, berm blasting energy
Inner energy and heat make a great BMX feat
A hot start makes for a cool easy ride
They're warm on the inside and hot on the track
Hot wheat inside, hot seat outside
Central heating for kids is the best stunt of all
They take everything in their ride
Seeing hunger disappear puts mind and body into top gear
They won't be saddled with an inferior breakfast
They've got stamina for stunts and weather the bumps
All that nutrition makes a stunt magician
They've got the strongest frames to enjoy fun and games

Spices/Stuffing

PRODUCT: Spices

One racks the spices, the other cracks the prices
This sage knows her onions

Sugar Puffs

PRODUCT: Breakfast cereal

Honey Monster, you're my pal, cos I love your cereal
Honey Monster, you're no fool, Sugar Puffs are really cool
Sugar Puffs are so fantastic, wish my tummy were elastic
Sugar Puffs are my mecca, for a super creamy, milkier brekker
They came, I poured, they conquered

Bread and Cereals in General

Nothing's a test when you're fuelled by the best
They always compete with a number one plateful
They often come first because their energy lasts
For stamina and skill this breakfast is real brill
They have the get up and go that champions show
Delicious French flavour from a super British store, as a good European I
      couldn't wish for more
Its matured grains make it the toast of the town
At a cheese and wine party if you're a real smarty you'll provide each head with
      some tasty French bread
Early reports that a hungry up-rising was over-whelmed by soldiers
A high fibre content other loaves may favour, but none can equal the granary
      flavour
In summer I could go for a long 'loaf' and get 'Sunblest'

Every morning, wheaty whole, they vanish from the breakfast bowl
Cereal, fruit, almonds too – nature grows the best for you
Prices at my Asda store, make Hovis worth returning for
My little charges love Hovis, I love Asda's little charges
Asda prices lead the way, helping Hovis starts my day
They win awards for the best cereal
At the box opening they always bring the house down
They get so much hyperaction from their breakfast satisfaction
Their perfectly balanced start help them overcome all obstacles
These 'super natural' nourishing packs work 'miracles' on hunger attacks

BREAK

▶ **There's no need to BREAK the bank because shopping at the Co-op means...**

PRODUCT: Supermarket foods

You get a much bigger haul without breaking the law

▶ **Mr Kipling makes the perfect weekend BREAK because...**

PRODUCT: Cakes
PRIZES: Weekend breaks at THF hotels

His recipe is beyond compare – THF Hotels and loving care
Whilst you fish or swim, safely leave the baking to him
Every day's a holiday with Mr Kipling's cakes on the tray
His cakes, small and large, make every trip bon voyage
Saturday and Sunday means relaxation with Mr Kipling's baked creations
Getting away, having a rest – Mr Kipling's cakes are best
From Friday suppers to Sunday dinners – his cakes are weekend winners
Check out the teatime treat and check into a weekend retreat
Mr Kipling's mouthwatering 'cakeaways' make scrumptious breakaways
Unparalleled luxury and outstanding confection equals 48 hours exceeding
    perfection

▶ **I'd love a Bonus BREAK because...**

PRODUCT: Dog food
PRIZE: Holiday in Greece

Sunny Zante, Ouzo, Feta, good kennels, Bonus, happy setter

▶ **I would like to win a DER/Lufthansa Berlin BREAK because...**

PRODUCT: Supermarket foods
COMPETITION: Safeway/DER Lufthansa Berlin break

Berlin presents a traditional fest, and Germany's Wurst is undoubtedly best
Sampling DER's German array, my fancy took flight for this weekend away
Flying DER, in Lufthansa's care, the perfect ingredients for a Berlin affair
Bierwurst, strudels, beer from a Stein, these enjoyments would be all mein
Deutschland beckons, something to savour, a superb flight with German
    flavour

BREAKTHROUGH

▶ **Wall's microwave sausages are a great BREAKTHROUGH because...**

PRODUCT: Microwave sausages
COMPETITION: Tesco/Wall's microwave sausages
PRIZES: Microwave ovens

Wall's have found the missing link, a microwave sausage that isn't pink
Even my husband Harvey can cook this Wall's banger
No frying-pan needed, no splashing fat, just succulent hot sausages in 50
    seconds flat
No longer a kitchen slave, with super sausage and microwave
Now when I say 'dinner in a minute' I mean it
You made me buy some and I haven't got a microwave ... yet
Now I can cook 'em as fast as they can eat 'em
With the microwave brainwave my cooking has entered the saus-age
Quality fare of renown is quick to heat and already brown
Quick to heat, delicious to eat, a combination hard to beat

BRIGHTEN

▶ **Pledge and Sparkle BRIGHTEN up my home because...**

PRODUCT: Furniture polishes and cleaners

My vote is pledged to this coalition, I reject the opposition
This brace sets the pace for a fresher cleaner place
All my little treasures are seen and not blurred

BRILLIANT

▶ **MAZDA softglow lights are BRILLIANT because...**

PRODUCT: Electric light bulbs
PRIZES: Texas Homecare £25 shopping vouchers in each store

They colour the moods of all cool dudes
They pale into significance
They let me see my home in a whole new light
Whether apricot, apple or rosy, with softglow you'll always be cosy
A subtle lighting combination soothes stress and means relaxation
The mood-making magic of softglow lights enhances colours with softer whites
Everyone has a soft spot for the way they conduct themselves
True romantics always know, Mazda's soft and subtle glow
Mazda bulbs lift up my light, apricot, apple or rose – all white
Out of the darkness, into the light, Mazda gets the mood right
Whilst others diminish and fade, Mazda continue into another decade
Outshining the rest, you will have a soft spot for the best
Their subtle magic can turn on the dullest of husbands
'Watt' was once clearly dull, Mazda's made colourful
A subtle introduction – a soft touch – sheer seduction
Their pastel colours shining bright, bring summer's warmth to winter nights
Their soft, restful tones, give style and flair to homes
They fill my home with gentle light, so soft, yet bright
They are 'CURRENT'ly the best, H'OHM'ES, 'ELEMENT'ary my dear
    'WATT'son
They needn't dazzle in your daze, but could in your nights
With apricot, rose, apple white, nature's finest colours are captured in light
For a home that's softly bright, switch to Mazda softglow lights
They put all others in the shade
It's hard to see how romance could survive without them
'Element'ary my dear 'Watt'son subtle ambience, Mazda has 'volt' it takes
Bought Mazda lights, I feel elated, the neighbours think I've decorated
Without a shadow of a doubt, Mazda reveals what good lighting's about
Apricot apple or rosy, they make rooms comfy and cosy
They spotlight beauty, without putting colours in the shade
Mazda illuminate each room to perfection, packing a superbly softglowing
    selection
New soft colours now enhance – a subtle scene set for romance
They illuminate your home and enhance your decor with warmth and colour
Mazda minds perfect them, perfectionists select them
Apricot, rose or apple white, create ingenious shades of difference at night
Decor complete with a softglow effect, pastel power is simply perfect
Pretty colours, cleverly made, leaves the others in the shade
Softly, softly is the way, for hardly any cash outlay
They softly illuminate the parts that no other light can reach
Befitting the god of light, they transform mundane interiors with heavenly
    ambience
They boldly glow like no bulb has shone before
They're the light sensation for a dynamic transformation
They provide superior lighting for the standard lamp

If lighting sets the mood for love – switch on
Whatever you choose for decoration – they enhance its effect – result sensation
Their subtle tones enhance the theme of whatever colour scheme
They outshine the rest by highlighting the best
Their warmth invites, their mood excites – Mazda always de-lights
Softglow 'reflect' a flair for fashion that 'colours' our creative passion
With subtle colour and softglow shade the welcome home is easily made
They create the perfect 'room with a hue'
With illumination so romantic, my love life has never been so frantic
Our house transformed to cherished home 'cause light is no more monochrome
Switch them on, dispel the gloom, bring instant comfort to every room
Romantic nights with 'er indoors with no bright beams to spotlight chores
Mazda at Texas till, means softer glow and lower bill
For atmosphere beyond compare, gives furnishings a touch of flair
Choosing apricot, rose or apple white enriches rooms with softglow light
It's watt to choose at ohm for a brighter shade of pale
It's the greatest glow on earth
Conversations blossom and friendships flower, even Cupid uses Mazda's
     'atmospheric' power
They are the bulbs that make a home blossom
With Mazda's soft and subtle lighting, every room is 'glowriously' inviting
This modern genie of the lamp makes this room easy to revamp
They glow where others have never shone before
For arousing desire they beat a coal fire
For 'highlighting' your chosen desire, Mazda takes the 'limelight'
Why redecorate when Mazda can illuminate
They make for soft landings
They add a little bit of chic and a shade of mystique
Romantically, candles can't hold a torch to them
Bulbs 'planted' in my room, produce a lovely 'bloom'
You can switch on to a great innovation, creating a colourful transformation
It's the warm glow watt brightens our lives and ohms
Mazda softglow are the modern genie of the lamp
Even Swan and Edison would agree, softglow improves their pedigree
Softglow brightens up the gloom, it makes a home in every room
They're room enhancing, simply entrancing
Glowing softly upon my wife, together harmoniously the light of my life
Whatever feeling you want to project, Mazda softglow will give the effect
Colours are calming, shades are neat, without Mazda no room is complete
They are the ultimate in soft furnishings without a shadow of a doubt
Softly glowing throughout the night, and they need not be all white
Softglow gives a colourful hue as Mazda brilliance comes shining through
A hint of colour bathes each room, enhancing decor, banishing gloom
Their hues sublime, and quality superior, transform interior design into
     designer interior!
When the world appears harsh, they know how to soften the glow
Each performs separate duty, adds shades of difference with spotlight on beauty

Their subtle illumination enhances your decoration
If you're after setting scenes, softglow lights outshine has-beens
Pastel pictures are created by magic, faded rooms updated
They make a big change to a room with only small change
Subtle highlights, soft-style glows are secrets only Mazda knows
Their colour co-ordinated atmosphere, makes a lovely change from pearl or clear
They let everyone have a room with a hue!
Your decor takes hints from their subtle tints
Their pastel shades leave other bulbs in the dark ages
Gently glowing, subtly hued, they soften the decor and mellow the mood
They add a touch that says welcome home
Their warming tones make loving homes
Sleeping baby, sparkling wine, excellent food, Mazda completes the romantic mood
The glow they impart is 'state of the art'
They enhance your decor at the flick of a switch
They create warm tones and harmonious homes
I can redecorate a room for the price of a Mazda bulb
Soft on colour but always bright, watt better form of man-made light
Softly, softly the softglow collection reflects my style and adds to perfection
What Edison made for duty, Mazda perfected for beauty
They give depth to your decor and bring colour to your chic
They add colour to life, blotting out the strife
The light with warm tone, that makes a house a home
A soft white light coloured right, turns twilight into cosy night
For a softer touch of style, Mazda's sure to beguile
I sat here in the gloom, 'til Mazda brightened up my room
Painting up your home in subtle light, gives a Mazda-piece of sheer delight
For ceiling, lamp or spot, they've so amp'ly displayed watt's watt
When Mazda glows, my son beams
Pretty in pink, gorgeous in green – Mazda's magic transforms the scene
The cost is nominal, yet the effect – phenomenal
Subtle hues and gentle glow, set the scene and spoil the show
Warm as firelight – soft as moonlight – Mazda lights are always the highlight
Not only do they banish gloom, but touch with magic, every room

▶ Scatch is a BRILLIANT game because...

PRODUCT: Board game
PRIZE: Family holiday to Euro Disney

It is a Super Catch And Throw game which is Challenging and Healthy
(SCATCH = ACROSTIC)

BRITISH

▶ **I like to buy British at Budgens because...**

PRODUCT: Supermarket foods
PRIZE: Mini Sprite car packed with British products

When quality and taste are a must, British and Budgens are names to trust

▶ **I like to buy British at Asda because...**

PRODUCT: Supermarket foods
PRIZE: Classic MGB roadster car

Everyone knows British is best, shopping at Asda knocks spots off the rest, for quality, value it passes the test

▶ **Trex helps produce the best of British cuisine because...**

PRODUCT: Cooking fat
PRIZES: Hostess trolleys

The great Trex tradition gives nouvelle cuisine the guillotine
Perfect pastry, better batter, Trex improves our favourite platter
Quality that delighted gran has been improved for modern man
Foreign sauces aren't required when British food is Trex inspired
Its reputation's sure to rise with the Star Trex Enterprise
By royal command they're changing the lard at Buckingham Palace
The kitchen runs smoother when it's well oiled
British food and Trex make the perfect union, Jack

▶ **Proton is Britain's fastest-selling new make of car because...**

PRODUCT: Fruit malt loaf
COMPETITION: Soreen/Proton
PRIZES: Proton cars

Pro design, pro built, pro me, pro you, Proton
The classy chassis – affordable dream, leaves money over – for fruity malt Soreen

BUY

▶ **I BUY Spillers products from VG Foodstores because...**

PRODUCT: Dog food
COMPETITION: VG/Spillers

I get the trademark I trust with a price tag that's just

▶ **I BUY Wall's meat products at Tesco because...**

PRODUCT: *Meat pies*
COMPETITION: *Tesco/Wall's*
PRIZE: *Metro car*

They have that 'Metro Gold-Win' star quality

▶ **I BUY McVities biscuits from Morrisons because...**

PRODUCT: *Biscuits*
COMPETITION: *Morrisons/McVities*

When it comes to the crunch I want value
When it comes to the crunch, once bitten – nice buy
They're fresh, they're crisp and they pack a great crunch
The crunch comes in the packet and not in the pocket

▶ **I BUY MFP's children's records because...**

PRODUCT: *Records*
COMPETITION: *Woolworth/MFP records*

Whilst kids are listening, parents get a long playing rest
Whilst I am a busy body, my busybodies are kept quiet and content
By hook or by crook they're the best in the book
Children's skills are alive with the sound of music
Mum finds pleasure in her children's leisure
They're a revolving world of pleasure for every child to treasure
I like their variety of well-produced sound, economically priced to help our
    money 'go round'
They are good family listening at mum's favourite prices

▶ **Asda shoppers BUY Varta batteries because...**

PRODUCT: *Batteries*
COMPETITION: *Asda/Varta*

Varta are to power what Asda is to savings
Like solaras, Asda and Varta are the perfect chargers
Shopping at Asda they're obviously smarter, so naturally they buy Varta
Asda shoppers are always smarter for value volts they veer to Varta
No other battery, no other store, pocket the difference, who wants more
Varta and Asda are a team with one theme – power to save

▶ **International shoppers BUY Varta batteries because...**

PRODUCT: *Batteries*
COMPETITION: *International Stores/Varta*

For power so bright, Varta's right, International shoppers have seen the light
Varta make light of being international champions

Varta is an international source of power
Many enlightened shoppers carry a torch for International – Varta powered of
    course
International shoppers expect the best, Varta batteries outlast, outshine,
    outclass the rest

▶ I BUY Unwins packet seeds at the Co-op because...

PRODUCT: Horticultural seeds
COMPETITION: Co-op/Unwins seeds

Garden, greenhouse, tub or pot, Unwins grow in any plot
For years Unwins and I have been great co-operators
Superb results are achieved with ease, thanks to Unwins' expertise

▶ I BUY Snappies cling film because...

PRODUCT: Cling film
COMPETITION: Tesco/Alcan Snappies
PRIZES: Picnic hampers

For hygiene and protection, they're the obvious selection
Picnics, sandwiches or frozen dinner, versatile Snappies are a winner
From Marrakesh to Bangladesh, Snappies cling film keeps the world's food
    nice
It seals in goodness, keeps things fresh, wraps up lunches, it's the best
I leave the rest and cling to the best
Freshness and flavour – sure to retain when cling film's got the Snappies name
They go to great lengths for value and strength
For keeping food fresh and preserving flavours, Snappies quality never waivers
Food keeps fresh and doesn't spill which helps reduce my grocery bill
It's what the best-kept food is wearing today
Snappies wrapping is better cover to keep food fresh for the good food lover
From fridge to fridge cross the land Alcan and Snappies go hand in hand

▶ I BUY Tetley tea bags at Tesco because...

PRODUCT: Tea
COMPETITION: Tesco/Tetley

Tetley's excellence, Tesco's flair, together they're a winning pair
Tetley tea at Tesco till, super taste and lower bill
Tetley for flavours – common sense, Tetley at Tesco – fewer pence
Torvill-Dean, Peaches-Cream, Tetley and Tesco partners supreme
Tesco supplies me, Tetley revives me

▶ I always BUY my Tetley tea at Safeway/Presto because...

PRODUCT: Tea
COMPETITION: Safeway/Presto/Tetley tea

Safeway's prices are money spinners and Tetley's blends are all-round winners
Tetley's my ticket, Safeway's my scene, London weekend – oh what a dream!
Superb tea, splendid store, put together, who needs more
Top performers, second to none, Tetley at Safeway show how it's done
The Tetley tea express is the Safeway to a starlight address
Busy housewife, little time, Tetley and Safeway suit me fine
Safeway's savings deserve congratulations, along with Sydney and his
    perforations
All-round flavour, Safeways impress – maybe two seats on the 'Starlight
    Express'
With affordable prices and quality in profusion they create the perfect infusion
It's that Tetley flavour which entices (not to mention Presto's prices)
Every bag is full of flavour – rounding up a taste to savour
Presto is the place to go, where Tetley stages one big show

▶ I BUY Van Nelle traditional coffee because...

PRODUCT: *Filter coffee*

No fancy gimmicks, passing trends, just finest beans, perfected blends
Taste of Holland superbly presented leaves palates pleased, pockets contented
I quaff like a toff without selling the Van Gogh
It perks me up and filters my cares away
Here's one Dutch masterpiece I can afford
The blend justifies the beans
I'll Netherland a better brand
It's a cup above the rest
Even Van Gogh's brother wouldn't 'ear of any other
It 'Can Al' Ways help unwind the 'windmills' of my mind
It's the only coffee you should put 'Tulips'

▶ I BUY Johnson's baby products at Savoury and Moore because...

PRODUCT: *Baby care*
COMPETITION: *Savoury & Moore/Johnson's*

Busy mums with no time to spare, can rely on you both for babycare
With two Johnson's babies and soon a third, at Savoury and Moore Mum's the
    word
I can shop with pleasure and use with confidence
I only buy the best, for the best, from the best
I can be sure of finding the complete range for baby and me
At Savoury and Moore, baby isn't the only one who's smiling

▶ BUY Swiss Emmenthal cheese at Safeway because...

PRODUCT: *Swiss cheese*
COMPETITION: *Safeway/Swiss cheese*

Emmenthal excellence, Safeway flair, together they're a perfect pair
Quality counts, prices please, unique flavour, 'gratest' cheese
King of cheeses, principal store, who could ask for anything more
Switzerland's across the sea, but Safeway is right next to me
Safeway sells singularly super Swiss cheese
For quality and selection, Safeway's Emmenthal is perfection
From Safeway its taste is assured, fresh as the day it matured
For fondues with an alpine flavour, Safeway is the store I favour
The delicious taste drives me mildly nutty
Alpine fresh, 'holesome' flavour, Emmenthal is the taste to savour
Emmenthal – a temptation 'alpine' for
Flavour outstanding – fondues divine, Swiss on the label, the pleasure is mine
It's the best there is, it gives this Miss Swiss bliss
I love Swiss cheeses and the best are at Safeway
I put great store by a great cheese
I'm just 'nuts' about Emmenthal
The best treasures are always kept in a Safeway
There's no mountains to climb in Safeway to find your dream
Both have a good history, recognised by all perfectionists
Both are monuemmental in the spread of good taste
Their Swiss cheese display draws me to it every day
It's a gourmet's invitation to forget inflation
I am fond(ue) see of good quality
Close your eyes, smell and taste, Safeway's Emmenthal the delight of
    Switzerland
This taste of Switzerland, superbly presented, leaves palates pleased and
    pockets contented
They both bring delight to the 'bored'
Their alpine selection makes fondue perfection
Its taste once acquired is forever desired
It is wholly the finest place for cheese and service alike
Flavour's delightful, taste divine, with the Emmenthal label, the pleasure is
    mine
Safeway's expertise at keeping Swiss cheese, means superb flavour, sure to
    please

▶ **I BUY Robertson's Golden/Silver shred and jams from Hillards
because...**

PRODUCT: Conserves
COMPETITION: Hillards/Robertson's

There's more than a shred of evidence to prove they're as good as gold
They are jam packed with flavoursome bargains
I can buy more Robertsons's gold for my silver at Hillards
They get my 'toast' every day
It's the gold and silver taste at copper prices
Robertson's prices butter the bread that goes between my golden shred

At such economic prices it would be folly not to enjoy warranted goodness by golly

Spotting the difference in the rest – for quality and value – they're the best

My little bits of silver buy pots of gold

Both take pride in the quality inside

Robertons's put on an old fashioned spread

They encourage the spread of good taste

Value is tastefully preserved

Delicious quality, each a money saver, they've so much 'in their flavour'

▶ **I always BUY the Galaxy range at John Menzies because...**

> PRODUCT: *Confectionery*
> COMPETITION: *John Menzies/Galaxy*

Galaxy produces gastronomic thrills and Menzies reduces astronomic bills

Big bar Galaxy sorts out the Menzies from the Boyzies

The Galaxy range is sweet temptation – Menzies prices beat inflation

Galaxy taste, John Menzies style – plus service with a smile

▶ **I BUY my wine in Peter Dominic because...**

> PRODUCT: *Wine*
> COMPETITION: *Peter Dominic wine/Silk Cut cigarettes*

Like Silk Cut Extra, they go to great lengths to ensure perfection

Their selection is sheer perfection

It's the store from which bargains pour

They are always a solid investment and not just a liquid asset

They're a cut above the rest

For drinks with class I wouldn't put anything else in my glass

Be it red or white, heavy or light, Peter Dominic choose right

They successfully combine a good price with fine wine

▶ **For peace of mind I BUY MB jigsaw puzzles because...**

> · PRODUCT: *Jigsaw puzzles*

MB symbol stands supreme, setting standards seldom seen

Pictures are perfect, pieces fit true, lovely to look at, great fun to do

Piece by piece and hour by hour a lovely picture is sure to flower

Experts perfect them, we connoisseurs select them

They perk me up, calm me down, and take away that worried frown

The pictures please and the puzzles tease

I treasure my leisure time quiet and free, and find it relaxing with puzzling MB

The colours are bright, the quality's right, forget the rest, they are the best

For quality, value and picture selection, MB has the fully interlocking collection

In life's muddled box of mis-matched bits, there's magnificent bounty when every piece fits

▶ **I BUY Wilkinson blades and razors from Asda because…**

PRODUCT: Blades and razors
COMPETITION: Asda/Wilkinson Sword

Their range is extensive but never expensive
A good save is as satisfying as a good shave
Ease of shaving comes with a saving

▶ **I BUY Pampers at Tesco because…**

PRODUCT: Disposable nappies
COMPETITION: Tesco/Pampers
PRIZES: Maclaren baby buggies

It's a damper without a Pamper
I'm not potty, just well trained
There's a better change for baby and more change for me
They have an absorbing interest in the changing needs of my family
They cater for my baby's every whim at rock 'bottom' prices
With quality you can't deny, with both you're home and dry
One is bottom on prices, the other is priceless on bottoms
With lower prices and leak proof elastic, I think they're just fantastic
When it's all change they're on the right lines
They have the best credentials for babies bare essentials
Baby stays drier, price is a perk, motherhood is such 'absorbing' work
They ensure that I rock-a-dry baby
There's no leeks, except on the vegetable counter
They have the dri-way code for the crawling lane
It's a crèche course in simple economics
Brood's enormous, budget's small, Tesco and Pampers says it all
Tesco solves my shopping problems from here to Maternity
In these changing times I'm sure of watertight bargains
The bare facts are simple, they protect every dimple
Like my baby I'm choosy where I spend a penny
There's so much change to use – so little time to 'loos'
They changed my favourite lullaby – home n' wear to home n' dry

▶ **I BUY Pampers Phases at Toys 'R' Us because…**

PRODUCT: Disposable nappies
COMPETITION: Toys 'R' Us/Pampers Phases

We 'R' full of praises for big value Pampers Phases
One is bottom on prices, the other is priceless on bottoms
They're a dynamic duo beyond compare, relied on for babycare
Super absorbent fits like a glove, Pampers Phases for the one you love
Toys 'R' Us offers wide aisles and selection, Pampers wide tapes for leakproof
    protection
Designer nappies heaven sent, and a penny saved for each one spent

Those nappies keep my baby nice, and shopping there's kids' paradise
It's superstore for kids and mums, unbeatable prices, driest bums
There's both nappies and toys bringing mother and baby joys

▶ I BUY Eden Vale natural cheese slices because...

PRODUCT: Processed cheese slices
PRIZE: Two-week holiday for two in the Seychelles

It's my favourite cheese, reasonably priced, nutritious, delicious and already
sliced

▶ I always BUY Asda Bunny bags because...

PRODUCT: Plastic bin bags
COMPETITION: Asda/Bunny bags
PRIZES: Raleigh mountain bikes

2-ply strength, ears that knot, Bunny bags have got the lot
Where quality is a must, Asda products I can trust
They're extra strong with a clever tie, saving trees a greener buy
While other brands split and sag, Bunny is the strong green bag
Part recycled, 2-ply strong, easy to tie, I can't go wrong

▶ For the highest standard in coffee, I always BUY Melitta from Tesco because...

PRODUCT: Filter coffee
COMPETITION: Tesco/Melitta
FIRST PRIZE: Holiday in Rio

Melitta from Tesco – Ooh! that nice penthouse taste, basement price!

RUNNERS-UP: Rio coffee makers

I save an awful lot of coppers on ze-bill!
I can quaff like a toff without selling off the Van Gogh
When spirits flag they turn Blue Peters into Jolly Rogers
Its strength is my weakness
It's quality is not to be snuffed at, snuff said, just taste!
Both have changed me from an instant housewife into a real hostess
Tasty temptation, free from inclination and imagine the sensation – a Rio
vacation
From mountain top from ship to shop, Melitta/Tesco crown the crop
It's a pricey taste at a tasty price
Backing winners makes good sense, this classic double saves the pence
No fancy gimmicks, passing trends, just finest beans, perfected blends
Tesco's a girl's best friend while Melitta's a man's best blend
They both give their competitors a good roasting
Coffee scoffers become coffee quaffers when it's Melitta Tesco offers
Taste and aroma take you over, feet start doing the Bossa Nova

Traditional cup or cappuccino – Tesco prices leave cash for the vino
It's like Wembley – easily the finest ground for success in the cup
Choicest beans, tip-top selection, served with a smile, priced to perfection
Always it gives elevenses out of ten
Their sealed blocks of gold whisper promises of aromas untold

▶ I BUY Philips products at Argos catalogue shops because...

PRODUCT: Electrical goods
COMPETITION: Philips/Argos catalogue
PRIZES: Shopping sprees

When put to the test they beat the rest
Their range is extensive and far from expensive
The quality is supreme and the price is keen
Philips are the best and at Argos cost less
You can select at leisure and buy with pleasure
Philip's too lazy to buy them himself!

▶ I BUY my hot cross buns at Asda because...

PRODUCT: Bread buns
COMPETITION: Asda/Easter

Bargains, great lines throughout, leave 0 to be X about
Where Asda leads, others follow, Asda prices beat them hollow
Asda means shopping's fun
Who needs to rave? Their prices help me save
I get value for money and there's plenty of choice
With value so a'bun'dant, shopping worries are redundant
In shopping games, Asda shines, always having winning lines
I'm certain of emerging a winner with every entry
I find the whole atmosphere totally relaxing
Top quality goods at reasonable prices is all I want
Life is never a 'drag' with their bargains in my bag

▶ I BUY French cheese at Asda because...

PRODUCT: French cheeses
COMPETITION: Asda/French cheeses
FIRST PRIZE: Luxury weekend in Paris for two

Forget about costly channel hopping, Asda's ideal for French cheese shopping

RUNNERS-UP: Sets of Sabatier knives

Choice of eight, flavours taste great, open late, no check-out wait
Whatever the occasion, they're a winning liaison
Quality cheese, standards so high, Asda – the place to buy
Lots of choice, lots of taste, lower prices, little waste
Asda value is sure to please, and nothing surpasses fine French cheese

▶ **I BUY Cow & Gate for my baby's needs at Boots because...**

PRODUCT: Baby food
COMPETITION: Boots/Cow & Gate

They're the weaning combination for the younger generation
We will never grow too big for our Boots
For choice and style I needn't walk a mile
From head to toe there's nowhere better to go
Boots care about the little things I care for
Boots Offer Outstanding Trusted Supplies *(BOOTS = ACROSTIC)*
Boots' goods start baby off on the right foot
The choice and quality are really superb, the prices unbeatable
A baby never gets too big for his 'Boots'
They help keep a baby 'Bootiful'
With Cow & Gate they guarantee quality, choice and economy
When good taste suits, I shop at Boots
It makes sense to get the best at least expense
Starting with Boots ensures a well heeled outlook on life
Like all good mums, they care

▶ **I BOUGHT my product from Superdrug because...**

PRODUCT: Superstore goods

I was tempted by the colourful range, and I wanted a little change

CALENDAR

▶ **I always keep a Jarrold calendar on the wall because...**

PRODUCT: Calendars

This is one 'hang-up' I don't mind having
I'd not find a better one in a month of Sundays
Then I have a room with a view
There's no better way to view the day

CALL

▶ **There's always a CALL for Rowntree's jelly because...**

PRODUCT: Dessert jellies
COMPETITION: Presto/British Telecom/Rowntree's jelly

Jelly-communications is the direct line to party success

Party line set to please – clearest answer from Rowntree's
Those engaging little numbers make a tasteful setting
Everyone knows Jellyphants make trunk calls for Rowntree's
Freshness and flavour – sweet sensation – a 'British Jellycom-bination'
With eleven extensions it's the hot line to cold treats
Trifles, mousses, sundaes too, bring smiles to 'dials' without ado
Hey Presto! another fruity favourite on the party line
On a Rowntree's receiver you're a Jelly 'Bell-iever'
Jelly communications is understood by every tongue
You'll soon get the message with those sweet little numbers
I would never switch once connected with a Rowntree's jellyphone
The bells are ringing for me and my 'Jell'
Everyone wants a share of British jelly-com
Every colour a different flavour, hey Presto a ring-a-ding saver
They make taste buds ring with fresh 'n' fruity flavours
Presto tills keep ringing up Rowntree's eleven fruity lines
It's a direct line to desserts divine
Your number's up if you haven't made one for T (*Telecom)
Sweet? treat? party line? A Rowntree's number springs to mind
It's engagingly fruity but without any pips
When sweet inspiration goes astray, Rowntree's call saves the day
When unexpected guests arrive, it gets you off the hook
It goes such a long distance for cheap rate

CAPITAL

▶ **A Woolworths spending spree is CAPITAL because...**

PRODUCT: *Chain store goods*

Woolworths leaves cash in my kitty, finest store, whichever city
You can ROME around PEKING and seldom KU or WAIT

CAPTION

▶ **Entrants had to devise the following captions for:**

...a picture of a man dressed in Oakland clothing

PRODUCT: *Men's clothing*

I like to think I'm wearing well
From little acorns mighty wardrobes grow
Extensive choice, helpful advice, lovely to wear, sensible price

...*a picture of a lady holding Mr Sheen and Windolene as she was standing, smiling in a fitted kitchen*

PRODUCT: *Cleaners*
COMPETITION: *Tesco/Mr Sheen and Windolene*
PRIZES: *Stag occasional tables*

Sheen and Windolene are the perfect 'partners in grime'
It's the powerful collection that gives lasting protection
Sheening is believing? No sooner said than shone
Armed with a pair of beauties
Like me, choose 'Sheen' the 'Mr' that never 'Mrs'
Banish dirt, dust and grime – use these products every time
Cross my heart, these two give me a real uplift
I am fully armed to win the war against dirt
Can I really go to the ball?
What a difference a spray makes
With Mr Sheen and Windolene – the difference is 'Stag'ering
Kitchens should be sheen and not blurred
Thanks to Tesco's price buster, Mr Sheen pilots mum's duster
Beforehand the dust shows, afterwards the place glows
Keep your home jolly clean, grasp Windolene and Mr Sheen
Meet my partners in shine
Come Sheen, come shine, Windolene saves time
A dazzling scene, both bright and clean, a housewife's dream
Mr Sheen's her 'man about the house'
All things bright and beautiful
Help is never far from hand

...*a picture of a lady standing in a bathroom*

PRODUCT: *Toilet cleaner*
COMPETITION: *Tesco/Harpic*
PRIZES: *Stanley handyman toolkits*

The H Team undercover action for overall satisfaction
It's 5 star and 'cistern-matic'
Harpic means never having to say you're sorry
Harpic Applied Regularly Produces Instant Cleanliness *(HARPIC = ACROSTIC)*
The bees knees whether you flush or squeeze
'Lav'ishly clean
Jet and Harpic in our loos cures sanitary blues
'Bowl'ed over by Harpic and 'flushed' with success
Bathed in glory and flushed with success
I skip to m'loo with Harpic
On my troops I rely if germs try to multiply
Har-pic those products because I'm no scrubber
With my Harpic drill, I've no germs to kill

At ease with Harpic expertise
Harpic fresh, Harpic clean, perfect on the hygiene scene
Harpic protection means gentle action – peace of mind and satisfaction
Every housewife worth her salt puts Harpic onto germ assault
Bath, basin or loo, Harpic you'll never outdo
Handy Harpic beats a brush, seeking germs with every flush
Harpic flush or squirt says goodbye to germs and dirt
It's spic and span – she's a Harpic fan
Get rid of your cleaning blues, use Harpic for those dirty loos
Using Harpic makes common sense, it lightens labours, lessens expense
Jet away dirt and grime with Harpic in double time
Housewives never 'loos' confidence with Harpic

...a picture of a smiling lady holding a single rose and standing in a lounge

> PRODUCT: Air Fresheners
> COMPETITION: Tesco/Airwick
> PRIZES: Raleigh bicycles

That small pack magic has me under its spell
Recommended by my Granny, Airwick freshens every nook and cranny
Conjure up a fresh room with an Airwick magic mushroom
Rosy cheeks and shapely hips, come from healthy cycling trips
Har Raleigh Pic anything else
Reckitt 'scent' magic into the air and freshness mushroomed everywhere
Now that's odour and done with
Airwick really means Toodle-oo to a room with a phew
Es-scent'ially Airwick and 'roses' again, I would prefer him to be more
    Raleighable
No room for odours here, Airwick recycles the atmosphere
And here is one I pre-aired earlier

...a lady in a room containing a cot, a teddy bear, a few other toys and also holding a bottle of Dettol

> PRODUCT: Disinfectant
> COMPETITION: Tesco/Dettol
> PRIZES: Exercise bicycles

This amber liquid gives the red light to germs
Happy kids make happy days, Dettol safety always pays
For peace of mind – Dettol's strong but kind
Stronger than Mr T. but gentle enough for the nursery
Home destroyed by kids? Germs destroyed by Dettol
For maximum protection – Dettol is the obvious selection
Dettol means in every sense disinfectant excellence
For infection prevention, Dettol's the No. 1 invention
With gentle antiseptic cleansing care, Dettol disinfectant gets me there

Dettol clean, Dettol happy, shame it doesn't change a nappy
Allaying fears, soothing tears, simple solution, Dettol appears

...a lady in a supermarket looking at cans of Mr Sheen in Tesco supermarkets

> PRODUCT: Cleaner
> COMPETITION: Tesco/Mr Sheen

Mr Sheen is much easier to find than French chickens
If only all men were so reliable
He must be the man who 'can'
This gives me satisfaction without putting my arm in traction
Just my type – diligent, attractive, brilliant and fluent in Polish
Mr Sheen saves my vigour, only question, can or trigger?
This is just what the duster ordered
My name's Sheen – the shine's my Bond
At least one man in my house works
Photo opportunity – Mr Sheen for Dustin Off Man!

...a picture showing a woman in a lounge holding a can of Mr Sheen

> PRODUCT: Cleaner
> COMPETITION: Tesco/Mr Sheen

A legend in their own grime
Sheening is believing
No sooner said than shone
Like Mr Sheen, the Mr that never Mrs
Don't have a grey day, have a spray day
Armed to win the war against dirt
My favourite winning team – every surface sports a gleam
Top names for the cabinet, reduces labour with conservative prices
Nightmare chores become a dream
What a difference a spray makes
Kitchens should be sheen and not blurred
Cleanliness is my mission, so I'm armed with the ammunition

CAR, ENGINES & TRANSPORT

▶ **Heinz and Budgens are my automatic choice because...**

PRODUCT: Supermarket foods

These great 'distributors' offer a 'bumper' range and 'manifold' savings to 'boot'

▶ **Twix and Volvo cars go well together because...**

PRODUCT: Confectionery
COMPETITION: Twix/Volvo/Twin to win

My pleasure is doubled, my pocket less troubled
Whether buying wheels or chocolate snacks, for satisfying power I make tracks
It's Twix 'buy a long weigh' and Volvo 'buy far'
Goods that last outrun the rest, Twix and Volvo pass the test
Money's tight, must spin far, enjoy Twix bars, drive Volvo cars
I know my share's fair with this carriage and pair
Like Twix and Volvo it's their value that clicks

▶ **Silkience is the driving force in haircare because...**

PRODUCT: Shampoo

Using Silkience care before hitting the road is the golden rule of the Hairway
code

▶ **I motor to the Co-op because...**

PRODUCT: Supermarket foods

For feeding the nation it's the best filling station

▶ **Lennons make me a happy motorist by...**

PRODUCT: Food store foods

Having a large range, I don't need to be a Rover
Customising their prices and range, each economy has automatic change
Providing the bumper bootful, that makes a low-cost car-go

▶ **I wear Arai motor bike clothing because...**

PRODUCT: Motor bike wear
COMPETITION: Belstaff Shops/Arai clothing

With Arai to hand, a jacket to boot, Belstaff prove they're the ultimate suit

▶ **If I shop at the Co-op I can afford to run a car because...**

PRODUCT: Supermarket foods

They are geared for fast shopping, keeping the brakes on prices
The divi I save, I can bank in my tank
A clutch of bargain brakes give manifold savings from a great distributor
On prices less than they 'Auto' be, I can run my automobile
Co-op cuts cover the cost of the care of my car
A trolley full of goods constitutes an 'Economy Drive'
I can 'Wheel in' the bargains as prices 'Change Down'

Automobile organisations

It's a fact quite undeniable, no one else is so reliable
Whatever the trouble, they're there at the double
Their expert mechanics mean nobody panics
They offer more than a 'hard shoulder' to cry on
In time of need it's a friend indeed
If your car has a breakdown, you won't
Peace of mind beats a nervous breakdown
What's under their berets understands what's under my bonnet
They know any C.A.R. backwards (*R.A.C.)
The motorist's ABC begins with the letters RAC
SOS-RSVP-RAC-ASAP

Car slogans

Noticing lights turning red, adjusting speed, planning ahead, changing gear to
    steadily slow, arriving as they change to 'go'
The car you can trust is a family must
It goes where other vehicles fear to place their tread
It's a tonic for a 'tyred' world
It can change its appearance at the drop of a hood
It's tough in the rough, fun in the sun and great for a run
It's thrusty and trusty and triffic in traffic
It's got everything except an equal
It's sporty like Le Mans and stylish like La Woman's
Under the bonnet it's more than just a pretty face
Its mobility gives 'tooting car men' the hump!
A little Austination goes a long way
I'm impressed with Leyland's notion to put poetry in motion
Although it sounds like a sneeze, it goes like a breeze

Engine maintenance

Its superb quality, protective care, gives higher performance, reduces wear
Friction is reduced to a fraction
One small squeeze will ease, unseize and please
It's tough with the rough but smooth on the move
The squeaks disappear and it's easy changing gear
For a life of ease, point the tin and squeeze
Noise annoys and rust ain't funny, lubrication saves you money
It prevents a spanner in the works
Little maintenance, no fuss, saves me running for the bus
Friction lessens, speed increases, wheels now happy, hard work eases
It gives friction the slip
It ensures you always keep your bearings
It makes an engine richer for the pourer
It protects all moving parts, that's fact *not* 'friction'
The GEC recommend it for pouring oil on troubled quarters

It eases the panic of the car mechanic
It would rather pay for the protection than the cure
From motorway melee to city crawl, designed for tomorrow, protects over all
Whatever my route or general direction, it gives me full engine protection
I'm less likely to need a hard shoulder to cry on
It's designed and refined with perfection in mind
Years ahead of time, it keeps cars in their prime
When you need the endurance it's the best insurance
When it comes to running endurance, it provides protective insurance
In a world of automation BP leads to lubrication
To lighten labour and lessen expense Visco 2000 is common sense
It's the one injection I'd give my right arm for
Improvements like this are too good to 'miss' (*spark plugs)
Petrol, diesel, turbocharged too, this miracle oil will easily do
The restriction of friction smooths the action of traction
The garage guidance council recommend it for pouring oil on troubled waters
Although you can't spot the difference, your engine will
It's the most 'engin-ius' of its kind
After this oil-change you'll never change oils again
It's a new solution to an age-old problem
It's the space-age oil brought down to earth
Excellent quality is certified, high performance verified, motorists everywhere
    satisfied
Its efficient lubrication foils runaway inflation
Its formula has three-way perfection, quality, performance and protection
Although the seasons change, its protective quality never dates
In Sahara sun you'll continue to run, yet in Arctic snows still it flows
It's stronger when hot, freer flowing when not
It's the oil that foils the affliction of friction

Fiat cars – Italian theme

Adds 'Pazazz' to the motoring scene
This machina saves much benzina
Meaner than Scrooge with benzina
A real mean machine on benzina
It's a 'Fiat Accompli'
With its molto vivace demeanour
Streets ahead is this prima carina
She purrs like a bella felina
An ex-Strada-nary cuta bambina
She's a bellissima buona bambina
It's Fiat's most bonny bambina
When parking she's called 'Thumbelina'
De car with delightful demeanour
Is bella – this bustling bambina
They are every driver's dream of perfection, which is no mean Fiat

Ford cars

For family man and sporty guy, there's only one car – XR3i!
A man likes to be seen around with the best looking Escort in town
Having two eyes on the road is good but 3 i's R X-cellent
The i's have it, the others don't

The Maestro car with a musical theme

From the very first movement you know the score, the Maestro performs
    without a flaw

Service stations/Service areas

They give a lift to tired travellers
They're convenient and cheery for someone who's weary
Aching limbs and rumbling tum, a perfect stop for dad and mum
By car or by coach they have the right approach
They're a bright spot on any horizon
They've really put comfort and service on the map
They're the welcome stop to get you re-started
I call at my Murco Service Station because it's a real gas
Petrol I require, clean forecourts I desire and the promotions I admire

Short and punchy

XR4i – XR4 who? – XR4 me!
MPH, MPG – XR3 OK 4 Me

Spark plugs

They spark me off in the right direction
They're a sure fire way to start each day
Copper heart gives a sure fire start
They are the best tips for the highest performance
Their firers and sweepers are cold weather beaters
They're a copper bottomed investment right down to the core
They plug the performance gap
Bosch produce the master stroke – not a carbon copy

THF hotels

After miles at seventy, it smiles at Forte
Though my car may be sporty, it won't go past Forte

CARE

► **Pure and Simple CARE for me because…**

PRODUCT: *Cleansing lotions and soap*
COMPETITION: *Asda/Pure & Simple jewellery*

They turn a demanding woman into a woman in demand
It puts a pure complexion on my simple reflection
Beautiful skin and shining hair – hallmarks of their expert care
A pure and simple service gives me a happy dermis
It is pure and I am simple
Every product's carefully planned – that's the beauty of the brand
I'm watching my crow's feet like a hawk
It even treats this 'rough diamond' gently
Pure ingredients, expertly blended, keep me looking as nature intended
Completely unlike the rest, simply they are the best

CARNIVAL & PARTY

▶ **Cabana Blanca rum gives me the CARNIVAL spirit because...**

PRODUCT: *Rum*

I get a rum feeling I want to celebrate

▶ **Diamond White and Diamond Blush are the perfect CARNIVAL drinks because...**

PRODUCT: *Ciders*

For extra sparkle and laughter, these little gems are what you're after

▶ **Campari and CARNIVALS go together because...**

PRODUCT: *Vermouth*

Campari's the drink that never goes in disguise
One is well asked for, the other is well masked for
Distinctive taste, definite hue, even masked the fun comes through
Campari is in full employment wherever there's enjoyment
Campari in St. Marks could lead to fun and larks

▶ **A Colman's wine cask makes a great PARTY because...**

PRODUCT: *Wines in boxes*
PRIZES: *£200 cash*

It's the liquid asset that earns capital appreciation
Parties without Colman's are like knickers without elastic – they fall flat
It's the only 'square' that makes a party swing
It takes the 'cant' out of decanting
Happiness always reigns where Colman's pours

Successful hosts always back it – thus ensuring a good binge and racket
It stays lively till the last drip has gone
This brilliant invention allows surplus retention, not to mention its spillage
    prevention
It's a knockout with its clever boxing
You just press the button if you want a lift
From the grapevine, you have a great wine on tap
It makes everyone happy, from the VAT man to the Co(a)lman
It's got taste with no waste, and to pour is no chore
Colman's wine on tap puts your party on the map
Right on tap, in handy pack, keeps those connoisseurs coming back
Who needs a lot of bottle, when they've got a lasting cask?
Anytime, day or night, red or white
It's easy to store, easy to pour, economical, versatile, success for sure
It's so easy to pour when guests shout for more

▶ **It's neat to PARTY at 40,000 feet with Smirnoff vodka if...**

PRODUCT: Vodka
COMPETITION: Virgin Airlines/Smirnoff vodka
PRIZE: A party on the upper deck of Virgin Airlines 747

The Smirnoff's ready, so you can Jet Set and Go
Your music is quadrophonic, the trip is supersonic served with vodka and tonic
A Virgin case of Smirnoff is all you have on take-off
It's all plane sailing with Smirnoff
You enjoy Smirnoff's supertonic with a Virgin supersonic
My friends agree, it's a one-off spree, and the spirit's free
You mix this cocktail, it's pure seven-forty-seventh heaven
Smirnoff's Magical Ingredients Reward Nobly Our Finest Fantasies
    (SMIRNOFF = ACROSTIC)
Smirnoff is on the menu, it will be a really great venue
On cloud eight, rising nine, you're with Smirnoff and doing fine
The flight is as smooth as the Smirnoff
Your vodka and tonic is supersonic
The music's hot, the booze free, there's a Virgin stewardess on my knee

▶ **What would you call a play or musical about Uncle Ben's stir-fry rice?**

PRODUCT: Rice

Pillau talk
Uncle Ben's – licence to fill
Annie get your chopsticks
Wok on
One night in Ben'swok
Stirway to heaven
The Fried A-Stir story

Uncle Ben's Hi 'Sauciety'
Ben if from Heaven
Stir rice express

▶ **The new look Mardi Gras makes a colourful addition to any occasion because...**

PRODUCT: Cocktail drink

Sparkle zest and razzmatazz, Mardi Gras has 'all that jazz'
For a cost so nominal the 'palette effect' is phenomenal
Bright and bubbly just like laughter, and no regrets the morning after
This sparkling creation makes it a gala, even in a humble parlour
Exotic, passionate, delicious, beguiling, adds fizz to your party – leaves your friends smiling
Drinks for two of party action, it sparkles as the star attraction
This sparkling drink can bring alive a welcome home or nightclub dive

▶ **Tefal's table top entertainment products bring a new dimension to entertaining at home because...**

PRODUCT: Heated trays

The sizzling secret of your party's success is just to let Tefal do its best

▶ **Wall's Viennetta and Moët & Chandon make that celebration special because...**

PRODUCT: Viennetta ice cream dessert and Moët & Chandon champagne
PRIZES: Bottles of Moët & Chandon

Both are in a glass of their own
Two teasing temptations, champagne vintage sensations of revelations
They complement each special date, bet Terry found them worth the 'Waite'
They're the height of 'fizzical' delight
When excellence is required, they're the taste that's admired
They're perfect for a bit of a do
Aristocrats of labels grace the most discerning tables
They are always top of their class
Any table would be 'graced' by their label
Guests know you care when you serve this special pair
Who could resist the delicious sensation of succumbing to a sparkling sensation
Their cool sophistication makes it impossible to resist temptation
Superior products of high esteem, grace the table for a celebration supreme
Alluring, delicious, beguiling – the perfect pair to keep you smiling
Both are cool, smooth and chic and quite unique
The 'course' of true love runs 'sweet'
What an entertaining pair, here's to their gastronomic fare
They set the scene for 'haute cuisine'
Luxurious taste, bubbles that explode, everyone's in the celebration mode

They're a great combination for a taste sensation

Such a delectable double make any party bubble

They make 'grape' minds think alike

With luxury beyond compare, I'd feel like a millionaire

Champagne excellence, Viennetta's flair, like Bonington's Everest, beyond compare

Scrumptious slice, sparkling glass, to any repast, brings a 'taste of class'

Deliciously iced and served in glasses, jubilation to anniversaries or university passes

They have sparkle and style, making the occasion worthwhile

Bubbles pop, taste buds flow, you feel that extra special glow

Moët & Chandon and Wall's Viennetta, make celebration days truly 'Red Letter'

Delicious, refreshing, taste beguiling, they add fizz to parties, keep guests smiling

This ice cool combination with warm congratulations will crown the jubilation

'Sin'tillating Viennetta, Moët & Chandon zing, makes a celebration a very classy fling

One pops the cork, the other tops the fork

One provides the starter, the other the ultimate finish

Both rich and cool and ostentatious, they make any celebration outrageous

With Viennetta and bubbly, any party's doubly lubbly

For that special date – they're the nicest way to celebrate

Moët & Chandon tickles my nose and Wall's Viennetta tickles my fancy

Composed by Wall's, this suite is best accompanied by the finest flute

They taste wickedly expensive but are wonderfully affordable

They're both designed with good times in mind

You cannot beat this 'bubble and sweet'

They are the connoisseur's dream of richness supreme

This perfectly blended pair adds cherished moments to any romantic affair

Whether cosy liaisons or family invasions, their unsurpassed taste complements all occasions

Rich and sparkling, they're merry making and so cool they're brrr-eathtaking

They're a marriage of equals – for richer and pourer

The unashamed luxury without the scandalous price

They make a cool party go with a bang

A tasteful twosome oozing class has all the grandeur none can surpass

They're supercalawallsfantastic extra bubbles – oh shucks!

You can bank on the interest they create

They're made by the makers of happy ever afters

Wall's Viennetta is the bizz, Moët & Chandon has the fizz

A wickedly rich ice queen and bubbly French aristocrat always sparkle together

The celestial combination is hellishly rapturous

Lilt Caribbean fruit drink

PRODUCT: Soft drink

Pulling the ring unleashes the 'zing', completing the sparkle of a Caribbean
   fling
It gives you a sparkling view of life
Lilt's taste, never boring, lifts me up with every pouring

CHALLENGE

▶ **Princes meat the CHALLENGE every time because...**

PRODUCT: Meats
COMPETITION: Princes/Kwik Save/Meat the challenge
PRIZES: Commodore Amiga computer systems
RUNNERS-UP: Computer games systems

Can-venient meals of value undefeated, key-in 'Princes' and hunger's deleted
Princes meats are really yum and only cost Amiga sum
Princes prime 'programs' – easy to learn – enter 'Kwik Save' – 'Save' – 'Return'
One 'byte' you Kwikly 'disc'over, you're a Princes input lover!
I monitored the range ... input – nutritious, family feedback ... keyword –
   delicious
Tastee sensashun, means evry bytes an edukashun
Candlelit dinner, family invasion, Princes are 'programmed' for every occasion
For busy mums – sheer paradise, quality meat at 'Amiga' price

▶ **I would CHALLENGE ... (Personality) to eat Shredded Wheat
because...**

PRODUCT: Breakfast cereal
PRIZES: Weekend breaks for two plus £150

Arnold Schwartzenegger ... he is so big and tough, but I bet two would be
   enough
Everyone ... Shredded Wheat wheaters are healthy eaters
Frank Bruno ... every crunch packs a punch that lasts till lunch
The Maxwell Brothers ... it's the whole wheat and nothing but the wheat
Eddie the Eagle ... only Shredded Wheat eaters can become world beaters
Nigel Mansell ... he'd lap it up
The three little pigs ... Shredded Wheat is sure to keep the wolf from the door
Andrew Lloyd Webber ... he'd appreciate Welgar as well as Elgar
The British Olympic Squad ... to be world beaters you need to be healthy
   eaters
Mary Whitehouse ... moral fibre isn't enough, our bodies need the dietary stuff
Robin Hood ... he wouldn't retreat with Shredded Wheat

My Budgie ... he can only manage to eat 'two wheat'
Oliver Twist ... after three would he ask for more?
Jerry Lee Lewis ... goodness gracious great bowls of fibre
Ronnie Barker ... after years of porridge to eat, he'd enjoy three Shredded Wheat
Captain Kirk ... he'd try to boldly eat what no man has ever eaten before
Magnus Magnusson ... once he'd started he'd have to finish
Uri Geller ... one on spoon, two on platter, three's too much for mind over matter
Humpty Dumpty ... the whole wheat cereal is good stuff for making softies eggstra tough
Midas ... Shredded Wheat is worth it's wheat in gold

CHAMPAGNE

▶ **I would like to visit the champagne country because....**

PRODUCT: Wine

Of the nature of the BRUT

▶ **Wall's Viennetta and Moët & Chandon make that celebration special because...**

PRODUCT: Viennetta ice cream dessert and Moët & Chandon champagne

Both are in a glass of their own
Two teasing temptations, champagne vintage sensations of revelations
They complement each special date, bet Terry found them worth the 'Waite'
They're the height of 'fizzical' delight
When excellence is required, they're the taste that's admired
They're perfect for a bit of a do
Aristocrats of labels grace the most discerning tables
They are always top of their class
Any table would be 'graced' by their label
Guests know you care when you serve this special pair
Who could resist the delicious sensation of succumbing to a sparkling sensation
Their cool sophistication makes it impossible to resist temptation
Superior products of high esteem, grace the table for a celebration supreme
Alluring, delicious, beguiling – the perfect pair to keep you smiling
Both are cool, smooth and chic and quite unique
The 'course' of true love runs 'sweet'
What an entertaining pair, here's to their gastronomic fare
They set the scene for 'haute cuisine'
Luxurious taste, bubbles that explode, everyone's in the celebration mode
They're a great combination for a taste sensation
Such a delectable double make any party bubble

They make 'grape' minds think alike

With luxury beyond compare, I'd feel like a millionaire

Champagne excellence, Viennetta's flair, like Bonington's Everest, beyond compare

Scrumptious slice, sparkling glass, to any repast, brings a 'taste of class'

Deliciously iced and served in glasses, jubilation to anniversaries or university passes

They have sparkle and style, making the occasion worthwhile

Bubbles pop, taste buds flow, you feel that extra special glow

Moët & Chandon and Wall's Viennetta, make celebration days truly 'Red Letter'

Delicious, refreshing, taste beguiling, they add fizz to parties, keep guests smiling

This ice cool combination with warm congratulations will crown the jubilation

'Sin'tillating Viennetta, Moët & Chandon zing, makes a celebration a very classy fling

One pops the cork, the other tops the fork

One provides the starter, the other the ultimate finish

Both rich and cool and ostentatious, they make any celebration outrageous

With Viennetta and bubbly, any party's doubly lubbly

For that special date – they're the nicest way to celebrate

Moët & Chandon tickles my nose and Viennetta tickles my fancy

Composed by Wall's, this suite is best accompanied by the finest flute

They taste wickedly expensive but are wonderfully affordable

They're both designed with good times in mind

You cannot beat this 'bubble and sweet'

They are the connoisseur's dream of richness supreme

This perfectly blended pair adds cherished moments to any romantic affair

Whether cosy liaisons or family invasions, their unsurpassed taste complements all occasions

Rich and sparkling, they're merry making and so cool they're brrr-eathtaking

They're a marriage of equals – for richer and pourer

The unashamed luxury without the scandalous price

They make a cool party go with a bang

A tasteful twosome oozing class has all the grandeur none can surpass

They're supercalawallsfantastic extra bubbles – oh shucks!

You can bank on the interest they create

They're made by the makers of happy ever afters

Wall's Viennetta is the bizz, Moët & Chandon has the fizz

A wickedly rich ice queen and bubbly French aristocrat always sparkle together

The celestial combination is hellishly rapturous

CHAMPION

▶ **Robinsons Barley Water is the CHAMPION refreshment because...**

PRODUCT: Fruit juices
COMPETITION: Tesco/Robinsons/Wimbledon
PRIZES: Collections of tennis accessories

Singles, doubles, indoor or out, Robinsons wins without a doubt!
Robinsons tasty fruity zing, gives my racquet extra swing
Smashing taste, cool on court, Robinsons is ace for sport
Robinsons in my trolley, helps me serve, lob and volley
Robinsons is seeded number one, for people everywhere having fun
Wimbledon without Robinsons? You cannot be serious!
McEnroe shouts, umpires overrule, but Robinsons keeps everyone cool
Robinsons seeded number one, bottles opened and it's gone
Whatever sport, whichever star, Robinsons made 'em what they are
Feeling refreshed, playing great, Robinsons is your best team-mate
Playing tennis with all accessories, Robinsons' one of the necessities
Every serving down the line, Robinsons aces win every time
There is nothing bigger than Robinsons liquid vigour
Being unknown or seeded, Robinsons Barley Water is always needed
Tennis champions come and go, Robinsons keeps the status quo
Robinsons serve a refreshing ace, quenching thirst at sparkling pace
For Wimbledon, or just for fun, Robinsons is No. 1
Robinsons and tennis a team, traditional as strawberries and cream
When parched with thirst, champions reach for Robinsons first
For seasoned pro, or a beginner, Robinsons' an instant winner
When Seles grunts, Agassi gasps, they down a Robinsons glass
When thirst is under attack, Robinsons wins game set and match
A Wimbledon champion continuously hears, Robinsons groupies raising cheers
Full flavour takes the tennis seed, Robinsons is No. 1 seed!
Robinsons on the label, means trophies on the table
Robinsons serve the perfect deuce, the ace winning liquid juice
When McEnroe's temper feels aflame, Robinsons restores a peaceful game
Whether rally, return or ace, Robinsons refreshes whatever the pace
Like Borg and Connors, Robinsons have earned the highest honours
What Wimbledon is to tennis, Robinsons is to squash
Monica grunts, Agassi grins, but Robinsons taste always wins
Every player tells the story, of Robinsons their best accessory
To play or just observe, Robinsons' the best to serve
Even McEnroe agrees, refreshing Robinsons never fails to please
Prize ingredients in every glass, Robinsons Barley is world class
Super taste, refreshingly mysterious, no Robinsons you cannot be serious
On merit, Robinsons seeded first, faultless service when quenching thirst
British finalist may be rare, but Robinsons is always there

Players come, players go, Tesco and Robinsons continue the show
Players of the highest grade, love their Robinsons thirst aid
With Robinsons' great drinks, even the opposition clutches at straws!
'A gassi' drink is no competition, compared to Robinsons' great tradition
Robinsons has the finest flavours, Wimbledon tennis the greatest players
Steffi grins, Agassi may run, but Robinsons stays number one
In singles or mixed fours, success reigns when Robinsons pours
Robinsons is on the ball, serving aces to us all
Back garden or centre court, Robinsons rewards games well fought
For Agassi or mere beginner, Robinsons always serves a winner
Victory signs up all around, means Robinsons is being downed
Robinsons always win the thirst serve!

CHARACTER

▶ **Who is your favourite Disney character and why?**

PRODUCT: *Electrical goods*
COMPETITION: *The magic of Philips/Argos catalogue*
PRIZES: *Family trips to Euro Disney*

Peter Pan ... because I'm hooked on Philips' products at Argos
Sleeping Beauty ... because with marriage pending, shop at Argos for a happy
    ending
Mickey Mouse ... because really unique, like Philips and Argos, c'est
    magnifique
Walt Disney is the man for me, the magician behind the fantasy
Fairy Godmother ... Cinderella's dreams came true, with Philips, maybe mine
    will too?
Cinderella ... at Argos Cinders' life did change, after choosing from the Philips
    range

▶ **Bertie Bassett is my favourite character because...**

PRODUCT: *Confectionery*

Tasty figure of a man, forget Chippendales, I am Bertie's fan
For Allsorts of reasons this man's for all seasons
Bertie Bassett's a dandy with swanky doodle candy
He remains constant passion when Simpsons or Turtles go out of fashion
He ain't Warren Beatty but he's a real sweetie

CHOICE

▶ **You find great CHOICE for holiday shopping at Boots because...**

PRODUCT: Holiday accessories

They enable you to get away with top quality goods at rock bottom prices

▶ **Heinz and Budgens are my automatic CHOICE because...**

PRODUCT: Supermarket foods

These great 'distributors' offer a 'bumper' range and 'manifold' savings to 'boot'

▶ **Daler-Rowney has been the artist's CHOICE for over 200 years because...**

PRODUCT: Artists' materials
PRIZES: Replica watercolour boxes

Daler-Rowney creates inspiration
They have made quality a fine art
Daler-Rowney helps to make art work
Consistent good quality can never be brushed aside
Fine art demands the finest materials

▶ **My first CHOICE is always Robinsons because...**

PRODUCT: Fruit juices
PRIZES: Sports bags filled with sports gear

Smashing thirst, tasting ace, Robinsons is perfect served any place
Though John McEnroe sometimes sins, Robinsons always wins
Singles are savoured, doubles are favoured
Robinsons always serve up an ace sparkling performance champion taste
If it isn't Robinsons, it isn't tennis
Tennis matches? Keep your nerve, Robinsons is what they'll serve
Centre court or on the beach, Robinsons goes down a treat
You cannot be serious! No Robinsons? I must be delirious
For taste and satisfaction guaranteed, Robinsons' the number one seed
Super value is the ruling theme, tasty Robinsons reigns supreme
When it's thirsty on court, Robinsons is first in sport
Robinsons is ace, putting a smile on even McEnroe's face
Serving Robinsons fruit deuce will give you an advantage
Wimbledon's past and gone – Robinsons taste goes on and on
Serving the best, only Robinsons leaves everyone refreshed
It is the most refreshing sensation to sweep the nation
My family love me to co-operate by serving Robinsons drink

This juice has advantage every time it is served
Robinsons in any event always comes first

▶ **Hamilton is my CHOICE for decorating products because…**

PRODUCT: D.I.Y. materials
PRIZE: £1,000 worth of antiques

Hamilton expertise, means perfect results with expert ease

CHOOSE

▶ **I CHOOSE my biscuits at Jacksons because…**

PRODUCT: Biscuits

The tills are alive with the sound of savings

▶ **I CHOOSE to install Honeywell radiator thermostats because…**

PRODUCT: Plumbing materials

Experts perfect them – perfectionists select them
For valves you can trust – Honeywell is a must
Like all Honeywell products they are 'moneywell' spent

▶ **I CHOOSE Cadbury's strollers above all others because…**

PRODUCT: Confectionery

Choice selection, taste divine, the label is Cadbury's, the memory's mine

▶ **I CHOOSE Vidor batteries at Asda because…**

PRODUCT: Batteries

Vidor power and Asda prices, just 'watt' we need for the 'current' crisis

▶ **I CHOOSE JVC tapes because…**

PRODUCT: Video tapes

You car'n't A-Ford to 'Sierras' (*you can't afford to see errors)
Of their record quality
Other tapes do not measure up to this tape

▶ **I CHOOSE my favourite Pearl because…**

PRODUCT: Soap
PRIZES: Trips to Holland

For skin care, fragrance rare, lather to spare, none compare
It pays to be choosy, shower or Jacuzzi
I'm a vulture for culture and I'd rather a lather

RUNNERS-UP

Cussons are my oyster
Bathing with Cussons is a heaven-scent sensation
Each tablet of scent is my pick of the bunch
It brings out the zest in me
Naturally, I'm a smooth customer
It's a small price to pay for such luxury
Perfect skincare and scented sophistication gives a sublimely luxurious
     sensation
Its luxurious skin treatment is well worth diving for
It's a jewel among soap
Fragrant pink Pearl every day and the world's my oyster
A little soft soap is always flattering
Every bath becomes a personal blue lagoon
I'm tickled pink because it matches my sink
It's a jewel untold, worth its weight in gold
It's like nothing on earth, must be scent from heaven
A connoisseur of soap perfection chooses Pearl for her complexion
It brings the grime out of its shell
It treats me as precious – costs but a drop in the ocean
It's special lustre keeps me feeling like a gem
I'm sold on previous Pearl, it captivates me
It cares for my bare essentials
For skin like silk it's better than milk
Experts perfect it, connoisseurs select it
It cares for my treasured chest, and all the rest
It keeps my birthday suit as good as new
It's the perfect solution to skin pollution
It's a clear favourite with all the family
I'm an oystercatcher 'bird'
It's a smoothie for an old softie
It's soap 'soaperior' to others
It's a jewel of a find for me
I'm no gran, I like to look naturally glam
Lather is rich and beautiful for features great and small

► **I CHOOSE Sadolin wood protection for my home because...**

PRODUCT: Wood preservative
PRIZES: £500 Sainsbury's vouchers

On all things exterior, the result is superior
It protects from rain, falling mainly on the frame
If the wood is well treated, the weather's defeated

▶ **I CHOOSE Pye because...**

PRODUCT: Hi-fi equipment
COMPETITION: Pye International/Index catalogue
PRIZES: Holiday breaks

Sold by Index, made by Pye – such a tribute made me buy
My little car, an absolute treasure, deserves the finest of listening pleasure
Speaking from experience, that's no lie, I know I can rely on Pye

CHRISTMAS

▶ **I buy Mr. Bassett's at Morrisons because...**

PRODUCT: Confectionery
COMPETITION: Mr. Bassett's/Morrisons Christmas

A sweet yule enjoy at a price that will sleigh you
A santapplause selection
All together sweeter holly days
A sweeter Christmas 'stock in' with fewer hang ups
Tills ringing – ding dong merrily on low with all sorts to show
A stocking full of goodies and all sorts of prices
All sorts of altogether excellent ways to wish goodwill to all men
An enterprising Mr. Bassett's making his presents felt
A tasty stocking filler from Mr. Bassett's, a bargain at Morrisons for cert

▶ **There's more reasons to buy Jeyes at Morrisons because...**

PRODUCT: Cleaners
COMPETITION: Morrisons/Jeyes at Christmas

Jeyes provide good cheer, Morrisons never reign dear
Yule always get bargains so true, yule never feel bloo
You get a clean bill of health at the checkout
With their fayre deal yule have a real Christmas spread
Wise men know Morrisons is the place for star bargains
These Jeyes that they sell fayres me well
A welcoming home saving ensures ye faithful all come
Whether they flush or squirt their action's a cert
Prices low, products great, win Xmas dinner on a plate
Star value and stable price is Inn Jeyes clean tradition
Jeyes Santariffic bargains price is Claus for celebration
Everything they do means I'm never bloo
I celebrate all my shopping days with Morrisons and Jeyes
Only a turkey would shop elsewhere
Their spotless reputations are legend, not fairy tales
The money is heaven scent

Of the convenience
Jeyes put the joy back into cleaning
Clean home, low price, Christmas Dinner – that's nice
Bathroom, kitchen, drains, loos depend on Parazone, Ibcol and Bloos
With their fayre deal yule have a real Christmas spread
On value you can depend with lots of healthy dividend
For holidays and high days – buying cleanliness at Morrisons pays
More hygienic, powerful, quick, its multi cleansing span is spick
Jeyes do a good job, Morrisons save you a few bob
Quality tells, quality sells
You can't get a word in sledgewise for good value buys
They make records cuts in the costa my Chopin Liszt
Their stores are bright and clean 'cos Jeyes already been
The outlook is brighter, the bills so much lighter
Budget tight, price right, shine bright, dynamite
I've never had it so bright
No germs will roam in your Jeyes clean home
There will be money to spare for Christmas fayre
They've a sparkling display to keep germs at bay
Having discovered perfection, why risk random selection
Paired to perfection, freshness and fragrance is their connection
Their reliable safety guarantee making extra change for me
Morrisons value, Jeyes care, quality and perfection everywhere
Everywhere is germ free, what more reasons could there be?
I can clean up in more ways than one
At Christmas feel lazy, as Jeyes Bloo works like crazy
They don't charge the earth to freshen your world
With freshness complete it's time for a treat
With these quality brands our health is in safe hands
It's a must to use names you can trust

▶ I'd like a Co-op Christmas hamper because...

PRODUCT: Hamper

A biscuit, a basket, I'd have a Co-op casket

▶ Christmas shopping at Asda is a bonanza because...

PRODUCT: Supermarket foods

They have that special gift of giving more for a lot less
You can stuff more in your stocking without feeling the pinch
Wise men know the way to star bargains
Hark the Asda angels sing, heralding the bargains that they bring
It's where Santa does his stocking up

▶ **Quality approved Scottish salmon makes Christmas special because...**

PRODUCT: *Fish*

Scottish salmon, the quality fish, makes the perfect Xmas family dish

▶ **Mrs Peeks puddings make my special treat because...**

PRODUCT: *Christmas puddings*
COMPETITION: *Tesco/Mrs Peeks Christmas puddings*

Know Mrs Peeks. Know Xmas cheer. No peeks. No Xmas here
They add distinction to my courses without draining my resources
Lucky me, no kitchen slave, with super pud and microwave
I'm plumb chuffed about 'em, plum duffed without 'em
It's peekier, perkier and a whole lot tastier
Impulsively bought, compulsively savoured, Mrs Peeks puddings, beautifully flavoured
No need for preparation, more time for celebration
They put the warming 'ember' in December
Hark! the Herald Angels Sing, Mrs Peeks – just the thing
Mrs Peeks on the label puts perfection on the table
Yule get the low-down on Santa's presents
A Dickens of a choice to please even Scrooge
The gift at the price that won't make Santa pause
Goodwill, a good fill and a smaller bill

▶ **We buy Quality Street at Christmas because...**

PRODUCT: *Confectionery*
PRIZES: *Tickets for trips to a pantomime*

With a house full, Quality Street takes centre stage, satisfying kids of any age
The quality in the name makes choosing a traditional family game
It's simply the best of 'present' day sweets
Quality Street proves like pantomime – you can please all the people all the time
For Claus encounters of the family kind, sharing Quality Street helps us unwind
Opening the colourful wrapper adds an extra tasteful gift for everyone
Quality Street keeps the ding dong going merrily on high
Quality Street makes for good cheer, not only at Christmas but all through the year

▶ **Coca-Cola and Schweppes always give me something to sing about at Tesco because...**

PRODUCT: *Soft drinks*
COMPETITION: *Tesco/Coca-Cola and Schweppes Christmas Carol*

While shepherds watch 'you know who' is stocking up
Slimline Schweppes or Diet Coke brand lead Tesco's healthy keep fit band
They are a classical pair and harmonise with other fare
Every be-bopping bubble bounces to the beat
Mix and mingle or straight and single, they make me swingle
I saw three Schweppes coke sailing by, tonic, coke and ginger dry
Coke and Schweppes keep me young, and like Cliff, Tesco's number one
They're a cracking Christmas double, loadsa savings, loadsa bubble
Whenever people gather and mingle, Tesco and Schweppes provide the jingle
Party time is tickety-boo with Tesco, Coke and Sch... 'You know who'

▶ I want to visit Father Christmas because...

PRODUCT: Chain store goods
COMPETITION: House of Fraser/Lapland
PRIZES: Trips to Lapland

Like visiting House of Fraser, it would be bliss, a Santastic trip, I hope I don't
     miss
He gives everyone so much pleasure it would be nice to thank him personally
My children's glowing faces, glimpsing magical scenes, Santa, snow and
     reindeer, please fulfil their dreams
A Frasercard buys you time to pay, for the gifts you send from Santa's sleigh
The spirit of Christmas is giving, so I hope he gives me first prize
Skidoo through the snow, where's Santa? Let's go, what a delight, let's win that
     flight
My little 'deer' with starry gaze, asks every year, where Santa stays
I want to put the Fraser logo above the entrance to Santa's grotto
Childhood fantasies only come true, for the House of Fraser fortunate few
He is childhood's most magical and enchanting memory
I'd sit on the lap of that wonderful chap and give him gifts to unwrap
He travels fast just like a laser, he is quick like House of Fraser
He'll then see me in the land of lap and not in the land of nod
With reindeer ready, his sleigh full of toys, Santa brings happiness to girls and
     boys
Searching for Santa at the end of the year, beats sitting at home in the reindeer
     (*rain, dear)
Visiting Santa on skidoo, beats travelling by coach on the M62
We could skedadal in a skidoo and see Father Christmas in an igloo
Now we've got a gas fire he won't be coming down our chimney

▶ I like Christmas pantomimes with Cadbury's because...

PRODUCT: Confectionery
COMPETITION: Tesco/Cadbury's at Christmas
PRIZES: Trips to Christmas pantomimes with overnight accommodation

Baddies to boo, goodies to eat, Cadbury's and panto – a spectacular treat
All kids at heart, we guzzle chox, wishing the genie would refill the box

Pantos are fun, Cadbury's are yummy, with two ugly sisters, daddy and
    mummy
Each magical assortment takes centre stage, appealing to kids of every age
This British tradition, unique to these Isles, like Cadbury's, brings happiness,
    laughter and smiles
Cadbury's chocs, at front seat stalls, I'm kept inspired till the curtain falls
Hotfoot to Tesco for Cadbury's chocs – Frank Bruno playing Goldilocks
A comical dame, the villain that's scary, please wave your wand, oh Cadbury's
    fairy

▶ **Cranberry sauce is the perfect accompaniment to my
Christmas Turkey because...**

PRODUCT: Cranberry sauce
COMPETITION: Ocean Spray cranberry sauce
PRIZES: Christmas hampers

Fruity, juicy, sharp yet sweet, makes any turkey taste unique
The rich fruit, the bright berry, Ocean Spray makes Christmas Merry
Its fruity flavour enhances the day, but only if it's Ocean Spray
The best part of tradition is Ocean Spray's addition
No doubt about it – can't eat my turkey without it!
Cranberry sauce by Ocean Spray complements turkey in every way
The perfect partners for Christmas Day, turkey served with Ocean Spray
The cost is nominal, the taste phenomenal
The cranberries in Ocean Spray keep the taste buds popping on Christmas Day
Ocean Spray is 'jolly' fruity – turns our bird into a festive beauty
All the trimmings I can boast, if Ocean Spray completes my roast
Christmas turkey isn't dressed, unless it wears the 'berry' best
My dish of the day is 'made' with Ocean Spray
Always fresh, always sound, always a joy to pass around
Our Christmas wouldn't be Merry, without this little red berry
Ocean Spray on Christmas Day, delicious in its 'saucy' way

CLEAN

▶ **Flash, Hoover and Wm Low help you CLEAN because...**

PRODUCT: Cleaners
COMPETITION: Wm Low/Flash Aquamaster bathroom
PRIZES: Hoover appliances

Wm Low's Flash through the tills, like Aquamaster with your spills
This trio means in every sense, cleaning aids of excellence
With this trio of masters, there's no more housework disasters
They form a winning team, guaranteed to make the whole house gleam
Flash and Hoover reduce cleaning chores by reducing prices WM LOW scores

This team answers a housewife's prayer, with performance and value beyond compare

They have a scratchless reputation for power, drive and acceleration

For savings, service, spotlessness, speed, they fulfil every housewife's need

Hoover brings power, Flash removes stains, at William 'Low' prices – everyone gains

Upstairs, downstairs, inside or out – the cleanest winning team without a doubt

CLEANERS

► **I would like to win a Presto Panda with Ajax because...**

PRODUCT: Cleaner
COMPETITION: Presto/Ajax panda car
FIRST PRIZE: Panda car

I'd get clean away after passing the M.O.P. test

RUNNERS-UP: Panda toy bears

It would drive me clean round the bend with delight

Performance of both is smooth, brilliant and outshines all rivals

They each give a guarantee – low price, high quality

One is a dream machine, one has the gleam supreme

Presto and Ajax panda to all my cleaning tasks

It will sweep me off my knees

Round the house or around the block they are sparkling performers

Hey presto their performance is magic

They both drive the dirt off the opposition

Getting around would no longer be PANDAmonium

The only Panda I can afford is a chest-ex Panda

I can't 'bear' being without one

► **I use Dry Magic on my Oriental carpets because...**

PRODUCT: Dry carpet cleaner

You cannot be experimental, it's Dry Magic for your oriental

Oriental or wall to wall, Dry Magic safely cleans them all

► **My family and I would have fun under the sun this winter because...**

PRODUCT: Washing-up liquid
COMPETITION: Tesco/Morning Fresh holiday in the sun

Gleams really do come true, when Morning Fresh washes up for you

We'd holiday on the Corinth Canal with Morning Fresh – both cut through Greece

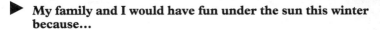

Providing Morning Fresh fulfils our wishes and all will enjoy those foreign
　　dishes
With warming sun and gentle breezes – we'd forget our coughs and sneezes
Sun, sand and family treat – like Morning Fresh's shine it's hard to beat
Morning Fresh makes dishes and wishes come shining through

▶ **I would like to win a super Kershan rug with 1001 because...**

> PRODUCT: *Liquid carpet cleaner*
> COMPETITION: *Co-op/1001*
> PRIZES: *Kershan rugs*

Even with grandchildren at play, 1001 saves the day
I would be a Co-op slave, with this gift from Aladdin's cave
I know it would stay good as new, using 1001 foam shampoo
It would keep its colour after 1001 colour schemes
They are supercarpetfragilisticexpialidocious
I know I can trust 1001 to keep the rug A1
A Kershan rug would be the first luxury item in my new home
With a combination like that I'd have the world at my feet
No need to journey too far east for a Kershan rug and Co-op feast

▶ **I get a golden handshake every week at Tesco because...**

> PRODUCT: *Household gloves*
> COMPETITION: *Tesco/Marigold gloves*
> PRIZES: *£500 cash*

It is hand in glove with cash in hand

▶ **I use Johnson Pledge and Sparkle because...**

> PRODUCTS: *Cleaners*

Routine cleaning I abhor, with Pledge and Sparkle it's no chore
Sparkles are a girl's best friend
I'm a Johnson's buff
My vote is pledged to this coalition, I reject the opposition
This brace sets the pace for a fresher cleaner place

▶ **Jeyes is the secret weapon of germ warfare because...**

> PRODUCT: *Disinfectant*

Wherever deadly germs may lurk, Jeyes fluids and powders do their work
Jeyes products used each day really do keep germs at bay
Although germs can't be seen, Jeyes kills them quick and clean
Whether floors, drains, sinks or loo, Jeyes kills germs with freshness too
Pick up Jeyes, give a squirt, say goodbye to germs and dirt
Goodbye germs, goodbye infection, Jeyes gives me complete protection

▶ **I buy Ariel washing powders at Tesco because...**

PRODUCT: Washing powder
COMPETITION: Tesco/Ariel/Sports

They're the leader of the brands and I'm the keenest of their fans
Automatically programmed to my need, they give value, economy and speed
Both are tops for a spin around
Terrific product, splendid store, matched together 'who needs more?'
I've cleaner cuffs and fresher socks without those dreaded check-out shocks
They give the very best from your pocket to your vest
Team-mates should go round together, hope these two go on forever
It would be nice and clean before it took a tumble
From clothes to base-line I have an advantage
It's quick off the mark at getting marks off quick
I like to win with flying colours
I'm tired of getting booked by the ref for playing dirty
It tackles stains and kicks dirt into touch without trying
It would shine on the line
Through tries and tests it scores the best
It gives spotless performance in a dirty game
Whatever cycle or machine, my gear change would turn out clean
What works better 'on your marks'?
It likes to play inside left and outside bright
Our family makes a glowing team, spick and span with Ariel clean
Walking, running, fitter and thinner, Ariel guarantees my kit is a winner
Feeling fresh, looking great, Ariel's your best team-mate
Clean washing is what appeals and Tesco offers the best in deals
Tesco eases shopping strains, Ariel zaps washing stains
Tesco's my prop, Ariel's my line, washday blues are never mine

▶ **I would like to win a Miralec Supreme shower with Oz from Tesco because...**

PRODUCT: Limescale cleaner
COMPETITION: Tesco/Miralec and Oz
PRIZE: Miralec Supreme shower

I'd have the whole spray and nothing but the spray, so help me Oz

▶ **Filetti with a softness theme**

PRODUCT: Swiss washing powder

Whitens safely, effective, mild – only the best for you my child
Alpine fresh, Swiss and new, fluffy Filetti means softness for you
Hush-a-bye baby, comfy soft clothes, washed in Filetti, from head to your toes
Filetti's purity is my baby's security
Skin soft and silky, your clothes are the same, washed with Filetti, remember
    the name

Gentle Filetti works with me, to keep your clothes soft and your skin trouble free
Filetti is pure, its softness appeals, it shows the others a clean pair of heels
Your beautiful skin says 'handle with care' – the secret of softness with Filetti I share
Thank heavens for my little 'Swiss Made'
Thanks to Filetti the gnomes are not the only people who enjoy 'Zu-riches'
For a whiter wash without irritation, Filetti belongs to a new generation
Skin so tender, skin so new, Filetti powder is the choice for you
Bye bye tears, bye bye troubles, all washed away on Filetti magic bubbles
Mummy doesn't make rash decisions, I never use anything else but Filetti
Filetti knocks spots off the rest, it cleans so gently, but whitens best
Your dirty clothes of yesterday, Filetti washed them clean away

Disinfectants

Upstairs, downstairs, inside and out, sterling trio seeks germs out
It's not money down the drain, it's sterling well spent
When they pour, they reign
Neat or with waste – they send germs to the slaughter
I don't pay a packet for their protection racket

Freshness

It's fresh, strong and picked up for a song
It always gives an air of freshness
A breath of spring each day it brings
They always excel, leave a nice smell and the job's done well
Money well spent, it's heaven scent
Its vibrant performance makes sound scents

Hoover vacuum cleaners

A quick turn with Hoover makes me a wonderwoman
With Hoover automation I keep a spotless reputation
Whatever the sentence there's no hard labour with Hoover
For domestic manoeuvre, depend on Hoover

Jeyes Bloo toilet cleaner

Now the loo is seen to be Jeyes Bloo clean
Germs don't stop on Bloo sprayed loos
It makes my loo too blootiful for words
Blue is the colour, hygiene is the game
It gives my loo true blue sparkle

Killing germs with Dettol disinfectant

It keeps our household germ-free and that's clean enough for me
Killing all germs, not just a few, home's healthy, helps gardeners too
It kills germs discreetly and freshens completely
It stops those germs from singing in the drain
From cellar to attic, they keep homes safe and aromatic
It's the powerful collection that gives lasting protection
For maximum protection it's the obvious selection
Our health's in safe hands with these quality brands
Supersanitational it's really quite sensational
Toilets flip their lids and sinks go round the bend without it
A sparkling house is what I'm after, it's my slave and I'm the master
Everywhere that germs are lurking, mums trust Dettol to keep on working
Recommended by my granny, Dettol cleans every nook and cranny
This Mrs Whitehouse prefers the Dettol name for her clean up campaign

Other cleaners

As they outshine all opposition, they fully deserve wide recognition
For cleansing and bleaching their range is far-reaching
An end to chores of grease and grime and jobs are done in record time
To sweep, perchance to clean, ay, there's the rub
All my little treasures are seen and not blurred

Toilet cleaners

Pine trees, floral breeze, rooms filled with smells that please
They keep odours at bay leaving nice smells to stay
Their protection rackets don't cost a packet
I just can't get it out of my cistern
It protects my toilet on a grand scale
It doesn't run away until it's finished its work
It brings the whoosh to my loo
It always makes me skip to m'loo
It leaves the loo as clean as a whistle
It guards like a sentry, germs find there's no entry
Every flush is a penny well spent
It flushes with success and fragrant cleanliness
It's the one that leaves the loo smelling like Kew
It gives rhapsody in blue with a royal flush
When you pull the handle they compose 'water music'
Used at one's own convenience, they're reasonably priced
It kills germs discreetly and freshens completely
Everywhere that germs are lurking, mums trust Bloo to keep on working
Upstairs, downstairs, in the loo, Bloo kills germs and smells good too
Good habits need no words – B Y'S U'S J'S (*Be wise, use Jeyes)
Racasan has a flair for transmitting freshness through the air
Freshening the air, cleaning the pan, nothing can beat Racasan

Washing powders

It brightens, freshens and whitens to give excellent results
It's the soft option that brings out the worst in clothes
Every bubble washes double
The cost is nominal, the performance phenomenal
The formula's just right, everything's clean and bright
At last at my 'Special Branch' the 'Grime Squad' and the 'Gentle Touch' work
    together
All things bright and beautiful for people great and small

COFFEE

▶ **Douwe Egberts is a great taste to wake up to because...**

PRODUCT: *Filter coffee*
COMPETITION: *Philips/Douwe Egberts coffee*
PRIZES: *Philips coffee filter machines*

A bedtime coffee at its best, leaves me feeling quite refreshed
A cupful taken early morning helps me stop persistent yawning
Delicious coffee right on cue with rich aroma filtering through
Douwe Egberts brews, catch the news, arise enthused, goodbye blues
Freshly brewed, piping hot, aroma, flavour, it's got the lot
Full-bodied flavour is so appealing when facing that Monday morning feeling
Full-bodied flavour is so appealing when looking at the mirror in the ceiling
Perfection when we awaken, far too tempting to save for the bacon
That first refreshing fragrant cup ensures your day is on the up
The full-bodied flavour revives enough, leave jogging to the fitness buff
Aroma and flavour, following my snooze, Douwe Egberts' real good news
A Douwe Egberts cuppa is the perfect wakenuppa
Arousing aroma, flavour divine, are fillups for loafers to rise and shine
At the dawn of the day it gets me up and away
With best flavour yet from Douwe Egberts and Philips duet
Delicious aroma from this smoothie, encourages everyone to discard their
    duvet
It has to be said, it's delicious in bed
It turns a rude awakening into a gentle dawning
The perfect start to any day, fresh coffee in bed, favourite DJ
Wakey wakey rise and shine, Douwe Egberts coffee tastes just fine
Whatever your taste of radio band, everyone agrees this coffee's grand
Who needs wakening with a kiss with fresh aromatic coffee like this

▶ **I prefer the taste of Douwe Egberts coffee because...**

PRODUCT: *Filter coffee*

It adds the touch that makes dinner a winner

Second to none it reigns when it pours

It is by far and away the finest ever to filter through

It's pure, full-bodied, rich and fine, smells delicious, tastes divine

I can sip luxury without having to swallow bitterness

Dinner Over Unanimously We Enjoy Every Grain Because Egberts Really Tastes Supreme *(DOUWE EGBERTS = ACROSTIC)*

It's the cream of the coffee and I'm not milked

It gives me no grounds for complaint

They filter the best discarding the rest

It puts eloquence in any after-dinner speaker

Its blend and roast is first choice for the perfect host

In a world of imitations Douwe Egberts gets my seal of approval

Its worldwide popular flavour grinds the rest into the ground

Its the flavour I can bank on without losing my balance

Everybody knows you'd be a mug to drink anything else

It 'perks' me up so much I can't 'stir' without it

Every succulent sip is great. Douwe Egberts is my coffee mate

They boast the roast I like most

Dutch Originality Utilising Worldly Experience Ensures Great Blends, Exquisitely Refreshing To Savour *(DOUWE EGBERTS = ACROSTIC)*

With aroma and flavour intact – perfection's assured and freshness a fact

Four countries in my cup give me international co-offee-ration at its best

Driving it's reviving, working it's perking, resting it's zesting

It keeps me perked up and full of beans

▶ **For the highest standard in coffee I buy Melitta from Tesco because...**

PRODUCT: Filter coffee
COMPETITION: Tesco/Melitta coffee

I save an awful lot of coppers in ze-bill

I can quaff like a toff without selling the Van Gogh

When spirits flag they turn Blue Peters into Jolly Rogers

Its strength is my weakness

Both have changed me from an 'instant' housewife into a 'real' hostess

Taste temptation free from inclination and imagine the sensation – a Rio vacation

From mountain top, from ship to shop, Melitta/Tesco crown the crop

It's a pricey taste at a tasty price

Backing winners makes good sense, this classic double saves the pence

No fancy gimmicks, passing trends, just finest beans, perfected blends

Tesco's a girls best friend while Melitta's a man's best blend

They both give their competitors a good roasting

Traditional cup or cappuccino, Tesco prices leave cash for the vino

It's like Wembley, easily the finest ground for success in the cup

Always it gives elevenses out of ten

Melitta from Tesco – a nice penthouse taste at a basement price

Coffee in general

As jaded hostesses would endorse, it's the best refresher course
It gives the end of the meal gourmet appeal
It's the after-dinner guest that speaks for itself
It provides grounds for success without the grind
It's the pick me up that never lets me down
Thermal goodness in a tin, it pushes cold out from within
It puts a glowing 'ember' into Nov'ember and Dec'ember
It would be the only smart mug there
I'd get a thrill each time the cup is lifted
I gave it a 'try', now I'm converted
Lyons blend in their vacuum pack the full fresh flavour others lack

COMBINATION

▶ **I think Tesco and Hoover make a winning COMBINATION because...**

PRODUCT: Washing machines

They wave the wand while I read James Bond
Both use technology as an aid to economy
They are a legend in their own grime
Economically and ecologically washloads are easily overcome
They are both value for money
Their clear action brings clean satisfaction
They're both fast and efficient
Green plus green adds up to a laundry bright white
Tesco keeps the prices right, while Hoover gets the whites bright
Together they are a mean cleaning machine

▶ **Heinz and the Co-op are a winning COMBINATION because...**

PRODUCT: Supermarket foods

Heinz flare and Co-op care, make a winning pair
They co-operate and care, looking after your 'wealthfare'

▶ **Heinz and Kwik Save are a winning COMBINATION because...**

PRODUCT: Supermarket foods
PRIZES: Trips to Florida

Of the price on the tin and the goodness within
They squeeze prices like Miami Vices
The odds are in their flavour, quality brands from a money saver

▶ **Andrex and Morrisons are a strong COMBINATION because...**

PRODUCT: *Toilet rolls*
COMPETITION: *Morrisons/Andrex/Cruise down the Nile*

Even the enigmatic Sphinx could not find two stronger links

▶ **Robertson's and Seville are my favourite COMBINATION because...**

PRODUCT: *Conserves*

Moorish flavour is their boast, golden and sumptuous, that's my toast
This fruity twosome, it is said, dragged Sleeping Beauty from her bed

▶ **Abbey National and American Express make the perfect COMBINATION because...**

PRODUCT: *Travellers' cheques*
COMPETITION: *Abbey National/Travel money*
PRIZES: *Travellers' cheques*

Lost or stolen or otherwise stray, this combination is best when away
Peace of mind is at hand, when you're in a foreign land
Local service is simply divine, with worldwide access and helpful helpline
They make travel fun, speedy, safe, reliable service to the sun
At home there's security with interest, when travelling they've interest in
   security
It's all under one brolly and takes care of your lolly
With minimum fuss, maximum speed, this global alliance is all I need
It's the connection that gives you worry-free travel perfection
Hand in hand, together they'll find carefree travel and peace of mind
A National abroad needs Express service for the perfect holiday
Top two companies give tip top rates and service
Wherever you stay, they go out their way, to make your day
You can relax while you're away, knowing your money's OK
They are the best combination for service, safety, simplicity and satisfaction
They link before you can blink, providing an unbeatable service
By giving you peace of mind, travel is made the easy kind
If storm clouds gather, clearer skies are only a telephone call away
Good friends never let you down
They look after your money interests while you enjoy your holiday
Their safe combination is number one
Business or vacation there's no hesitation, our service is the very best
You get hi-rate exchange, not an irate exchange
With friends like these, you may travel with ease
They are easily bought, easily carried and easily spent
The combination gives peace of mind, the best protection you can find
Expert service and smiling faces, they're my passport to exotic places
Peace of mind is your most important piece of luggage

While the best things in life are free, money gives you security
You will enjoy your vacation without aggravation
They're internationally acclaimed – world wide their fame – always ahead of the game
No-one goes further to make travelling easier
They are a passport to trouble-free cash
No matter how far away, they give fast efficient service without delay
It is reassuring that good service at home can be taken abroad

▶ **Asda price and Kenco coffee is a COMBINATION worth preserving because...**

PRODUCT: Filter coffee
COMPETITION: Asda/Kenco Coffee/National Trust
PRIZES: Annual membership to National Trust

Kenco coffee is a must, Asda price has National Trust
They let the best filter through to the Englishman's castle
Their national trust is upstairs value at downstairs prices

▶ **Mars ice cream and the Olympics is a winning COMBINATION because...**

PRODUCT: Ice cream
COMPETITION: Safeway/Mars ice cream/Olympics
PRIZE: Trip to Florida

Ice cool Mars, Olympic flame, 'Safeways' to board the Florida plane

▶ **Hale Trent cakes and Presto stores COMBINED together give...**

PRODUCT: Cakes

Quality cakes without a doubt and shoppers with something to yodel about
A chance for this lass to enjoy a Swiss pass
Chances to climb mountains if you come in and take your pick
We have a cracker of a Jamboree when they club together
People have always associated Presto with the best in biscuits
They provide a delectable destination for my economy drive

COMBINATIONS in general

Just like Dud and Pete a winning combination, quick to 'Cook' and 'Moore' to eat
So quick to heat and eat, such delicious combinations that you'll find them hard to beat
Come pre-paired for us that's neat
Paired up to perfection to make any meal complete
For sheer elegance and chic their combination c'est magnifique
One selects superior stock, one arrests my hunger clock

For choice, value and nutrition, both surpass all competition
Both look after your interest and give value for money
It's a reliable combination which gives good service
When two greats meet, their fame is hard to beat

COMMUNITY

▶ **We think of Wavy Line as our community grocer because...**

PRODUCT: Food stores foods

They know that good family fare is a family affair
As my nearest not dearest I spend on fare but not fares

COMPUTER

▶ **Every home should have a computer because...**

PRODUCT: Biactol medicated skin cleanser
COMPETITION: Biactol/Computers

Like Biactol they are the future for every face
Basic Information Applied Completely To Spot On Learning *(BIACTOL =
    ACROSTIC)*
Like Biactol it ensures you face the future with confidence
It knocks spots off pencil and paper
In our house it has put a brand new complexion on things

COSMETICS

▶ **If my Eastern promise companion could make one promise to
me, it would be...**

PRODUCT: Cosmetics
COMPETITION: Cover Girl/Far East
PRIZE: Holiday for two in Far East

An exotic eastern holiday – social life a whirl – waltzing with the King of Siam
and me, a Cover Girl

▶ **I would like to experience RoC at Ragdale Hall because...**

PRODUCT: Skin care

COMPETITION: *Tesco/RoC/Ragdale Hall*
PRIZES: *Weekends at Ragdale Hall*

With RoC's supreme skin care and Ragdale's style and splendour I should come away refreshed, relaxed, supple and slender

Once upon a time a lovely girl married, mothered, worked, became jaded, please RoC and Ragdale revive what has faded

For relaxation, health and good skin care, RoC and Ragdale are the perfect pair

Stress wreaks havoc on figure and face, RoC and Ragdale are my saving grace

RoC and Ragdale Hall – beauty is their theme – rest and rejuvenation – this harassed mother's dream

▶ Foster Grant sunglasses look great on my face because...

PRODUCT: *Sunglasses*

They add a little bit of cheek and a shade of surprise

▶ High Definition defines make-up because...

PRODUCT: *Foundation make-up*

Such technological innovation used to be a 'pigment' of my imagination

Charlie perfume

Has the knack, she's in the know, always prepared and ready to go

The 'scents' of freedom, adventure, pazazz, that only a Charlie user has

Confident, independent, determined to be an achiever – she also needs an irrepressible Joie de Vivre

A taste for adventure, an air for fun and keeping Charlie as my No. 1

Perfume products

It announces my arrival and delays my departure

With that spray which makes things happen, I would catch myself a Latin

I am a girl with a touch of class because more than a touch would be just too much

The perfect spray to last all day

The perfume's terrific, the effect stunning, a welcome addition to feminine cunning

Putting on Babe at '45' makes me feel like '33$\frac{1}{3}$' and more alive

Cool and trendy Babe is the talc of the town

Revlon cosmetics with an Italian theme

Beautiful clothes, Revlon faces, handsome men and romantic places

The magic collection gives British girls perfection

Long enchanted nights and dreamy days thanks to Revlon's Roman gaze

Visions of perfection because Revlon provides the Italian Collection

An Italian Collection that's enough to make you blush

Looking good even when feeling the pinch

I just adore a Latin close encounter starting with a 'Revolutionary' pinch

A touch of class by Chianti, a pizza resistance by Revlon of course

No more Rome-ing since Revlon colours, so Ve-Nice makes looking beautiful a Pisa cake

Revlon cosmetics give it to me, delicious eyes cream, from Italy

Two thousand years from the glory of the Caesars to the elegance of Rosa di Roma

Like my Revlon lipstick – Latin style with a satin smile

Vichy skin care products

Years simply fade away as Vichy keeps the lines at bay

Vichy's pure, Vichy's simple that's why my skin has not a wrinkle

Vichy every day, keeps wrinkles at bay

Super selection, pampered protection, Vichy at Boots suits my purse and complexion

Vichy slenderising cream

When hips and thighs are oversize, Vichy cream will slenderize

Experts perfected this cream that takes a firm hand keeping me lean

I used Vichy every day and saw the flab just melt away

It keeps hips and thighs trim and is kind to the skin

The plant extract helps remove past excesses

Just a thimble full each night, fights flabby thighs and cellulite

My Vichy minimises where cellulite emphaTHIGHSes

It firms me up and slims me down

Twice a day use the cream and you look twice as lean

COSTS

▶ **Housekeeping costs are always low at Tesco because...**

PRODUCT: Supermarket foods

Bargains and offers make me richer, but guaranteed value completes the picture

Lightening reductions are always followed by thunderous applause

▶ **Associated Biscuits help me to cut costs by...**

PRODUCT: Biscuits

Providing the lion's share of bargains to the family's roar of approval

COUNTRIES, CITIES AND TOWNS

AMERICA

▶ I would like to eat my Cadbury's eclairs in Belair because...

PRODUCT: Confectionery

Mingling with millionaires, I'll share my mints if they share theirs
After the weekly grind, this sweetie needs to unwind
I could pic'n'mix with the Hollywood chicks
Amongst the glamour, glitz and action, Cadbury's eclairs are the star attraction
They are twentieth century chox (*20th Century Fox)

▶ Uncle Ben's rice and Texas theme

PRODUCT: Rice

Barbecuing courtesy of Uncle Ben's foods, just the life for active dudes
Uncle Ben's gourmets rice – Texas my Wild West paradise
I may be a dude but I know good food
Exciting experience, welcome change, always at home on their range
With Uncle Sam's welcome, Uncle Ben's rice, ranching rivals paradise
Lone Star State and alfresco cuisine, kindles my American dream
Texan food is finer than the junk from China
Uncle Ben's is no greenhorn, it complements everything perfectly, especially
　　Texan longhorn
Riding, fresh air, ribs and rice, is western style paradise

▶ Lee jeans use the copy line 'The Jeans that built America' because...

PRODUCT: Denim jeans
PRIZE: Trip for two to the MTV Video Music Awards in Los Angeles plus £500

'Coast to Coast' across the nations, quality and style, 'Build Great
　　Foundations'

▶ I would love to win flights to Orlando with Virgin Atlantic because...

PRODUCT: Airline tickets
PRIZES: Air tickets to Florida

They're first for value, second to none and like Orlando Number One
Even a kid like me was made to feel like a V.I.P.

America in general

I'm a sucker for tall storeys
I'd meet Mickey Mouse and Goofy too, they really exist, I always knew
Horses roam free, cactus grows high, it's the kind of place money can't buy
I enjoy the Big Apple to the Core (*New York)
Midas touched this golden state, millions filter through its gate

AUSTRALIA

▶ **Why don't Australians give a Castlemaine XXXX for anything else?**

PRODUCT: Lager

No other Australian brew has more hops than a kangaroo
Other lagers, couldn't drink 'em, only Castlemaine is fair dinkum
It matches the land – smooth and gold like Bondi sand
Not even Bondi sands feel like XXXX in the hand
This Aussie brew gave the kanger its OO!
Like boomerangs and didgeridoos, XXXX is the one to choose

▶ **'Neighbours' and Willow are the perfect teatime treats because...**

PRODUCT: Butter
PRIZES: Camcorders

For double pleasure use your loaf, relax, switch on and enjoy both
Crumpets with Willow, wonderful treat, with daily fix of Ramsay Street
Finding 'Neighbours' hard to swallow? Spread some Willow enjoy a wallow
Willow for tea, kids' squabbles cease, letting me watch 'Neighbours' in peace
Tears and laughter sandwiched together, friendships rewarded with spreadable pleasure
Love thy neighbour as a friend, love thy Willow as a blend
They're an un'Koala'fied success, 'transporting' you after a day's duress
Busy housewife, little time, 'Neighbours' and Willow suit me just fine
They're a 'put your feet up' combination – fascinating viewing and taste sensation
Like good friends, they 'Will O W'ways be there
Willow always tastes the tops, 'Neighbours' tops the TV slots
'Neighbours' tops the viewers poll, Willow tops their teatime roll
Together they make teatime absolutely 'Madge-ic'
'Neighbours' for taste, Willow for cream, put together, a teatime dream
Without them my koala can't bear it and my Eucalyptus leaves!
Your camcorder at school teatimes could record Willow and 'Neighbours' being adored
For style and performance unsurpassed, Willow and 'Neighbours' are perfectly cast
From Ramsay Street to Dairy Crest, their producers 'churn out' the best

Being upper crust and well bred, like Willow, 'Neighbours' fame has spread
Gossip from 'Neighbours', Willow on bread, both as tasty and easily spread
They're both legends in their own teatime
'Neighbours' cliffhangers may get you excited, but Willow's flavour leaves you
     delighted
These two for tea, make tea for two, an essential daily rendezvous
It's Kylie likely there's no better taste
My favourite programme is churned out down under, while Willow is churned-
     out wonder
Once – completely devoid of charm, had tea with 'Flora' and 'Emmerdale
     Farm'
Both 'Neighbours' and Willow have recipes clever, winning ingredients mixed
     in together
Dreamy Willow with a slice of 'Oz' – Wizard fare if ever there was
Both have the quality that matters most – consuming interest, coast to toast
Willow brings taste to every occasion, family, party or 'Neighbours' invasion

BELGIUM

▶ **I would like to eat my Cadbury's eclairs in Brussels because...**

   PRODUCT: Confectionery

In Poirot's country I'd d'eclair, their flavour's just great anywhere

▶ **I would like to go to Bruges because...**

   PRODUCT: Wall planners

Like Rexel Wallplanners it 'encapsulates' everything European within one place

BRITAIN

▶ **Britain is great for holidays because...**

   PRODUCT: British holidays

Rain or sun resorts are fun, hills and moors make lovely tours
The Kingdom is united in wishing you were here
This traditional package has it all wrapped up
It always delivers a first class package
It's better the village you know than 'de villa' you don't
You'll find the best of Beautiful Resorts Impressive Towns Idyllic Scenery Here
     (BRITISH = ACROSTIC)
No language snarls or airport hassle, scenery's great by shore or castle
Of country walks, golden beaches, vales, hills and mountain reaches
There are sands, bands, tours, moors, piers, fairs, follies, lollies for all
There's so much to see besides the sea
North, South, East and West, places, food and people are best
It is a beautiful island with a royal stamp of approval

If the world's your oyster, Britain's the pearl
Holidays in Britain are fun because the mother-in-law lives in France
There's so much ado for next to nothing
Good food, scenery, lots to do, England's bonus, the dog comes too
It's not like holidays spent in Spain, it's sterling value, guaranteed gain

▶ **I buy British because...**

PRODUCT: British foods

Making do with second best is foreign to me
They're British, they're best and can beat all the rest

▶ **I would like to go to Westminster because...**

It's the only way I'll get a seat in the Lords

EGYPT

▶ **Andrex and Morrisons are a strong combination because...**

PRODUCT: Toilet rolls
COMPETITION: Morrisons/Andrex/Cruise on the Nile

Even the enigmatic Sphinx could not find two stronger links

▶ **I prefer Crown paint because...**

PRODUCT: Paint in tins

I used to 'Peer-Amid' the gloom 'till Crown White brightened up my tomb

▶ **Sainsbury's new potatoes are the best because...**

PRODUCT: Potatoes
PRIZE: Cruise on the Nile

With tasty tubers to grace your meal, Sainsbury's offers a Pharaoh deal

▶ **I would love to cruise down the Nile with Cleopatra at Asda because...**

PRODUCT: Supermarket foods
PRIZE: Cruise on the Nile

Asda prices are a dream come true, a cruise down the Nile would be one too
I could sit on the bank of the Nile with my mummy

FAR EAST

▶ **If my Eastern promise companion could make one promise to me, it would be...**

PRODUCT: *Cover Girl cosmetics*
PRIZE: *Holiday for two in Far East*

An exotic eastern holiday – social life a whirl – waltzing with the King of Siam and me, a Cover Girl

▶ Sharwood's is the natural choice for the full flavour of the Orient because...

PRODUCT: *Spices and chutneys*

They make wholesome, authentic Chinese fare, with that extra ingredient – Sharwood's care
For authentic flavour, find Sharwood's display, it's the ultimate Chinese takeaway
Eastern spices I unlock, so I can be wicked with my wok
With crackers, marinades, oils, sauces, Sharwood's great for all courses

▶ Dry magic carpet cleaner Oriental theme

PRODUCT: *Dry carpet cleaner*

You cannot be experimental, it's Dry Magic for your oriental
Dry magic, best on the market, guaranteed even for your oriental carpet
Dry magic cleans without harm, restoring oriental charm
Oriental or wall to wall, Dry Magic safely cleans them all
Oriental or roll end – Dry Magic is the pile's best friend

FRANCE

▶ We can say without doubt that our holiday in France is...

PRODUCT: *Paper towels*
COMPETITION: *Fiesta kitchen towel roll*
PRIZES: *Trips to Paris with spending money*

Scottfree – that's the besta Fiesta
A fiestaval we'll resort to again
Like Fiesta, everything rolled into one

▶ I enjoy French food and wine because...

PRODUCT: *French foods*
COMPETITION: *Grandways/French food & wine*

From simple meal to festive treat, French food and wine are hard to beat
With the French connection and Grandways selection I taste perfection
Fresh varieties, wines supreme, it's a Grandway to haute cuisine
La crème de la crème – a gourmet's delight – many Grandways to tempt my appetite
The French taste is unique and choice c'est magnifique

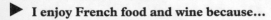

The taste drives me in-Seine

Vin de pays excites me, pâté de champagne delights me, hope Grandways invites me

Grandways' vin de pays, French bread and brie, conjure up Paris for me

Be it for pleasure or celebration, perfect for every occasion

It tastes out of this world but doesn't cost the earth

Have gourmet tastes they suit my palate

For Grandways to dine the French are sublime

▶ I enjoy the taste of Baxter's French pâté because...

PRODUCT: French pâté

Buy a Baxter's French pâté and turn your meal into a banquet

Its fame is spread from coast to toast

Baxter's French pâtés take some beating, turning ordinary snacks into gourmet eating

Baxter's French pâté c'est si bon, it's soon all gone

Baxter's French pâté perfect for a tasty spread

For a toast of Britain buy the taste of French Baxter's pâtés

Baxter's French pâté, the starter that finishes ahead of the rest

First class fare with continental flair

Make your day bright with the gourmet's delight – Buy French pâté

Let's be Franc, a taste of France from Baxter's makes Cents

Paris

▶ A weekend in Paris is exciting...

PRODUCT: Sanitary towels
COMPETITION: Minima Bodyform/Shopping spree in Paris
PRIZES: £100 cash

Because by the time you see the Mona Lisa you'll know why she is smiling

Marvellous Irresistible Nightlife Intimate Magnetic Atmosphere, Beyond Ones Dreams Yes Fabulous Occasion Really Magic *(MINIMA BODYFORM = ACROSTIC)*

Because Paris, a lady of many charms, welcomes lovers with open arms

Its romantic, relaxing atmosphere, good cuisine and friendly people, makes it the perfect getaway

Like Dior – fun like Gaultier, romantic like Chanel, wicked like Mugler and always in Vogue

C'est à la Mode, C'est très chic pour moi, Paris est magnifique

It's exciting and absorbing in any shape or form

It makes me feel forty and naughty, instead of fifty and thrifty

Wining and dining, dancing chic to chic, would make a weekend in Paris magnifique

Eiffel tower – lots to view, fashion houses, dreams come true, romantic dinners just we two

Between visiting the Louvre and shopping I'm torn, Paris modes may improve my 'Body Form'

Shopping and sightseeing by the mile, it's 'Amour' romantic city, remember Mona Lisa's smile?

Cos there's so much to see and do, The Seine, Louvre and Eiffel Tower too

Because a secret assignation in romantic Paree reminds me of Minima – discreet just like me

And having left your old pad behind, there's now more absorbing things in mind

Modern art, a peep at the past, gastronomic delights, I'm packing fast

Shopping, sight-seeing, café-au-lait, then 'Joie-de-Vivre' at the cabaret

For a Hyde bound lady who has de Gaulle to dream of winning

Paris has variety, the spice of life which makes a body feel on top form

UK Adieu, Paris à Deux – sights and sounds inviting

Leisurely, Interesting, Beautiful, Relaxing, Entertaining, Surprising, Sensational and Educational (LIBRESSE = ACROSTIC)

One part sightseeing, two parts shopping spree, stir in romance and voilà, pour out Paree

It's romantic but at all times discretion is the better part of Minima

Perfect, Ambience, Romance, Interludes, Sensational (PARIS = ACROSTIC)

Romantic, chic, with a special pazazz, the joie de vivre only Paris has

I could climb the tower, sip champagne, dine at Maxims, then sail up the Seine

Let's be Franc, to win a trip would be my 'M'Arc de Triomphe'

Because with the Minima of fuss you get your body formed into chic French fashions

Capital of love, vibrant, sincere, puts Spring in my heart anytime of the year

Because we live in Leeds (honest)

Because it's the fashion capital and I love French dressing

Spreeing is believing

To the woman who expects the 'Maxim-um' satisfaction from life with the 'Minima-m' effort

Because an Eiffel of Paris makes me in Seine

The haute cuisine, sights and shops are ample, for a girl like me to sample

▶ Paris takes the biscuit because...

PRODUCT: Biscuits

It's the à la carte venue with romance on the menu

Eiffel Tower with latticed legs, vivacious girls like powder kegs, Boulevards with coiffured trees, crowded bistros, great strip-tease, Mistress Paris, quite contrary, lovable, extraordinary

Onion soup, vin ordinaire, garlic, Gauloises everywhere, pavement cafés, bal musettes, taxis, lovers, midinettes, sounds and secrets, a pot pourri, evocative of gay Paris

GERMANY

A German trip would more than suit, the scenery's great, the good 'sehr gut',
   so keep your Bombay, Rome or Dallas, I prefer Deutschland über alles

GREECE

Under the sun where myths were begun, I'm like a goddess having fun
I don't want to leave my holiday in the lap of the gods
For once in my life I'd like everything to be Greek to me
And a 'steak' in the prizes would be one 'Hel-i-os' of a treat (*Berni Inns)
On those idyllic islands for the classical style seeker this is my chance to say
   Eureka
This charter holiday is a visa to avoiding a Greek tragedy
The poise and style of classical Greece make wonderful holidays my Golden
   Fleece
Alpha, Beta, Gamma, Delta, stop me when I get to Rhodes
Going Greek in Rhodes would make a change from Going Dutch at the
   beehive
The Greeks had their 'Rhodes' before the Romans had even thought of them

HOLLAND

► **I buy Van Nelle traditional coffee from Holland because...**

PRODUCT: Filter coffee

No fancy gimmicks, passing trends, just finest beans, perfected blends
Taste of Holland superbly presented leaves palates pleased, pockets contented
I quaff like a toff without selling the Van Gogh
It perks me up and filters my cares away
Here's one Dutch masterpiece I can afford
The blend justifies the beans
I'll Netherland a better brand
It's a cup above the rest
Even Van Gogh's brother wouldn't 'ear of any other
It 'Can Al' Ways help unwind the 'windmills' of my mind
It's the only coffee you should put 'Tulips'

► **Caption Competition showing a Gouda cheese saying to an
   Edam cheese 'Why are we so popular?', to which Entrants
   replied...**

PRODUCT: Dutch cheeses

They can slice us, cube us, grate us, grill us - even scoop us out and fill us
After trying my red and your amber, they know where to go for the tastiest
   cheese
We're from the low countries – low price, low fat, low calories
We're a colourful pair crammed full of flavour, less fattening but nice with a
   taste that folks savour

For losing pounds or saving pence, double Dutch makes more sense
Once people taste so Goud-a cheese, they don't give Edam for anything else
Like Dutch tulips we're colourful, cut beautifully, are ideal for parties and
cheer up slimmers
'We try to please everybody', as the actress said to the bishop
Once bitten twice buy, the simple explanation why

▶ **I would like to fly to Amsterdam with Toilet Duck because...**

PRODUCT: Toilet cleaner

It could show the Dutch its magic touch
In the city of flowers, I'd smell of roses
Me and the Duck's gonna clean up this town
I can smell fragrant flowers swaying in a springtime breeze
I'm hooked on Holland and flushed with success
I'd go clean round the bend at such luck
If I scoured the world I couldn't choose better
His streamlined jet reaches clogs and canals fastest and safest
Pot-pourri puts me in mind of tulips in springtime
Loo-tips from Amsterdam couldn't make a cleaner pan

HONG KONG

We could take our clothes back home for a holiday

INDIA

▶ **Why would you like to make a trip to INDIA?**

Land of palaces and princes, land of temples, minarets, land of mystery and
magic
Contrasts you will not forget. Scented spices, jasmine, roses, sights and sounds
Beyond compare, I would give a royal ransom just to be transported there

ITALY

▶ **Napolina pasta gives me the real taste of Italy because...**

PRODUCT: Pasta
PRIZE: Panda car

To this dedicated pasta eater, Napolina is the dolce vita

► **You can experience a taste of Italy with perfect pizza because...**

PRODUCT: *Pizza*

Authentic? Delicious? Proved for you – Julius ate one – Brutus et tu

► **Ragu brings out the Italian in me because...**

PRODUCT: *Pasta sauce*

The door to the Dolce Vita is now a-jar

► **Presto biscuits and cakes in Venice competition**

PRODUCT: *Biscuits and cakes*

A perfection in confection and that wins my selection
An exciting tea time menu, from a bright inviting venue
Cakes to please for family teas
A Venetian whirl for the price of a Swiss roll
The chance to say hello to a good buy
Sweet encounters of the preferred kind
A sweet response within your grasp helping to make your money last
A friendly hello and lots of good buys

► **Dolmio Italian Lire competition**

PRODUCT: *Pasta sauce*

Dolmio Lid, 500 quid, sightseeing Italy, me and our kid
What Mama Mia cooks in Rome, Dolmio perfects at home
With it to pep up fare I feel like a millionaire
Its wealth of flavour brings memories to savour
The taste is the best when put to the test
I bank on it to enhance-a my pasta
Its Italian aroma turns a house into a home-a
Dolmio saves time and time is money
It's a priceless treasure for meal time pleasure

Italian foods

Spaghetti Junction becomes a Pizza cake
It was mama's spaghetti that led to confetti
Like Pisa it's always on the list
Magic on ze lips – murder on ze hips
A winner – it's pippa ze pasta pasta ze posta
Pizza deep, value high, they're the round square meals that satisfy
Their flavour by Jimminy takes you straight to Rimini
You don't knead a lot of dough for the taste Italians know
Vrom Reading to Roma zey Asda diploma
Asda prices and pizza spices make our teatimes extra nice

Chocolate freckled cappuccino, double-decker ice, towering mountains of
    Trentino, my Italian paradise
Gondolas, fountains, art works on view, pasta, vino and ice cream too
Gondolas, Bridge of Sighs, leather shoes, silk ties, classic buildings, Venetian
    glass, all first class
Julius Caesar, pizza pies, Eternal City, and Bridge of Sighs
Aristocratic splendour, stylish beauty, cappuccino, tutti frutti, silhouetted
    cypress trees, pink washed villas, sunlit seas
Piano Pollini, measured Martini, lifts in Lamborghini, films by Fellini, calories
    by Crespolini
Opera singers, film stars, fashion houses, Fiat cars, villages, cities, mountains,
    sea, beautiful, unique Italy
Capri, Loren, Gucci shoes, vibrant life, sunswept views, Carino colour
    everywhere, Muscatel, Barbera flair
Dolce Vita, with the blessing from St. Peter

MONACO

▶ **I would like to win a trip to the Monaco Grand Prix because...**

PRODUCT: Supermarket foods
COMPETITION: North West Co-op

Thanks to NWC it's Monte Carlo 'not' bust

MOROCCO

▶ **I think the best place to drink Norfolk cider would be...**

PRODUCT: Cider

Morocco because there's no place like the Kasbah

POLAND

▶ **Zamoyski Warsawthis is the spirit of Poland because...**

PRODUCT: Polish vodka
PRIZES: 2,000,000 Zloty

One glass-is-not-enoughski
I love it, lodz and lodz and lodz
It makes you want to Gdansk all night
I'm Russian off to study Perestroika
It is the liquidarnosc of good taste

SOUTH AMERICA

A lifetime's dream is Rio-lised
I could squat by a handsome gaucho instead of my old groucho

SPAIN

▶ **I would like to discover the real Spain because...**

PRODUCT: Fundador brandy

Spanish hospitality, warm and inviting, Fundador brandy, smooth and exciting
Spain excites me, Fundador delights me, hope you invite me
Peaceful pueblos and castles unfold, like Fundador, true Spanish gold

▶ **Drinking Pepsi Cola in Spain**

PRODUCT: Soft drink

Pepsi's a real cool winner amongst hot properties
As the temperatures go up, Pepsi's cool taste goes down
Under Spanish sun with spirits soaring, happiness is Pepsi pouring
Señores and señoritas agree, Pepsi reigns in Spain for me
When tourists shout 'Pep', the locals shout 'Si'
Pepsi peps zi flagging man, Marbella peps zi fading tan
Marbella's planned for leisure, Pepsi's canned for pleasure
International jetsetters all report Pepsi's favourite in this resort

SWITZERLAND

▶ **I like cheese from Switzerland because...**

PRODUCT: Swiss cheeses

Whatever the venue, Swiss cheese fits the menu
Rival products can't compare, Swiss cheeses are unique
Cheese Has Essential Elements Specially Emmenthal from Switzerland
    (CHEESES = ACROSTIC)
Pure ingredients and traditional care make Emmenthal and Gruyère
They are tasty, nutritious and simply delicious
Alpine meadows with clean fresh breeze produce a fuller flavoured cheese
Quality food, standards high, from Safeway, the best place to buy
Flavour outstanding, dinners are divine, Suisse on the label, the pleasure is
    mine
The Swiss symbol stands supreme and Safeway sets standards seldom seen
For taste and flavour no cheese can compare with nutty Emmenthal and
    matured Gruyère
As a mature student who enjoys delicious cheeses, Swiss are a Safeway of
    guaranteeing satisfaction
My palate is hard to please, I only eat the finest cheese
It's the Safeway to guarantee quality
I've tried the rest and I know what's best
They're a GRATE idea for any occasion, from fondue supper to a family
    invasion
For lunchtime temptation or evening treat, tasty Swiss cheeses are hard to beat

Cheese is only bliss when it's real Swiss
It's irreswisstibly the taste for me
I like to savour the flavour of an alpine fondue
My mother Swiss, a childhood treat, a cheese fondue, the memory sweet
Their taste is a mountainous experience, like a yodel in fresh air
They're always at the peak of perfection
A connoisseur I love to savour, their unique and distinctive flavour
It has the flavour my tastebuds love to savour
Mountainous flavours, outstanding to eat, standard never wavers, a fresh alpine
    treat
They have wonderful taste, superb textures and are so versatile
Emmenthal has 'hole'some flavour, Gruyère – spicy taste to savour – delicious
    'two' in a Swiss fondue
They taste so delightful, meals are divine, Suisse on the label, the pleasure is
    mine
Eaten alone or with bread or wine, Swiss cheese are great, there's none so fine
I know that the alpine horn blower on the label means satisfaction around the
    table

▶ **Buy Emmenthal Swiss cheese at Safeway because...**

PRODUCT: Swiss cheese

Emmenthal excellence, Safeway flair, together they're a perfect pair
Quality counts, prices please, unique flavour, gratest cheese
King of cheeses, principal store, who could ask for anything more
Switzerland's across the sea, but Safeway is right next to me
Safeway sells singularly super Swiss cheese
For quality and selection, Safeway's Emmenthal is perfection
From Safeway its taste is assured, fresh as the day it matured
For fondues with an alpine flavour, Safeway is the store I favour
The delicious taste drives me mildly nutty
Alpine fresh, 'holesome' flavour, Emmenthal is the taste to savour
Emmenthal – a temptation 'alpine' for
Flavour outstanding – fondues divine, Swiss on the label, the pleasure is mine
It's the best there is, it gives this Miss Swiss bliss
I love Swiss cheeses and the best are at Safeway
I put great store by a great cheese
I'm just 'nuts' about Emmenthal
The best treasures are always kept in a Safeway
There's no mountains to climb in Safeway to find your dream
Both have a good history, recognised by all perfectionists
Both are monuemmental in the spread of good taste
Their Swiss cheese display draws me to it every day
It's a gourmet's invitation to forget inflation
I am fond(ue) see of good quality
Close your eyes, smell and taste, Safeway's Emmenthal the delight of
    Switzerland

This taste of Switzerland, superbly presented, leaves palates pleased and pockets contented

They both bring delight to the 'bored'

Their alpine selection makes fondue perfection

Its taste once acquired is forever desired

It is wholly the finest place for cheese and service alike

Flavour's delightful, taste divine, with the Emmenthal label, the pleasure is mine

Safeway's expertise at keeping Swiss cheese, means superb flavour, sure to please

▶ Filetti washing powder with a Swiss theme

PRODUCT: Swiss washing powder

Alpine fresh, Swiss and new, fluffy Filetti means softness for you

Thank heavens for my little 'Swiss Made'

Thanks to Filetti the gnomes are not the only people who enjoy 'Zu-riches'

THAILAND

▶ I can really go places with Uncle Ben's because...

PRODUCT: Stir-fry sauces

Travel is easy, just need my wok, Thai Curry Sauce – Hello Bangkok!

▶ I would enjoy this trip to Thailand because...

PRODUCT: Stir-fry sauces
COMPETITION: Uncle Ben's sauces
PRIZES: Trips to Thailand

Perfect results every time, thanks Uncle Ben's for mine

Jar + Wok = 4-star Bangkok

Love the sauce, but the perfect result is to visit the source

I'm Thai-d of Thai-ping, Thai-m for a Thai-fling

▶ I would like to beanfeast in ... (Country of your own choice) because...

PRODUCT: Packet meals

French Riviera ... Beanfeast! A treat! France hard to beat! Together – dreams complete

The West Country ... wholesome, tastiest and best fills me with 'Summerzest'

Mexico ... climates warm, Chillis hot, for me just the spot

Venice ... in a gondola I could laze, eating plates of Bolognese

Sri Lanka ... tropical Island, Beautiful Life, take the Beanfeast, not the wife

Spain ... that 'package deal' named 'paella' tastes extra good in Marbella

▶ **I would take my deck chair to ... (Place of your own choice) because...**

PRODUCT: Cigars
COMPETITION: Henri Wintermans Cigars

The Caribbean ... dat's de place to be in de 'Winterman'
Anywhere where I could get Henri Wintermans cigars
Egypt ... I could sit on the bank of the Nile with my mummy
Westminster ... it's the only way I'll ever get a seat in the Lords
Bali ... I'm browned off now, why not get a good tanning in paradise
Bermuda ... I know no better place to 'Winterman'
Zuiderzee ... I do like to be be-Zuiderzeezside

CRACKERS

▶ **I'm CRACKERS about Asda shopping because...**

PRODUCT: Wheat crackers
COMPETITION: Asda/Ritz crackers

Crazy low prices persitz, I snap packitz of bargains I cannot resitz

CREDIT CARD

▶ **Barclaycard is the best credit card to use overseas because...**

PRODUCT: Credit card

It simply makes sense of sign language
Under 'present' circumstances they are an aid to finances

▶ **Mastercard and Thomas Cook go together well because...**

PRODUCT: Credit card
PRIZES: Trips to New York to see the film 'Hook'

With minimum fuss, maximum speed, this global alliance is all I need
Perfect planning, pay with plastic, together they trip the flight fantastic
When travel requirements must be met, they make the best combination yet
Together they give a travel style, without hook, hitch or crocodile

▶ **American Express credit card**

PRODUCT: Credit card

Tried and trusted, safe and quick – it's my financial one-card trick
All losers can be winners
Easy to buy, simple to cash, lost or mislaid? Replaced in a flash
When it comes to selection, I simply go for 5-way protection
They unravel the hassle of travel
They're so readily accepted in every land that only gamblers travel with cash in hand
I would rather be cashing my cheque than checking my cash

▶ **Eurocheques**

PRODUCT: *Travellers' cheques*

Speaks all languages so let your chequebook do the talking
Simple, easy, safe, quick, it's my bank's own one-card trick
Their Eurocheques mean cash in hand in every European land
While money talks, Eurocheques go without saying

CUT

▶ **The Co-op helps me CUT costs by...**

PRODUCT: *Supermarket foods*

Never putting a foot wrong when it comes to outstanding bargains
Presenting a permanent wave of good buys
Lightening reductions followed by thunderous applause

▶ **A Danish bacon joint from Tesco is a CUT above the rest because...**

PRODUCT: *Bacon*

Its 'Joint' advantages are tender taste and little waste

▶ **Spar CUTS the cost of living because...**

PRODUCT: *Food stores food*

Quality goods at sensible prices with courteous service by co-operative assistants

DAIRY

▶ **Which is your favourite English cheese and why?**

PRODUCT: English cheese

Smooth double Gloucester do I favour with its rich and mellow flavour

Mature English Cheddar reigns supreme, fit for every king and queen

English double Gloucester's best, it's smooth and creamier than the rest

Mature Cheddar strong in taste makes home dishes made in haste

Leicester waste, Leicester pay and Leicester find in the fridge every day (*less to)

I always 'Caerphilly' choose – as it would take nothing 'Leicester' please me

For a snack or main meal, Cheddar has 'grate' appeal

'Tis tangy when mature, a Derby winner for the connoisseur

▶ **I like cheese from Switzerland at Safeway because...**

PRODUCT: Swiss cheeses

Whatever the venue, Swiss cheese fits the menu

Rival products can't compare, Swiss cheeses are unique

Cheese Has Essential Elements Specially Emmenthal from Switzerland
    (CHEESE = ACROSTIC)

Pure ingredients and traditional care make Emmenthal and Gruyère

They are tasty, nutritious and simply delicious

Alpine meadows with clean fresh breeze produce a fuller flavoured cheese

Quality food, standards high, from Safeway, the best place to buy

Flavour outstanding, dinners are divine, Suisse on the label, the pleasure is mine

The Swiss symbol stands supreme and Safeway sets standards seldom seen

For taste and flavour no cheese can compare with nutty Emmenthal and matured Gruyère

As a mature student who enjoys delicious cheeses, Swiss are a Safeway of guaranteeing satisfaction

My palate is hard to please, I only eat the finest cheese

It's the Safeway to guarantee quality

I've tried the rest and I know what's best

They're a GRATE idea for any occasion, from fondue supper to a family invasion

For lunchtime temptation or evening treat, tasty Swiss cheeses are hard to beat

Cheese is only bliss when it's real Swiss

It's irreswisstibly the taste for me

I like to savour the flavour of an alpine fondue

My mother Swiss, a childhood treat, a cheese fondue, the memory sweet

Their taste is a mountainous experience, like a yodel in fresh air

They're always at the peak of perfection

A connoisseur I love to savour, their unique and distinctive flavour

It has the flavour my tastebuds love to savour

Mountainous flavours, outstanding to eat, standard never wavers, a fresh alpine treat

They have wonderful taste, superb textures and are so versatile

Emmenthal has 'hole'some flavour, Gruyère – spicy taste to savour – delicious 'two' in a Swiss fondue

They taste so delightful, meals are divine, Suisse on the label, the pleasure is mine

Eaten alone or with bread or wine, Swiss cheese are great, there's none so fine

I know that the alpine horn blower on the label means satisfaction around the table

▶ **Buy Swiss Emmenthal cheese at Safeway because...**

PRODUCT: Swiss cheese

Emmenthal excellence, Safeway flair, together they're a perfect pair

Quality counts, prices please, unique flavour, gratest cheese

King of cheeses, principal store, who could ask for anything more

Switzerland's across the sea, but Safeway is right next to me

Safeway sells singularly super Swiss cheese

For quality and selection, Safeway's Emmenthal is perfection

From Safeway its taste is assured, fresh as the day it matured

For fondues with an alpine flavour, Safeway is the store I favour

The delicious taste drives me mildly nutty

Alpine fresh, 'holesome' flavour, Emmenthal is the taste to savour

Emmenthal – a temptation 'alpine' for

It's the best there is, it gives this Miss Swiss bliss

I love Swiss cheeses and the best are at Safeway

I put great store by a great cheese

I'm just 'nuts' about Emmenthal

The best treasures are always kept in a Safeway

There's no mountains to climb in Safeway to find your dream

Both have a good history, recognised by all perfectionists

Both are monuemmental in the spread of good taste

Their Swiss cheese display draws me to it every day

It's a gourmet's invitation to forget inflation

I am fond(ue) see of good quality

Close your eyes, smell and taste, Safeway's Emmenthal the delight of Switzerland

This taste of Switzerland, superbly presented, leaves palates pleased and pockets contented

They both bring delight to the 'bored'

Their alpine selection makes fondue perfection

Its taste once acquired is forever desired

It is wholly the finest place for cheese and service alike

Flavour's delightful, taste divine, with the Emmenthal label, the pleasure is mine

Safeway's expertise at keeping Swiss cheese, means superb flavour, sure to
  please

▶ **Mars ice cream is the perfect way to end a meal because...**

PRODUCT: Ice cream

For a melting moment unsurpassed, Mars wins by finishing last

▶ **You can taste the good life with Longboat butter because...**

PRODUCT: Butter

Its natural flavour is tops and sails ahead of the others

▶ **I make sure I get enough milk because...**

PRODUCT: Milk

My son shouts 'au lait' every day
That's the threshold agreement I have with my milkman

▶ **Milk's a winner because...**

PRODUCT: Milk

It's nutritionally foremost and first past the door post

▶ **Kraft cheese slices**

PRODUCT: Processed cheese slices

Kraft's our best seller, so we profit together
The grocers delight with crafty bite selling on site
Slice for slice, portion for portion they are brand leaders
They are first in their class, so hard to surpass
The product and pack keep the housewife coming back
Nobody can 'slice' into their share of the market

English cheese

Just a little grating gives meals the perfect rating
It takes an English cheese to make a perfect cracker
I always 'Caerphilly' choose – as it would take nothing 'Leicester' please me

Dutch cheese

They can slice us, grate us, grill us, even scoop us out and fill us
We're from the low countries – low price, low fat, low calories
When people taste so Goud-a cheese they don't give Edam for anything else

Cream

One good churn deserves another
It's the elite treat you can whip but can't beat
It's simply the best cream yet for turning a pancake into a crêpe Suzette
The taste of Devon is beyond compare, but frozen for convenience, quel savoire faire

Eggs

Sinking the yellow and the white is the best break of the day
It's one of the oldest wise cracks
They're everything they're cracked up to be
It's a cheep meal without having to shell out a fortune
I like my soldiers with egg on their faces
My soldiers don't like shells
It's a three-minute crash course
A break in the oval gets me an all round square meal
It's the ready packed snack
With such little time to spare, breakfast is always a scrambled affair
Hopeless are the yokeless for they shell not
Smashing their cover gets them put inside
The freshest eggs I've tried, boiled, scrambled or fried
I love a spot of GBH – Great British Habit
I could follow one up with a-salt and buttery
I find an egg tastes better if it's a-salted
Eggs brighten up my 'male' in the morning
They're so fresh I get a quick coddle
It causes quite a scramble in our household
It takes one mad scramble to top the upper crust
If at first I don't succeed, I fry, fry again
I've joined the frying pickets
It's the easy way to strike rich by panning for gold
There's gold in them thar eggs
It would bring me face to face with a heart of gold
I love a good yolk without making an oeuf of myself
By George, I like my little YOLK-elele in me hand
I've always wanted to play OMELETTE
I'd pot the yellow with the white and score a maximum break
If I miss the yellow and white I'm snookered alright
It's the only time we win at the OVAL
It's the only Oval I'll open for England
Great EGGspectations means a Dickens of a meal
Sportsman or spectator, I'm healthier hitting the eggcelerator
EGGSecutions make topping meal solutions
My EGGRessive tendencies always lead to mad scrambles
I'd whisk everything for a smash and grub raid
You can beat 'em and butter 'em but you can't better 'em

It's one of the oldest wise cracks
It's the cracking taste that's launched a thousand chips
A few wise cracks cheer me up a treat
It's a cracking bit of activity on the cheep
I've got ten soldiers waiting to take the plunge
With soldiers at the ready it's a smash and dab raid
If you're hungry, feeling plucky, smash a chucky

DANCING

▶ **Pepsi Cola keeps me DANCING because…**

PRODUCT: *Soft drink*
COMPETITION: *Pepsi Cola dance to the beat*

It's liquid potion, for poetry in motion
The be-boppin bubbles burst to the beat
It bubbles through my lips, putting wiggles on my hips
With the taste so alive, you just got to jive

DELIGHTFUL

▶ **Delicious Danish is DELIGHTFUL because…**

PRODUCT: *Bacon*

The sizzle 'siz' it all
The Co-operative Viking makes bacon to my liking
It is a succulent sizzler and has no spitting image
Once fried, never forgotten
When appetites tend to roam, tender Danish brings them home
That sizzling sensation is the Co-op's recommendation
Food of the Viking 'leans' to my liking
It is the star attraction for knife and fork action
Grill it, fry it, bake it – you can't beat it
The true fresh taste means there's never any waste
The nice flavour never wavers
Bacon butties, haute cuisine, with Danish as the go-between
It's cured with caring for flavour fresh sharing
They're a cut above the rest, don't buy second best
With bacon or ham it's always 'grand slam'
It's a delectable dish that deserves a degree
Tender, tempting, full of taste, none ever goes to waste
We are a healthier nation with their food innovation

Ideal barbeque, Danish on prong, funfilled party, cannot go wrong
It's freshly sliced and nicely priced
It's a money saver with a perfect flavour
Its appetising nutrition is part of our Great British tradition
In lean times it's streaks above the rest
Nobody can be rashernough to claim otherwise
Its lean back style makes my purse smile
The aroma from the sizzle makes the homeward drizzle fizzle
It sizzles superbly, fries fantastically and tastes terrific
It saves the busy housewife's bacon
Denmark achieves perfection in the dairy product section
It's the perfect way to sail through the day
It recalls happy memories of dazzling Denmark
When it comes to rashers the Danes are price bashers
Like the Co-op I can always 'Seaways' of tastefully satisfying everybody
Eggs just beg for it
On lean streaks you can make a pig of yourself
When it comes to Norse code it's word perfect
Quality, taste, healthy nutrition, have always been a Danish tradition
The Danes take great pains to ensure quality never wanes
Having fresh Nordic flavour it's the perfect invader
The taste lives up to the aroma
Bacon that is Danish cured is bacon for the connoisseur

DIAMOND

▶ **For which special diamond occasion would you wear the exquisite jewellery collection and why...**

PRODUCT: Ice cream dessert
COMPETITION: Wall's Viennetta/Diamond collection
PRIZES: Diamond necklace and ear-rings worth £5,000

Romantic dinner with fantastic fella, thank you Viennetta – signed Cinderella
My next Viennetta – because this hallmark of desserts deserves a sparkling
    setting
Vienna ball – masked mysteriously, sparkling bright, a Viennetta queen for a
    night
When the last slice of Viennetta, like the diamonds would last forever
Saying to Liz 'mine are better', then softening the blow, offering Viennetta
Sparkling Claridges dinner 'gems' of haute cuisine, flawless Viennetta
    completing the brilliant scene
Enjoying Viennetta's taste of renown the tantalising jewel in Viennetta's crown
Candlelit dinner, soft music and wine solitare-y-setting, Viennetta's all mine
Wimbledon – forget the strawberries and cream, Viennetta is my dream
To go to paradise where there is always a second slice

▶ **Diamond White and Diamond Blush are the perfect carnival drinks because...**

PRODUCT: Ciders

For extra sparkle and laughter, these little gems are what you're after

▶ **I think Gloria Hunniford is the perfect jewellery wearer because...**

PRODUCT: Jewellery

She embodies the style, elegance and charm of pure gold
Precious pieces, worn with style, are matched by Gloria's golden smile
Gloria always pays attention to that precious touch you mention
Like gold, she is a shining example of timeless elegance

I regard Silk Cut as the diamond of cigarettes because...

PRODUCT: Cigarettes

Skilled cutters perfect what Silk Cutters select

DIFFERENCE

▶ **Bisto makes all the DIFFERENCE because...**

PRODUCT: Gravy browning

Bisto tops off meat a treat
The taste and flavour do the meal a favour
When the boat comes in, it's full of flavour
It's made with ease and sure to please
Rich, dark and inviting, it makes meals exciting
From simple meal to festive treat, Bisto complements the meat
It's the dishy addition that's now a tradition
Smoothly blended, piping hot, Bisto flavours top the lot
It makes any meal m-AHH-vellous
Bisto gets everyone's vote, nobody wants to miss the boat

▶ **The DIFFERENCE with Mum Solid is...**

PRODUCT: Ladies' deodorant

Its performance you can spot
It gives solid protection from odour detection
Its great underarm action
It's the starting block that results in a personal best
It means success without excess
My aroma keeps my husband home-a

When things get sticky, Mum sticks around
It's better to be chunky than a little squirt
I'm home and dry – best antiperspirant money can buy
Odourwhelming
Easy to spot
It's simply fantastick
It's made for secret armies
It's a problem shifter and confidence lifter
My favourite has a new twist to the ending
Easy to choose – delightful to use
Odour is defeated in underarm combat with Mum's Solid defences
It turns up again and again
No more shake, rattle and roll
Solid protection, second to none, for cool confidence, number one
It's the only Mum I take on a date
It's here to stay not sprayed away
It's selective, protection and extremely effective
It's a stick up at a price that's a steal

DIFFERENT

▶ **Norwegian cheeses are DIFFERENT because...**

PRODUCT: Norwegian cheeses
COMPETITION: Tesco/Norwegian cheese
FIRST PRIZE: Weekend breaks for two in Oslo or Bergen

Like Norwegian Railways they are smooth, tasteful and offer great enjoyment

RUNNERS-UP: Salter digital weighing scales

Say 'Ya' for Jarlsberg – Norwegian please, when you're talking tasty cheese
These tasty flavours of the Norse, make welcome invaders of any course
Green grass, fresh air and no pollution, Norwegian cheeses are the solution
Where summer's short and winter's long, their delicious cheeses aren't too
    strong
Norway's cows know the secret, but they won't grass
Norway's Jarlsberg is cheese supreme, Ridder a midsummer knight's dream
Ridder deep, Jarlsberg high, milkiest meadows: 'Tes-Bes-Buy'
Land of legend, skiing, hiking, produces cheese you find to your Viking
Golden as the midnight sun, they're 'hole'some, tasty, second to none
Keep your Edam, Brie and Cheddar, cheeses from Norway taste far better
Naturally the Jarlsberg crest, ensures I can Fjord the best

DISH

▶ **My favourite dish from around the world is ... because...**

PRODUCT: Washing-up liquid
COMPETITION: Goodtime Magazine/Fairy Liquid .

Moussaka ... I don't mince words, it just tastes superb

Haggis ... for taste and thrift the Scots have it sewn up

Vindaloo ... like Fairy it's a hot favourite ending in clean dishes all round

Zabaglione ... it's something I never could say but had no problem putting away

Spaghetti Bolognese ... it's magic on ze lips but murder on ze hips

Fondue ... like fairy 'bubble, bubble' no toil or trouble

Fondue ... it's the taste that launched 1,000 dips

Coq au vin ... it's something to crow about

Paella ... it reigns from Spain but is far from plain

Russian borscht ... even though it's 'red' there's no chance of it being 'left'

Pizza ... for a square meal you can't beat a round one

Frogs legs ... I'm never caught on the hop

Russian fish pie ... it's the Crème de la Kremlin

Lamb en Croute ... the French know how to 'case the joint'

Mushy peas ... they're mild, green and fairly liquid

Suckling pig ... there's nothing like a piece of crackling

Baked Alaska ... it stays cool when the heat is on

Chilli con carne ... it's the ultimate Mexican 'Taco Way'

Spaghetti Bolognese ... like Pisa I have a 'leaning' towards it

English lamb ... it's a winner in its field

Haggis ... I enjoy it 'Piping' hot without the 'Burns'

A Fondue ... it's always fun do

Muesli ... I'm a connoisseur of 'oat' cuisine

Boiled eggs ... it's the only Oval I'll open for England

Sausage and mash ... Britain's succulent sizzler has no 'spitting' image

Hot dogs ... I always eat them with relish

Shepherd's pie ... it never fails to please my flock

DISNEY

▶ **Timex watches give you the time of your life because...**

PRODUCT: Watches
PRIZES: Holidays in Florida

Whatever your age, the time, the place, Timex has the perfect 'face'

A slip in time and Mickey's mine

Reliable, attractive, durable too, Timex for me, how about you?
They are all things bright and beautiful, on faces great and small
Handsome face, a fashion must, more precisely, a name to trust
One timely purchase from Argos and four could be shaking Mickey's hand
Whilst others simply tick along, a Timex watch keeps going strong

▶ **Why would you like to win a cruise and Disney week with Percy Daltons Famous Monkies?**

PRODUCT: Monkey nuts
COMPETITION: Percy Daltons Monkey Nuts
PRIZES: Trips to Disneyland

To win a cruise and Disney week would really make my family freak
No longer in our boring ruts, we'll holiday with monkey nuts
Original monkeys natural food, has put us in a nutty mood
Winning would be a dream come true, so crack my shell it's up to you

▶ **I would like to drink Coca-Cola at Euro Disney because...**

PRODUCT: Soft drink

Coca-Cola's classic tingle makes Mickey's magic multi-lingual
I like my 'mice' with coke and ice

▶ **Mars and Walt Disney are the super selection at Christmas because...**

PRODUCT: Confectionery
COMPETITION: Presto/Mars

Top attractions, second to none, Mars and Walt Disney are number one
The Christmas Hulla 'Baloo' is fun when Mars and Pluto Plan-et for you
Presto, Mars and Lady Luck could lead me straight to Donald Duck

▶ **My mum deserves her dreams come true because...**

PRIZES: Family holidays in Florida

I'm obnoxious, dad gets snappy, time that someone made mum happy
She's always caring, always fair, always loving, in all ways rare
She gives me love and affection, advice and direction
She deserves her 'American dream' for loving management of our home team
Loving, caring, funny and wise, fairly small but her heart's outsize
Every day mum takes the flak, Orlando's magic would pay her back
Caring for me can cause despair, this will show I really care
Driven mad by sis and me, she dreams of regaining sanity
Her life's no fairy tale, full of monsters, each one male
She's my best pal, my favourite chum – loving, caring, sharing mum
Children cares, housework done, goes to work and still she's fun

▶ **I would like to visit Disneyworld because...**

Dumbo has 'Big Ears' – Noddy has asked me to fetch him back

▶ **Why are Princes spreads in jars like Disney characters?**

PRODUCT: Meat pastes
COMPETITION: Tesco/Disneyworld spreadables

Like Cinderella, if I press buttons, Princes appear
Just like Pooh, small, dumpy and always in the cupboard
Like Cinderella I found Princes charming and gone by midnight
Like Disney's dalmations they knock spots off imitations
Minnie trapped unsuspecting Mickey by spreading Princes on her biccy
After Princes kissed her bread, Sleeping Beauty leapt from bed
Like the Cheshire Cat they disappear and leave a smile

▶ **My family would enjoy the magic of Disney because...**

PRODUCT: Soft drink
COMPETITION: Coca-Cola/Euro Disney at Littlewoods
PRIZES: Family trips to Euro Disney

This wonderland at last we'd see, Coke and Littlewoods – merci!
Coca-Cola and Disney, you know, both give that tingle you never outgrow

▶ **Who is your favourite Disney character and why?**

PRODUCT: Electrical goods
COMPETITION: The magic of Philips/Argos catalogue
PRIZES: Family trips to Euro Disney

Peter Pan ... because I'm hooked on Philips' products at Argos
Sleeping Beauty ... because with marriage pending, shop at Argos for a happy
ending
Mickey Mouse ... because really unique, like Philips and Argos, c'est
magnifique
Walt Disney is the man for me, the magician behind the fantasy
Fairy Godmother ... Cinderella's dreams came true, with Philips, maybe mine
will too?
Cinderella ... at Argos Cinders' life did change, after choosing from the Philips
range

DISTINCTION

▶ **Choicest Blend tea is the tea of DISTINCTION because...**

PRODUCT: Tea

Thirsting for the best leaves me dramatically refreshed
Passing trends quickly go, perfect blends steal the show
Outstanding selection and brewing technique, guarantee flavour truly unique
Distinct refreshing morning cuppa – lifts at luncheon, soothes at supper
Its good taste is never left to pot luck
With finest leaves expertly blended, choicest blend tastes absolutely splendid

DO-IT-YOURSELF

▶ **Ronseal quick drying woodstain is the best woodstain because...**

PRODUCT: *Wood varnish*

While rival stains fail and fade, Ronseal lasts another decade
What used to take hours can be done between showers

▶ **Sikkens Masterstroke offers me an excellent range of woodcare products because...**

PRODUCT: *Wood sealant*

Sikkens quality guarantees perfect results with expert ease
From indoor timbers to garden seat, the Sikkens treatment is hard to beat
Wood staining and varnishing inside and out, is simply long lasting without any doubt
A Masterstroke of genius in woodcare, a brush with Sikkens is beyond compare
Whatever the surface, interior or exterior, the natural finish is simply superior
Extensive choice, helpful advice, easy to use, sensible price

▶ **I like using Wolf tools because...**

PRODUCT: *D.I.Y. tools*

Whatever the task, Wolf tools are winners, giving expert results for pros and beginners

▶ **I always use 3M adhesives in the studio because...**

PRODUCT: *Spray adhesive*

They make art work

▶ **I buy Loctite products at Morrisons because...**

PRODUCT: *Adhesive*

To be 'franc' they both give Xtra value

▶ **I would recommend Tru-tile because...**

PRODUCT: Tile grout

It gives professional skills for handyman bills

▶ **I watch for Loctite because...**

PRODUCT: Adhesive
PRIZES: Portable TVs

Its vertical hold is visibly superior
Loctite 'screen' every product then 'stick' with the best
I'm glued to their set

▶ **Unibond is simply more professional because...**

PRODUCT: Wood sealant

Seal, fill, stain, stick, Unibond's the one to pick
It's the glue to restore shattered faith
For easy bonding it meets all demands, completely safe in my hands
The fella with the filla gets the decorating spirit

▶ **I buy Graham and Brown wallcoverings at Great Mills because...**

PRODUCT: D.I.Y. materials
PRIZES: Luxury weekends in Paris

Perfection comes at such little cost, ugly plain walls are forever lost
Simple to find, pleasing to eye, lovely to hang, easy as pie

▶ **If a job's worth doing I head down to Texas Homecare because...**

PRODUCT: D.I.Y. materials

Professional or handy man, everyone's a Texas fan
Every job, great and small, demands the best, they have it all
The selection and prices are right, Sandtex will protect and make bright
I know there's never a snag with a Texas price tag
Texas service is the best and their prices beat the rest
Choosing is easy, paying no pain, so I return, time and again
There's free parking, cheerful service and pound-saving practical ideas – thanks
    Texas
Everything I need is there and the Texas people care
For a perfect finish I need to start at the right place
Why go round the corner when the big ones are at Texas
That's the direction for home care perfection
The quality, range and price, make it D.I.Y. paradise

▶ I use Crown paint because...

PRODUCT: *Paint in tins*
PRIZES: *Camcorders*

You can knock it but you can't chip its reputation
Prepared with precision by experts with vision, Crown's award-winning colours
    bring dreams to fruition
It gives perfect results and that's no shaggy dog story
Its wide range of beautiful colours adds a touching finish to your finishing
    touches
Kitchen in white, loo in blue, whichever you choose there's a Crown paint for
    you
From undercoat to overcoat they make your technicolour dreamcoat
Whatever the surface from ceiling to floor, the range is extensive, the coverage
    more
It covers my husband's mistakes so well
Twinkle twinkle little flat, Crown paint covers, just like that
If you like brush marks on your wall, don't use Crown – there's none at all
No other can can do what this can can
Degas work taken out, less Monet, what have you Toulouse?

▶ Hamilton is my choice for decorating products because...

PRODUCT: *D.I.Y. materials*
PRIZE: *£1,000 worth of antiques*

Hamilton expertise, means perfect results with expert ease

Climatube

PRODUCT: *Tube lighting*

With it you can go round the bend easily
A Climatube is a real pipe dream

Window blinds

Your room's decor picks up the stylish hints they drop

DOUBLE

▶ Princes tomatoes and button mushrooms give us DOUBLE the choice at Kwik Save because...

PRODUCT: *Canned vegetables*
COMPETITION: *Kwik Save/Princes double your choice*
PRIZES: *Amstrad double decker video recorders*

Fast forward, stop, Kwik Save wins, get your pause on Princes tins
It's another fine meal you've put us into
Wise shoppers knew it, Princes and Kwik Save help us du-et
Being canned-did, Kwik Save value is top name brand-did
Princes veggies always nice, double delicious at Kwik Save price
For marvellous mushrooms, tomatoes canned, Princes is the finest brand
Princes quality, Kwik Save economy, they duet in perfect harmony
Fried, grilled, casseroled or baked, Princes have got it taped
Kwik to open and cook, who needs a recipe book?
Kwik Save incre-doubly crops the price of Princes incre-double crops
Tempting meal with price appeal, giving shoppers twice the deal
With this twosome a Princes user is never a loser
Perfect Princes, great store, that's a double you can't ignore
Om-e-letting my wife shop there now
We're veggie healthy happy shoppers
Double, double, no toil or trouble, Princes makes casseroles bubble
With plum prices, chopped lids peeled, a meal just 'mushrooms'
Princes double feature bill, cuts horror stories at the till
My pleasure is double, my pocket less troubled
Double vision on display, loads to choose, buttons to pay
Princes are twice as nice at Kwik Save price
They're two super super goodies, from the super super store
Delicious duo from super stores, always popular with 'er indoors
A credible, edible combination, they make a Kwik meal sensation
Hard acts to follow are double the fun to swallow
Kwik-ly prepared, no trouble, another Princes tasty double
Others are soso against a cancan of these tutu
No pantomime with these buttons, because Princes are quite charming
Once bitten, nice buy, Princes know the reason why
Kwik Save and Princes socialise, like the mushrooms, real 'fun-gi's' (*fun guys)
Double choice, double take, double vision, no headache
Double deals at every trip, extra value, what a snip!
Without this tasty twosome, our meals would be gruesome
Who else puts 'More-can and Prize' on the bill?
Twofold value fills my trolley, outstanding products, little lolly

▶ **Blue Riband and Breakaway are the best DOUBLE since...**

PRODUCT: Chocolate biscuits

John and Olivia – they're the ones that I want
Rodgers and Hammerstein whose sweet bars always scored a hit

DREAM

▶ **Shopping at Morrisons would be a DREAM shopping spree because...**

PRODUCT: *Chocolate biscuit*
COMPETITION: *Morrisons/Rowntree's Kit Kat*
PRIZE: *£200 in shopping vouchers*

Morrisons' low prices, it is said, Rip-ped Van Winkle out of bed

▶ **Using Imperial Leather in the bathroom is a DREAM because...**

PRODUCT: *Soap*
COMPETITION: *Cussons Imperial Leather bathroom*

Its value impresses me, its lather caresses me, and its fragrance un-stresses me
It soothes away my cares and troubles, doesn't burst my South Sea bubbles
It creates a bathroom transformation, creamiest, dreamiest soap in the nation
With its luxurious scent and lather like cream it's surely soap fit for a dream
It has the feel and quality of a luxury soap at a wide-a-wake price
Cussons soap makes dreams come true, leaving skin like morning dew
Imperial Leather will reign supreme, an affordable luxury is everyone's dream
Luxurious bubbles as light as a feather, transport me to cloud nine with
    Imperial Leather
Jacuzzi or tin bath tub, Imperial Leather's the luxury rub
A dream lasts forever with Imperial Leather
The lather of leather keeps me soft and clean, an altogether pleasant
    imperialistic dream
Imperial Leather creates magical mornings, dreamy days and shining knights
Imperial Leather's everyone's dream, lets you spend like a pauper but bathe
    like a queen

▶ **If I had the chance my American DREAM would be...**

PRODUCT: *Peanuts*
COMPETITION: *Planters peanuts*

To fast talk in New York, disco in San Francisco, get legless in Texas
About 19, blond, suntanned Californian. My companion on a nutter's holiday
    of a lifetime
Meeting Heston, Olivier, Lennon, Loren, Yul, Wayne, Omar, Orson, Dustin –
    Stallone, Tatum, Astaire, Redford (*HOLLYWOOD STAR = ACROSTIC*)
To wake up in America and know I wasn't dreaming
To have a nice day in every state of the USA

▶ **Philips and Argos will make my DREAM come true because...**

PRODUCT: *Electrical goods*
COMPETITION: *Philips/Argos*

The Argos collection of Philips perfection satisfies every customer's selection
Argos offers economy on Philips modern technology
In Argos Philips products appeal – competition won – fantasy becomes real
Philips products lead the rest, Argos prices are the best
Philips reduces boring chores, by reducing prices Argos scores
Argos value, Philips innovation epitomise a dream combination

▶ **On which of six islands would you choose to have your DREAM and why?**

PRODUCT: *Cigarettes*
COMPETITION: *Martin & Lavells/Silk Cut cigarettes*

Sicily ... Silk Cut duty free, only Etna could outsmoke me
Cyprus is the one for me, a silken cut in azure sea
Crete ... because I enjoy the unknown and Crete's all Greek to me
Ibiza ... what more could a Silk Cut nut bask for?
Cyprus ... to drink all their sherry and end up Silk Cut
Smoking Silk Cut in Crete would be one Hel-i-os of a treat
Sicily 'Godmother' ... because I'm 'branded' for life and can't leave the 'Pack'
I've a S'Silly notion to see Mount Etna smoking
Seven days, seven nights, off come the silks and cut the lights
Crete ... Greek men trip the light fantastic, I'll light the tip, fantastic
I'd cut loose for a week, live like Zorba the Greek

▶ **Zanussi appliances are DREAM machines because...**

PRODUCT: *Electrical goods*

Competitors are a pest but Zanussi is best
Every drum has a silver lining
Zanussi allow you forty winks without faulty jinks, let your memories flood
    back, not your washing
The best daydream decision is choosing Zanussi precision
Only Zanussi inspires this dreamer's desires with guaranteed reliance from my
    hi-tech appliance
When washing makes you blue, your dreams can come true, with machines
    from Zanussi you'll make music like Debussy
Washing and cooking were nightmares to me so my husband bought me a
    Zanussi, now he wants the XR3i
'White' out of the blue, Zanussi makes dreams come true
Whether wet or dry, it's no illusion Zanussi are the washday blues solution
Zanussi turns washday into a soap opera, now I'm Krystal in suspenders
    instead of Pauline in Eastenders

▶ I'm a DREAM Topper because...

PRODUCT: *Synthetic cream for desserts*

I make a heavenly approach to a sweet course

▶ My mum deserves her DREAMS come true because...

PRIZES: *Family holidays in Florida*

I'm obnoxious, dad gets snappy, time that someone made mum happy
She's always caring, always fair, always loving, in all ways rare
She gives me love and affection, advice and direction
She deserves her 'American dream' for loving management of our home team
Loving, caring, funny and wise, fairly small but her heart's outsize
Every day mum takes the flak Orlando's magic would pay her back
Caring for me can cause despair, this will show I really care
Driven mad by sis and me, she dreams of regaining sanity
Her life's no fairy tale, full of monsters, each one male
She's my best pal, my favourite chum – loving, caring, sharing mum
Children cares, housework done, goes to work and still she's fun

▶ I would love to cruise down the Nile with Cleopatra at Asda because...

Asda prices are a dream come true, a cruise down the Nile would be one too

▶ DREAMS are made of this...

PRODUCT: *Orient Express train*

Posh and pampered all the way, a first class start to my holiday
In surroundings such as these, we'd both feel like VIPs
It spells luxury from the start and happiness in the finish
For a touch is history with a hint of mystery, all laced with luxury
Sights to be seen, marvellous dream, comfort and luxury and treated like a
    queen
Sights to see, a peep at the past, a romantic dream fulfilled at last
Travelling elegance, revelling in style, lapping up luxury, I'd savour every mile
My imagination could run riot, living in luxury and forgetting my diet

DREAM places

Sights to see, a peep at the past, a romantic dream fulfilled at last
If you dream of castles in the air, come with us we'll take you there
Their supermarkets reign supreme, where services and choice are a shopper's
    dream

EASY

▶ **Entertaining in style is EASY if you shop at Wavy Line because...**

PRODUCT: Food stores food

They add distinction to your courses without draining your resources

ENJOY

▶ **I ENJOY Princes pastes/pâté because...**

PRODUCT: Pastes and pâtés
COMPETITION: Kwik Save/Princes Pastes/Pâté, Outdoor
PRIZES: Raleigh bikes/Luxury Karrimore fleece leisure jackets

Mountainous appetites are 'Kwikly' suppressed, Princes 'Raleigh' are the best
Hunger attack! Kwik Save located – Princes purchased, inner tubes inflated
Delicious Princes 'Elite' of spreads, 'Karrimore' flavour onto my bread
Tasty fish, leanest meat, like Boardman's cycling, cannot be beat
Dolphin friendly with quality inbred, Princes is the 'Elite' spread
Indoor, outdoor, any place – it's minimum price with maximum taste
Well balanced and nutritious, Princes spreads are 'Raleigh' delicious
Countless others taste alike, swap my Princes? On your bike
I relish it in my 'Rolls' or on my Raleigh
Super flavours, super store, our inner tubes say 'Kwik buy more'
They 'pump' up the appetite, but don't 'puncture' my purse
It's the spread I adore for the go-ahead store!
When my 'tyred' frame needs a 'brake', Princes is appropriate

▶ **I ENJOY chewing Dentyne chewing gum because...**

PRODUCT: Chewing gum
COMPETITION: Dentyne/Levi's jeans

It gives me the taste of confidence
The hot taste of Dentyne ensures I'll stay cool on the scene
Its fresh spearmint flavour does your mouth a great favour
It's a cool fresh taste with a hint of Jeanius
It's a pleasant solution to breath pollution
In a rush, no toothbrush, teeth still clean, thanks Dentyne
It prevents any 'dirty film' from becoming a 'regular feature'
Once I got my teeth into it, I can't Levi-t alone
I'm chew-sy
It doesn't lose its flavour on the bedpost overnight

It was love at first bite
My fresh breath has just one source, this pocket size refresher course
I've tried the rest, now I chew-s the best
Every day is a chews-day
Dentyne fresh and gay, is my daily 'breath bouquet'

▶ I ENJOY entertaining with Kenco because...

PRODUCT: Coffee

A jaded hostess would endorse, it's the best refresher course
It gives the end of the meal the gourmet appeal
Traditional coffee costs less pounds, so select with finest grounds
It provides the grounds for success, without the grind

▶ I ENJOY Diet 7 UP as part of my calorie controlled diet because...

PRODUCT: Diet drink

Tastes a treat, makes ends meet, in the pocket, around the seat
It quenches thirst throughout the day, in a tasty calorie controlled way
Its light refreshing taste helps take inches off my waist

▶ What I most ENJOY about Californian wine is...

PRODUCT: Californian wine
FIRST PRIZE: Holiday to California

It's Classical, Aromatic, Lively, Invigorating, Fruity, Often Romantic, Never
  Insignificant, Always Nice *(CALIFORNIAN = ACROSTIC)*

RUNNERS-UP: Guides to New World wines

It puts you in the Sunshine State
Californian sun grows fruit so fine, they produce the most superior wine
It epitomises all the vitality, glamour and sunshine of the New World
The combination of Old World promise with New World zest
It pampers the palate, mellows the mood, and complements almost any food
Party, lunch, formal dinner, rich smooth taste, certain winner
It's Crisp, Appetising, Luscious, Innovative, Full-bodied, Outstanding,
  Rounded, Notable, Inviting and Avant garde *(CALIFORNIA =
  ACROSTIC)*
Party time or romantic dinner, it never fails to be a winner
Tasting this liquid sun, what pleasure, makes every bottle such a treasure
Whether rosé, white or red, tasting proves it's well bred
The taste, the body, the sunshine – the Californian dream
No pretention, no pomposity, just sheer taste generosity
One swallow makes a summer
The flavour, that's forte, with a body that's decidedly naughty
That fruity warmth of the West, so no need for your vest

It's Charming, Aromatic, Light, Innovative, Fruity, Original, Refreshing, Nectar, Inexpensive And News! *(CALIFORNIAN = ACROSTIC)*

Forget Français, Deutschland and Yugoslavia, the best value wines come from California

Native Zinfandel, intense berry flavour, buttery Chardonnay, so perfect to savour

Fragrant, delicious distinctive nose, but impossible to capture in short prose

With weather so stable, it's great on the table

It is nectar based, sunshine laced, always appealing to my good taste

Every bottle brings its guarantee, a perfection of consistency

From simple meals to festive treats, Californian wines cannot be beat

It makes every occasion a celebration

It tastes nice and sunny and it's 'grape' value for money

Rouge, rosé or blanc – it's the sunniest plonk!

Quaffing wines so much superior, they bring a glow to my interior

The wine from Monterey really makes my day

▶ **I would ENJOY this trip to Thailand because...**

PRODUCT: *Stir-fry sauces*
COMPETITION: *Uncle Ben's sauces*
PRIZES: *Trips to Thailand*

Perfect results every time, thanks Uncle Ben's for mine

Jar + Wok = 4-star Bangkok

Love the sauce, but the perfect result is to visit the source

I'm Thai-d of Thai-ping, Thai-m for a Thai-fling

▶ **I ENJOY McEwan's lager whilst watching football on TV because...**

PRODUCT: *Lager*
COMPETITION: *Tesco/McEwan's lager*

I always enjoy the result: McEwans's v Competitors – Home Win

I raise it in triumph, and down it in defeat

Cold McEwan's, grandstand view, hassle nil, enjoyment two

McNificent McEwan's – always a winner whatever the competition

Switching on to McEwan's, lends support to the blue'ns

▶ **I ENJOY French food and wine from Grandways because...**

PRODUCT: *French foods*

From simple meal to festive treat, French food and wine are hard to beat

With the French connection and Grandways selection I taste perfection

Fresh varieties, wines supreme, it's a Grandway to haute cuisine

La crème de la crème – a gourmet's delight – many Grandways to tempt my appetite

The French taste is unique and choice C'est magnifique

The taste drives me in-Seine

Vins de pays excites me, pâté de champagne delights me, hope Grandways invites me

Grandways vin de pays, French bread and Brie, conjure up Paris for me

Be it for pleasure or celebration, perfect for every occasion

It tastes out of this world but doesn't cost the earth

Have gourmet tastes they suit my palate

For Grandways to dine the French are sublime

▶ I ENJOY eating Nuttall's soft mints because...

PRODUCT: Mints

These melting, crumbling, cool creations give monumental taste sensations

They're the mintiest sensation without a doubt, softness bursts from inside out

They are cool, minty, sweet and light, in every way exactly right

They don't stint on the mint or overdo the chew

A cool refreshing minty flavour gives that icy taste to savour

Soft mints are hard to beat, crisp and cool a real treat

They are smooth, minty, quite unique, in my opinion 'C'est magnifique'

I don't need to own the royal mint to enjoy a packet

They are heavenly mints at a down to earth price

Crumbling, delicious, they're cool perfection – a pure white melting mint selection

▶ My family would ENJOY a holiday in Florida because...

Mum and the kids deserve the thrill of seeing Donald Duck without the bill

▶ Fine cheeses from France can be ENJOYED at any time of the day because...

PRODUCT: French cheeses
COMPETITION: Wm Low/French cheeses

They're perfect for breakfast and lunchtime's a treat, these fragrant fromages are cheeses elite

They're the taste we adore from-a-gem of a store

Quality, taste and healthy nutrition makes a cheeses from France a family tradition

Be it picnic, party, mild or mature, there's always something new for the connoisseur

Au matin or déjeuner, they bridge that gap for le gourmet

Whatever the time, whatever the event, cheeses from France are heaven sent

Like Wm Low, and French cheese, good taste wins with ease

Wm Low's French collection guarantees a good selection

From anytime suppers to grand Sunday dinners, cheese from France are everyday winners

Such timeless quality second to none, makes French cheese (h)our numéro un'

There's a wedge divine from every segment of time

For variety and taste, French cheese wins first place
The French know the tasteful way to enjoy the whole day
With a cup of tea or a glass of vin, fromage français tastes just fine
Flavours outstanding, delicious to eat, with aromas enchanting an anytime treat

▶ **I ENJOYED the American adventure experience because...**

America's finest and all it entails, brings terrific adventures to Derbyshire's
Dales

EXCELLENT

▶ **Sikkens Masterstroke offers me an EXCELLENT range of woodcare products because...**

PRODUCT: Wood varnishes

Sikkens quality guarantees perfect results with expert ease
From indoor timbers to garden seat, the Sikkens treatment is hard to beat
Wood staining and varnishing inside and out, is simply long lasting without any
doubt
A Masterstroke of genius in woodcare, a brush with Sikkens is beyond compare
Whatever the surface, interior or exterior, the natural finish is simply superior
Extensive choice, helpful advice, easy to use, sensible price

EXCITING

▶ **I think the Fiat range is EXCITING because...**

PRODUCT: Italian car

A Fiat simply smiles at miles
The extras are standard and the standard is superior
It combines economy with style for mile after mile
It has an air of quality with a flair for style
They are top of their class and are built to last
Fiat gives each mile comfort, speed and style
There's a wider range of perfection in style and comfort
They are styled with flair to get you there
You can drive the cars of the future today
It's the Italian collection that stands British inspection
It's the range that gives me plenty of change
Fiats are fun, Fiats are fast, Fiat cars are made to last
They are every driver's dream of perfection, which is no mean Fiat
Fiats have style, economy, pace, first by a mile, Fiats are ace

EXHILARATING

▶ **Shopping at Selfridges is an EXHILARATING experience because...**

PRODUCT: Chain store goods

It's a shopper's delight that reaches great heights

FAMILY

▶ **Plumrose and Hyundai are part of the FAMILY because...**

PRODUCT: Canned meats
FIRST PRIZE: Hyundai car

Plumrose means happy smiling faces, Hyundai means we're going places

▶ **Heinz and Wm Low are a winner for FAMILY shopping because...**

PRODUCT: Supermarket foods

Both are 'parent' companies, going 'father' for mother, sister and brother
Of wide variety of Heinz and other products, cleanliness and friendly staff
They've found the formula to succeed – more 'per pound' is guaranteed
Healthy taste – budget price, together make the spice of life

FAMOUS PEOPLE

▶ **I prefer Teatime biscuits because...**

PRODUCT: Biscuits
COMPETITION: Nabisco/Alice in Wonderland

Never plain, said Alice through the cellophane
Without a shadow of a doubt, what the Hatter's mad about

▶ **Which pop star would you invite to your party and why...**

PRODUCT: Confectionery
COMPETITION: Bertie Bassett's party

Bob Geldof ... he'd be a real live aid to any party, singing Allsorts of songs with mixtures of interesting chat

Bob Geldof ... he'd make sure there'd be enough food to go round

Bob Geldof ... he's a great fun raiser

Shakin' Stevens ... he is a colourful character with a sugar sweet voice and liquorice-like legs – a King of Allsorts

Shakin' Stevens ... when he dances my knees turn to jelly, baby

Shakin' Stevens ... with quivering jelly and shivering ices, it's got to be Shakin' Stevens

Boy George ... it takes Allsorts to make a world, and he's a real sweetie

Boy George ... it takes all sorts to make a Bert-day party

Boy George ... he would be popular with Allsorts

Paul Nicholas ... because at 'Granmas Party' he was a 'Sweet Illusion' with 'Personality' who could 'Rock this Town' 'Tonight'

Cliff Richard ... a 'Living Doll' like Bertie for Allsorts he's a fixture from 'Deep Purple' to 'Hello Dolly' mixtures

Russ Abbot ... never short of fun and laughter – what every party needs and is after

Russ Abbot ... because he would add atmosphere to the party with Allsorts of fun, a true madhouse

Sting ... like Bertie Bassett all the best things in life begin with a 'Bee'

George Michael ... he stars with the Wham, goes off with a bang, Allsorts he's sang and still a batchelor man

Bruce Springsteen ... because even if the lights go out we could still go on 'Dancing in the Dark'

Cheryl Baker ... Cheryl and Bertie Bassett have enough Fizz to Buck Allsorts of parties

Madonna ... like Bassett's she's colourful and sweet, terrific to bring in for a party treat

Dearest Bertie ... without you there'd be no party, so I'd like to invite 'U2'

▶ **I would most like to have morning coffee at Selfridges with ... (Personality) because...**

PRODUCT: Coffee
COMPETITION: Selfridges/Lyons coffee

Jeffrey Archer ... I 'thirst' between sequels to meet this 'first among equals'

Marcel Marceau ... I like a quiet cup of coffee in the morning

Sacha Distel ... he is the original continental always to be held in special reserve

George Thomas (*Lord Tonypandy) ... conversation wouldn't be laboured with this speaker, and who better to 'order'

▶ **If given the opportunity to sing a duet with a famous celebrity who would it be? What would you sing, and why?**

PRODUCT: Cocktail drink
COMPETITION: Mardi Gras great sounds

Tom Jones ... 'Green Green Grass of Home' – People say I hover around the dance floor like a Flymo

Benny Hill ... 'Ernie' (the fastest milkman in the west). Fun song, fruity star, please two extra bottles of Mardi Gras

Cyndi Lauper ... 'Girls just want to have fun'. Because girls DO just want to have fun and that's why I drink Mardi Gras

Me ... 'I did it my way' – A duet yourself kit

Cher ... 'Ticket to Ride' – All I want is my fare, Cher

▶ **I would most like ... (Person) as an ideal travelling partner because...**

A Knight of Olde ... he'd be bold

Bob Geldof ... he would be my Live Aid for perfect Knights

Ian McCaskill ... depressions lift, clouds float away – his warm front would brighten each day

Neptune ... he would keep his trident working in air-traffic controllers' disputes

Sir Harry Secombe ... the Highway leads to Safeway

Steve Davis ... he's got what it takes to make perfect breaks

Marcel Marceau ... I enjoy a quiet holiday

Frank Muir ... because he can 'Call my Bluff' any day

Ian McCaskill ... he'd keep a 'weather eye' out for me

Richard Branson ... balloon, boat or plane, records can be broken – again and again

Andre Previn ... his charm isn't phoney, even on 'conducted' tours

Cyril Smith ... we'd always get two seats

Patrick Moore ... I'd feel like a star in his company

Bamber Gascoigne ... in case of breakdown he'd provide a 'starter for 10'

Montague Burton ... his 'tailor-made' companion would be sure to 'suit' me

Nigel Mansell ... life's more fun in the fast lane

Paul Daniels ... be under no illusion – the trip would be pure magic

▶ **If I was stranded on a desert island the companion I would choose is ... because...**

PRODUCT: Sun tan lotion
COMPETITION: Piz Buin/Classics

Richard Branson ... his 'record' for water resistance is 'Virgin' on the incredible

Barry Manilow ... who 'nose' what might happen

Claire Francis ... there we would stay alone and remote, I'd build up my tan, she'd build a boat

Frank Bruno ... with Frank and Piz Buin I'd have double protection (know what I mean Harry?)

Jimmy Savile ... he'd be kind and caring whilst island sharing and would easily fix-it for a speedy exit

Patrick Duffy ... if anything nasty took place it would only be a dream (*Remember the shower scene in the soap, 'Dallas')

Man from Del Monte ... he says 'Yes' it's all go

Piz Buin Combination pack ... I'd just fry without it

Portfolio of shares ... they would hopefully enable me to make a quick return

▶ **I would like to share a bath with … (Personality) because…**

Tarzan … I heard it through the grapevine he's a real swinger
Venus de Milo … it would be a perfectly clean 'armless experience
Sir Les Patterson … I love to have a good 'soak' in the bath
David Owen … as a liberal minded lady, it's the perfect alliance

FARM FRESH

▶ **I shop at Kew Farm Fresh shops because…**

PRODUCT: Food store foods

They bring the essence of the country to the heart of the town

FAVOURITE

▶ **Imperial Leather is Britain's FAVOURITE soap because…**

PRODUCT: Soap

Imperial Leather will reign forever, reproduction in the bathroom – never

▶ **My FAVOURITE place to eat Princes canned food would be…**

PRODUCT: Canned food

London, Paris, Brussels, Rome, but 'Prince'-ipally here at home

▶ **British trout is a firm FAVOURITE because…**

PRODUCT: Fish

Greater variety, calories in check, you never become a 'fishical' wreck
For healthy living there's no doubt, treat yourself to British trout
Capt'n Birdseye take a hike, it's tasty British trout we like
Poached, fried, baked, barbecued or grilled, the trout quintet leaves us all
    fulfilled
We're 'soled' on the taste of trout at our 'place'
It's quick, versatile, British and best, head and 'shoal-ders' above the rest

▶ **Sun Maid is the world's FAVOURITE raisin because…**

PRODUCT: Dried fruit

It's the unseeded number one

▶ **Bertie Bassett is my FAVOURITE character because...**

PRODUCT: Confectionery

Tasty figure of a man, forget Chippendales, I am Bertie's fan
For Allsorts of reasons this man's for all seasons
Bertie Bassett's a dandy with swanky doodle candy
He remains constant passion when Simpsons or Turtles go out of fashion
He ain't Warren Beatty but he's a real sweetie

▶ **I always buy my FAVOURITE Jacob's biscuits at Gateway because...**

PRODUCT: Biscuits
COMPETITION: Gateway/Jacob's biscuits/Raleigh
PRIZES: Raleigh mountain bikes

Gateway's service never sours, Jacob's biscuits pedal power
In the BUY election, both get my vote for selection
Super biscuits, superstore.... Inner tubes say 'mum buy more'
Like Gateways, my kids' mouths are always open

▶ **When I shop at Kwik Save, Princes are my FAVOURITE spreads because...**

PRODUCT: Meat and fish pastes in jars
PRIZES: Kwik Save shopping vouchers

No waste, super taste, makes sense, saves pence
They have the best selection of the Princes collection
Kwik Save the price saver, Princes has perfect flavour
They're the top of my pots and don't cost me lots
For perfect taste, a royal munch, with pennies saved, it packs punch
I get Kwik service, Kwik flavours and Kwik savers
They help me make ends 'meat'
Lunches, picnics, snacks, dinners, with Kwik Save they are 'breadwinners'
It's value shopping, family fed, provides quality, princely spread
Lower priced, super tasting, they give rivals a proper pasting
The round pot's petite, the variety's very elite
Buying Princes at Kwik Save really spreads your bread
Competition, there is none, lower prices, best brands for everyone
Sealed in their pot, Princes beats the lot
Salmon, beef, pâté, paste bought with confidence, spread with taste
For old, young or teens, they're great for go-betweens
Bread becomes haute cuisine with Princes as the go-between
I want the tastiest topping and lowest-priced shopping
Once opened, soonest eaten, Princes spreads just can't be beaten
Kwik Save is my money saver, Princes offer perfect flavour
Largest choice, lowest price, nothing else half as nice
Watching movies late a night, Princes make the perfect bite

The best dressed bread wears Princes spread
A Princes spreader makes a better gorge than Cheddar
More choice in my trolley, pots more for my lolly
Chuffed to bits, my sarnies are fit for the Ritz
I'm completely besotted, with every spread potted
Bargain buys, big brand name, other spreads are not the same
Princes provide tasty bites, Kwik Save saves me check-out frights
With tastebuds teased and pockets pleased, excellent value is guaranteed
The humble loaf becomes well-bred, decorated with Princes spread
Tired of scampi, caviare, squid, answer lies under Princes lid
Princes is quick to spread satisfaction

▶ **Glenmorangie is my FAVOURITE purchase from Victoria Wine because...**

PRODUCT: Whisky
COMPETITION: Victoria Wine/Glenmorangie

Tain refrain from casks fae Spain, and let it soak – in oak
With pleasure in every measure, Glenmorangie is Victoria's gold liquid measure
It's the supreme malt from the shop without a fault
It's the Monarch O' the Glen for all whisky-drinking men
It's highland dew, Ross-shire air – bottled and priced beyond compare
The highlands beckon take me forth, to Glenmorangie 'spirit' of the north
I've tried the rest and like Glenmorangie the best
The supreme malt from highest still, is supreme value from lowest till
Good service, without fault, serves me the best malt
From Tarlogie springs, pleasure it brings, unique and fulfilling, the Scotman's
    Darjeeling
After years of trying the rest, Glenmorangie is still the best
The taste is luxurious, my wallet's victorious
What the sixteen men of Tain perfect, I at Victoria Wine select
Glenmorangie is a malt beyond measure, smooth, distinctive and always a
    pleasure
From a range inspired, its taste once acquired is forever desired
Fresh and fragrant delicately flavoured, Glenmorangie is made to be savoured
Delicate and distinctive, king of malts, my favourite drink from Victoria's vaults
For me, the taste is premier with Glenmorangie 'The Malt the Merrier'
I can't fault Glenmorangie malt, from Victoria Wine's extensive vaults

▶ **Cadbury's Roses are my family's FAVOURITE because...**

PRODUCT: Confectionery

A boxful of Roses helps the medicine go down

▶ **My little expert's FAVOURITE Milupa variety is ... (favourite variety) because...**

PRODUCT: *Baby food*
COMPETITION: *Boots the Chemists/Milupa*

Porridge oat breakfast ... my Goldilocks leaves no spares – pity those three bears

Harvest muesli breakfast ... she ploughs through the plate until every grain is gone

Rice dessert ... he never gets into a paddy

Spring veg dinner ... she's a bouncing baby girl

7 cereal breakfast ... this serial can be on the programme every day of the week

Garden veg ... he's always full of beans

Oat breakfast with apple ... as a connoisseur in this specialist subject he knows it's so 'appletizing'

▶ I choose my FAVOURITE Pearl because...

PRODUCT: *Soap*
COMPETITION: *Cussons Pearl*
FIRST PRIZES: *Trips to Holland*

For skin care, fragrance rare, lather to spare, none compare
It pays to be choosy, shower or jacuzzi
I'm a vulture for culture and I rather a lather

RUNNERS-UP

Cussons are my oyster
Bathing with Cussons is a heaven-scent sensation
Each tablet of scent is my pick of the bunch
It brings out the zest in me
Naturally, I'm a smooth customer
It's a small price to pay for such luxury
Perfect skincare and scented sophistication gives a sublimely luxurious sensation
Its luxurious skin treatment is well worth diving for
It's a jewel among soap
Fragrant pink pearl every day and the world's my oyster
A little soft soap is always flattering
Every bath becomes a personal blue lagoon
I'm tickled pink because it matches my sink
It's a jewel untold, worth its weight in gold
It's like nothing on earth, must be scent from heaven
A connoisseur of soap perfection chooses Pearl for her complexion
It brings the grime out of its shell
It treats me as precious – costs but a drop in the ocean
Its special lustre keeps me feeling like a gem
I'm sold on precious Pearl, it captivates me
It cares for my bare essentials
The world's my oyster and Cussons my pearl
For skin like silk it's better than milk

Experts perfect it, connoisseurs select it
It cares for my treasured chest, and all the rest
It keeps my birthday suit as good as new
It's the perfect solution to skin pollution
It's a clear favourite with all the family
I'm an oystercatcher 'bird'
It's a smoothie for an old softie
It's soap 'soaperior' to others
It's a jewel of a find for me
I'm no gran, I like to look naturally glam
Lather is rich and beautiful for features great and small

▶ **Which is your FAVOURITE English cheese and why?**

PRODUCT: English cheeses

Smooth double Gloucester do I favour with its rich and mellow flavour
Mature English Cheddar reigns supreme, fit for every king and queen
English double Gloucester's best, it's smooth and creamier than the rest
Mature Cheddar strong in taste makes home dishes made in haste
Leicester waste, Leicester pay and Leicester find in the fridge every day
    (*Leicester = less to)
I always 'Caerphilly' choose – as it would take nothing 'Leicester' please me
For a snack or main meal Cheddar has 'grate' appeal
'Tis tangy when mature, a Derby winner for the connoisseur

▶ **Bubblicious is my FAVOURITE bubble gum because...**

PRODUCT: Bubble gum

Bubblicious bubbles are the best, they grow much larger than the rest
I've tried the rest, now I 'chews' the best
It is half the trouble to blow twice the bubble
Its bubbles leave me speechless
Hubba Bubble toil and trouble, Bubblicious bubbles blow up double

▶ **Which is your FAVOURITE Asda brand French wine and why?**

PRODUCT: French wines
COMPETITION: Asda 'Wine and cheese'

To choose just one would be sheer folly, such a choice to tempt your trolley

▶ **Treasure hunters eat Jacob's Club and Trio as their
FAVOURITE chocolate biscuits because...**

PRODUCTS: Chocolate biscuits

Real thick chocolate '4T'fies those who hunt for better buys

Chocolate so rich, fillings supreme; to find them together is a prospector's dream

Pirates searching the seven seas, never found booty as good as these

Like Christopher Columbus they open up a new world of delight

Even Tutankhamen would come alive, could he taste this pack of five

As Tutankhamen said to mummy, 'Jacob's are so very scrummy'

Every bite is 18 carat, quite a change from eating parrot

Chocolate Lovers Uncover Bargains, They Really Insist On Jacob's *(CLUB TRIO = ACROSTIC)*

You can't beat a man with a Club

With a different flavour every day, who needs treasure anyway?

Specialists perfect them, perfectionists select them

In their quest for the best, real thick chocolate passed the test

▶ **My FAVOURITE Disney character is … because…**

PRODUCT: Soft drink
COMPETITION: Coca-Cola/Euro Disney competition
PRIZES: Holidays in Euro Disney

Pongo Dalmation … like Coca-Cola – he knocks spots off the rest!

Mary Poppins … like Coca-Cola, she lightens life, banishing household strife

Snow White … she's 'une étoile' – everything worth wishing for

FIESTA

▶ **Associated Biscuits makes teatime into FIESTA time because…**

PRODUCT: Biscuits

Looking fancy and tasting delicious – the most humdrum days become highly auspicious

FINISH

▶ **Mars ice cream is the perfect way to FINISH a meal because…**

PRODUCT: Ice cream

For a melting moment unsurpassed, Mars wins by finishing last

FIRST

▶ **Swish is the FIRST choice in curtain tracks because...**

PRODUCT: Curtain tracks

Swish is quality, the number one name, to dress with style, your window frame
They're styled for beauty and made for duty
They glide, they slide, they open wide, doing their duty, with silent beauty
With effortless ease they glide and sail, curtains are honoured to hang from this rail
My curtains were on the wrong track until I discovered I could swish them back
For each curtain and blind, a Swish system you'll find
From lounge to hall they are easy to install, a smooth performance every curtain call
Nets, curtains, swags, tails, you are on the right track if you pick Swish rails
The smoothness of the glide, helps my curtains hang with pride
No need to pull, tug or jerk, the smooth Swish action does the work

▶ **My FIRST choice of prize from Cadbury's at Boots is ... because...**

PRODUCT: Confectionery
COMPETITION: Boots the Chemists/Cadbury's
PRIZES: Choice of either Sharp midi system (SMS) or Sharp video recorder

Sharp Video recorder ... it allows you to chew over the fruity bits twice
SMS ... I've eaten the choc, now husband wants to rock
SMS ... after a two bar introduction, that's real easy listening
SMS ... Aled's voice will never break nor Simon's symphonies rattle
SMS ... like Cadbury's – quality supreme, from a 'Wispa' to a scream
SMS ... with Boots and my midi this system won't catch cold

▶ **My FIRST choice of Cadbury's home improvements is ... because...**

PRODUCT: Confectionery
COMPETITION: Presto/Cadbury's
PRIZE: Choice of fitted units

A fitted bedroom ... my bedroom furniture's quite appalling – hey Presto, Cadbury's are re-installing

FISH

▶ **Princes canned fish products are a hit with my family because...**

PRODUCT: Canned fish
COMPETITION: Kwik Save/Princes
PRIZES: Personal CD players and cassette players

They are tastier than 'New squids on the block'
Hey Hey we're the chunkies
We would rather 'Roe with Cod' than 'Sail with Rod'
You can't CD bones
'Down Down' tastily they go – Princes – forever our 'Status Quo'
For taste they're 'The Temptations', for quality 'The Supremes'
They're too tasty for their tins
Before Princes we all lived in a yellow soup tureen
Dolphins without tears brings music to my ears
Princes 'Bridge over troubled waters' – pleasing dolphin-friendly daughters
You'll be hooked on this line

▶ **British trout is a firm favourite because...**

PRODUCT: Fish

Greater variety, calories in check, you never become a 'fishical' wreck
For healthy living there's no doubt, treat yourself to British trout
Capt'n Birdseye take a hike, it's tasty British trout we like
Poached, fried, baked, barbecued or grilled, the trout quintet leaves us all
    fulfilled
We're 'soled' on the taste of trout at our 'plaice'
It's quick, versatile, British and best, head and 'shoal-ders' above the rest

▶ **Why would you like to win an angling break with Argos?**

PRODUCT: Catalogue
COMPETITION: Argos Angling
PRIZES: Two-day angling breaks

'Becod' it sounds like a nice 'plaice' and it would really knock me off my
    'perch' to win
Angling Times are few and far between, so on the river bank I'd like to be seen
No more freezer fish shop bought, but fish by me freshly caught, a unique
    experience – food for thought
Holme Pierrepoint the venue, maggots on the menu, the fish they will dine,
    let's hope for a tight line
A chance to learn from the experts how to fish, is me and my son's greatest
    wish
Rudd, roach, tench, bream, how I like to dream, it would be my cup of tea,
    hooked on fishing, that's me!

New tackle at hand, bigger fish we hope to land, our prize weekend out angling will keep lines from entangling

Treasures I would forsake, for an angling break, teachers to hand, showing how to land, wellies that clutter the lake!

I've never won a 'fin' on such a 'scale' and this new 'line' would have me 'reeling'

Because I want to get the fishing angles from the anglers

Hook, bait, rod, line, cast out, weather's fine, keep-net full of bream, Argos win – angler's dream

Once you're 'hooked' on Argos, you're right on 'line' to 'tackle' any competition

It would be A Really Great Outdoor Surprise, if I could win this smashing prize *(ARGOS = ACROSTIC)*

My dad and me, we're in despair, we catch no fish – not anywhere, help is needed for this daft pair

I'd like to tell a fishy tale, I caught no eel, it was a whale

I'd like to win the break because fishing makes me unwind faster than a 4lb line from a match spool

Being a girl who's just started fishing, I think there should be more women anglers like my nan, mum and myself

To be a 'King Fisher' would be brill, with expert schooling in angling skill

At my age it's never too late to learn

To win a fishing break would be a 'reel' catch

Tackle, lakes, bream, angling's in my dreams – chance to be coached to catch big roach, that is now my dream

FIXED

▶ **Obo Seals and Trims FIXED it for me because...**

PRODUCT: Plumbing accessories
PRIZES: Holidays of a lifetime

For a professional finish at little expense, Obo made such common sense

Gaps between worktops spread diseases, Obo prevention is a cure that pleases

FLAVOUR

▶ **I'd like to win a holiday with a real Italian FLAVOUR because...**

PRODUCT: Pasta sauce
COMPETITION: Tesco/Dolmio

Dolmio's recipes savoured at home, inspire this Papa to travel to Rome

Mamma Mia, this cook at home needs a 'pasta port' to Rome
Saucy Dolmio's my inspiration to savour a classical Latin sensation
'Aroma' and authenticity would herald my freedom from domesticity

▶ **Safeway brings me FLAVOURS from afar because...**

   PRODUCT: Supermarket foods

They give you exotic tastes, mysterious spices, faraway places at affordable
   prices

FLOCK

▶ **Shoppers FLOCK to our stores because...**

   PRODUCT: Lamb
   COMPETITION: Gateway/New Zealand lamb
   PRIZE: Trip to New Zealand

The Gateway shopper, discerning folks, buy prime products, not pigs in pokes

▶ **Zealous customers FLOCK to the Co-op because...**

   PRODUCT: Beds
   COMPETITION: Co-op/Slumberland beds

They know they can feather their nest with a little down

FLYING

▶ **I would like to FLY to Amsterdam with Toilet Duck because...**

   PRODUCT: Toilet cleaner
   COMPETITION: Tesco/Toilet Duck
   PRIZES: Trips to Holland to visit the Dutch bulb fields

It could show the Dutch its magic touch
In the city of flowers, I'd smell of roses
Me and the Duck's gonna clean up this town
I can smell fragrant flowers swaying in a springtime breeze
I'm hooked on Holland and flushed with success
I'd go clean round the bend at such luck
If I scoured the world I couldn't choose better
His streamlined jet reaches clogs and canals fastest and safest
Pot-pourri puts me in mind of tulips in springtime
Loo-tips from Amsterdam couldn't make a cleaner pan

▶ **I'm FLYING high with Del Monte and Morrisons because...**

PRODUCT: *Canned fruit*
COMPETITION: *Morrisons/Del Monte fruit*
PRIZE: *Trip in air balloon*

Morrisons' prices are surprisingly light, for such a truly juicy Del-height

▶ **We wish we could take off in the Cadbury's Crunchie FLYING circus because...**

PRODUCT: *Confectionery*

Flying fun we could share, family clowning in the air

▶ **I would like to win the Lil-lets flight of fantasy on Concorde because...**

PRODUCT: *Tampons*
COMPETITION: *Lil-lets flight of fantasy/Concorde*
PRIZES: *Trips on Concorde with champagne lunch*

It's a supersonic philharmonic holiday tonic
My husband wants to see if Concorde's nose is bigger than mine
I would gladly replace the stress in my life with Strauss
A flying start certainly won't end by going off the rails
Our tent leaked this year

▶ **When we buy Princes we zoom into orbit because...**

PRODUCT: *Canned fish*
COMPETITION: *Kwik Save/Princes*
PRIZES: *Satellite dishes*

We go to Ma's for tea
Waistline friendly, little bread Princes Kwik Save 'light' years ahead
Kwik Save empire strikes back, blasting prices off every pack
A 'star' buy from Kwik Save's aisles, 'dishy' Princes satellite smiles
Princes dishes without exception, always get a great reception
Together they proffer an Unbeatable Family Offer *(U.F.O. = ACROSTIC)*
It's a capsule of health from a store saving wealth
We know we'll come down to earth tuna or later
Princes tuna to our choppers, Kwikies programmed to save coppers
In a galaxy of tins Princes always wins
Quick, cheap, no waste, satellite your sense of taste
They're light years ahead in the store wars
Princes tuna quick and zippy, healthier than a Martian chippy
Sky's the limit, great selection, 'dishing up' Princes' sheer perfection
No alien fish will we receive on our dish
Armstrong first on lunar lands, Princes first for tuna brands
It's Princes network transmitted by Kwik Save received by shoppers

Kwik Save's Princes tuna dish'll taste heavenly – that's O-fish'all
Princes tuna tasty dish Kwik Save prices every woman's wish
Such Fishical pleasure in store even Patrick asks for Moore!

▶ I would like to go up up and away with Wings because…

PRODUCT: *Water biscuits*
COMPETITION: *Huntley & Palmer/Wings*

I fancy Wings on the menu and Paris as the venue
They are the ideal pick up to help a drink down
I would then know that an aperitif is not a set of dentures
I'd avoid attacks of inferior flying snacks

▶ Jacob's crackers are like Concorde because…

PRODUCT: *Crackers*

They came, they saw, they 'Concorde' the market – the cream of crackers
One excites the palate – the other unites the planet
Home is 'Teethrow'
Concorde flies the flag, Jacob's raise the standard
Outstanding qualities they combine are 'original and best' – by *sound* design
For top flight taste I'mach two (*Mach 2) with cheese and get cracking

▶ I take off with Cover Girl cosmetics because…

PRODUCT: *Cosmetics*

Its 'great base' gives me a 'perfect lift-off' to a 'sparkling splash down'

▶ I would like to take the Pepsi challenge in a hot air balloon because…

PRODUCT: *Canned drink*

Drinking Pepsi on a cloud, raises me above the crowd
Then I can have an up-up and away day
I'd like to be high not dry
Drinking Pepsi on cloud nine would be so divine
Nothing can compare with Pepsi in mid air
Sipping Pepsi in the skies, what a breathtaking surprise
At any height Pepsi's the tops
Every drop gives me a lift

Air travel

At high level they excel, planely they've no parallel
If you dream of castles in the air, come with us and we'll take you there
With reliability and service guaranteed they ensure many happy returns
To err is human but to Air with Italia is divine
They bridge the skies to the Bridge of Sighs

BA is a degree above the rest
Flying was an ordeal, now I lie back and think of Britannia
With duty free goods and in-flight meal, Britannia's service is ideal
They rule out all the waves

▶ **Flying with Concorde to Paris**

PRODUCT: Airline

On Concorde you'll be a high flyer
'Eiffel' for 'Concorde' as soon as I'd 'Seine' it

FORTUNE

▶ **Princes are my fruits of FORTUNE because...**

PRODUCT: Canned fruit
COMPETITION: Kwik Save/Princes fruits
PRIZES: Isle of Man holidays with a visit to the Casino

Placing bets across the table, nothing beats the Princes label
Isle wager there's no better cert than a Princes dessert
Winners in themselves I draw lots from Kwik Save's shelves
They've finest fruit, expertly canned, I ca'sino better brand
I've got Princes gambling feeling, fruits that are so appealing
Princes label on my can, my ticket to the Isle of Man
Isle of Man-aged transportation kitchen table to gaming table
Quality fruits, canned at prime, hits the jackpot every teatime
Princes tea aces win over poker faces
I never get the pip with Princes fruity lucky dip
Never a gamble, always a cert, praiseworthy Princes, delicious dessert
Chips down, worried frown, I need fix, Kwik – cocktail mix
Enjoying Princes for tea, lady luck has smiled on me
Breakfast, lunch, tea and dinner, delicious, versatile, what a winner
A Princes canny gambler has the odds in his flavour
Oranges, apricots, peach or pear, I casino others that compare
Luscious treasures in a tin, Manx Casino if I win
One gamble true, scores a look with a view
Partnering Princes, with fortune's grace wins me this three legged race
Laying my cards on the table, they're the winning label
Every winning line will reveal fruits with such great ap-peel
Small payout, fruit divine, hitting the jackpot every time
The Midas touch they guarantee means golden taste for family tea
With their perfection as afters I ca-si-no disasters
Confucius say for Kwik Save win – need nod from Princes mandarin
E Manx-ipated from boring puds, the Princes jackpot delivers the goods

Gambling on other brands lands me in custardy
Princes fruits with cream are a Manx cat's dream
Give any tin a spin – you win

FREEZERS

▶ **I buy Bird's Eye at Tesco because...**

PRODUCT: Frozen vegetables

They have mountains of choice at frozen prices

▶ **North West Co-op are the great price freezers because...**

PRODUCT: Supermarket foods

They try to keep their customers cool – but never on the rocks!
It gets a warm reception at our house

▶ **The ice creams from Mars are cool classics because...**

PRODUCT: Ice cream

Summer heat, sheer delight, a taste remembered with every bite
Unlike classics past, Mars ice creams aren't meant to last
Discerning shoppers never miss them, even Eskimos can't resist them

▶ **Mars cool chocolates from the fridge**

PRODUCT: Confectionery

We like our chocs served up on the rocks, delicious and nice garnished with ice
Chilled chocolate puts the 'umm'! back into summer
Chocolate chilled is biteably sweet – puts the 'ice' in nice and the 'eat' in treat
Kept safely chilled, makes quite sure they melt in the mouth and not before
There's no messy paper and no sticky fingers, with ice chilled chocolate it's the
    flavour that lingers
Cool on the tongue makes the taste buds tingle, when delicious chocolate and
    flavours mingle
Delicious bars the ice cold way are red-hot favourites every day
Chocolate with a chill gives an extra thrill, so make it a rule to eat it cool
Hot cross mums become real cool customers after this kitchen treat
Mars from the fridge is all the rage, is this the beginning of a new ice age
Picture of summer, deckchairs and sun, chilled chocolate complete it for
    everyone
Whether the weather is sunny or grey, I forecast Mars bars will brighten any
    day
Run a marathon, land on Mars, always reach for the fridge cooled bars to give
    you energy

Out of this world, chocolate is chilled to perfection, the sky is the limit for Mars confection

Winter or summer, autumn or spring, eating chilled chocolate gives you a zing

FRESHNESS

▶ **Easy-On gives your ironing day-long FRESHNESS because...**

PRODUCT: Spray starch
COMPETITION: Easy-On/Rowenta Irons

When using Easy-On, worries cease, fresher and crisper laundry, 'wrinkles decrease'

Its freshness will never cease, its wonders will never crease

Outdoor freshness and inner pride come when Easy-On's applied

My clothes will go wherever I please and please wherever I go

Laundry takes in a fresh air aroma - deserving of a hygiene diploma

One small squirt keeps your shirt alert

Without it you're left with ironing bored clothes

Easy-On smoothes the way to a perfect finish every day

It's the easy way to a crease-free day

It's the finishing touch that counts so much

Clean and fresh form starch to finish, crispness lasts and won't diminish

It's my laundry's first aid

Such freshness, comfort, crispness, flair, puts springtime into every wear

We both know our job and press on together

Its speedy smooth spray, is starch the easy way

Clothes smell sweet, they feel right, looking neat from morning 'til night

It contains every right ingredient, it's excellent and expedient

It sprays back a new look in seconds, with lasting impressions

The lasting 'iron on' chic is quite unique

A little spray keeps the creases at bay

FRIEND

▶ **Whitworths are a girl's best FRIEND because...**

PRODUCT: Dried fruit

Like diamonds, the result is a dazzling success

Making cakes is a fruitless task without them

Men enjoy fruity beauties, juicy peels and outstanding cherries

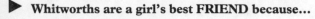

▶ **Access is your flexible FRIEND because...**

PRODUCT: *Credit card*

Even when your budget's tight, Access is your friendly knight

FUTURE

▶ **I'll enjoy a golden FUTURE with Mars because...**

PRODUCT: *Confectionery*
COMPETITION: *Mars/Anglia Building Society*
FIRST PRIZE: *£20,000*
SECOND PRIZES: *4 x £5,000*
THIRD PRIZES: *5 x £1,000*

Anglia is the better building society but Mars is building society better
From every angle, Mars is best – a capital investment giving new interest
For value, goodness, taste and size, Mars will always win my prize
Their superior criterior makes life much cheerier
Quality and value will never date, so interest in Mars will appreciate
An investment of a Mars a day will yield a high dividend
Fifty years and never surpassed, years ahead – still top of their charts
It's the big bar investment the family love to share
Each generation has tasted variety but only Mars is building society
For quality, value and nutrition, Mars is the great British tradition

GASTRONOMY

▶ **I buy Wall's sausages because...**

PRODUCT: *Sausages*
COMPETITION: *Tesco/Wall's sausages/Moffat cookers*
PRIZES: *Moffat cookers*

They're a gastronomic thrill, without an astronomic bill
Tesco savings gastronomic makes a meal so economic
Gastronomic Wall's are fine, Tesco please make Moffat mine
They fulfil my gastronomical wishes with economical dishes
The price is right for this gastronomic delight
It combines gastronomy with economy

GET ON DOWN

▶ **When we buy Princes fruit juices at Kwik Save we GET ON DOWN to the juiciest flavours around because...**

PRODUCT: Fruit juices
COMPETITION: Kwik Save/Princes fruit juices
PRIZES: Midi CD hi-fi systems and personal CD players

Six fruit juices to select, no nonsense prices – sounds perfect
It's a disc-tinctive drink at a disc-ount price
Like the Right-Juice Brothers – 'we lose that thirsty feeling'
Fruity construction – pure seduction, sound deduction a Princes production
Quality juices, small expense, Princes and Kwik Save sound sense
For record savings, it's jolly cartons' (*Dolly Parton's) greatest hits
Every drink they do, they do it juice for you
Princes flavours and the Temptations, Kwik Save stores the Supremes
This top of the shops has the best juice box
For a price that is nominal, the taste is phenomenal
The family's hit quencher is no money wrencher
They are thirst quenching, purse quenching, leaders of the brands
Princes juices are enticing, Kwik Save has attractive pricing
We've disc-covered disc-tinctively fruity flavours at disc-idedly fruity prices
It's liquid sunshine that makes the pourer richer
The taste like fruit drinks oughter, not just flavoured water
It's the CD-uctive taste that re-45s me
Wholesome juices, little lolly, make me lambada with the trolley
Perfect taste in every pack, something other juices lack
Princes quality is traditional, Kwik Save low prices are additional
Princes juices twist and squeeze, popular Kwik Save prices please
Princes great, Kwik Save ace, no more wild juice chase
Taste temptations, supreme tang, Princes Kool for all the Gang
I can't get no satisfaction without Princes juice extraction
Tastebuds atingle, tills ajingle, top names unite, sounds just right
Princes strikes a fruity note, Kwik Save value gets my vote
There's always thirst choice on my Chopin Liszt
We're getting D'major fruit juices at D'minor prices

GOLD & TREASURE

▶ **Krona is as good as GOLD because...**

PRODUCT: Margarine

Krona sets the standard by which others are judged
It outshines all the others

From prospecting shoppers, hear the roars, there's Krona gold in them there stores

Krona and gold's hallmark connection is a stamp with the crown of pure perfection

It transforms a plain meal into a glittering success

Van den Berghs do the donkey work, the consumer gets the carats

The taste all eaters treasure, the price all buyers dig

Precious little gives a lot of enjoyment

It's Krona ore nothing

Its 250g ingots crown both cottage loaf and upper crust

It might be mined down under but it's never undermined

It's a favourite of mine and all my little minors

It has rich deposits of natural goodness

It's got a 24-carat taste without costing a mint

The taste is ore inspiring

Even King Midas couldn't touch Krona for taste

It's the find of a lifetime, the rush is over, but it's still spreading

Its rich fine texture and superb taste is such a fine prospect

You can take your pick at the supermarket

For taste it Midas well be butter

It has an aura of perfection unsurpassed by ore-dinary margarines

Troy Krona and you're sure to dig it

▶ Cider is as good as GOLD because...

PRODUCT: Cider

Looking forward to drinking 'mine' is a great prospect

Like gold, each measure sets a standard

It sets the standard all others are judged by

▶ I think that San Miguel is a GOLD medal winning premium lager because...

PRODUCT: Lager
PRIZES: Trips to Olympic Games at Barcelona

Like all winners it has a strong clean finish

Unlike the Olympics, no-one should have to wait four years for another

Every 'Opening Ceremony' is followed by a lap of honour

To Cat-a-lan story short, in the race for perfection it can't be caught

It's sharp as a javelin, smooth as a rink, a winner in Spain and our favourite drink

They haven't made a platinum medal yet

▶ Asda coffee is as good as GOLD because...

PRODUCT: Coffee

Its flavour you treasure, its prices you dig

▶ **Rowenta and Comet/Currys make a GOLD winning team because...**

PRODUCT: Electrical goods
COMPETITION: Comet/Currys and Rowenta

Together they are joint firsts in product popularity and professional
    presentation
For quality and service they are both front runners
Their 24-carat gold reputation is never tarnished
The elegant technology and shining prices provide the most glittering of prizes
With every purchase a glittering prize they cut ironing down to size
Experts perfect them connoisseurs select them.
Rowenta steam past the rest and Currys only choose the best
Top performer second to none, Rowenta and Currys show how it's done
Names of such 'esteem' together reign supreme

▶ **Dole Californian raisins and prunes are ideal for health-conscious people because...**

PRODUCT: Dried fruits
PRIZES: Trips to Barcelona including Olympics, therefore GOLD a theme

Gold medal performance is Dole's tradition, first for taste, first for nutrition
If health and fitness is your dream, Dole's track record reigns supreme
Tended with love in Californian sun, Dole's dried fruits rate No. 1
Naturally healthy, full of nutrition, if going for gold is your ambition
Natural, dolelicious, packed with sun, they're gold medal winners for everyone
They're packed with energy, wholesome, sweet, a sustaining snack, a mealtime
    treat
For snacks, breakfast, lunch, dinner, nutritious, delicious Dole's a winner
Essence of sunshine, guaranteed zest, Dole is the Gateway to personal best
They're 'Dole'liciously fruity, energy giving, ideal for a healthier style of living
Californian sweet sunshine in every pack, the truly 'gold' medal snack
In the race for a healthy today, Dole's the winner all the way

▶ **I buy Robertson's GOLDEN/Silver Shred and jams from Hillards because...**

PRODUCT: Conserves
COMPETITION: Hillards/Robertson's

There's more than a shred of evidence to prove they're as good as gold
They are jam packed with flavoursome bargains
I can buy more Robertson's gold for my silver at Hillards
They get my 'toast' every day
It's the gold and silver taste at copper prices
At such economic prices it would be folly not to enjoy warranted goodness by
    golly
Hillards' prices butter the bread that goes between my golden shred

Spotting the difference in the rest – for quality and value – they're the best
My little bits of silver buy pots of gold
Both take pride in the quality inside
Robertson's put on an old fashioned spread
They encourage the spread of good taste
Value is tastefully preserved
Delicious quality, each a money saver, they've so much 'in their flavour'

▶ **Shopping at Spar is a GOLDEN opportunity because...**

PRODUCT: Food store foods

You don't have to dig for treasure, it's at your finger tips
It provides the perfect setting for a gem of bargains
The sweet buy and buy makes your basket a casket
Their new ideas and old ideals make Spar a mine of happiness
There is a load of bargains stamped with hallmarks of excellence
You get timeless quality with up-to-the-minute value
Anyone with a grain of sense collects gold by saving pence
The sign of the tree points to savings for me
I dig their bargains, treasure their prices and save myself a fortune
The watchword is quality and value the mainspring
The savings are golden the staff are gems, it's a golden combination
Spar prices are a golden oasis in the sands of inflation
I dig their rich seams of bargains and quickly make them mine
It raps inflation on the knuckles

▶ **The Pledge shine is a GOLDEN shine because...**

PRODUCT: Furniture polish
PRIZE: Bag of gold dust worth £3000

Pledge dust worth £3K would put a shine on any day

▶ **The Simpsons are GOLDEN Wonders because...**

PRODUCT: Snacks

Dudes dig the mega crunch, small fry love this radical bunch
Wild and wacky, bags of fun, family favourites every one
The sky's the limit for these cheeky Wotsits

▶ **I'll enjoy a GOLDEN future with Mars because...**

PRODUCT: Confectionery
COMPETITION: Mars/Anglia Building Society
FIRST PRIZE: £20,000
SECOND PRIZES: 4 x £5,000
THIRD PRIZES: 5 x £1,000

Anglia is the better building society but Mars is building society better

From every angle, Mars is best – a capital investment giving new interest
For value, goodness, taste and size, Mars will always win my prize
Their superior criterior makes life much cheerier
Quality and value will never date, so interest in Mars will appreciate
An investment of a Mars a day will yield a high dividend
Fifty years and never surpassed, years ahead – still top of their charts
It's the big bar investment the family love to share
Each generation has tasted variety but only Mars is building society
For quality, value and nutrition, Mars is the great British tradition

▶ **I think Gloria Hunniford is the perfect jewellery wearer because...**

PRODUCT: Jewellery

She embodies the style, elegance and charm of pure gold
Precious pieces, worn with style, are matched by Gloria's golden smile
Gloria always pays attention to that precious touch you mention
Like gold, she is a shining example of timeless elegance

▶ **I'm worth my weight in pounds with Douwe Egberts because...**

PRODUCT: Filter coffee
COMPETITION: Leo's/Douwe Egberts win your weight in gold
PRIZE: Winner's weight in £1 coins

I'm endowed with the Midas touch of old, all my coffee from Leo's turns
Continental Gold

▶ **'99' is my most treasured of teas because...**

PRODUCT: Co-op tea

Other teas velly sloshy, make tea that is wishee woshy
The best from the chest is brought out under water
One drink and I'm no longer a sunken wreck
The swag's in the bag
There's nothing finer to cure a Mao-Tse tongue
Any other brand would make a mandarin duck
It's a thirst quencher and also an oriental taste adventure
It's collected with care to give a flavour that's rare
You get a precious lot for precious little
You can stir it but you won't beat it
Richer, poorer, sickness, health, with '99' who needs wealth?
Richness flavour every sup, with fortunes found inside every cup
Steve Davis couldn't make a better pot
Stock markets crash but '99' slips down gracefully
Such a tea beyond compare, makes me feel like a millionaire
A great tasting tea is enough riches for me
Its secret is in the bag

Its flavour is priceless and priced less
You never get a short measure with this tea treasure
Its great wall of flavour is a real life savour

▶ Toffifee is delicious because...

PRODUCT: Confectionery
COMPETITION: Woolworths/Toffifee GOLDEN toffee cup

They're the taste I treasure at a price I dig
Inside each caramel cup there's a hoard of golden promise fulfilled
It's a golden cup with a 14-carat taste
... Well – it's different!
This tasty hoard good to eat when required pop up a treat
There's no need to speculate just sit back and appreciate
The taste drives you 'nuts' which leaves others behind
With hazelnut and caramel shell, chocolate and nougat, they taste swell

GOOD LIFE

▶ Tesco and Hilton give you a taste of the GOOD LIFE because...

PRODUCT: Supermarket foods
COMPETITION: Tesco/Hilton hotels
PRIZES: Luxury breaks in London Hilton hotel or weekend breaks in Britain

Champagne, smoked salmon and Stilton, bought at Tesco, eaten at the Hilton
Their superb quality, cleanliness and style, mean every visit produces a smile
Careful attention to customer needs, means satisfaction and pleasure are
    guaranteed
High Street or Park Lane, their quality is the same
Dedication to excellence knows no bounds, at Tesco and Hilton – paradise
    found
However Important Luxury, Taste Or Needs, Their Excellent Service Creates
    Outstanding Satisfaction (HILTON TESCO'S = ACROSTIC)
Both richly deserve EGGceptional praise – Hilton for style, Tesco for
    mayonnaise
Each with own brand of care, add quality to life beyond compare
Luxury put Hilton on the map, Tesco's put luxury on your lap
Each deserves a standing ovation, for giving elevated prices a welcome vacation
Five star value, five star praise, plus crème de la crème mayonnaise
Tesco and Hilton are streets ahead, tasteful quality from A–Z
Luxurious quality with prices right, a traveller's dream, a shopper's delight
Forget 'Onassis' yacht in Med – try Tesco champagne in Hilton bed
Tesco's Mayo – best taste around, Hilton's hospitality – world renowned

GREAT

▶ **Melitta one-cup filters are GREAT for every occasion because...**

PRODUCT: Coffee filters
PRIZES: Picnic baskets

Adding water off the boil, gives fresh ground coffee without the toil
Easy to use fresh every time, taste and aroma simply divine
Every cup freshly brewed, ensures the last is never stewed
Fresh, tasty, rich and smooth – handy packs when on the move
Freshly roasted then individually packed, all the flavour stays intact
It is the taste sensation, to be taken, at any location
Now I can impress my guests without doing silly sound effects
Picnics, barbecues, whatever the venue, they have to be on the menu
They suit solo occasions, cosy liaisons, even unexpected family invasions
With morning toast or evening brandy, Melitta is deliciously handy

▶ **To win a mountain bike with Twist 'n' Squeeze would be GREAT because...**

PRODUCT: Fruit drinks
COMPETITION: Kwik Save/Twist 'n' Squeeze
PRIZES: Mountain bikes

I can have the thrills on the hills without spills
When kids are on vacation these are the perfect combination
Climbing hills non-stop is just as easy as opening top
Superb bike makes speedy trip, to purchase favourite fruity sip
Cycling would be a breeze with refreshing Twist 'n' Squeeze
A crucial cycle fun galore, delicious drink, who needs more?
Freewheeling fun, open air thrills, never saddled with messy spills
Thirst from biking makes Twist 'n' Squeeze even more to my liking
They send my tastebuds on migration, cycling to my destination
Both handle with ease and go where I please
Both give pleasure, one to drink, the other to treasure
When you reach the top you'll relish every drop
Its chain reaction gives me thirst satisfaction
This fruity feeling keeps you moving, when the going's gruelling
It would combine the pleasure when it's enjoyed together
You can overtake any burst of thirst
With this fruity blend, it's top gear to journey's end
This juice gives more miles per hour of pedal power
To be dramatic, I'd be wheely ecstatic
This fruity drink brings satisfaction, leading me to pedal action
Six packs without seals means a new set of wheels
They double the pleasure when enjoyed together
Amid biking bumps and thrills, Twist 'n' Squeeze never spills

Paper round done with ease, thanks delicious Twist 'n' Squeeze
Over vale and hill, not one drop will spill
Speedy drink, wheelie speed, this alliance is what I need
It goes down well, on the rocks it's swell
I'd have the gear and bottle for riding high
Twist 'n' Squeeze mountain biking, how refreshing, no more hiking
It's every cyclist's dream to be a winning team
Like Twist 'n' Squeeze extraordinaire, you can take your bike anywhere
On yer bike, having fun, Twist 'n' Squeeze number one
The taste is won, this juice is number one
Bike plus Twist 'n' Squeeze a tandem sure to please
I could keep my frame thinner while drinking a winner
This kid likes adventure with his favourite thirst quencher
Mountain high, river deep, the cost of refreshment isn't cheap
Bike, Twist 'n' Squeeze, Ben Nevis – what a breeze
That Twist 'n' Squeeze action leads to cycling satisfaction
This great combination fulfils my inclination – thrills without spills
On yer bike, down the street, drinking Twist 'n' Squeeze, what a treat
One chilled to thrill the other has thrills that chill
As a drink and bike selection they reach the peak of perfection

HAPPY & FUN

▶ **I like making people HAPPY with Pomagne because...**

PRODUCT: Sparkling wine

Its sparkling bubbles dispel their troubles

▶ **Lennons make me a HAPPY motorist by...**

PRODUCT: Food store foods

Having a large range, I don't need to be Rover
Customising their prices and range, each economy has automatic change
Providing the bumper bootful, that makes a low-cost car-go

▶ **HAPPINESS is a packet of Nik Naks and...**

PRODUCT: Snacks
COMPETITION: Rowntree's/Nik Naks
PRIZES: Sony CD players

Ecstasy is a boxful
Crunching to the best of their rhythm sticks
Knowing that they're nice 'n' spicy and not too pricey
Relief that the packets aren't compact
Having the nak of eating them before somebody niks them

ExCDingly good sounds in my ears 'Sony'
A sound perception of savoury perfection
And sadness when they're all gone
Singing nik nak paddy wak dog's got the scampi pack

▶ It's FUN to be blonde with Clairol because...

PRODUCT: Hair colourant

In any setting, Clairol's attention getting
When it's so easy you just can't keep it bottled up
It shows in a crowd and makes you feel proud
Blondes succeed where others concede
Clairol gives a fair deal
It turns plain into pearl
Clairol perfects them, so gentlemen select them
You're streaks ahead
Girls who use flashlights soon discover they have a winning streak
Clairol's blonding range is like champagne, it makes you bubbly and
    lightheaded
It's the ideal tonic when you want to curl up and dye
It's attention-getting whatever the setting
Wolf whistles abound, heads turn around and my ego is crowned
I feel on a par with a Hollywood star
You become the main attraction, driving men to sheer distraction
Blondes make more Bonds
Flaxen, tawny, ash or highlighted, gentlemen prefer us, we are delighted
Formerly mousy, frumpish and forty, now I frolic as a blonde quite naughty

▶ Vileda makes housework more FUN because...

PRODUCT: Cleaning cloth

It's 'Kelly's Eye' for my 'Housey Housey' (*'No. 1 for my house' as in the
    game of Bingo)
When cleaning is snappy, the cleaner is happy
I don't have to do repeat performances
Once I've started I've soon finished
Their varieties make light entertainment of chores
I'm char-free, chore-free and care-free
Together we've a polished act
It cleans up without wiping you out
Whatever the sentence, there's no hard labour
They've dusted down many an old favourite
Dirt is eliminated in the first round
It reflects the life I lead
Vileda brings the sparkle back into my life
It takes the aches out of panes
Good views should be seen and not blurred

▶ **Owning a Silver Burniston caravan would be FUN because…**

PRODUCT: Horticultural seeds
COMPETITION: Woolworths/Cuthbert Seeds

Fun is easy going, easy towing, knowing my Cuthbert seeds are growing
Pulling style for many a mile means arriving with a smile
With Woolworth and Cuthbert I've grown to enjoy the best by miles
It would lighten my load and make me king of the road
The world would be my oyster and I could really come out of my shell
Never again would I have to leave the kitchen sink behind

▶ **I buy Mars FUN size chocolates for my children because…**

PRODUCT: Confectionery

Handy bars mean happy faces, nicest nibbles for all places
Though pocket sized, they give monumental pleasure
They go far, these maximum goodness, mini bars
Children always bag a prize with every single fun size
Small bars bring smiles to all little faces
Active children may flag, the cure is in the bag
The right bite size suits little pint size
Tops for tots this mini measure – guarantees them maxi pleasure
They're choc full of gusto
A little of what you fancy is fun-tastic
Young tearaways have such a ripping time with them
Fish for Mars, catch a bite, net gain, pure delight
Where fun sizes are found, there are smiles all round
Small bars bring smiles to little faces
Once bitten, nice sigh, dreams come true for small fry
It's the big dipper for the little nipper
Between the red, white and blue, kids are tickled pink
When they please little fingers they get a big hand
They are full of magic moments
Active children may flag, the cure is in the bag
The small pack magic has youth under its spell
They may be small but the taste stretches for smiles
They are like Christmas stockings, full of little surprise prizes
Whether outdoors or in, here your pleasures begin
Just open the bag and out comes the fun
Easy to take anywhere, share the fun of the 'fare'
When the kids drop in I won't be caught out

▶ **Bathtime is FUN time because…**

PRODUCT: Moist tissues
COMPETITION: Tesco/Freshtex/Tiffany bathroom suite
PRIZE: Tiffany bathroom suite

With Freshtex and Tiffany I'm no longer a Moaning Lisa in the Loo'vre

▶ **Robinsons make racing for Raleigh at Leo's more FUN because...**

PRODUCT: Fruit juices
COMPETITION: Co-op Leo's/Robinsons
PRIZES: Raleigh Supreme bicycles

'Thirst' prize – a Raleigh bike, other drinks can take a hike
Wheels in motion, mind on the road, drinking Robinsons, the best Highway
    Code
Amongst a multitude of tins, this coolest carton always wins
It's the flavour I like when I'm riding a bike
The fruit in the juice makes the wheels run loose
I went to Leo's, bought a drink, won a bike, wicked I think!
Robinsons and Leo's are a winning team, I hope they win me a Raleigh
    Supreme
The juice of the fruit reaches down to your boots
Robinsons juices, brill fuel injection, I'm 'genRALEIGH' transported in Leo's
    direction
Robinsons fruit flavours bring energy and smiles, to race Raleigh down Leo's
    aisles!
Refreshed by Robinsons juices by golly, we'll beat the fast supermarket trolley
They're on the right tracks to quash thirst attacks
With Robinsons drinks in my trolley, I'm extremely refreshed and 'Raleigh'
    jolly
On yer bike, round the aisles, wild, extreme but like Robinsons, brings smiles
Exciting taste buds, quenching a thirst, Robinsons and Leo's pedal quality first
Open the carton, pour out the sun, pedal the power, Raleigh's number one
Raleigh and Robinsons show such versatility, providing crucial street credibility
Robinsons the 'Raleigh-ing' cry, Leo's the 'chain' for the coolest buy

▶ **Gaymer's Norfolk cyder gives me lots of laughs because...**

PRODUCT: Cider

I am the lady who swallowed the spider, that giggled and giggled and giggled in
    cyder

HARVEST & FRUIT

▶ **I buy Harvest produce at Asda because...**

PRODUCT: Bread

Abundant Asda always sustains, finest food from home grown grains
What nature has perfected, Asda has selected
Whilst harvest produce keeps me healthy, Asda's prices keep me wealthy
British country food is a must from a store you can trust

Quality, taste and healthy nutrition, Asda reaps this British tradition
Asda's answer to customer care is reaping the benefits of British fare
Produce of British country mills, produces finer wholesome meals
First class food from finest fields, first class value Asda yields
Asda is beyond compare for the choicest British fare
From this green and pleasant land, quality and choice go hand in hand
Pure harvest produce, Asda skill, I 'reap' the benefits of the till
British produce, excellent store, harvested together, who needs more

Dried fruit

Making cakes is a fruitless task without them
They deserve an Oscar for the best role in a scone
They are plum goods to be picked from every branch, and all at pruned prices

HEALTH & FITNESS

▶ **Ribena, Lucozade and Horlicks means fitness, health and
energy because...**

PRODUCT: Fruit Juice, Glucose Drink, Malt Drink

They give triple satisfaction and energy in action
They keep my body working right, alert by day, relaxed by night
I always sip into something tasteful after a hard day
You get a clean bill of health at the checkout
Ribena ready, Horlicks steady, Lucozade – Go!

▶ **Yeoman is really fit for the family because...**

*PRODUCT: Dried mashed potato
COMPETITION: Yeoman/Raleigh bicycles
PRIZES: Raleigh bicycles and back packs*

It's a natural link in the nutrition chain
For great taste at high speeds it's geared to our needs
It boosts the figure – but not the vigour
Ride through the nineties with convenience and ease, healthy family, appetites
    pleased
It's passed the family proficiency test
We race to finish first to get seconds
It keeps them in top gear all year
Four-star fuel for family fill-ups
When the going gets tough, Yeoman is 'wheelie' fun-tastic stuff
After our cycling trips it's healthier than chips
It's instant nutrition for our inner tubes
Its benefits are clear, it keeps everyone in top gear

Its track record is second to none, always my number one
It's so quick you don't need to wait training
High fibre, energy, vitamin C – means no couch potato family
Other instant mash potatoes just don't work out
It is rich in fibre and value for Yeo-money
It never takes us for a ride but makes us warm inside
They wouldn't be saddled with anything else
It's an instant success we never tyre of
It's what active families like, showing great minds think abike
Wherever you wheel and deal, Yeoman puts you on the right track
It's the goodness from within that keeps my family trim
It's good for the diet and prolongs the life-cycle
High fibre and low calories mean no spare tyres
For speedy spuds it's the finest handle bar none
Seven days without it makes one weak
It ain't heavy and it's no bother

▶ **I enjoy Diet 7 Up as part of my calorie-controlled diet because...**

PRODUCT: Diet drink

Tastes a treat, makes end meet, in the pocket, around the seat
It quenches thirst throughout the day, in a tasty calorie-controlled way
Its light refreshing taste helps take inches off my waist

▶ **Shopping at the Co-op helps keep me healthy and happy because...**

PRODUCT: Supermarket foods

It's an exercise which pays dividends

▶ **Jeyes helps you lead a healthier life style because...**

PRODUCT: Disinfectant

Their contribution to national health is protecting the local body

▶ **KiteKat by Pedigree rewards my cat with 100% nourishment for life because...**

PRODUCT: Cat food

Pedigree knows without a doubt that health comes from inside out

▶ **Heinz and the Co-op are a healthy combination because...**

PRODUCT: Supermarket foods

They co-operate and care, looking after your 'wealthfare'

▶ **Dole Californian raisins are ideal for the healthy family because...**

PRODUCT: Dried fruit
COMPETITION: Gateway/Dole Californian raisins
PRIZES: Holidays in sunny California

California's the 'Gateway' to America's West, Dole the 'Gateway' to nature's best

Quality taste and healthy nutrition, Californian sun the Dole tradition

Seedless, sensible, tasty too, Dole Californian raisins spell fitness for you

They're dolelicious, delightful and delectable

Full of goodness, tasting divine, Dole Californian raisins are packed with sunshine

High in fibre and nutritious, sun dried raisins, they are dolelicious

Wholly natural, naturally whole, there's only nature's best in Dole

Naturally perfected, grown by the sun, naturally selected for a growing sun

Soaked in sunshine, tended with care, there's nothing more natural – anywhere

They make all things 'dried and fruitful' for eaters great and small

Super in salads, sweet tasty snacks, pleasures in puddings, perfect lunch packs

For raisin' standards seldom seen, we plump for Dole, seedless supreme

With fruity nibbles all the rage, Dole raisins take centre stage

Dole standards never waiver, first for goodness, first for flavour

Sun-drenched, sun-dried, naturally sweet, Dole raisins are wholesome and ready to eat

For a tasty treat that's highly nutritious, nature ensures they're purely dolelicious

They are sunshine packed Californian gold, nutritious enjoyment for young and old

Sun packed and nutritious, they are naturally dolelicious

Quality stamped in American tradition, they are natural, delicious, full of nutrition

Breakfast, lunch, tea or dinner, Dole's high fibre versatility is hard to beat

They're grown and dried in Californian sun, natural goodness for everyone

Dole don't risk random selection, every raisin is picked for perfection

Tasty, versatile, healthy, nutritious, Dole Californian raisins are simply dolelicious

Full of fibre, soaked with sun, regular nourishment for everyone

Their sweet nutrition, sun soaked fun, suits growing children, dad and mum

Family fitness, that's my goal, I'm always sure to score with Dole

▶ **I take Ladycare in my daily health and beauty routine because...**

PRODUCT: Ladies' vitamins

To be specific its formula is terrific

It ensures a correct balance of vitamins and minerals

Evening Primrose, B6 and E keep me A1 and PMT-free

They do what they should to keep me looking and feeling good

They fulfil my dream for an interior and exterior healthy, happy sheen
Ladycare takes good care of me
It treats the whole woman, the whole time
I know without a doubt that good health comes from inside out
It keeps me fit and healthy all month through
It makes me feel great, makes me look great – so why hesitate?
Ladycare supplements which I lack, keeps me fit and on the track

▶ **I take Healthcraft vitamins because...**

PRODUCT: Vitamin tablets

They've helped me join the 'fit brigade'
Their sound quality ensures record vitality
They keep me healthier and thinner, so we are both a winner
My health is No. 1 with me and Healthcraft are the tops
Correct addition helps the sum of good health
Experts perfected them, the healthy selected them
They keep me bright and beautiful, improve all features great and small
They're instrumental in keeping body and soul in tune
Music makes the world go round but complete vitality is Healthcraft found
Healthcraft purity is my security
I like to keep as fit as the young ones
They're the best 'minister' in my 'cabinet'
They make fitness first and beauty last

▶ **I use Marvel milk as a healthy lesson in my diet because...**

PRODUCT: Low fat dried milk

No need to 'weight and see' – more of lesson, less on me
Lesson one – Marvel's fun, lesson two – less on you, lesson three, less on me

▶ **Dole Californian raisins and prunes are ideal for health-
conscious people because...**

PRODUCT: Dried fruit
PRIZES: Trips to Barcelona including Olympics

Gold medal performance is Dole's tradition, first for taste, first for nutrition
If health and fitness is your dream, Dole's track record reigns supreme
Tended with love in Californian sun, Dole's dried fruits rate No. 1
Natural, dolelicious, packed with sun, they're gold medal winners for everyone
They're packed with energy, wholesome, sweet, a sustaining snack, a mealtime
    treat
For snacks, breakfast, lunch, dinner, nutritious, delicious Dole's a winner
Essence of sunshine, guaranteed zest, Dole is the Gateway to personal best
They're 'Dole'liciously fruity, energy giving, ideal for a healthier style of living
Californian sweet sunshine in every pack, the truly 'gold' medal snack
In the race for a healthy today, Dole's the winner all the way

Health foods

It improves your health without damaging your wealth
Harvest fresh, country fare, goodness to munch, just anywhere
Nothing added, plenty gained, goodness to munch, never strained
There's nothing added, nothing removed, because nature's best can't be
    improved
The remedy's simple, purely pleasure, nature's store of country treasure

HELPS

▶ **Nevins HELPS me to cut costs by...**

PRODUCT: Food store foods

Keeping prices low, so whenever I go, inflation is on go-slow

HIT

▶ **Princes canned fish products are a HIT with my family because...**

PRODUCT: Canned fish
COMPETITION: Kwik Save/Princes
PRIZES: Personal CD players and cassette players

They are tastier than 'New squids on the block'
Hey Hey we're the chunkies
We would rather 'Roe with Cod' than 'Sail with Rod'
You can't CD bones
'Down Down' tastily they go – Princes – forever our 'Status Quo'
For taste they're 'The Temptations', for quality 'The Supremes'
They're too tasty for their tins
Before Princes we all lived in a yellow soup tureen
Dolphins without tears brings music to my ears
Princes 'Bridge over troubled waters' – pleasing dolphin-friendly daughters
You'll be hooked on this line

HOLIDAY

▶ **I selected Tefal at Argos to win a holiday for two in Hawaii because...**

PRODUCT: Electrical goods
COMPETITION: Tefal/Argos catalogue
PRIZE: Holiday for two in Hawaii

The brand is grand, the price is right, to get away would be a delight

The Tefal brand is reliable and neat and Argos prices are hard to beat

Of Tefal's outstanding technology, reliability and safety together with Argos's unbeatable value for money

Guaranteed quality and reliability, a small price to pay, plus Hawaii too, a dream holiday

For efficiency and style it stood out a mile

▶ **I would like to win a desert island dream holiday because...**

PRODUCT: Electrical goods
COMPETITION: Rumbelows holiday

With travel iron, kettle, cordless tong, Rumbelows ensures I can't go wrong

By replacing one old electrical castaway, two others gain a rejuvenating holiday

HORTICULTURE

▶ **I buy Unwins seeds at the Co-op because...**

PRODUCT: Horticultural seeds
COMPETITION: Co-op/Unwins

Garden, greenhouse, tub or pot, Unwins grow in any plot

For years Unwins and I have been great co-operators

Superb results are achieved with ease, thanks to Unwins expertise

▶ **The next Expert should be ... (Book) because...**

PRODUCT: Books

Garden Design ... mansion or cottage with statue or gnome, a well designed garden makes 'house' into a 'home'

The Garden for Children ... a successful future stems from careful nursery training

The Water Garden ... without an Expert I'm wet behind the ears and out of my depth

▶ **Concorde gardening books are a boon to the gardener because...**

PRODUCT: Gardening books

Gardening becomes a bed of roses with Concorde grow-how

Bulbs and plants

Their packs costing pence make blooming good scents
I fork out less and rake in more
All kinds of everything reminds me of Kew
I plant with confidence and pick with pride
They tidy my 'bed' with 'blankets' of colour
They give me growing confidence
I know my 'beds' will have wonderful 'springs'
My wallflowers dance, snapdragons smile, and runner beans win by a mile
For growing needs of plants and seeds, this fitting solution always succeeds
It's tough, well designed, lasts many seasons, British made, what better reasons
It's the best formula for getting right to the root of the problem

Lawn products

It gives my lawn a velvet sheen and the richest green I've ever seen
You can dig for success without forking out a fortune
It does the groundwork
It goes down with the rain, comes up with the sun, growing no pain and cutting
    is fun
It combines the marvels of science with ease of appliance
It gives a dazzling display for a modest outlay
It's the thoroughbred feed that turfs out any weed
With this excellent tonic, its growth is bionic
It stops us from getting 'browned off'
I like to keep up with the Greens next door
It feeds the blades as they arise and starves inflation down to size
It prevents a young blade from going to seed
To keep 'law-n-order' you need a 'super-grass'
When the kids have abused it, Greenup renews it
Without a monthly Greenup feeding, its long term future would be 'receding'
With Greenup who needs green fingers?
The cost is nominal but the effect is phenomenal
For less work and less pence, the grass is green on my side of the fence
The easy to use three-way feed, protects a lawn right from seed
It's the health food, the complete treat, for the living carpet beneath my feet

Lawn sprinklers

Ballbarrow, sprinkler, hose or spray, they help create gardens the easy way
Connect or spray, shower or mist, precision built it tops my list

I COULD...

▶ **With a Hotpoint Slimline dishwasher I COULD...**

PRODUCT: *Washing-up liquid*
COMPETITION: *Hotpoint/Sunlight washing-up liquid*
PRIZES: *Hotpoint dishwashers*

Do many things of which I dream whilst Hotpoint brings that Sunlight gleam
Have time on my hands – not wrinkles
Have my dishes sparkling aglow by pressing the button for H2O
Economise on space and bills as well as breakages and spills
Kiss goodbye to daily drudgery – Hello hubby, wink, wink, nudge, nudgery
Be like Eliza, do little and dance all night
Sip some champagne – make mine pink, bubbles in glass – not in sink
Down gloves, release the chains, see some Sunlight outside for a change
Relax, unwind, become a new man, thumb my nose at Nanette Newman
Lever myself from the kitchen sink and bathe in Sunlight

▶ **If I had a Bosch Slimline dishwasher I COULD...**

PRODUCT: *Washing-up liquid*
COMPETITION: *Bosch/Sunlight washing-up liquid*
PRIZES: *Bosch dishwashers*

Say me Jane, you Bosch, me sit, you wash
Throw in the tea towel and admit defeat – this marvellous machine has
    dishwashing beat
Spend more time on haute cuisine now Bosch will get pots Sunlight clean
Retire my old dishwasher 'hubbie' – low tech, slow and frankly tubby
Fit it in
Add magic to my kitchen's smallest space, making dirty dishes disappear
    without a trace
Say goodbye grease, hello shine, now to relax I've got time
Entrust my precious 'crocks' to super-automation – award my two-legged
    dishwasher a permanent vacation
Banish rubber gloves for good, my husband too (as if I would)
Free my family from the chores and eradicate domestic wars
Become a lady of leisure and entertaining would be more of a pleasure

IDEA

▶ **Give your IDEA of a perfect holiday location**

PRODUCT: *Knitwear*
COMPETITION: *Jaeger knitwear/British Airways*

Up and away with caring BA
To scenic and historic sights
Wearing Jaeger for style
Whilst exploring a while
And enjoying the Hyatt's delights

Peaceful pueblos
Smart tapas bars
'Mañana' the key word
Donkeys, not cars

Charming chalets on sophisticated streets
Spotless shops with scrumptious sweets
Mountains, meadows and sparkling springs
These are a few of my favourite things

Delicious chocs, cuckoo clocks
The festival when Montreux rocks
A lake, a mountain, a chic hotel
The combination goes down well

All smart in Jaeger gear
Off for the holiday of the year
On a BA flight – forgetting diet
To swim and play at Hotel Hyatt

Guaranteed the sun would shine
Of course on perfect food we'd dine
Some golf and riding and the sea
Would be perfect bliss for me

A BA flight to somewhere cool
Dressed in Jaeger, he's no fool
Staying at Hyatt resort
California must be the ultimate port

BA would be jetting me there
In style and comfort beyond compare
A Hyatt hotel the crowning glory
Australia with Jaeger – what a story

▶ **I think the Mercury music prize is a great IDEA because...**

> *PRODUCT: Communications*
> *COMPETITION: Mercury Communications/Mercury music prize awards*
> *FIRST PRIZE: Caribbean cruise*
> *RUNNERS-UP: Philips Bitstream CD players*

Corporations have a duty to contribute to society, this is a great way
A full-range company is sponsoring awards for a full range of artists
It brings together two winners in communications
The range is extensive and prices remain inexpensive
Established, emerging, classical or pop, quality acknowledged by the
    communicator – that's top
Sounds wonderful, sounds different, sounds cooler than the rest, proves biggest
    isn't best
A regular listener I would be, with a sound investment from Mercury

The best of British/Irish musical innovation, acclaimed by the new kings of
    communication
A communication prize from the prize communicators
The choice of today's music from the people who bring you choice

IDEAL

▶ **Kraft cheese slices are IDEAL for outdoor snacks because...**

PRODUCT: *Processed cheese slices*

Sealed in freshness, ready in a flash, peel off a slice for nourishment first class

▶ **Boots the Chemists sports preparations are IDEAL for me
because...**

PRODUCT: *Sports preparations*

Keeping fit meant strain and grief before Boots worked out pain relief
Out of form in distress, Boots have a formula for success
When pain stops play, Boots save the day
Champion I'll never be, but Boots keeps me pain free
When every muscle feels aflame, Boots restores me to my game

▶ **Dole Californian raisins are IDEAL for the healthy family
because...**

PRODUCT: *Dried fruit*
COMPETITION: *Gateway/Dole Californian raisins*
PRIZES: *Holidays in sunny California*

California's the 'Gateway' to America's West, Dole the 'Gateway' to nature's
    best
Quality taste and healthy nutrition, Californian sun the Dole tradition
Seedless, sensible, tasty too, Dole Californian raisins spell fitness for you
They're dolelicious, delightful and delectable
Full of goodness, tasting divine, Dole Californian raisins are packed with
    sunshine
High in fibre and nutritious, sun dried raisins, they are Dolelicious
Wholly natural, naturally whole, there's only nature's best in Dole
Naturally perfected, grown by the sun, naturally selected for a growing sun
Soaked in sunshine, tended with care, there's nothing more natural – anywhere
They make all things 'dried and fruitful' for eaters great and small
Super in salads, sweet tasty snacks, pleasures in puddings, perfect lunch packs
For raisin' standards seldom seen, we plump for Dole, seedless supreme
With fruity nibbles all the rage, Dole raisins take centre stage
Dole standards never waiver, first for goodness, first for flavour

Sun-drenched, sun-dried, naturally sweet, Dole raisins are wholesome and ready to eat

For a tasty treat that's highly nutritious, nature ensures they're purely dolelicious

They are sunshine packed Californian gold, nutritious enjoyment for young and old

Sun packed and nutritious, they are naturally dolelicious

Quality stamped in American tradition, they are natural, delicious, full of nutrition

Breakfast, lunch, tea or dinner, Dole's high fibre versatility is hard to beat

They're grown and dried in Californian sun, natural goodness for everyone

Dole don't risk random selection, every raisin is picked for perfection

Tasty, versatile, healthy, nutritious, Dole Californian raisins are simply dolelicious

Full of fibre, soaked with sun, regular nourishment for everyone

Their sweet nutrition, sun soaked fun, suits growing children, dad and mum

Family fitness, that's my goal, I'm always sure to score with Dole

▶ **My IDEAL Intense Woman is...**

PRODUCT: Perfume

Helen of Troy because she was loved and treasured by Paris

Romantic with common sense because her perfume is Lancôme Intense

Elegant because Intense of such quality makes dreams reality

Very chic because her choice of perfume makes her unique

My wife because she is exciting, chic, has personality and wears Intense

Always irresistible because her new fragrance is so Intensely bewitching

Utterly desirable because she wears my favourite perfume

Individual because Intense fragrance instills interest and inspiration

Juliet because Romeo's passion so Intense, love truly heaven scent

Romantic because she creates Intense past, present and future memories

Special because she intensifies the feeling of love

Full of flair because Intense puts romance in the air

Discerning because she's tried the rest, now selects the best

Sensually vibrant because the perfume itself complements her femininity

IMAGINATION

▶ **My idea of a journey beyond imagination would be...**

PRODUCT: Aftershave
COMPETITION: Journey/Camcorders
PRIZES: Camcorders

To leave before yesteryear and arrive in my mind's eye

To go pasta Italia, curry on to India and wok to China with 'Journey' the

perfect companion
Journeying Over Unknown Realms, New Excitement You never forget
  (JOURNEY = ACROSTIC)

IMPORTANT

▶ **Home care value is IMPORTANT to me because...**

PRODUCT: Supermarket foods

Every product tried and tested, super value can't be bested

IN...

▶ **I would most like to be seen wearing my personalised Budweiser jacket IN...**

PRODUCT: Beer
COMPETITION: Safeway/Budweiser beer

Style ... because like Bud's beers it stands out a mile
St. Louis ... bat in hand, playing for the Cardinals band
St. Louis ... and drink a toast to the king of beers
A 'home run' to 'first base' Safeway for a twelve-can case
Safeway ... providing I won, whilst stocking up Budweisers for a home run
Audience with the king of beers, supporting Red Sox with Safeway's beers
Busch gardens Florida USA ... that would really make my day
St. Louis ... a city where you don't ask for beer – ask for Buddy
My local ... because it surpasses the best in the taste 'Bud' test
Ten years' time ... when I'm an older 'Budweiser' person

INSIST

▶ **I INSIST on buying John West because...**

PRODUCT: Canned fish
PRIZES: Weekend breaks at Dalhousie Castle in Scotland

The standards never waver, first for value, first for flavour
John West's tradition for healthy nutrition, the natural selection when seeking
  perfection
Quality fish – a Scottish tradition – provides a meal with healthy nutrition

They're delicious, nutritious, conveniently canned, at pleasing prices for a
    quality brand
John West feeds the hungriest clans, with delicious saucy fish in cans
Authentic ingredients, ready to savour – just open up for fresh Scottish flavour
A gourmet meal is a guarantee, without going on a spending spree
Delicious cold, tasty hot, for flavour and value it's 'Scot' the lot

INVENT

▶ **Invent a slogan for Little Chef restaurants**

PRODUCT: Motorway restaurant

Arrive as our guests, leave as our friends

▶ **Invent a 5-word slogan using each letter of the word 'Bisto'**

PRODUCT: Gravy browning

(These are jumbled acrostics of Bisto)
Tasty Bisto, Sauce Of Inspiration
Oh Boy It Tastes 'Stew'pendous
Stir In Bisto – Outcome Tastier
Try Bisto It Surpasses Others
Take Stock, Insist On Bisto
It's The Original Sunday Best
On Sundays I'm Thoroughly Bisto-ed
Bisto Is The Savourite One
Only Bisto Stirs The Imagination
Indispensable Bisto Suits The Occasion
Supermeals Owe It To Bisto
Bisto On Table, Success Inevi-table
Bisto Offers Instant Satisfaction – Thanks
Out To Impress? Select Bisto
Only Bisto Tastes So Inspirational
Thank Bisto It's Sunday

▶ **The first thing Mr Perky said after inventing Shredded Wheat
was...**

PRODUCT: Breakfast cereal
COMPETITION: Safeway/Shredded Wheat
FIRST PRIZE: Holiday in North America

Eat Shredded Wheat and walk Niagara

RUNNERS-UP: Victorian style telephones

Competitors tumble, Niagara must fall, but Shredded Wheat will survive them
    all
I'm no crackpot, I've hit the jackpot
Wholesome and tasty, give three cheers, the perfect breakfast for pioneers
If Pinky was here he wouldn't be able to eat three
We'll have real good health and plenty of wealth
My secret's safe, I've shredded the recipe
It's the little of wheat you fancy that does you good
People will eat Shredded Wheat as long as Niagara Falls
I bet someone invents sliced bread now
It's ready to wheat
It's the natural and Safeway for healthy eating every day
This will bowl them over
Try them, feel free, they're so good, I eat three
Euwheata!
This wheat I have shred will Rip Van Winkle out of bed
Three to one won't go
Nothing added or taken away – delicious and nutritious any time of day
Now what do I do with this third one
Without a shred of doubt, this will be a long running serial
Wow, that takes the biscuit, it was worth the wheat
For a healthy energy-giving treat, I invented Shredded Wheat
Now I can really enjoy my breakfast every day
A million dollars for anyone who can eat three – who dares wins
Nothing – it's rude to talk with your mouth full
Goodness high fibre, sugar free – a healthy wholesome breakfast thanks to me
Shucks! This is sure the darndest fine cereal pardners
Now the Americans won't oversleep, arise for breakfast Shredded Wheat
It's a square bite that's just right for the sleepy eater
I'm staking a claim to breakfast fame
Shredded Wheat will be as famous as Niagara Falls
Father always said I make a mesh of things
2 to eat a yummy treat, but 3 never, an impossible feat
Wow, this is great, but what shall I call it?
Bless my bowl
You are what you wheat
Just wheat, this will prove to be one hundred per cent successful
Mr Niagara, I've just added another wonder to the world's list
Small step for man, a giant step for cereal kind
This invention will last for 100 years
Eureka, it's 100% pure wheat
Bring me my bowl of burning gold
This cereal will make compulsive chewing
Time for breakfast
No, you can only have three when I've made two more
Pride always comes before a falls
What a natural start to the day

This will be the salt of the earth – made without salt

A snappy breakfast, bursting wheat nutrition, will never be beaten

My feat's complete called Shredded Wheat a neat treat to eat

Call me early between the sheets, for breakfast tomorrow is Shredded Wheats

Even though I'm soaking wet, best health food I ever ate

It's the next natural wonder of the world

Ready to eat, pure wholewheat, high fibre measure, a breakfast treasure

Jot down the date in 1922 a centenary we'll celebrate

Now, who's going for the first triple helping

I've Shredded Wheat without taking the goodness out

I made Shredded Wheat the natural way, because it is the Safeway

Wow, they really take the biscuit

Shredded Wheat has made my day, taste and goodness here to stay

Never mind the bull, where's the cow, Pat

By golly, without any question, Shredded Wheat will aid my digestion

At last a tasty way to eat hundred per cent natural wholesome wheat

Purest wheat shredded with talent, a journey of wonder for the palate

One hundred years from now Shredded Wheat will still take the biscuit

Goodbye beans, goodbye jerky, welcome quick wholesome breakfasts from me
     Mr Perky

Pure and wholesome I declare, no tastier health food found anywhere

Unbeatable first for taste second to none but a third impossible

This scrumptious goodness will for sure, breakfast the whole world for
     evermore

Now I've completed my feat, they'll have a treat

100% wheat that's a treat to eat, that's a real wholesome treat – I'll call it
     Shredded Wheat

Go milk the cow mother, the West is about to be won

They said it couldn't be done but victory's wheat

Yippee – this'll do for breakfast and tea

At last, a food ready for eating, definitely a serial worth repeating

Don't be an unhealthy breakfast eater, become a fitter Shredded Wheater –
     100% perkfection

Family treat, healthy to eat, wholesome grain, Shredded Wheat's the name

Niagara Falls, Shredded Wheat rises, by eating three you win the prizes

Shredded Wheat's the other natural force and completely healthy of course

Wheat a treat – a cereal worth repeating

Shredded Wheat's real neat – its taste you can't beat

First three Shredded Wheat – then off to carve Mount Rushmore

This is the perky way to really have a nice day

Goodness and mercy will nourish and keep the whole family perky

Milk please!

Now here we have perky breakfasts for perky people

As the great Niagara Falls, Shredded Wheat reigns as it pours

Giant or pint size, you are one hundred per cent wholewheat

Breakfast time won't be the same, Shredded Wheat will bring me fame

I create masterpieces wheat after wheat

IS...

▶ **The difference with Mum Solid IS...**

PRODUCT: Ladies' deodorant

Its performance you can spot
It gives solid protection from odour detection
Its great underarm action
It's the starting block that results in a personal best
It means success without excess
My aroma keeps my husband home-a
When things get sticky, Mum sticks around
It's better to be chunky than a little squirt
I'm home and dry – best antiperspirant money can buy
Odourwhelming
Easy to spot
It's simply fantastick
It's made for secret armies
It's a problem shifter and confidence lifter
My favourite has a new twist to the ending
Easy to choose – delightful to use
Odour is defeated in underarm combat with Mum's Solid defences
It turns up again and again
No more shake, rattle and roll
Solid protection, second to none, for cool confidence, number one
It's the only Mum I take on a date
It's here to stay not sprayed away
It's selective, protection and extremely effective
It's a stick up at a price that's a steal

▶ **The man who wears Sergio Tacchini IS...**

PRODUCT: Aftershave

Polar cool and in command, smooth, refreshed and in demand

▶ **Monergy IS...**

PRODUCT: Energy-saving scheme

Increasing awareness of energy spills, so reducing the cost of incoming bills

▶ **Home brewing with Tom Caxton IS...**

PRODUCT: Home brewing kit

The fun thing to do for the best way to brew
A recipe for instant success
Hopping good

In a glass of its own
Like betting on the favourite, but Tom Caxton's a dead cert

▶ **I enjoy Lancers wine because it IS ... and...**

PRODUCT: *Wine*

Born in Portugal and raised in glasses everywhere
Bright ... and ... bubbly

▶ **My favourite place to eat Buitoni IS...**

PRODUCT: *Pasta*

Nowhere exotic, just at home, reliving the pleasures of dining in Rome
In Jules Verne's time machine – perfect pasta deserves future projection
La Scala Opera House and sing praises accompanied by 'Strings and Bows'
Gazing into gondolier's eyes, dark handsome looks to Bridge my Sighs
St. Marks Square because Buitoni pasta always makes time with loving care

▶ **Gardening with Fisons IS...**

PRODUCT: *Garden soil in bags*

Never gardening alone
The route to success
A perfect plot on the landscape
A pleasure – my beds always have wonderful springs
Not feeling ready to throw in the trowel
Deeply satisfying
Knowing the fruits of your labours will outdo your neighbours
Like having a helping hand at making the beds
Down-to-earth confidence
The way I lead admirers up the garden path
Like an excellent author bringing elegance to an undistinguished plot
Having a friend to do the spadework
Knowing that the earth's going to move for you

▶ **To me, Dutch Royal Crest bacon IS...**

PRODUCT: *Bacon*
PRIZES: *Luxury hampers*

Tasty, nutritious, quite a dream, in my kitchen it reigns supreme
Food to savour, full of flavour, perfect to taste, without any waste
Perfectly cured, reasonably priced, a Dutch of class, slice after slice
A cut above the rest, I can tell by the crest
Such a tasty rasher – no wonder it's a smasher

ITEM

▶ **What other ITEM would you take to London if you won and why...**

PRODUCT: Cigarettes
COMPETITION: Preedy Newsagents/Silk Cut cigarettes
PRIZES: Weekend for two in London at Ritz hotel

My personal cigarette lighter, because it is a cut above the average
Silkateurs to snip off more above the mean
Husband because it would be 'wholly' more enjoyable with my 'other half'
Comfortable shoes. London shoes paved with gold make your feet very old.
An invitation to dine at No. 10 Downing Street.
Set of luxurious luggage to match the luxury of the Ritz
Evening dress, set to dazzle, out on the town, on the razzle
A video camera to record my moment at the top
Some dancing shoes to do the Lambeth walk and the Piccadilly glide
Some sellotape – I intend to pick up a bit of fluff
Pure silk, there's nothing like the feel of it against your skin

JUICES

▶ **When I shop at Kwik Save, Princes fruit juices are a refreshing sight because...**

PRODUCT: Fruit juices
COMPETITION: Kwik Save/Princes fruit juices
PRIZE: Nova Carlton car

Princes packs always hearten when 'gaspin' for a Nova Carlton
Where else can three litres turn into a four seater
The number plates you see are Kwik Save – 63P
They're always guaranteed to 'win-Nova' your taste buds
Princes at Kwik Save are a sight for more buys
I am highly 'motor-vated' by the flavours they've created
Princes juices reign supreme: is the Nova just a dream?
They're the greatest reviver for a thirsty driver
Three packs minus seals equals brand new set of wheels
They are the greatest revivers for thirsty trolley drivers
Offering luscious appetisers, there's nova a nonsense with breathalysers
Kwik Save 'loaded trolley drivers' need Princes juices as revivers
Princes stand out like a 'Nova' brilliant star performer
For finest juice without inflation Kwik Save is an inNOVAtion
Princes juices – thirst choice – Kwik Save prices – first choice

My taste buds come alive spinning me into overdrive
I'm on the right road for the good bodywork code
Quality – Princes rule of thumb renders me a NOVAjoyed mum
Princes juice brings satisfaction replacing thirst with five speed action
When I thirst for the best I drive away refreshed
On a long distance shop it's my pit stop
Such cool juices, no 'Novalty' always trust in Princes quality
Quality seal, price appeal, gives Kwik Save shoppers twice the deal
Their 'thirst' gear sends my trolley into 'Nova-drive'
Their many varied flavours are the starters for Kwik Savers

▶ **When we buy Princes fruit juices at Kwik Save we get on down to the juiciest flavours around because...**

PRODUCT: Fruit juices
COMPETITION: Kwik Save/Princes fruit juices
PRIZES: Midi CD hi-fi systems and personal CD players

Six fruit juices to select, no nonsense prices – sounds perfect
It's a disc-tinctive drink at a disc-ount price
Like the Right-Juice Brothers – 'we lose that thirsty feeling'
Fruity construction – pure seduction, sound deduction a Princes production
Quality juices, small expense, Princes and Kwik Save sound sense
For record savings, it's jolly cartons' (*Dolly Parton's) greatest hits
Every drink they do, they do it juice for you
Princes flavours and the Temptations, Kwik Save stores the Supremes
This top of the shops has the best juice box
For a price that is nominal, the taste is phenomenal
The family's hit quencher is no money wrencher
They are thirst quenching, purse quenching, leaders of the brands
Princes juices are enticing, Kwik Save has attractive pricing
We've disc-covered disc-tinctively fruity flavours at disc-idedly fruity prices
It's liquid sunshine that makes the pourer richer
The taste like fruit drinks oughter, not just flavoured water
It's the CD-uctive taste that re-45s me
Wholesome juices, little lolly, make me lambada with the trolley
Perfect taste in every pack, something other juices lack
Princes quality is traditional, Kwik Save low prices are additional
Princes juices twist and squeeze, popular Kwik Save prices please
Princes great, Kwik Save ace, no more wild juice chase
Taste temptations, supreme tang, Princes Kool for all the Gang
I can't get no satisfaction without Princes juice extraction
Tastebuds atingle, tills ajingle, top names unite, sounds just right
Princes strikes a fruity note, Kwik Save value gets my vote
There's always thirst choice on my Chopin Liszt
We're getting D'major fruit juices at D'minor prices

KEY

▶ **Johnson's baby products are the KEY to...**

PRODUCT: Baby care
COMPETITION: Boots the Chemists/Johnson's

A smoother way of life – you can bet your Boots
Happy babies, kind mums, bubbly baths and powdered bums
A contented mum because with value and flair, Johnson's share the care
Happy faces and clean little places
Proving no-one's too small for their Boots

LANDMARK

▶ **Woolworths is a LANDMARK because...**

PRODUCT: Chain store goods

You get a good sight more for a good sight less

LEADERS

▶ **Bejam are the LEADERS in frozen foods because...**

PRODUCT: Supermarket foods

They know the ropes which enables them to sail ahead
Wherever I go, whatever my needs, Bejam quality always leads

LIKE

▶ **I would LIKE to win a Presto Panda with Ajax because...**

PRODUCT: Cleaners
COMPETITION: Presto/Ajax Win a Panda
PRIZE: Panda car

I'd get clean away after passing the M.O.P. test

RUNNERS-UP: Panda toy bears

It would drive me clean round the bend with delight

Performance of both is smooth, brilliant and outshines all rivals
They each give a guarantee – low price, high quality
One is a dream machine, one has the gleam supreme
Presto and Ajax 'Panda' to all my cleaning tasks
It will sweep me off my knees
Round the house or around the block, they are sparkling performers
Hey presto, their performance is magic
They both drive the dirt off the opposition
Getting around would no longer be PANDAmonium
The only Panda I can afford is a chest-ex Panda
I can't 'bear' being without one

▶ **I LIKE Apt and Village products because...**

PRODUCT: Food store foods

With their brands of wholesome fare, you've baskets full and money spare

▶ **People LIKE Galaxy because...**

PRODUCT: Confectionery

It rates best in the taste test
It soars through any test
In the field of confection Galaxy's grown to perfection
It's munch, munch better
The taste tells, the quality sells
Once they try it, for ever they'll buy it
It smooths the way to a perfect day
Galaxy confection is sheer perfection
It's a luxury chocolate at a practical price
It opens the tastaway to creamland
It simply gives more pleasure
The taste sends them over the moon

▶ **People LIKE Mars because...**

PRODUCT: Confectionery

At today's living pace, nourishing Mars keeps me in the race
It gives pleasure and power through every strenuous hour
It's a small price to pay for big bar value every day
It picks me up, gives me a rest, Mars forever, it's the best
It's the tastiest way to see me through the day

▶ **I would LIKE to win an Ambrosia desserts country cottage
holiday because...**

*PRODUCTS: Desserts
COMPETITION: Dairy Diary/Ambrosia desserts county cottage holiday*

PRIZE: Holiday in a country cottage

Fresh air, freedom and Devonshire cream, make Ambrosia cottage a wonderful dream

▶ **The Simpsons LIKE Golden Wonder crisps and snacks because...**

PRODUCT: Snacks
COMPETITION: Golden Wonder/Simpsons
PRIZES: Satellite dishes

Hunger strikes, turn volume high, crunch and continue watching sky
They're the thing to eat to the Bartman beat
Their street-cred crunch suits a street-wise bunch

▶ **There is nothing I LIKE better than sausages cracking in the pan. Bowyers sausages are the best...**

PRODUCT: Sausages

The ones my family most request, delicious, juicy, plump and porkful – the undisputed favourite forkful

▶ **I LIKE Pez candy because...**

PRODUCT: Sweets
PRIZES: Skateboards

Every happy minute has Pez candy in it
They're the chosen chew
They're the sweet sensation for my generation
The flavours make you flip your lid
They are the indispensable dispensers
Pez candy, perfect selection, add a skateboard – perfection
They are 'minni' sized with a mega taste
Fun dispenser, Minni candy, mighty flavour, always handy
To be specific, they taste terrific
They refresh the parts other sweets can't reach
They're so fizzy, my tongue goes dizzy
Out on the Street, Pez is THE sweet
I get flavour-fun-thrills and unlimited refills
The wrappers are bright, the taste sheer delight
I feel more optimistic when I get pessimistic
Fruity beauties for little cuties
They fizz and whizz like a skateboard
They're cool and compact with tastebud impact
Enjoyed at leisure a mouth-watering pleasure
Cartoon capers, family fun, sweet sensations for everyone
They're sweets ahead of the rest

Small in size but BIG in fruity flavour
Just one taste turns my frown upside down
I go overboard to savour the juicy flavour
They flick and have a fruity kick

▶ **I would LIKE to eat my Cadbury's eclairs in Belair because...**

PRODUCT: Confectionery

Mingling with millionaires, I'll share my mints if they share theirs
After the weekly grind, this sweetie needs to unwind
I could pic'n'mix with the Hollywood chicks
Amongst the glamour, glitz and action, Cadbury's eclairs are the star attraction
They are twentieth century chox

▶ **I would LIKE to experience RoC at Ragdale Hall because...**

PRODUCT: Skin care
COMPETITION: RoC/Ragdale Hall
PRIZES: Weekends at Ragdale Hall with full beauty treatment

With RoC's supreme skin care and Ragdale's style and splendour I should
    come away refreshed, relaxed, supple and slender
Once upon a time a lovely girl married, mothered, worked, became jaded,
    please RoC and Ragdale revive what has faded
For relaxation, health and good skin care, RoC and Ragdale are the perfect pair
Stress wreaks havoc on figure and face, RoC and Ragdale are my saving grace
RoC and Ragdale Hall – beauty is their theme – rest and rejuvenation – this
    harassed mother's dream

▶ **I would LIKE to win the wonderful wildlife weekend with Ajax because...**

PRODUCT: Cleaners
COMPETITION: Asda/Ajax wildlife

It would be twiffick to wander awound in a wange wover
We could enjoy the goodlife watching the wildlife
Adventure reaches the parts everyday life cannot reach
It will make a change from hunting bargains and snapping them up
It's a Gnu-dimension in family entertainment
I'm sure I could adapt to my husband's natural habitat
'Jungle Book' was terrific, I'd love to see a live performance
Then the children would not complain I was 'Beastly' to them again
Without liquid assets I could clean up a cream of a dream
It pandas my need to monkey around and if fine, toucan play
My 'tribe' would love it
On safari without financial care cos Ajax paid the lion's share
It would stop my lazy monkey 'lion' in bed all weekend
With my 'kids' I have no 'bucks' and only a little 'doe'

My weekends are always the same, really 'tame'
Workaholic Tarzan and housewife Jane need to learn to 'swing' again

▶ **I LIKE Knorr soups at Tesco because...**

PRODUCT: Packet soups

There's a 'royal' variety at my command without any 'performance'
They both offer a standard to salute
Living on my JACK this perfect pair makes INDOOR BOWLS a delight
It's the hot soup served by warm people at cool prices
Flannelette drawers, thermal jackets, can't beat the warmth in these little
    packets

LIMERICKS & RHYMES

▶ **A young windsurfer named Foster...**

PRODUCT: Lager
COMPETITION: Tesco/Foster's lager
PRIZE: Surfboard

Saw a Sheila and tried to accost her
Her assets he squeezed
She wasn't pleased
He ended up on the court rosta

▶ **There was a young Scot in New York...**

PRODUCT: Lager
COMPETITION: Tesco/McEwan's Export lager/Kestrel lager

Positively expressing his thought
Malt's fine
Burger's divine
But refreshment's – McEwan's Export

Enjoying flattering thought
Kestrel inspired
Immensely admired
Highland flinging along the sidewalk

Drinking companions he sought
Unfortunate saga
No Kestrel lager
Or McEwan's Export

Hopscotching every sidewalk
McEwan's in hand

Exported and canned
Attracting complimentary talk

Whose incomprehensible talk
Amazed and astounded
Completely confounded
Pedestrians taking a walk

▶ **There was a young lady called Clair, who went to Ireland by air, she was met with a smile...**

PRODUCT: Butter
COMPETITION: Tesco/Kerrygold butter
PRIZE: Trip to Ireland

As she sailed down the Nile,
(The pilot was trained by Dan Air)

By the men in customs' 'Green aisle'
But satisfaction was all she'd declare

Knew her trip was worthwhile
When she found herself walking on 'Eire'

From a cow by a stile
It's the grass that makes Kerrygold rare

By a cow from the isle
who said 'No udder butters compare'

▶ **Our prizes are all Britain's best, the Minis and also the rest, we think Britain's great, it's never too late...**

PRODUCT: Chocolate biscuits
COMPETITION: Viscount biscuits
PRIZES: Mini Metro cars

So gird up your coins and invest
So look for the pack with the Crest
If they've sold out of 'Viscount' – protest
Our UK's OK not US
So buy goods with the British made Crest

▶ **There was a young lady called Jess, whose carpets were in a real mess...**

PRODUCT: Liquid carpet cleaner
COMPETITION: Boots the Chemists/1001 Clean Up
PRIZES: Rowenta cordless vacuum cleaners

To Boots she did walk, 1001 Troubleshooter she bought, her carpets are now just the best

So Santa Claus sent her, a Cordless Rowenta, by Rudolph the Reindeer express
But 1001, made cleaning up fun, and ended poor Jess's distress
She said, I know what I'll do, use 1001 carpet shampoo, then vacuum with
    Rowenta Cordless
So she went round to Boots, where they do give two hoots, and one thousand
    and one did the rest

▶ **Panasonic's CD appeal, is that all your artists sound real, to
picture the scene, just sit back and dream...**

PRODUCT: *Electrical goods*
PRIZE: *Choice of holiday*

Of the visions the sound will reveal

▶ **Une jolie young lady from France, bought Burnez Frères for
preference, she said 'Eet's so handy, zis all-purpose brandy...'**

PRODUCT: *French brandy*
PRIZE: *Holiday in France*

From hors d'oeuvres to pièce de résistance
But too much eez not good for le bonce
It's something I would never be 'sans'
Grape value – with French elegance
And ze price is un bit de bonne chance
For ze cook and ze 'slurp' – par excellence
From Lundi right through to Dimanche
Could I 'ménage' without it? No chance!
Eet cures all my aches en Provence

▶ **Princes make the nicest hot dogs, their ham tastes quite
divine...**

PRODUCT: *Canned meats*

Lunch tongue glides along alimentary canals, while meatballs in gravy untwine
Kisses make Princes of frogs, I got meatballs out of mine
Chicken breast is quite delicious, send Dudley Moore for mine
Served on Delft these top dog products could enhance that fine design
Which 'quillistrates' (*illustrates) the 'point' that it's for Princes Porc-u-pine
    (*pork you pine)

▶ **Savoury and tasty, that's the Findus Double treat, Findus
Double Deckers...**

PRODUCT: *Potato/Meat fritters*
COMPETITION: *Findus Double Deckers perfect partners*
PRIZES: *14-inch Decca portable colour TVs and Decca cassette radios*

Make peas and chips complete
Paired up to perfection to make any meal complete
Frozen or fried, tout de suite
Make the meal you love to eat, have them as the main course, or serve them as
    a pecker, whichever word you choose, you'll never top this decker
Just like Dud and Pete, a winning combination, quick to 'Cook' and 'Moore' to
    eat
Meals 'wrapped up' all nice and neat
So quick to heat and eat, such delicious combinations that you'll find them
    hard to beat
Makes the children's teas complete
Come pre-paired for us – that's neat
The eighties way to eat, quick and simple to prepare – come on, pull up your
    seat

▶ **There was a young man from Woodford Green...**

PRODUCT: Medicated facial cleanser
COMPETITION: Boots/Oxy Clean
PRIZES: £10 vouchers

Who fell into a hot soup tureen
The crown heard a splash
He climbed out with a rash
But it went thanks to Boots' Oxy Clean!

Who needed no make-up on Halloween
'Witch' left him feeling foolish
And looking quite 'ghoulish'
'til cured with a 'spell' of Oxy Clean

LIMIT

▶ **The Sky's the LIMIT with Braun at Asda because...**

PRODUCT: Electrical goods
COMPETITION: Asda/Braun
PRIZES: Sony satellite kits

Seeking to reach the discerning buyer, Asda features Braun – quality couldn't
    be higher
Braun offers a galaxy of quality devices and Asda's switched on to lower prices
They dish up a galaxy of selection, but Braun gets the best reception
Braun 'channel' their new devices, to Asda's 'low-zone' friendly prices
Quality, value and five-star care, make Braun and Asda a higher-flyer pair
Braun products I conceal between groceries with skill – hubby happily paying
    my bill

Down to earth, that's Asda price, while Braun on reflection, twice as nice
Asda value, Braun precision, both could bring me heavenly vision

LINK

▶ **I think Snickers and the NFL American Football weekends are an ideal LINK because…**

PRODUCT: Confectionery
COMPETITION: Snickers/NFL
PRIZES: Trips to the American Superbowl

Miami Dolphins would swim a mile/Philadelphia Eagles swoop in style/New England Patriots wave the flag/Pittsburgh Steelers hide their swag/St. Louis Cardinals hail the people/Dallas Cowboys do it with the rope/San Diego Chargers being thrifty/the 49ers make it to 50/Green Bay Packers pack a whack/Nutty packed Snickers the perfect snack

Spend a dollar on Snickers, get a quarterback
You've got to be 'peanuts' not to be 'running back' for more
They both cheer me up when I'm a touch down
Snickers is full of nutty chunks, NFL is full of chunky hunks
NFL excites me, Snickers delight me, hope you invite me
Amongst the glamour, glitz and action, snickers are the star attraction
At home or away they're the match of the day
When excitement rises and energy gets low, snickers provides the get up and go
I'd be a 'touch down' in the mouth if I had to 'pass' on either
Snickers, Snickers, Snickers, Rah, Rah, Rah in our league you'll go far
Energy, Entertainment, Excitement - both have the 3E's that are sure to please
Top attractions, second to none, Snickers and Superbowl are number one
When you drool over Snickers you never miss a dribble

LOOK & LOOK GOOD

▶ **The fresh LOOK of Lyons Original will always be on my shopping list at Tesco because….**

PRODUCT: Coffee

It's blended with care, then vended with flair
The eyecatching packs of unequalled flavour are another Tesco money saver
The green and gold vacuum pack captures flavours others lack
Superior taste, distinctive pack, Tesco value, draws me back
Light, dark or medium, it helps to beat the tea-dium
When flavour is the main attraction, Lyons gives sealed satisfaction

► **Clairol gives me a great new LOOK because...**

PRODUCT: Hair colourant

Its use guarantees me confidence in my appearance
It's the instant beauty treatment for tired hair

► **I always LOOK for VDQS because...**

PRODUCT: Wine

It is a guaranteed sign that spells superior wines from superior vines

► **I LOOK for Scottish salmon carrying the tartan quality mark in Safeway stores because...**

PRODUCT: Fish

Where quality's a must, this hallmark I can trust
The quality is unquestioned, the value unsurpassed

► **Boots the Chemists are always worth a close LOOK because...**

PRODUCT: Chemist goods

Close inspection means no rejection, quality, range and right selection
You might miss a chance with only one glance
It's no illusion, you always see good value

► **Vidal Sassoon products make me LOOK GOOD because...**

PRODUCT: Hair care

Every step is carefully planned, that's the beauty of the brand
The Sassoon routine with its step-by-step care, brings a bloom to my skin and a bounce to my hair
They give me the protection I desire, the selection I require, and the reflection I admire
Those shining highlights in my hair, skin deep beauty cleansed with care, three simple steps combine to show, Sassooning gives that polished glow
They're carefully balanced, expertly blended, so keep me looking as nature intended
This unique collection, provide care and protection, giving hair and complexion, a look of perfection
They lavish care on my skin and hair
Beautiful skin and shining hair, are hallmarks of their expert care

LORD, KING & QUEEN

▶ **Shopping at Woolworths makes me feel like a LORD because...**

PRODUCT: Chain store goods

Their bargains galore enable me to buy more

▶ **Lyons sponge sandwich will always be my traditional teatime treat cos...**

PRODUCT: Cake

Like Madam, I'm adamant that only the best is served

▶ **Budweiser is the KING of beers because...**

PRODUCT: Beer

It's the leader of the packs and so don't blush, it guarantees a Royal flush
This lager spelt backwards describes the taste (*lager = regal)
Only Budweiser can put the 'King' into drinking
Flavoured by Henry VIII they say it stayed cool whilst the others lost their heads
It makes every Knight special

An upper class standard

Time saved, super taste, guests arrive, table graced
It's fast becoming a tradition for quality, value and nutrition
Its taste transports me into raptures of delight
You don't have to be extravagant to buy the best
It's a gastronomic thrill without an astronomic bill

At the races – the sport of KINGS

I always choose from these labels, coming from distinguished stables
I never lose my shirt backing these dead certs
I wouldn't be saddled with anything else
They are runaway winners with my party punters

LOVE

▶ **I LOVE Vendona French Style because...**

PRODUCT: French Style coffee
COMPETITION: Tesco/Vendona coffee

This taste of France, superbly presented, leaves palates pleased and pockets contented

▶ **I would LOVE a Neville Johnson kitchen because...**

PRODUCT: Kitchen units
PRIZE: Fitted kitchen

Quality, range, craftsmanship abound, with value and professionalism all round

▶ **I LOVE Harvest bran flakes because...**

PRODUCT: Breakfast cereal

They are tasty, tempting and nutritious, not to mention quite delicious

▶ **You can't help falling in LOVE with Wall's individual Viennetta because...**

PRODUCT: Ice cream dessert

It sends a thrill down my spine knowing it's all mine

▶ **I LOVE my Lolobal because...**

PRODUCT: Toy ball

The bounce, fun and magic, Lolobal created, would make Mickey Mouse super animated

▶ **I LOVE pancakes with Lyle's because...**

PRODUCT: Golden syrup

Yummy, nutritious, sticky and sweet, Lyle's on pancakes is our regular treat

▶ **I LOVE French prunes because...**

PRODUCT: Dried fruit
COMPETITION: Food & wine from France/Safeway
PRIZES: Johnston's French cookery courses

Français Pruneaux, always in fashion, tenderly grown, consumed with passion
Pruneaux are a tempting treat, succulent, healthy, ready to eat
For flavour, fibre, fitness and fun, Pruneaux are the Number One
Full of fibre, soaked with sun, very nutritious for everyone
Every wrinkle hides a twinkle – n'est-ce pas?
Selected plums kissed by sun, resulting in Pruneaux, pleasing everyone
Perfectly grown, perfectly dried, the tastiest prunes ever tried
Beginning life as a humble plum, how flavoursome French prunes become
Sunshine grown to French tradition, wholesome, delicious, full of nutrition
Tender Pruneaux, every day, evoke the taste of French soleil

▶ **Tony the Tiger and I LOVE the Gr-r-reat Taste of Frosties because...**

PRODUCT: Breakfast cereal
COMPETITION: Kellogg's Frosties mega music machine
PRIZES: Philips music equipment

Tony, me and Venus, like ours with Banana-rama
So CD-uctive, they're deeply dippy and too crunchy for their packets
They have an itsy, bitsy, teeny, weeny, sugar frosting, really dreamy

LUXURY

▶ **Shopping at Discount for Beauty is a LUXURY because...**

PRODUCT: Beauty shop goods

It's my passport to see a fair sale

▶ **What is your idea of the ultimate LUXURY weekend?**

PRODUCT: Confectionery
COMPETITION: Elizabeth Shaw mint chocolates

A weekend at Raffles in Singapore, fresh melon for starters and cocktails galore, but don't tell the wife who I'm taking because I'll be spending the time with Elizabeth Shaw

Hired Porsche to stay at Miller House, Windermere, best suite, delicious meals, wine, return to find house cleaned, laundry done, garden tidied so we don't spend next week 'paying' for our weekend off – that's luxury

Exotic location, Barbados not Bedford, macho companion, Eastwood or Redford, five star hotel, drinks by the pool, intimate barman, long dark and cool, lunching on linen, candlelit dinner, Elizabeth Shaw, the weekend's a winner

Centre court seats for Wimbledon finals weekend, strawberries and cream teas, and Elizabeth Shaw chocolates, plus the outfit and tickets to go to their dance afterwards and dance with the stars

I'm getting on so let it be soon: float me to the Neuschwanstein Castle by balloon, silent skies, breath-taking height, a room at the top, unforgettable night

A weekend in Vienna is my dream come true, a night at the opera and dinner for two, a ride in a carriage, the music of Strauss, then enjoying Shaw mints in a quaint coffee house

It's fantasy, but I should like to be a guest of Her Majesty (and I don't mean Wormwood Scrubs)

Neither of us can swim very well, a trip to the Dead Sea would be swell, to lie on our backs and float with ease, while eating our favourite chocolates please, is a weekend delightful indeed

I missed Halley's Comet when clouds got in the way, but I could view it from
    Australia – if Elizabeth Shaw would pay
A visit to a land of perpetual daylight, where for two nights at least, my
    nightmares must surely become daydreams
I'd like to go to Aintree races, in a car that really shows its paces, to drive a
    Porsche would please me the most, with my Grand National choice first
    past the post

MACHINERY

► **I can dish up perfect results every time with Moulinex
because...**

PRODUCT: Microwave

Food's done to a turn without risk of burn
For great cooking at quick speed, Moulinex fulfils your need
Technical expertise makes superb results a thing of ease
Kitchen cool, less to wash, every meal's a super nosh
Amateurs of the male sex find cooking easy with Moulinex

► **Every Biactol home should have a Computer because...**

PRODUCT: Facial spot cleanser

It knocks spots off pencil and paper

Appliances

They go hand in hand in the happy home
Appliances designed with the user in mind
Quality is remembered long after the price is forgotten
Now I'm char-free, chore-free and care-free
Housework becomes a hobby not a sentence
Freedom is mine thanks to their design
I have exchanged kitchen sink dramas for current affairs
Now my kitchen is my kingdom
An investment with Miele means a dividend daily
Twixt dishes and floor, I'd have time galore
It gives me time on my hands, not on my knees
Washing-up and brush and pan, went out with the Bogey Man
They're automatic, electronic – it makes this housewife seem bionic
The quality which delighted gran has been improved for modern man
They never err indoors
This electric team makes chez-nous gleam
They take cleaning on board with the speed of Concorde

Computers

'Digitally' delightful, economically 'keyed' with quality 'taped' there's all I need
For variety and 'visual display' they're a bargain 'byte' any day
Using 'logic' not 'memory' they have more flavour 'in store'
When I need a tasty snack they feed me correct information back
For a snap decision they never play pranks on my memory banks
'Dataday' they give more munch and less to pay
When added 'chips' carry less cash, it's dotty not to dash
When the 'chips' are down they're a great 'byte' altogether
For work and play they are the machine of the day
It would be an education in recreation
The computer age is here to stay, I'd like to join without delay
Atari's chips are a kids delight, memory shows they love Marmite
Input is healthier than chips and that's no silly con

Hoover appliances

There's no better life improver than an appliance made by Hoover
There's no hard labour with Hoover
Hoover products of renown never let the housewife down
Freezing, cooking, cleaning too, Hoover products help you through
Mug or rug, skirt or shirt, Hoover's supreme wherever the dirt
Wash, clean, freeze or chill, reliable Hoover fits the bill
With Hoover's dishwasher I'd trust my china, nobody makes products finer
Hoover changes a workhouse into a leisure centre
Chaos, crises, gremlins – gone, home sweet Hoover, home, you're on
Hoover's designers have used their brain – housework's done, no need to strain
My housework took the booby prize till Hoover opened up my eyes
Giving Hoover a twirl changes this Mrs Mop into Wonder Girl
Give Hoover a plug and it's top of the cleaning charts
With Hoover it's touch and go, go, go
I'm a Hoover-groover who's gone clean-keen
Whatever the challenge, whatever the grime, Hoover finishes in half the time
It's a fan for all seasons for all the best reasons
Blowing, waving, mixing, shaving, only Hoover's worth all the raving

Hoover vacuum cleaners

A quick turn with Hoover makes me a Wonderwoman
With Hoover automation I keep a spotless reputation
Whatever the sentence there's no hard labour with Hoover
For domestic manoeuvre, depend on Hoover

Hotpoint appliances – with the environment in mind

Through technology they've paved the way, saving energy every day
They make a valuable contribution towards a world without pollution
Protection of our earth's fragility needs man's utmost technical ingenuity

They're designed for today's chores and tomorrow's people
They provide today's clean home and tomorrow's green world
Whether energy, water or CFCs, the Green Machine considers these
Reducing power and CFCs protects the earth and seven seas
Their economy and fewer CFCs conserves ozone, lakes and trees
Carefully designed with green technology, these machines safeguard ecology
Hotpoint has the power to save more kilowatts per hour
For our environment's protection, Hotpoint appliances are the number one
     invention
Planetary rescue by you and me in partnership with Hotpoint
Hotpoint ecology is technology for future generations
Conservationists select what Hotpoint perfect

Irons

Best pressed man about town
We both know our job and press on together

KP mini chips – Computer theme

PRODUCT: Potato snacks

For small fry they're a big buy
Insert digits into mini chips, the finest snack to pass your lips
They are perfect 'pressed-digit-taters'
No other 'joy sticks' put a beam on my 'screen'
They're the experimental prototype (protatoe) chippy of tomorrow
Basically, it's no 'silli-con' they're crisp and crunch with salt on

Microwaves

Food cooked to a turn so incredibly fast, long hours in the kitchen are a thing
     of the past
Cook or thaw, they always score
They're a sight for thaw wise
Quick to cook to a turn without any burn
For great cooking and quick speed, a microwave fills your needs
I like to do my cooking on easy therms
They're built to wear without repair

Philips hairdryers and shavers

Even a goddess needs her Philips
Philips' fabulous flair for personal care
I need Philips care and protection for satin smooth skin and hair perfection
When I'm looking a wreck on some distant shore – Philips to the rescue, I'm
     ship-shape once more
Though I'll pack my bikini and nightie – it's Philips that gives me the fillip to
     feel like Aphrodite
I place more reliance on a Philips appliance

Philips is the 'best man' for a tidy 'groom'
Switched on to 'current' style
These 'light' travellers quickly adapt to the 'current' conditions
They're free and easy to plug into style and really socket to them

Video recorders

To watch breakfast TV with my supper or tea
I'll know all the answers the second time around
Many happy returns to yesterday
To record for pleasure and repeat at leisure
Break into snooker, advance each frame, no interference bars my game
While I'm out I'll miss nowt

Yamaha organs

The leader of the band
Open the door to musical pleasure – Yamaha have the key
Brahms, Bach or Kenny Ball, the Yamaha Electone plays them all
Yamaha organs are easy to play because of their 'teacher features'
Nip-pon your Yamaha organ and kick start to a new world

MAGIC

▶ **Shreddies and Shredded Wheat make a MAGIC breakfast treat because...**

PRODUCT: Breakfast cereals

They conjure up the double treat of 100% wholewheat
They conjure up goodness to bewitch us all day long
Shreds of evidence are never left on the plate
When hunger beckons, they disappear in seconds
They're worth their wheat in gold
These all-time greats are just wizard on our plates
You need no magician to make them disappear
This 'super natural' nourishing pack, works 'miracles' on hunger attacks
Every morning wheaty whole, they vanish from the breakfast bowl
At the 'bix' opening they always bring the house down

▶ **A New Maestro is MAGIC because...**

PRODUCT: Car

Its matchless performance, quality and style, carries you spellbound, mile after
mile

▶ **Vanish soap stick puts a little MAGIC in my home because…**

PRODUCT: Cleaner

Bar, stick or lotion it's a miracle potion
Upstairs, downstairs, the front doormat, cleaning made easy – 'just like that'
Rub it on, then sit back – out damned spot – just like that
With a flick of the stick it does the trick
Reviving upholstery and spilt on Wilton, turning my home into the Hilton
Kids' mess, spilled drinks, general grime; vanishcadabra, gone in no time
Without boil and bubble, toil and trouble, stains will vanish
It's quick, it's slick, it does the trick
Robots, supervacs, all very nice, but Vanish is my special cleaning device

▶ **My family would enjoy the MAGIC of Disney because…**

PRODUCT: Soft drink
COMPETITION: Coca-Cola/Euro Disney at Littlewoods
PRIZES: Family trips to Euro Disney

This wonderland at last we'd see, Coke and Littlewoods – merci!
Coca-Cola and Disney, you know, both give that tingle you never outgrow

▶ **I would go to see … (Show in London) because…**

PRODUCT: Confectionery
COMPETITION: Forbuoys/Rowntree's Mackintosh/Win a Starlight weekend
PRIZES: Weekends in London to see a show

Phantom of the Opera … a scarier aria raises eyebrows without being highbrow
… two's company, three's a shroud
… Crawford's influence still grabs 'em – some 'murders' do have 'em
… it would be phun
… it's a thrilling show Forbuoys and 'ghouls'
… the last Op I went to I slept through it
… Dairy Box in a box at the Opera – Phant(om)astic
… although I've seen it only once, I'd 'Stillgo' again
… it's my delight for a frighty night

Spirits to drink – Ghosts theme

They're worth coming back for
I could make one disappear tonight
Made for the right kind of ghoul, it brings the right spirit into the High Street
A better class of spirit is present at this haunt

Magic

Technical wizardry at a magical price
Say hello to a magical good buy

Food for kids and tiny tots

It's the famous disappearing trick for big and little 'uns
Their 'special effect' on tums, a 'picture' for discerning mums
They change an irritable imp into a charming prince
When hunger beckons they disappear in seconds

MAN

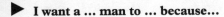 **I want a ... man to ... because...**

> PRODUCT: *Confectionery*
> COMPETITION: *Aero chocolate*
> PRIZE: *Win a man for a week*

I want a gypsy man to drive me in his horse-drawn caravan because of the gypsy in my soul

I want a water diviner/engineer man to supply my sheep with water because they live too high for mains supply

I want a toy boy man to flaunt (at the whist drive) because when I go to the OAP whist they are always talking about toy boys

I want an Otto man to keep a new bed company because my present man is of obscure antiquity, in fact prehistorical!

I want a Chinese chef man to cook Chinese dishes for a week because I've not yet got the wok technique

I want a Lord of the Manor man to hold a banquet at his residence because I'd like a taste of grandeur

I want a milliner man to design me a fabulous hat because then I could mix with 'The Royals' at Ascot!

I want a body building champion man to teach me French because my submarine is going to France and I'm the Liaison Officer

I want a body building champion man to 'pose' because I want my husband to see where the 'large bits' are meant to be

I want a clever man to help me in my Maths and English because I am not good at it

I want a puppet man to make my 'spitting image' because I've got a big nose to inspire him

I want a crafts man to teach me silver smithing because I'm allergic to gold and long for some silver jewellery

I want a council man to build a 'Toad Tunnel' because migrating toads are killed crossing the road

I want a nice plump Turkish wo-man to teach me belly dancing because at 57, 5' 3", 11 stone, I'm fascinated by it

I want a rock climbing guide man to assist scaling the Cuillins' inaccessible pinnacle because I want to reach for the 'Skye'

I want a woodcarver man to carve me as a genuine ship's figurehead because

I'd love to be a mermaid

I want a top photographer man to turn me into a cover girl because I am 74 and still get the glad eye

I want a mycological man to show me Destroying Angel because I long to see and photograph this rare fungus

I want a stunt man to show my daughter a real stunt because she thinks the actors really die

I want a mahout man to take me on his elephant to Sainsbury's because that would add spice to a weekly tusk

I want a golf professional man to perfect me because swing needs improving, grip needs a fix, stance is atrocious, handicap thirty-six

I want a lazy good for nothing man to prove to my wife I'm not that bad because she is convinced I am

I want a parrot trainer man to discipline 'Merlin' because all he does is screech and squawk, how I long for polly talk

I want an aero man to fly to Exeter because we're newborn triplets and are bubbling over to see great-grandma

▶ **What makes your romantic man so special that you would like to visit Rome with him as the weekend guests of Mills & Boon?**

PRODUCT: Books
COMPETITION: Mills & Boon Romantic Partner
PRIZES: Weekends for two in Italy

Paul buys me perfume, cards and flowers, loves good wine and happy hours

Italian panache, good looks to match, with Mills & Boon, he's my winning catch

He shares, is always there, he'd make this second honeymoon a perfect affair

MEANS...

▶ **To me, Country Choice Dutch Royal Crest bacon MEANS...**

PRODUCT: Bacon
PRIZES: Weekend breaks for two in Amsterdam

The tender Dutch

Excellent quality I 'canalways' rely on!

The country taste without the fat of the land

The continental basis of my English breakfast

A fuller flavour in every forkful – juicy tender, lean and porkful!

MEAT

▶ **Delicious Danish is delightful because...**

PRODUCT: Bacon

The sizzle 'siz' it all
The Co-operative Viking makes bacon to my liking
It is a succulent sizzler and has no spitting image
Once fried, never forgotten
When appetites tend to roam, tender Danish brings them home
That sizzling sensation is the Co-op's recommendation
Food of the Viking 'leans' to my liking
It is the star attraction for knife and fork action
Grill it, fry it, bake it – you can't beat it
The true fresh taste means there's never any waste
The nice flavour never wavers
Bacon butties, haute cuisine, with Danish as the go-between
It's cured with caring for flavour fresh sharing
They're a cut above the rest, don't buy second best
With bacon or ham it's always 'grand slam'
It's a delectable dish that deserves a degree
Tender, tempting, full of taste, none ever goes to waste
We are a healthier nation with their food innovation
Ideal barbecue, Danish on prong, funfilled party, cannot go wrong
It's freshly sliced and nicely priced
It's a money saver with a perfect flavour
Its appetising nutrition is part of our Great British tradition
In lean times it's streaks above the rest
Nobody can be rashernough to claim otherwise
Its lean back style makes my purse smile
The aroma from the sizzle makes the homeward drizzle fizzle
It sizzles superbly, fries fantastically and tastes terrific
It saves the busy housewife's bacon
It's the perfect way to sail through the day
It recalls happy memories of dazzling Denmark
When it comes to rashers the Danes are price bashers
Like the Co-op I can always 'Seaways' of tastefully satisfying everybody
Eggs just beg for it
On lean streaks you can make a pig of yourself
When it comes to Norse code it's word perfect
Quality, taste, healthy nutrition, have always been a Danish tradition
The Danes take great pains to ensure quality never wanes
Having fresh Nordic flavour it's the perfect invader
The taste lives up to the aroma
Bacon that is Danish cured is bacon for the connoisseur

▶ **I buy Farmhouse 1lb pork sausages at Co-op Leo's because...**

PRODUCT: Sausages
PRIZES: Sets of Prestige pans

So sizzlingly good they shout for more, Farmhouse at Leo's deserves 'oinkore'
They make a tasty feast for all my little beasts
Their bangers are bang on
The first prick with a fork brings sizzling aromas of Farmhouse pork
There's never a raw deal, just a sizzling good meal
You can't beef about the price or the contents
I get more pork on the fork, less bill at the till
There's fireworks if they don't get their bangers for tea
With these pieces of eight I can enhance any plate
Price keen, meat lean
I plump for the best and ignore the rest
Party, BBQ, or family dinner, delicious Farmhouse are a winner
Phenomenal taste, nominal cost
Farmhouse excellence and Co-op Leo's flair, together are a winning pair
These scintillatingly succulent sizzlers satisfy my scoundrels' stupendous
    stomachs
With their prestige I'm always sure of sizzling tasty value
These porkers are corkers
It adds distinction to my courses, without draining my resources
I want my pound of flesh without the fat
For sizzling good value Farmhouse and Co-op Leo's 'siz' it all
I get a top quality product with first class service
When I want some flavour, short of cash, Farmhouse sausages with mash
It's the pork you pine for
Co-op prices and Farmhouse sausages are 'pantastic'
These better sizzling link me and I scrap any other old bangers
The price is just right for a sizzling bite
Grandpa loved them, so did dad, now they're favourite with the lad
When my family commands a sizzling performance they're 'porky and best'
I always get my hot dogs from the coolest 'big cat'
I live in the city and they taste of the country
The quality 'links' they provide, are the tastiest sizzlers sold with pride
Both take pride in the quality inside
Buy in haste, repent at leisure, Farmhouse bangers are always fresher
Once fried – never forgotten
I get a gastronomic thrill without an astronomic bill
A bunch of bangers can bash the biggest appetite
They are the 'pork' of the town with prices renown
This succulent meal has purse appeal
When packing school dinners they're competition winners
There's less bread in the bangers and more in the purse
Hunches for lunches, winners for dinners, Farmhouse sausages are money
    spinners

For breakfast, lunch or tea, they fill the family with glee
For a sizzling occasion they are a sausage celebration
They pan out the taste for value

▶ **Wall's microwave sausages are a great breakthrough because...**

PRODUCT: Microwave sausages
COMPETITION: Tesco/Wall's microwave sausages
PRIZES: Microwave ovens

Wall's have found the missing link, a microwave sausage that isn't pink
Even my husband Harvey can cook this Wall's banger
No frying pan needed, no splashing fat, just succulent hot sausages in
    50 seconds flat
No longer a kitchen slave, with super sausage and microwave
Now when I say 'dinner in a minute' I mean it
You made me buy some and I haven't got a microwave ... yet
Now I can cook 'em as fast as they can eat 'em
With the microwave brainwave my cooking has entered the saus-age
Quality fare of renown is quick to heat and already brown
Quick to heat, delicious to eat, a combination hard to beat

▶ **Porkinson's sausages are the best because...**

PRODUCT: Sausages

They make bangers and mash incredibly flash
Porkinson's sausages sizzled to fame by placing taste behind the name
Porkinson's sausages are a beautiful sight, pork filled perfection in every bite

▶ **Bernard Matthews products are best for barbecues because...**

PRODUCT: Meat
PRIZES: Barbecues

You get succulent slices at sizzling prices
With standards so high they're an excellent buy
They're the money savers with the 'bootiful' flavours
There's no wasting, no basting, just wonderful tasting
Always tasty, always lean, they never ruin Dad's big scene
Norfolk flavour beyond compare, tastes even better in open air
They're handy, delicious, always tender and nutritious
No fuss, no waste, our Bernard's got taste
They are quick and delicious, lean and nutritious
The waste is removed and the taste improved – bootiful

▶ **To me, Dutch Royal Crest bacon is...**

PRODUCT: Bacon
PRIZES: Luxury hampers

Tasty, nutritious, quite a dream, in my kitchen it reigns supreme
Food to savour, full of flavour, perfect to taste, without any waste
Perfectly cured, reasonably priced, a Dutch of class, slice after slice
A cut above the rest, I can tell by the crest
Such a tasty rasher – no wonder it's a smasher

Bacon

They packa fresha rasha
In lean times it's streaks above the rest
Other brands of bacon are small fry
It's the best cure for an empty stomach
Its taste I adore so I streak back for more
Their porkers are corkers
Counter intelligence and grilling reveals Danepak's the secret of successful
    meals
When Danes find the best they put 'Walls' around it
Denmark's breakfast best is behind the writing on the walls
Wall's save my bacon, a Dane, and a Dane...

Dewhurst the Butchers

They're great value, no bones about it
They're great hunches for lunches and winners for dinners
Master butcher's made his point, variety, without a joint

MEET

▶ **Why would you like to meet the Flintstones?**

PRODUCT: Supermarket foods
COMPETITION: Tesco/Meet the Flintstones
PRIZE: Family holiday for four in Florida

Flintstones are great, Flintstones are funny, I love them all and so does my
    mummy

▶ **The 'Star Trek' character I would most like to meet is ...
because...**

Spock ... I would not need to do any decorating since everyone knows Vulcans
    have no 'emulsion'
Captain Kirk ... when everything is driving me potty, I just have to say 'Beam
    me up Scottie'
Scottie ... there's na miracle he canna work to get warp speed for Capt'n Kirk
Uhura ... with her sultry good looks and tuneful modulation, I'd have no
    problems with 'communication'

Scottie ... I could beam myself up in an Enterprising way, into Trekkie
    adventures every day
The Ship's Computer ... Mr Spock would always be running his hands over my
    software

▶ **Which famous person would you most like to meet and where
    would you like to go with them on a day out?**

PRODUCT: Chain store goods
COMPETITION: House of Fraser/Father Christmas
PRIZES: Amiga home computer consoles
Entries submitted by children

E.T. ... at home
The Queen ... go to Buckingham Palace and have a ride in her car
God and invite him to my house for a cup of tea and a chat
Frank Bruno ... take him to a local knitting club and watch him knit
Rapunzel ... first to the hairdressers then to the disco to let down our hair
Me and Merlin would collect frogs to make a magic potion to stop dad smoking
    so he can live longer
The man who makes stickers ... I would take him to the Isle of Wight
Queen Elizabeth ... to the seaside and I could build her a new castle
Jesus ... I would take him to my school nativity play, as I am playing Mary and
    it would surprise everyone
I would take Gorden Kaye to France for the day, so we can both practise our
    French

MILES

▶ **Johnson's products are MILES better because...**

PRODUCT: Baby care

Many coins make a mile but a little Johnson's makes baby smile
When you're in the crawler lane you need the right gear
To ignore their dri-way code would be a rash decision
They make important little extra savings

▶ **You're MILES better off with Orchid Travel and Soreen
    because...**

PRODUCT: Fruit malt loaf
PRIZE: Holiday to Menorca

Soreen delights me, Menorca excites me, hope Orchid Travel will invite me

▶ **I would drive MILES for Mayfair because...**

PRODUCT: *Cigarettes*
COMPETITION: *Mini Mayfair/Mayfair cigarettes*
PRIZES: *Mini Mayfair cars*

When quality and price are the main attraction, Mayfair gives most satisfaction
There's nothing mini about a Mayfair!

MILLION

▶ **Dolmio is worth a MILLION lire to me because…**

PRODUCT: *Pasta sauce*

That 'rich' tomato flavour is 'puree' gold
Dolmio's Italian fare makes me feel like a millionaire
Every jar creates with ease a true Italian masterpiece
It's the safe way to create a 'Pisa' Italy
It adds flavour to my courses without draining my resources
I 'bank' on Dolmio for meals with 'high interest'
Wherever I Roma it can't be surpasta
The cost is nominal and the taste phenomenal
Candlelight dinner to family invasion, Dolmio capitalises on every occasion
It's always affordable and richly rewardable
I can cook to impress and bank on success
It's the only sauce of income worth having
It's the currency my family are de-lira-eous about
Venice may sink, towers may lean, but Dolmio always reigns supreme
There's no need to speculate, merely appreciate
When dreaming of riches I crave Dolmio dishes
The gourmet pleasure is a priceless treasure
I can afford it on my Dole-mio
What other sauces lack in spice, Dolmio's worth any price
Figarotively speaking, pasta's a load of Bologna without Dolmio
It makes life richer for the pourer
It is my pasta-port to Rome
A richer sauce cannot be found
No longer a disaster, now I'm a pasta master
If it cost the earth I'd get my money's worth
For taste and presentation it's a noteworthy sensation
With Dolmio you can eat like a millionaire
It saves me 'Turin' Italia for the spicy a-Roma
The flavour is so rich, it's priceless
A Dolmio jar makes life richer by far
Dolmio delights me, Rome excites me, hope Asda invites me
I always hit the jackpot with this really tasty sauce
I can sample the taste of Italy without flight delays

Even millionaires surely know, pasta just hasta have Dolmio
Italian connection for gourmet perfection
It Asda be one in a million
With Dolmio's aroma, who needs a 'pasta' port to Rome
It's a luxury sauce that will complement any course
It's so much richer for the pourer
Found the best so now I never need to 'Rome'
Delicious flavour that tastebuds love to savour
I can bank on Dolmio and take all the credit
O' I'm a doll who's not past-a Rome-eo
You can bank on it to stop the family Rome-ing

▶ **I would like to share in the Bold/Ariel MILLIONAIRES spending spree because...**

    PRODUCT: *Washing powders*
    COMPETITION: *Hoover/Bold/Ariel Millionaires Spending Spree*
    PRIZES: *Hoover washing machines*

Moonlight, magnolia and a millionaire, but the girl wants the goods from
    Hoover
With Hoover products, made with care, I feel like a millionaire
You don't have to be a millionaire investor to clean up with Hoover
Walking on air like a millionaire, cleaning with Hoover I don't have a care

MISCELLANEOUS

Betting shops

Ladbrokes make every day a Bet-a-day

Calendars

This is one hang-up I don't mind having
I know if I fail to plan then I'm planning to fail
If you give a fig for efficiency you look after your dates

Camping equipment

I'm a back to nature enthusiast who wants to rough-it in comfort
Good tents, easy cooking, safety first and trouble free, everything so stylish
    looking, light a GAZ lamp and you'll see
Whatever the weather, wherever the site, GAZ will prove a camper's delight

Cash and carry

Traders keep buzzin' into Landmark knowing that elsewhere they could be
    stung

Corner shops

We get big shop savings in a trice, with small shop service and advice
Opens early, closes late. Choice, price, service – all are great

Double glazing

Whatever your outlook on life, they'll improve it

Estate agents

Their name is a 'House Sold' word

Flooring

It's the best in the long run
It has all the opposition floored
It cushions your pocket as well as your feet
Quality tells, quality sells
It puts spring in my tread for years ahead
It makes friends with my feet
What else could hold up to a stampede every mealtime?
With quality and price in mind, a better vinyl's hard to find
They floor the opposition with a clean sweep
It deserved my stamp of approval
Sa-far-I haven't 'herd' of anything to beat it

Glass and china

It's clearly cut above the rest

Insurance brokers

His advice and service is personalised, on the latest quotes he is computerised,
    so perfect policies materialise
He has the advantage of second sight to find the best cover at a price that is
    right

Money belts

If you care about the pounds, watch the waistline

Newsagents

There's so much to choose as well as your news
They are the best people to 'book' with
They serve me with more than the bare necessities

Non-stick pans

I'd like to make pan scrubbing a lost art – like Dodo plucking
I'm a one pan woman

It makes frying less trying
Tefal sticks to nothing but its promise
Tefal non-stick dishes out winners, while flashier rivals stick to dinners

Post Office aerogrammes

A reunion would be jubilation after years of aerogramme communication
My heart flies with every aerogramme – it's time I went too
Aerogrammes fly so why can't I?
Aerogrammes keep friendships strong, whilst parting has been much too long

Rugs

▶ **I would like to win a Super Kershan rug with 1001/Co-op because...**

PRODUCT: Liquid carpet cleaner

Even with grandchildren at play, 1001 saves the day
I would be a Co-op slave, with this gift from Aladdin's cave
I know it would stay good as new using 1001 foam shampoo
It would keep its colour after 1001 colour schemes
They are supercarpetfragilisticexpialidocious
I know I can trust 1001 to keep the rug A1
A Kershan rug would be the first luxury item in my new home
With a combination like that I'd have the world at my feet
No need to journey too far east for a Kershan rug and Co-op feast

Savings stamps

The caring sharing store that gives you so much more
It 'stamps' on inflation and that's quite a 'feat'
Better value, wider range, friendly service, stamps and change
For value they're champs with bonus stamps
The store that's stamped its reputation through Britain

Showers

I like to be 'showered' in luxury
I can make a splash without splashing out

Sky Satellite television

It sounds so good, I'm really tempted, with British TV I'm going demented
Sixteen channels of sheer bliss, sweet 'beams' are made of this
The scope of my viewing would rocket without leaving a space in my pocket
With 16 channels into which to tune, this telly addict would be over the moon
I'd reach for the sky without leaving home, a satellite system I'd love to own
Satellite TV is the one for me, am, pm and Sky TV
My ambition's quite specific, to see 16 channels would be terrific

Sport for him, movies are my wish, add music and lots more, the perfect dish
Five channels are not enough whenever you're a TV buff
No more snoring, watching the boring, let's rejoice at Sky's wide choice

Stationery (invisible and adhesive tape)

Its good connections give it a clear advantage
It's conspicuous by its absence
The best thing you never saw
It's transparently superior

The National Trust

They brought the English history books to life
Past, future and present were there. Heritage protected by people who care
It's the gift of the past to the generation of the future
It was a time capsule visit back into history and a gracious way of living
History became reality, the past came alive, our priceless heritage will always
    survive
Like a collection of good books, each one has a different story to tell

Toys

They're brightly coloured and easy to hold, sources of fun for a one year old
Tommee Tippee's bright ideas bring abundance of fun in the very first years
The colours are bright, the sizes just right, they're a sheer delight
They provide hours of play in a safe hygienic way
They're useful and fun and second to none
They are tough and colourful and easy to use, tuneful and noisy and hard to
    abuse
Safety tested, fun-filled teaching toys make learning child's play for girls and
    boys
They promote co-ordination and stimulate sensation
They make child's play of growing up
They're styled with appeal that makes toddlers gurgle and squeal
Even little hands appreciate unbreakable quality and unbeatable value
They are safe, attractive and constantly put to the taste
For a pram trip or kitchen crawl Tommee Tippee designs are superb overall
Eating is a chore and nappy time a bore but in-between times Tommee Tippee
    entertains galore

MIX IT

▶ **It's neat to MIX IT with Cockspur because...**

PRODUCT: Rum

Cocktails cockspurred win praise, shaken or stirred

This message in a bottle mixes harmoniously with a 'Sting'
Mixed or neat it tastes a treat
Shaken or stirred it's always preferred
That smooth, mellow flavour makes any drink 'One to Savour'
It's the record breaker mixer shaker
Specialists perfect it, connoisseurs select it
Every Judy falls for this Punch
Ice likes it, lemon adores it, and 'sodas' everyone else
An exotic potion sets the chemistry in motion
Mixing with Cockspur's Rum is like Britain without Queen Mum
Nine out of ten cool cats prefer it
It refreshes the bars other bars cannot reach
Mixed or neat it makes friends meet
Like the Titanic it goes down well with ice
It beats the Sch... out of you know who
It's the perfect combination for taste and presentation
It circulates with ease, getting to the parties that please
Everyone makes passes at Cockspur filled glasses

MORE

▶ **There's MORE reasons to buy Jeyes at Morrisons because...**

PRODUCT: Cleaners
COMPETITION: Morrisons/Jeyes at Christmas

Jeyes provide good cheer, Morrisons never reign dear
Yule always get bargains so true, yule never feel Bloo
You get a clean bill of health at the checkout
With their fayre deal yule have a real Christmas spread
Wise men know Morrisons is the place for star bargains
These Jeyes that they sell fayres me well
A welcoming home saving ensures ye faithful all come
Whether they flush or squirt their action's a cert
Prices low, products great, win Xmas dinner on a plate
Star value and stable price is in Jeyes clean tradition
Jeyes Santariffic bargains price is Claus for celebration
Everything they do means I'm never Bloo
I celebrate all my shopping days with Morrisons and Jeyes
Only a turkey would shop elsewhere
Their spotless reputations are legend not fairy tales
The money is heaven scent
Of the convenience
Jeyes put the joy back into cleaning
Clean home, low price, Christmas Dinner – that's nice
Bathroom, kitchen, drains, loos depend on Parazone, Ibcol and Bloos

With their fayre deal yule have a real Christmas spread
On value you can depend with lots of healthy dividend
For holidays and high days – buying cleanliness at Morrisons pays
More hygienic, powerful, quick, its multi cleansing span is spick
Jeyes do a good job, Morrisons save you a few bob
Quality tells, quality sells
You can't get a word in sledgewise for good value buys
They make records cuts in the costa my Chopin Liszt
Their stores are bright and clean 'cos Jeyes already been
The outlook is brighter, the bills so much lighter
Budget tight, price right, shine bright, dynamite
I've never had it so bright
No germs will roam in your Jeyes clean home
There will be money to spare for Christmas fayre
They've a sparkling display to keep germs at bay
Having discovered perfection, why risk random selection
Paired to perfection, freshness and fragrance is their connection
Their reliable safety guarantee making extra change for me
Morrisons value, Jeyes care, quality and perfection everywhere
Everywhere is germ free, what more reasons could there be?
I can clean up in more ways than one
At Christmas feel lazy, as Jeyes Bloo works like crazy
They don't charge the earth to freshen your world
With freshness complete it's time for a treat
With these quality brands our health is in safe hands
It's a must to use names you can trust

MUSIC

▶ **Mars, Twix and Tesco are MUSIC to my ears because...**

PRODUCT: Confectionery
COMPETITION: Tesco/Mars/Twix
PRIZES: CD players

Mars and Twix bars are as sweet as the bars in music
The bars of Mars and Twix make Tesco shopping a super (re)mix
Mars confectionery, best by miles, has Tesco shoppers cheering in the aisles
Tesco's prices give the best worth, Twix, Mars and earth
For sound, satisfying shopping trips, Tesco stock tons of Mars and Twix
Tesco shopping – hard to beat, Twix and Mars my planet 'sweets'
Perfect harmony, Tesco and Twix – always on my 'Chopin Liszt'
Tesco call the tune you're Mars-ter of the shopping parade
Record price beyond compare, Tesco and Mars are a classical pair
Mars and Twix a melody mix made a good trio with Tesco

NAME

▶ **I would name my Renault 5 ... because...**

> PRODUCT: Tampons
> FIRST PRIZE: Renault 5 car

SPY ... it's MI 5 (*my 5)

> RUNNERS-UP: Watches

Green bean ... she's green, French and a great little runner
Pickford ... she doesn't half shift
Fonda ... she'd be great to workout with
Soda Pop ... a little gas gives it a lot of fizz
Page 3 ... it looks good in or out of gear
Axminster ... it would be my little car pet
My Little Pony ... she's the best from the Renault stable
Lorna ... it would never let me Doone
Thompson ... I would use it Daley
A La Carte ... it's a tasty little number
Newman ... it's better then a Red Ford
La Rue ... like Danny it makes a joke of the drag factor
Top Gun ... the car I'd love to cruise with
The Mousetrap ... it's a long running success
Applause ... it goes like the clappers
The North Pole ... it's really nippy
Aperitif ... it's a wonderful little starter
The Graduate ... it has a degree of distinction
Prawn Cocktail ... it's a good starter
Major Tom ... its ground control is out of this world
Sahara ... a hot little number with plenty of space
Filofax ... it's bound to impress

▶ **Name the 18th hole on either of two French golf courses...**

Le Professeur
The ultimate Drop

▶ **Suggest a name for the Coalite Dragon...**

> PRODUCT: Coal

Burnie

▶ **Name a person and think of an occupation for his name...**

Claude Daley – Veterinary Surgeon (*clawed daily)
George Orr – Politician (*jaw jaw)
Mike N. Airey – Bird Breeder (*my canary)

▶ The car that most represents my personality...

Must be that old street car, the one named 'Desire', for I'm still a wild lady, (despite my spare tyre)

▶ Make up a Yorkie windscreen sticker

PRODUCT: Confectionery

Yorkie not on board – my caravan'ette' it
Yorkie's the hunk in the car in front
Yorkie drivers like a bite on the side
Yorkie, when size is everything

▶ Name a Trawler

Net Prophet

▶ Write an appropriate advertising slogan for Philishave

PRODUCT: Shaver

A Philishave a day helps you work, love and play

▶ My name for a film starring Jacob's crackers is...

PRODUCT: Crackers for cheese

You've got to pick a packet or two
One hundred and one temptations
He came, he saw, he ate them all
Come up and eat me sometime
The life and loves of a cheese devil
Romancing the cheese

▶ Suggest an advertising slogan to mark Yamaha's 100th anniversary in making musical instruments

PRODUCT: Musical organs

Listen and enjoy the difference
Pianos aren't our only forte
Chopin would have loved one
Easier to learn than Japanese
Even our portables are grand

▶ Suggest an apt, original and humorous name for Santa's reindeer...

PRODUCT: Soft drink
COMPETITION: Schweppes/Coca-Cola & Schweppes at Christmas

Fizzy-Fizzy Pop-Pop
Mr. F.R. Vescence
Rhu-You Know Who
Tonicocobelle

▶ Give an alternative name for the Distinctive 2CV6 car

PRODUCT: Coffee
COMPETITION: Asda/Melitta coffee

Aroma
Melitta express
Mic Moc (Melitta Individual Coffee, Melitta Original Coffee) *(MIC MOC =*
    ACROSTIC)
Sancho Panza's donkey
The grindaround
Cumfi cozy van
Blendy
Melitta special
Mylitta dual
Cappuccino
Citrolitta
Expresso
The mileater
Super bean
Melitta mile eater

▶ Submit an advertising slogan for Famous Grouse Whisky

PRODUCT: Whisky

The Famous Grouse it's class in a glass
Blended with past skills to meet present tastes
An old master in a modern world
From a great past they have created a great present
Upholding famous traditions
For those who appreciate the best
Scotch the birdie
Give any old whisky the bird, buy a Grouse
GAMEbird – SET apart – MATCHless whisky
Don't beat about the bush, ask for a Grouse
An elusive bird? An exclusive whisky
Ensure the bird in your hand is a Famous Grouse
From the best 'still' and still the best
The scotch not to be mist
Up with the lark but to bed with a Grouse
The blend of a perfect day
Measure for measure a real scotch treasure
Di'still'inguished

Aim for the Famous Grouse
Set your sights on the Famous Grouse
Dram-atic
Try the high flier – the Famous Grouse
Grouse puts other whiskies to flight
Scotsmen perfect it – scotchmen select it
Grouse from the hills and liquid gold from the stills
A well made choice for a choice well made
A taste of heaven doesn't cost the earth
Stock and share the Famous Grouse
Still the best
Be game – grin and share it
Great scot – great scotch
A little bird told me about the Famous Grouse
The moor Grouse the better
Grouse season – 12th August to 11th August
Famous to the last drop
Discover the spirit of the wild
The Highland Spirit
Born in Scotland raised worldwide

▶ My name for the new Lotus model for Lynx wearers would be...

PRODUCT: Men's toiletries
COMPETITION: Boots the Chemists/Lotus/Lynx

X-Capade

▶ Name a boat

Lather Nice (*Shield Soap competition)
Pep Sea King (*Pepsi Cola competition)

▶ Name the Fairy Liquid Baby

PRODUCT: Washing-up liquid

Justin-Credible

▶ Name a new cocktail

Green Cocktail – Glass Hopper
Tsar Struck
Rhuff n' Ready
Opti-mystics

▶ Give a name for the Kosset Cat

PRODUCT: Carpets

Walter Wall (*wall to wall)

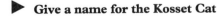

▶ **Name a sandwich…**

PRODUCT: Mayonnaise
COMPETITION: Hellmann's Real Mayonnaise/Childline

Childliner
Bib & Tuck in
Cherub's Choice
Openwider
Repeat After Me
Six-Decker
Mouth-Spreader
Munch and Chewdy
Cress Bang Wallop
Gorilla-Filler
Gannet-Grounder
Glorious Gungy Gob-Stopper
The Hunky-chunky Chew
Refrigeraider Taste Invader
Gourmaise Relish
Hamnaise in Buns-a-Daisy
Spacefiller

▶ **Name a crime novel for Scholl footcare**

PRODUCT: Pedicure items

'By Foot or by Crook?'
'A little Footwork Reveals a Gem'
'A Soft Spot for Sparklers'

▶ **Abbey National Building Society name an island**

PRODUCT: Savings account

Rum-tum-drum Island
Cashablanca
Bootyful Isle
Bone Idyll

▶ **My name for a film starring Princes spreads would be…**

PRODUCT: Meat and fish pastes in jars
PRIZES: Camcorders

'Rightspread revisited'
'The "Butty" Professors'
'Liz Taylor Story – (only "paste" you'll see me with)'

▶ **Name a baby elephant**

PRODUCT: *Paper towels*
COMPETITION: *Quilted Fiesta 'Trunk Call'*

Kitchener
Blotalot
The Incredible Pulp
Willie Wipeit
Justin Satiable
Phanta Size
Mustapha Fiesta
Wrinkle Quiltskin
Gloria Fiestaphant
Nuzzles

▶ **My name for the cruise ship is…**

PRODUCT: *Liqueur*
COMPETITION: *Bols/Make it Fun*
PRIZES: *£5,000 cruises*

'Sym-Bols of Success'
'The Spirited Swallow'

NATURAL

▶ **The Palmolive Collection makes you look and feel your NATURAL best because…**

PRODUCT: *Skin care*
COMPETITION: *Asda/Palmolive win a weekend at Henlow Grange*
FIRST PRIZE: *Weekend for two at Henlow Grange Health Farm*
RUNNERS-UP: *£20 Asda shopping vouchers*

Skincare is now a doddle, too bad my body needs a remodel
Its gentle care is beyond compare
It soothes and clears and takes off the years
I'm programmed to perfection with Palmolive's high-range selection
Only the best bubbles can soothe away your troubles
Palmolive's got zest so it's a cut above the rest
The caring Palmolive Collection makes it the natural selection
It's made tender and kind with people in mind
Now the exclusive is not so elusive
Purely and simply it outshines the rest

NEED

▶ **I NEED Woolworths because...**

PRODUCT: Chain store goods

I get a sense of direction for bargain detection

▶ **I NEED Dextrosol's extra energy because...**

PRODUCT: Glucose tablets
COMPETITION: Boots the Chemists/Dextrosol/Short tennis
PRIZES: Short tennis sets

Playing tennis without it would be courting disaster
Always game for anything, Dextrosol gives me that extra spring
Outmanoeuvring friend and foe necessitates the speed of Coe
I've got too few 'amps' in my pants
Tennis racket, really whack it, not without a Dextro-packet
Over 40 I need all the advantages I can get
Being a blood donor is a very draining experience
Nearing my alloted span, I pack in all I can
I'm at the age when my zip's gone zap
It gives me the advantage that nets the prize
Until Dextrosol came along I was well past sell-by date
It gives me the zip to fasten on to sport
Mum has to be good at 'serving' and rallying around
Whenever I reach 'break point' Dextrosol gives me the advantage
After going all out, I'm often all in
When playing basketball, I soon lose my bounce
Watching sports is my game, taking part is my aim
Being ambidextrous I need Dextrosol for my extra dexterity

▶ **Everybody NEEDS Johnson's sometimes because...**

PRODUCT: Baby care
COMPETITION: Boots the Chemists/Johnson's Miles of Money

Johnson's 'bridge' cradle to pension, gentle products for caring attention
This superb selection provides care and attention
It's become second nature to me, although my nipper's six foot three
They keep her fresh and healthy, even though I am not wealthy
For skin so tender, loving care they render
They keep my treasure in mint condition
She was heaven sent, and Johnson's keeps her heavenly scented
They're perfectly pure and purely perfect
For keeping him clean and content it's money well spent
Although a fine seventeen, she's fair as she's ever been
They're the best mummy can buy

She's the smoothest babe in Devon, 36.24.37
For a gentle touch, no one can touch Johnson's
They're the finest fare in baby ware
Many coins make a mile but a little Johnson's makes baby smile
When you're in the crawler lane you need the right gear
To ignore their dri-way code would be a rash decision

▶ **Travel NEEDS are well served at Savoury & Moore because…**

PRODUCT: Holiday accessories

Their capital selection has the right answer for every case

NUMBER ONE

▶ **Del Monte fruit juices are my NUMBER ONE choice because…**

PRODUCT: Fruit juices
COMPETITION: Del Monte super sleuth win a mystery weekend
FIRST PRIZE: Super Sleuth weekend

They're the fresh fruit taste and zest my taste buds love the best

RUNNERS-UP: £250 leisure breaks

Having detected superior blend, I long to play sleuth on a murder weekend
They're first for thirst and second to none
They are perfectly natural and naturally perfect
Quality and choice come first – the healthy way to quench that thirst
They're pure delight at a price that's right
I have found every pack has qualities its rivals lack
Picking Del Monte for me is like picking the fruit from the tree
Range and price is great with a price that is first rate
Del Monte catch the fruit, squeeze out the juice and trap the taste

▶ **Diet Coke is the NUMBER ONE selling diet drink because…**

PRODUCT: Soft drink
COMPETITION: Coca-Cola/Film festival
PRIZE: Family holiday to Hollywood

Its sparkling performance steals the show, office, home or studio

▶ **Carling Black Label and Sainsbury's are my NUMBER ONE choice because…**

PRODUCT: Lager
COMPETITION: Sainsbury's/Carling Black Label 'See the World'
PRIZE: £5,000 travel voucher

The Sainsbury's choice and the Carling tingle, make my taste-buds multi-lingual!

NUTS

▶ **I'm NUTS about Poundstretcher because...**

PRODUCT: Nuts
COMPETITION: British Airways/KP Nuts Poundstretcher

If BA isn't the best I'll eat my 'kepi'
I can nibble the world's favourite nuts on the world's favourite airline
I have confidence eternal in a BA captain and a KP kernel
I could 'book a rest' in Bucharest without getting in the 'red'
You can go round the world in KP days
I've a 'one snack' mind when choosing travel companies
It's around the world in thrifty ways
I fancy a world-wide nibble, leaving behind the English drizzle
No others can compete when putting the world at my feet
Like KP it still makes sense getting the best at least expense
The nibbles always strike in flight
Peanuts are yummy, peanuts are neat, Poundstretcher holidays make my life complete
UB nuts as well not to BA Jetsetter
After every daily grind, this ground nut needs to unwind
Like KP British Airways are miles above the rest
Just like KP they are Britain's No. 1
They take 'me soh fah' for a little 'doh'
Can-nut deny their attraction – they provide 'nothing to declare' but satisfaction

▶ **I go NUTS over Diamond walnuts because...**

PRODUCT: Walnuts

They're chosen pieces nut just crumbs, freshly shelled and sealed in drums

NUTS

A man struck by the nibbles has a one snack mind
By taking goodness from jacket, they put pleasure in a packet
They're super-crunchi-tasti-sticks-for-hunger-that's-ferocious
You can 'nut' be serious about others
Once tasted, always eaten, as for value never beaten
One's never snookered for choice and always in pocket
One bite turns you into a fan
Great combination, taste sensation, and the 'cash-ew' save ain't peanuts

You may have 'guest' KP is fancied best
One potato, two potato, three potato, four – KP crunch munch munch more

▶ **Why would you like to win a cruise and Disney week with Percy Daltons Famous Monkies?**

PRODUCT: Monkey nuts
COMPETITION: Percy Daltons/Win a week to Disney and cruise

To win a cruise and Disney week would really make my family freak
No longer in our boring ruts, we'll holiday with monkey nuts
Original monkeys natural food, has put us in a nutty mood
Winning would be a dream come true, so crack my shell it's up to you

OCCASION

▶ **For which special diamond occasion would you wear the exquisite Viennetta collection and why?**

PRODUCT: Ice cream dessert
COMPETITION: Wall's Viennetta/Diamonds collection
PRIZES: Diamond necklace and ear-rings worth £5,000

Romantic dinner with fantastic fella, thank you Wall's – signed Cinderella
My next Viennetta – because this hallmark of desserts deserves a sparkling
    setting
Vienna ball – masked mysteriously, sparkling bright, a Viennetta queen for a
    night
When the last slice of Viennetta, like the diamonds, would last forever
Saying to Liz 'mine are better', then softening the blow, offering Viennetta
Sparkling Claridges dinner 'gems' of haute cuisine, flawless Viennetta
    completing the brilliant scene
Enjoying Viennetta's taste of renown, the tantalising jewel in Wall's crown
Candlelit dinner, soft music and wine solitare-y-setting, Viennetta's all mine
Wimbledon – forget the strawberries and cream, Viennetta is my dream
To go to paradise where there is always a second slice

▶ **For any mealtime occasion, Princes products please because...**

PRODUCT: Canned meats
PRIZE: Car

Whether succulent fish or juiciest meat, Princes are in the driving seat

▶ **Melitta, the real name for coffee, brings sophistication to every occasion because...**

PRODUCT: Coffee

COMPETITION: Asda/Royal Doulton
PRIZES: Royal Doulton coffee sets

Now there are four ways to be seduced by a smooth dark sensation

Freshly brewed, piping hot, aroma, flavour, it's got the lot!

Tastefully enticed by rich aromas to savour, you always re-'fined' the real coffee flavour

Day or night, connoisseurs select and sophisticates prefer Melitta

Coffee mug and cup of bone china, when filled with Melitta, there's nothing finer

Served in Royal Doulton after dinner, Melitta completes the course – the outright winner

Serving Melitta will always impress, providing the 'grounds' for social success

The filtering taste of fine roast coffee, is perfect enjoyment, right down to the grounds

In chunky mug or fine bone china, this real coffee's flavour could not be finer

Fine fresh flavour, Doulton coffee cup, hostess me, fills a little one up

It gives me confidence to serve, fine coffee that guests deserve

Melitta's reputation well deserved, guarantees that fresh ground flavour, enhanced and preserved

Smooth taste and pleasing aroma, are awarded the coffee Diploma

For quality, charm or perfect style, Melitta coffee stands out a mile

Melitta knows what is proper and tasteful, the rich aroma gives grounds to be grateful

Whether best china, tin mug or Irish in a glass, Melitta always adds undeniable class

These elegant blends impress my friends and call for recognition

Whether mug on the rug or finer china, good taste filters through

Full bodied, smooth tasting, coffee supreme, served with Royal Doulton, what a team

Melitta's irresistible aroma, perfect brew, adds class to any 'bit of a do'

Even the pourer can enjoy the richness of Melitta coffee

I never spill the beans when it comes to haute cuisine

Melitta Original distinctive and classically blended, ensures all occasions are perfectly ended

That classic pure coffee taste makes Melitta elite-a

This super aromatic blending, ensures a satisfying ending

OUTDOOR

▶ **Kraft cheese slices are ideal for OUTDOOR snacks because...**

PRODUCT: Processed cheese slices

Sealed in freshness, ready in a flash, peel off a slice for nourishment first class

▶ **Princes spreads are the ideal OUTDOOR treat because...**

PRODUCT: Sandwich spreads
COMPETITION: Kwik Save/Princes/Raleigh Bikes & Karrimore Outdoor
PRIZES: Raleigh bicycles and Karrimore jackets

Tasty Princes, full of vits, smoothes away the bumpy bits
Picnic shopping for mountain hopping needs a whopping Princes topping
Princes 'holdall' the thrills when you 'haversack' to fill
Nature's door is ajar thanks to Princes spread
Tasteful sarnies made by mum, help make uphill cycling fun
Princes peddles picnic packing pleasure
The pot's petite, the taste's elite
Princes goes where others fear to spread
Kwik Save be very quick, for English summertime picnic
Yellow jersey, winning sash, Princes flavour in a flash

▶ **For picnics with a difference Waistline means...**

PRODUCT: Low calorie salad cream

That negative sandwiches suffering from exposure are instantly fully developed

PARADISE

▶ **Martini in the Maldives is my idea of PARADISE because...**

PRODUCT: Vermouth
PRIZE: Holiday to Maldive Islands

Soft silver beaches
Bright blue-lagooned
A 'twist' in my fist...
Please leave me marooned!

PARTNERS

▶ **Robinsons Hi-Juice and Wimbledon are perfect PARTNERS because...**

PRODUCT: Fruit juices
COMPETITION: Tesco/Robinsons juice at Wimbledon
FIRST PRIZES: Tennis kits

Never outglassed, it's superlative to the last
Robinsons Barley Waters never go against the grain
At an 'ace' price, it's a deuce juice

I single them out after any sporting bout
Robinsons – every drop gives me a lift
Robinsons always single themselves out for a refreshing doubles match
Measure for measure they add pleasure to leisure
For my brass I get class in a glass
Every swallow is a taste of summer
I pour out the best when I thirst for success

RUNNERS-UP: Tennis ball alarm clocks

The net result is a perfect serve that squashes the opposition
They both give you a real taste of the thirst to win
Both offer rich rewards for the highest concentration
No other in its class will fill a Wimbledon glass
Cordial companions made a deuce of a good time
Wimbledon's the supreme competition and Robinsons squashes the opposition
No other tennis partnership has lasted so long
Record breaking thirsts are made and matched
At Wimbledon Robinsons always win the thirst serve
They're both champion cups
As top attractions, second to none, each are seeded No. 1
They both rank number one for taste, enjoyment and old-fashioned fun
Robinsons is chilled to thrill, Wimbledon has thrills to chill
They serve a deuce of a juice
They are established favourites with a matchless record of service
They maintain interest to the very last drop shot
When it's pouring on centre court, Robinsons always serve an ace
It's a love match
When you serve them together, in a generous measure, it's an undiluted
    tasteful pleasure
Wimbledon wouldn't be the same without the bottles with Robinsons' name
They've style, they've taste, they're really ace
As a mixed double they are hard to beat
They are the originals others strive to imitate
They aim high, serve well and create winners
When the heat is on, the service is real cool
Even Wimbledon champions sometimes require 'thirst aid'
You can see first class squash and tennis at the same time
Top attractions, second to none, Robinsons and Wimbledon are both number
    one
They concentrate their energy on being purely the best
They serve the public well
They are an ace combination
As a doubles pair they're the perfect match
They're both legends in their own lines
They break all records for popularity
The deuces and the juices combine to make everyone cheer
The taste that's desired comes with the name that's admired

Wimbledon isn't Wimbledon without Robinsons
They are a deuce of a pair
Robinsons' is hard to beat, therefore Wimbledon's the place to meet
For refreshment and enjoyment they are a deuce of a pair
One without the other would be 'courting' disaster
Served together they're the perfect double
They both produce an excellent deuce
They go together like cricket bats, church clocks, honey and afternoon tea
Whether the weather is dry or wet, there's always great service down at the net
Robinsons refreshes the Wimbledon successes
Top quality ingredients, top quality players – both are winners
Robinsons serves original juices and Wimbledon deuced good serves
They have a traditional excellence that can't be faulted
They are the champions of tennis and squash
Robinsons are court favourites at all England's favourite courts
No other combination is game, set or able to match this dynamic duo
Known the world over as the very best of British
Premier event and prestige name, they combine to make the perfect game
For a perfect game Robinsons and Wimbledon ensure instant fame
They're the winning combination for a perfect match
They never alarm their fans
Wimbledon's fine in sunshine but when it pours, Robinsons scores
Tennis is the game, the scene is set, Robinsons the taste none can match
They are original, British and best
They are a great British tradition, unparalleled elsewhere
They break records every year
Centre court or under the covers they've poured through the reign
A mouth-watering quencher in every glass is welcomed by players of every class
The famous squash plus the mecca of tennis makes a winning combination for
    this nation
Whether playing or watching, on an English summer's day, you can't beat
    either of them
'Thirst' come 'Thirst' served
At every meeting it's a love match
Robinsons with every batch, squashes opponents, game, set and match
It's a thirst class blend
They're a mixed doubles team that really 'ticks'
Among all the aerated fizz of Wimbledon tennis, Robinsons remains the best
    'still'
Both take pride in the standards inside

▶ **The Airwick range and Tesco are ideal PARTNERS because...**

PRODUCT: Air fresheners
COMPETITION: Tesco/Airwick Fresheners ideal partners

Tesco shopping is a 'breeze' – 'fresh' food and 'solid' service
Pair to perfection, freshness and fragrance is their connection

They're the team with one theme – more for less
They give so much for so long for so little
Airwick fragrance, Tesco flair, give my home a fragrant air
They don't charge the earth to freshen your world
They give maximum freshness with minimum expense
They have everything you need with freshness guaranteed
You can trust Tesco to make your home maxifresh
Prices are right, fresh air is left

▶ **Electrolux and Carpet Fresh are great PARTNERS because...**

PRODUCT: Electric carpet cleaner

They make the pile smile without being a-frayed

▶ **New improved Ariel Automatic and the new Hoover Logic 1200 are the best cleaning PARTNERS because.....**

PRODUCT: Washing powder
PRIZES: Hoover washing machines

They love to take stains out for a spin
Partners should go around together, hope these two go on forever
Without phantom boast or masking fact, nothing equals their soap opera act
They are 'clothes companions'
When Hoover needs a fill, Ariel automatically fits the bill
They bring tomorrow's world to today's wash
Washing lined up for inspection, salutes these partners to perfection
Faced with such almighty foe, stubborn stains give up and go
Nice and cool and quickly spun, the partnership that gets it done
All housewives can profit from their merger
In their field they're no beginners, both clean favourites and clear winners
Their spin and tonic makes mums seem bionic
They're designed and refined for a performance stream-lined
Both take pride in the care they provide
Now I'm Krystal in suspenders instead of Pauline in Eastenders
Ariel provides the biology and Hoover 'chips' in with technology
This packet and model make washday a doddle
Clothes are no longer 'Les Misérables' since this brand new revolution

PARTNERS

With taste so supreme, these two set the scene
They both have no peers, turning tears into cheers
One has style, one allure for the true connoisseur
One pops the cork, the other tops the fork
One provides the perfect starter, the other the perfect finish
Rival products can't compete, this duo combined – what a treat
Every bite and every sip, puts a smile on every lip
Such a delectable double makes any party bubble
One turns a demanding man/woman into a man/woman in demand

▶ **Pommy Chips make the perfect PARTNER for any meal because...**

PRODUCT: Frozen chips
COMPETITION: Asda/Pommy Chips Partners
PRIZES: Non-stick bakeware

Any food would be their slave – they even make the micro wave
They are the new sensation for a chip loving nation
It's as clear AS-DA-light, they're easily the best chips
From speedy supper to distinguished dinner, every time you are a winner
You can't beat 'em, just heat and eat 'em
They're just like my husband, he'll go with anything

▶ **I would most like ... (Person) as an ideal travelling PARTNER because...**

Marcel Marceau ... with him there would be no language problems, anywhere
Captain James T Kirk ... we could boldly go where no man has gone before
Anyone other than Jonathan Ross ... he would would be 'The Last Resort'
Secret Agent 007 ... travelwise and wordly, this reliable 'Bond' is licensed to thrill
Nigel Mansell ... I'd show him a woman is Le Mans' best friend
Christopher Reeve ... airports would not apply – I believe this man can fly
Kate Adie ... conversation should be interesting as we shared a climatic hot spot
Chay Blyth ... he's seen many ports in a storm but never flounders
Mark Thatcher ... when lost, no effort would be spared to find us
Dumbo ... he'd remember the passports and save my air fares
Paul Daniels ... he'd ensure that every location was a magical experience

▶ **I would most like ... (Person) as an ideal travelling PARTNER because...**

A knight of olde ... he'd be bold
Bob Geldof ... he would be my live aid for perfect knights
Ian McCaskill ... depressions lift, clouds float away – his warm front would brighten each day
Ian McCaskill ... he'd keep a 'weather eye' out for me
Neptune ... he would keep his trident working in air-traffic controllers' disputes
Sir Harry Secombe ... the Highway leads to Safeway
Steve Davis ... he's got what it takes to make perfect breaks
Marcel Marceau ... I enjoy a quiet holiday
Frank Muir ... he can 'Call my Bluff' any day
Richard Branson ... balloon, boat or plane, records can be broken – again and again
Andre Previn ... his charm isn't phoney, even on 'conducted' tours
Cyril Smith ... we'd always get two seats
Patrick Moore ... I'd feel like a star in his company

Bamber Gascoigne ... in case of breakdown he'd provide a 'starter for 10'
Nigel Mansell ... life's more fun in the fast lane
Paul Daniels ... be under no illusion – the trip would be pure magic

▶ My ideal PARTNER for an English country cottage holiday would be...

Pauline Fowler ('Eastenders') ... from city strife to country air, the perfect
change from Albert Square
Steve McQueen ... it's time for the great escape
Ronnie Corbett ... not the man of my dreams, but he'll miss the low beams
Buttons ... romantic holiday with a fantastic fella, thank you Country Cottages,
signed Cinderella
Michael Palin ... he would entertain with tales of east and west, whilst
discovering Britain's best
Gandhi ... English country cottages are perfection and an Indian summer
would enhance my selection

▶ Ambre Solaire and Jet Ski Watercraft are a great summer PARTNERSHIP because...

PRODUCT: Sun tan lotion

They make leisure time a pleasure time
You'll 'jet' a perfect tan

▶ Braun and Rover Metro make the perfect PARTNERSHIP because...

PRODUCT: Electrical goods
PRIZE: Rover Metro car

When quality and performance are a must, Braun and Rover are names you can
trust
Quality, craftsmanship, style and precision make Braun and Rover an easy
decision

▶ Kodak Films and Dixons camera shops in PARTNERSHIP

PRODUCT: Photographic goods

Together they keep you in the picture
They are both continually developing better ways of keeping you in the picture
Both have long experience in supplying quality products but keeping value in
focus
Together they offer an unrivalled team which caters for all your photographic
needs
They are positively the best double act in films for miles around
These two together are surely tops, Kodak films and Dixons shops
Kodak's quality provides a perfect image, Dixons' image is to provide perfect
quality

Dixons' price snips match Kodak's prize snaps

Kodak's products are the tops, and Dixons sell them in all the shops

With Kodak productions and Dixons' directions, my pictures steal all the
limelight without casting reflections

If you rifle through Dixons you'll shoot a winner with Kodak

Whatever your budget, whoever you are, with Kodak and Dixons you're the
star

They're growing and developing with current technology

One says wine and the other says cheese

For sparkling eyes and sparkling buys, they're the pair that harmonise

Kodak's quality provides a perfect image, Dixons' image is to provide perfect
quality

If you rifle through Dixons' bargains you'll shoot a winner with Kodak

These two together are surely tops, Kodak films and Dixons shops

PASSPORT

▶ **Shopping for Old Spice at Discount for Beauty is my
PASSPORT to...**

PRODUCT: Aftershave

Duty free goods, to buy galore, whenever I go abroad the store

PERFECT

▶ **Sharwood's chutneys are the PERFECT complement to any
meal because...**

PRODUCT: Chutneys and spices
PRIZES: Hampers

To give appeal, give a meal the Sharwood's seal

The quality is unquestioned, the taste unsurpassed

Omitting Sharwood's spicy bite would be like eating black and white

One good taste deserves another

Sharwood's chutney is the passport to a world of exciting tastes

The door of flavour is always ajar on Sharwood's

They jazz up mealtime blues, my problem is which one to choose

Even to meals prepared in haste, they add that extra special taste

Whatever the season or hour, Sharwood's chutneys make tastebuds flower

The name invites, the flavour excites, fruitful delights for our appetites

They give that extra spice which makes it a veritable banquet

Sharwood's help anyone create winners out of ordinary dinners

With ingredients fine, since 1889, their expanding range has adapted to change
Exotic dish or British tradition, Sharwood's make a tasty addition
A fruity affair or spicy liaison, there's one to fit every occasion
Sharwood's adds the twist you can't resist
Supremely piquant – sweet too, they salute cuisine as no other can do
Pure ingredients plus traditional care, make Sharwood's complement all major fayre
They make the difference between an ordinary meal and a taste experience
They bring faraways tastes direct to your table

▶ **'Neighbours' and Willow are the PERFECT teatime treats because...**

PRODUCT: Butter
PRIZES: Camcorders

For double pleasure use your loaf, relax, switch on and enjoy both
Crumpets with Willow, wonderful treat, with daily fix of Ramsay Street
Finding 'Neighbours' hard to swallow? Spread some Willow enjoy a wallow
Willow for tea, kids' squabbles cease, letting me watch 'Neighbours' in peace
Tears and laughter sandwiched together, friendships rewarded with spreadable pleasure
Love thy neighbour as a friend, love they Willow as a blend
They're an un'Koala'fied success, 'transporting' you after a day's duress
Busy housewife, little time, 'Neighbours' and Willow suit me just fine
They're a 'put your feet up' combination – fascinating viewing and taste sensation
Like good friends, they 'Will O W'ways be there
Willow always tastes the tops, 'Neighbours' tops the TV slots
'Neighbours' tops the viewers poll, Willow tops their teatime roll
Together they make teatime absolutely 'Madge-ic'
'Neighbours' for taste, Willow for cream, put together, a teatime dream
Without them my koala can't bear it and my eucalyptus leaves!
Your camcorder at school teatimes could record Willow and 'Neighbours' being adored
For style and performance unsurpassed, Willow and 'Neighbours' are perfectly cast
From Ramsay Street to Dairy Crest, their producers 'churn out' the best
Being upper crust and well bred, like Willow, 'Neighbours' fame has spread
Gossip from 'Neighbours', Willow on bread, both as tasty and easily spread
They're both legends in their own teatime
'Neighbours' cliffhangers may get you excited, but Willow's flavour leaves you delighted
These two for tea, make tea for two, an essential daily rendezvous
It's Kylie likely there's no better taste
My favourite programme is churned out down under, while Willow is churned out wonder
Creamy Willow with a slice of 'Oz' – Wizard fare if every there was

Once – completely devoid of charm, had tea with 'Flora' and 'Emmerdale Farm'
Both 'Neighbours' and Willow have recipes clever, winning ingredients mixed in together
Both have the quality that matters most – consuming interest, coast to toast
Willow brings taste to every occasion, family, party or 'Neighbours' invasion

▶ **JVC tape is PERFECT for video because...**

PRODUCT: Video tapes

It makes a perfect present ... and past, and future
BBC and ITV are best repeated on JVC
Every 'once upon a time' stays 'Happy ever after'
It's crystal clear and not too dear
With JVC you'll never 'Look back in Anger'
Japanese velly clever tape makers
It prolongs video life and puts life into your video
They last forever, like your memory
The gain of the name is entertainment
You can touch it but no other tape can
You can definitely say it's not a video nasty
Judicious Videos Completely Justify Verbal Commendation *(JVC JVC = DOUBLE ACROSTIC)*
I've tried the rest, JVC is best

PERFORMANCE

▶ **Heinz at Morrisons means outstanding PERFORMANCE because...**

PRODUCT: Supermarket foods

Like Rolls and Royce they're the connoisseur's choice
Quality is excellent, prices right, choice extensive, service bright
They are 'Rolls Royce' products sold at 'Mini' prices
They are never overtaken for quality and service

▶ **Concorde and Cunard combine to give a 5-star PERFORMANCE because...**

PRODUCT: Air and sea travel

Each is the 'flagship' of a fleet – elegant, stylish and unique

▶ **Pierre Cardin OUT-PERFORMS the rest because...**

PRODUCT: Aftershave

Who dares wins
It's a winner on all Sir-faces
Going through other locations is just going through the motions
Its unique fragrance starts and finishes as the very best
For power where it counts – it's fast and it lasts
Down the straight, through the chicane, Cardin Messieurs win again
It's a formula one fragrance
Its sweet smell of success powers it over the line
Lasting qualities, drawback free, win the after shave grand prix
In the pits or in the Ritz – Pierre Cardin fits
A leader in its class – a formula one cannot surpass

▶ **I would like to go and see ... (Show in London) because...**

PRODUCT: Confectionery
COMPETITION: Forbuoys Newsagents/Rowntree Mackintosh/Win a Starlight Weekend
PRIZES: Weekends in London to see a show

'Starlight Express' ... from 'best box' – 'Chew-Chew' way through favourite chocs
'The Secret of Sherlock Holmes' ... I've always wanted to visit the Ideal Holmes Exhibition
'Phantom of the Opera' ... a scarier aria raises eyebrows without being highbrow
... two's company, three's a shroud
... Crawford's influence still grabs 'em – some 'murders' do have 'em
... it would be phun
... it's a thrilling show Forbuoys and 'ghouls'
... because the last Op I went to I slept through it
... Dairy Box in a box at the Opera – Phant(om)astic
... although I've seen it only once I'd 'Stillgo' again
... it's my delight for a frighty night
'Cats' ... the memory lingers long 'After Eight'
... it's purrfect entertainment
'A Midsummer Night's Dream' ... I doth much admire the work of 'Bill the Quill'
... Shakespeare Hath-a-way that cannot be written off
... someone else would be bottom for a change
... when Bottom's on stage, chocolates are tops
... if Rowntree's be the food of love, play on
'Chess' ... it's a Knight out for me and my mate
'South Pacific' ... it's nautical but nice
... there is nothing like a name – Forbuoys
... no harm in wishing I was afishin down there
... Forbuoys there's nothing like a Dame
''Allo 'Allo' ... listen carefully, I shall see 'eet only once...
... after 8 my resistance is low

'Budgie' ... my weekend would be chirpy, chirpy, cheep, cheep
'42nd Street' ... 42nd Street is a 'tap' quality show

Performing, personalities and shows

The unforgettable variety show for everyone
Their prices don't break the bankety bank
They have a good line in family favourites with regular repeats
They know everyone's lines by heart
For star quality without expense, shopping there is commonsense
The scene is set, a spectacular show, everything they've got carries names we
    know
They stage the best show in town with shelves full of star buys
It's the scene for best sellers, with shelves full of star buys
It spotlights good value for all the family
Variety shows...
Always on view with goodies galore, it's a great scene, this family store
They star in the shopping scene, for young, old and in-between
They take their cue from the family man with the economy plan

PERFORMERS

▶ **Fairy Liquid and Seat cars are gold medal PERFORMERS
because...**

PRODUCT: *Washing-up liquid*
PRIZES: *Seat cars*

They're pros, not beginners, fast favourites, clean winners
Both leaders in their class – a formula one cannot surpass
Peak performance is their intent, cleaning up in any event
Dirty dishes, city pollution, Fairy and Seat the perfect solution
Both are valuable liquid assets

▶ **Sony and Sony Music are great PERFORMERS because...**

PRODUCT: *Music accessories*
PRIZES: *Trips to superstar concerts, Sony equipment and CDs*

It is part of Sony's great tradition, to rock the world with their precision
If music be the food of love, then Sony provide the catering
Quality, clarity, power and precision, make choosing Sony an easy decision
When you hear the cry encore, you know it's Sony giving them more
Musical memories fade too fast – Sony sound ensures they last
Top of the bill and connoisseur's choice, only Sony fully capture that 'beautiful
    noise'
Great sounds sound best on a Sony

Sony artists always get standing ovations, thanks to Sony's technological innovations

Once heard, always preferred, for sound perfection, Sony's the word

Jackson, Springsteen or whatever you need, crystal clear sound is guaranteed

Experts perfect it, connoisseurs select it

They define sound better than the Oxford Dictionary

If Neil Diamond, Bruce Springsteen and Michael Jackson choose it, shouldn't you?

Music lovers won't compromise – they like excellence per'Sony'fied

Together they make the perfect pair, listening to them you'll think you're there

Leading the way in technology and art, has been Sony's strength right from the start

When it comes to music power, Sony know watt's watt

The stars and music in the collection, make Sony second to none to sound perfection

Together they're a great combination, always deserving a standing ovation

Critics give them rave reviews. Sony's collection is headline news

They grew to fame, by putting quality behind their name

Only Sony is music to my ears

Sony quality can be seen and heard

This great combination, defies imitation, for sound creation

They're a perfect match and I'm the winner

I always enjoy the superb music they both seem to produce together

With so many sound systems to choose from, only Sony jazzes up my summertime blues

The sizzling sounds they produce are an amazing show of top quality entertainment

They take the shake and rattle out of rock and roll

Sony the first letter in sound

It was Sony that Neil Diamond chose, to eliminate the cracklin' from cracklin' Rose

For technology and sound they are the best, out-performing all the rest

Pop, jazz, quality abounds, rock, classical, unsurpassed sounds

You can enjoy the sound of silence of 'The Sound of Music' with Sony

For pop, classics, jazz or rock, Sony's the epicentre of audio shock

While others may sound distorted or blur, Sony pleases the connoisseur

When you're listening to Sony, you know it's not phoney

The sound produced by their systems, means you can hear live music in your home

Michael, Bruce and Neil, don't go with just any deal

The Sony sound puts fun into funk and turns class into classic

Their technical merit and music interpretation is impeccable

On great occasions the pleasure is double, the finest sounds no hiss, no trouble

They bring together the world's greatest rock stars on the world's best record label

Sony quality is never under par, in Berlin, Jacko and I should wunderbar

The systems sound, the sound's sublime, Sony's the one, the one that's prime

Pound for pound they offer best value around, combined with quality and purest sound

From the opening you know the score, classic Sony receives an encore

They are leaders in a never ending race with no serious challengers

They are always out in front for reliability, purity of sound and entertainment value

The sound you hear, is always crystal clear

Jazz, soul, rock n' roll, funk or jive, treat your senses, Sony brings them alive

From Walkman to concert their performance astounds, being perfectly equipped for sensational sounds

Both are undoubted masters of their craft and bring pleasure to millions with their art

Designed for duty, produced with pride, they're stylish, distinct and dignhi-fied

Of their advanced technology, which always produces products of the best quality and top performance

They've got style and sound, the greatest performers to have around

The combination of quality and electronics, makes Sony equipment supersonic

Who is it makes such a beautiful noise, the entertainment bosses, those Sony boys

They're in perfect harmony with my needs, crystal clear sounds are guaranteed

They make your home host to a star, sounding so near and yet so far

When quality and pure entertainment are the main attraction, Sony gives most satisfaction

They keep my body working right, alert by day, relaxed by night

Supersonic Sony is a music megastar, tip top rock and pop, non-stop repertoire

Sony turns even the smallest event into a musical extravaganza

When quality and clarity are a must, Sony is the name to trust

Sony's reputation stands supreme, setting standards seldom seen

Sony's unrivalled levels of clarity and precision, provides virtual reality in sound and vision

Their track record is second to none, I've disc-overed they're number one

With Sony's swinging logo, it's all systems agogo

Without doubt, I have learned, they leave no tone unturned

All other labels just sound phoney, for perfect sound it must be Sony

Fantastic music, sounds that thrill, Sony technology sounds just brill

They've got everything except an equal

Market leaders again and again, bound to satisfy my yen

For clarity beyond parity, Sony is Number 1

I won't settle for anything phoney, for outstanding performance it has to be Sony

Reputations that are world renowned, guarantee the best sound around

Of that excitement of music played as the artist intended

Experts perfect them, perfectionists select them

The Sony double is the best thing, next to the stars in person popping in

They make everything come alive, for a young 33 or an old 45

The excellent sound quality produced by their systems is the boss over all the others

Sony delivers sound so perfectly, it can be heard all over the world

Their quality product and superb sound, ensure the performance of a life-time, everytime

They are the terminology for modern technology

Top performance second to none, Sony and Sony show how it's done

That sensational Sony sound, leaves us musically spellbound

They duet better than the rest, when Sony make music it's the best

The best only choose the best – Sony

Loud and clear, or sweet and low, Sony soundly steals the show

Sony's team beats the rest, they're noted, quoted and voted the best

Whatever the product, whoever's the sound, Sony starts what's goin' down

Sony sound is so near perfection and Sony music gives the best selection

Sony provide hi-tech perfection, so every track is number one, whatever your music selection

Recordings supreme, too good for the attic, only Sony systems can turn class into classic

Classics, jazz, blues or pop, Sony sound is always top

Their claim to fame is a quality name

Class acts and quality sound, make them the finest duo around

Their sounds abound with perfect pitch and the quintessential quality is music to the ears

Generations of innovations, ensure a truly superior selection, with world-wide perfection

I can't get no satisfaction from any other hi-fi action

Latest technology in tune and in style, pure entertainment with an ear to ear smile

Music makes the day seem sunny and all their products are good value for money

This winning team grew to fame, by putting quality behind their name

Music on Sony, jazz to symphony, is simply the best, better than all the rest

Jackson's quavers never waver, Springsteen's tones never drone, 'cos all Sony performances sparkle like Diamond's

Great sounds were made to be heard on a Sony system

Whilst rivals boom bang and blast, Sony sound is unsurpassed

With superb sound and Japanese precision, Sony music is a winning decision

Walkman, cassette, recorder or hi-fi, they are the best that money can buy

Jackson ain't bad, Springsteen can jive, but Sony systems bring music alive

You don't seem to CD difference, but you will hear it

They guarantee high quality and performance at all times

They're simply the best for quality, performance and value

Whatever the key, they're just right for me

They're Sony perfection you can't tell the difference

Paired to perfection, beautiful sounds is their connection

Together they provide a magnetic attraction, that could prove dangerous when listening to Jackson

They're as smooth as a love song and as modern as rap

Jackson, Diamond, Springsteen too, vote them tops like me and you

They're the highest tech for the lowest cheque

With their CD players and artists, Sony have man and machine working in perfect harmony

Sony systems superior sound, suits Sony superstars down to the ground

The quality is unquestioned, the sound's unsurpassed, Sony equipment made to last

First for innovation, second to none, a back catalogue of success that's born to run

PERSONALITY

▶ **I would like to go shopping in London with ... (Personality) because...**

PRIZES: Shopping trips to London, staying at the Savoy hotel and to see a show

Shirley Bassey ... sights, lights, weekend of splendour, my only chance to be a big spender

David Frost ... to turn the tables on him with a Savoy grilling

Michael Ball ... I'd coo just like a turtle dove if he would show me Aspects of Love

My mum ... working hard she wears a frown, the Savoy would turn her world upside down

Peter Bowles ... landed gentry, man-about-town, an endearing smile and shopping without a frown

Donald Sinden ... I am convinced his savoir faire would guide me through the Savoy fare

My mum ... teenage daughter, trendy mum, look out London, here we come

Nigel Mansell ... he needs a brake

Paul Daniels ... abracadabra and his spell I would be under, but toupee or not toupee I wonder

Geronimo ... everywhere else he's had 'reservation' problems

Ian McCaskill ... come rain or shine we'd get along just fine

Edwina Currie ... she would make sure you didn't swallow any old yolks

Kylie Minogue ... I should be so lucky

PICTURE & FILM

▶ **The Co-op keeps me in the PICTURE and...**

PRODUCT: Supermarket foods

Sets a trail of leading star bargains, definitely deserving an Oscar

▶ **Old Spice is always in the PICTURE at Goldbergs because...**

PRODUCT: Aftershave

Their all star cast is unsurpassed
No matter where you go it makes a lasting impression

▶ **We're in the PICTURE with Princes canned meats because...**

PRODUCT: Canned meats
PRIZES: Camcorders

Before mum says 'hocus pocus', delicious dishes are in focus
Roll camera, 'pan' meal, 'zoom' to table, 'cut' and 'eat'
Epic feasts or snappy eats, the highest standards Princes 'meets'
Lights – Princes – Action, a meal is 'produced' of satisfaction
The family tastebuds record delight, demanding replays every night
Always 'snapped' up the moment they're exposed
'Perfection' portrays Princes' name, tasting it quickly confirms that acclaim
'Meatballs' – take two – roll 'em (in gravy and cut)
Lights, camera, action, Princes is the star attraction
We know Mona's grin – was a Princes meatball – popped in
Even Hannibal Lector must have heard, succulent Princes are preferred
They taste great in Hollywood, but better in can(ne)s
You just 'snap' your fingers to 'develop' meals that 'click'
Meatier than Schwarzenegger! Spicier than Cher! Princes performance we
    prefer
Princes focus on quality – I zoom in for the take
Princes snap up brownie points for using finest quality joints
A 'slice' of this action means no 'cuts' in satisfaction
We 'focus' our attention on Princes and simply love rep'eats
Princes have MGM appeal – Magnificent Gourmet Meats
These excellent performers attract more fans than anything in 'Cannes'
We click for the meatiest 'roles' with no hidden 'extras'
With Princes setting the scene, ordinary dishes become haute cuisine
Everyone knows Princes ace – just an open and shutter case
Mum focuses on price cuts since dad got the 'chop'
They're always 'framing' tasty
In our 'joint', tasty Princes are the focal point
Princes winners in the can, turned dad into 'action' man
We can develop a 'reel' meal in a flash
All Princes fans like 'meating' stars in Cannes
We have auditioned the rest, Princes plays the part best

▶ **I buy Fuji FILM from Index because...**

PRODUCT: Camera film
COMPETITION: Fuji/Index catalogue
PRIZE: Fuji camcorder

Life's memories fade too fast, Fuji and Index ensure they last

► **I trust Fuji FILM to capture any image because...**

PRODUCT: Camera film

I can't picture life without it
Family memories fade too fast, Fuji film ensures they last

► **What to call the remake of a famous FILM featuring Dolmio pasta sauce?**

PRODUCT: Pasta sauce

A dish called wonder
Dolmio grande – a spaghetti western
Guess what's coming for dinner
Plateful attraction
Oh for a few Dolmio's more
Hello Dollymio
The goodmother
To stir with love
Plate it again, Sam
Goodbye Mr Chips
Goodbye Mr Chips, Hello Papa Dolmio
Pastablanca
Surround the whirls in 80 ways
From Dolmio with love
A jar is born
Antony and Cleopasta
1001 Dolmio creations

► **I believe Reala Film is a revolution in colour negative FILM because...**

PRODUCT: Camera film

Reala is now the terminology for accurate colour technology

► **Dolmio is the star ingredient in my kitchen because...**

PRODUCT: Pasta sauce

Forget Hoffman, Cruise and Swayze – Dolmio drives my tastebuds crazy
Dolmio is the only Safeway to have a saucy Italian
It is simply Supermovapastarrificexpertdolmiocious
Natural ingredients, guaranteed to please, Italian cuisine without any E's
No 'Casualty' for 'Fools and Sauces', it 'Masterminds' 'Blockbuster' courses
Its appeal is 'Universal' and its taste 'Paramount'
'Super' smashin' 'simply great' – bullseye scored on every plate
Like Pisa – it's always on the list
A prize performer in cuisine, Dolmio always steals the scene
Produce Dolmio – 'pan meat' – 'zoom' to table – 'action' – eat

▶ **With Jacob's crackers I get a super snap because...**

PRODUCT: Crackers

I never supper from over-exposure
I get 35mms to every packet
This winning line is so compact
Once exposed for tasting, a likeness soon develops
When I unwrap the film, good results always develop
Since 1885 Jacob's have always won in the photo finish
These delicious biscuits I just F.2.8. (*have to eat)
Like the camera, the taste never lies
They're always a delight, 35mms per bite
Say cheese and this cracker wins by a smile
They're the best biscuit since the boxed brownie
Just Anyone Can Obtain Brilliant Snaps *(JACOBS = ACROSTIC)*
Each pack oPEN TAX's my purse so little (*Pentax Camera)
They focus attention on never baking mistakes
I zoom in on the plate before it's too late
I like-a-da crackers so shutter your face
My husband's the photographer so I NAB 'IS COmpact camera *(NABISCO =
    ACROSTIC)*
Each bite means snappy days are here again

▶ **My image is complete with Drakkoir Noir because...**

PRODUCT: Aftershave

Though visually sound, I need Drakkoir Noir for close-ups
It's the signature that attracts admiring glances and closer inspection
Experts perfect it – connoisseurs select it
Handsome, not I, but its fragrance is a graphic equaliser
Pleasant aroma, expertly blended, the finishing touches that Laroche intended
We co-star in close-ups
It brings me sharply into focus
The situation 'lens' itself to zooming on good grooming
It announces my arrival and delays my departure
It has a sharp focus on style
It turned a demanding man into a man in demand
It's the finishing touch that brings everything into focus
Now she loves to share my close-ups
One touch programmes the extra-sensory reception
Drakkoir Noir develops it from negative reflection to positive projection

▶ **I would have my safari holiday photos developed where I see the
Kodak colour check sign because...**

PRODUCT: Photographic processing service

It's a sign of safety in the processing jungle

Why hunt for quality when it can be assured
Without Kodak Kenya's colours become a 'Pigment' of my imagination
If I want my prints up to spec I get them Kodak colour checked
Neither splash nor fleck escapes the Kodak colour check
Kodak ensures my prints are never endangered species
Kodak checked prints mean better wild life tints
Big game treks deserve big name checks
Lichfield, Snowdon or mere beginners, Kodak colour check – outright winners
It protects photographers from the predators of the developing world
Kodak knocks spots of the cheatahs in the game
Kenyan sunset? Dusty track? Perfect portrayal on the Kodak snap
This Kodak symbol stands supreme setting standards seldom seen
Kodak's inspection is my protection
Steady hands, nerves of steel, perfect photos with Kodak seal
Colours bright, day or night, Kodak colour check is right
I want the hue without the sty
They'd never bungle my snaps from the jungle

▶ **Agfa and BMW create the perfect image because...**

PRODUCT: *Camera film*
PRIZE: *BMW car*

You cannot escape their quality control, mile after mile, roll after roll

Other areas of filming

They turn my memoirs into renoirs
It ensures a clear winner at the photo finish
Kodak filter out the poor developers

Instant cameras

I can have a film 'premier' whilst I'm still on location

PLAY

▶ **Whatever game you PLAY, Blue Stratos is essential equipment because...**

PRODUCT: *Aftershave*
COMPETITION: *Blue Stratos 'Play the Game'*

Feeling fresh, smelling great, Blue Stratos – your best team-mate
Game for any 'Sport' it's 'Sport' for any game
When the going gets tough – Blue Stratos gets going
Squeeze or spray the Blue Stratos way will win the day
When under 'Blue Stratos Orders'... you've a clean sporting chance

Out of the Blue comes a fresh clean you
You're home and dry when it's Blue Stratos you buy
Healthy grooming, style, panache, Blue Stratos Sports the winning class
A Blue Stratos Blue in any sport is a clean winner
Sport's no sweat with Blue Stratos on your side
We're all good starters when wearing Blue Stratos
Blue Stratos showers me with confidence
Polo, diving, football, cricket, Blue Stratos Sport takes the wicket
Blue Stratos outlasts the heat and you finish a cool first
For sports gear that is ace, Blue Stratos wins the race
With the Blue Stratos smell, you know you played well
Win or lose, you will relish the Blue's
Blue Stratos Sport keeps the active fresh, cool and attractive
No-one outpaces Blue Stratos aces!
With Blue Stratos freshness, you always feel a winner
The Blue Stratos player always has the advantage
The Blue Stratos user is a winner not a loser
For a fast sporting pace Blue Stratos is ace
The Blue Stratos sporting collection is the winning selection
Whether home or away, Blue Stratos freshens the day
With the Blue Stratos name, I'm ahead of the game

▶ **I always eat Princes Pastes when PLAYING video games because...**

PRODUCT: Meat pastes
COMPETITION: Kwik Save/Princes pastes Wordsquare
PRIZES: Amiga video game consoles

With Kwik Save the 'end of level' jar is always 'a-jar'
Energy packed, flavours galore, they always improve 'Super Marios' score
Watch my fingers go, with a 'sandwich course' in Princes
Kwik Save Princes console winner, has turkey paste for Xmas dinner
Greatest paste by far, for battling the moustachioed megastar
Super fayre, Super Mario, what a pair, no compario
Tetris culminates in despair, Kwik Save's pastes win fair and square
Nine flavours plus Princes action, guarantee 25 'bits' of satisfaction
Kwik Save are prize 'Street Fighters 2' (*too)
They're scrummy, yummy, here's mummy with more for my tummy

PLEASURE

▶ **Shopping at the Co-op gives me PLEASURE because...**

PRODUCT: Supermarket foods

I save, as I spend, as I share

PLUS

▶ **Tea, coffee and biscuits PLUS the Co-op means…**

PRODUCT: Supermarket foods

A little taste of heaven, which does not cost the earth
I'm happy to live a hand-to-mouth existence
Pleasure for palate – and purse

POCKET GUIDE

▶ **My best friend when I travel is an Insight pocket guide because…**

PRODUCT: Pocket guide
FIRST PRIZE: Week in New York

From Greece to Grand Canyon the perfect companion

RUNNERS-UP: Sunglasses

Only Insight has twenty twenty vision
Insight's information incites exploration
Travelling East or West they're simply the best
Seven days in New York without Insight makes one weak
An Insight guide means a ticket to ride
It saves the task of having to ask
It gives me the lowdown on the high spots
I get right to the core of the Big Apple
A pocket guide is the best friend to 'resort' to
I take time out knowing Insight have put time in
It's colourful, concise and cheap at the price
I'm always in the picture without being out of pocket
It leads me safely through the tourist maze
It makes every trip an adventure, every arrival a homecoming
Insight ensures I never feel an outsider
Like a true mate it just tells me straight
It came, I saw, it 'Concorde' my heart
There's help at hand in every land
Holiday visit or scheduled meeting, pocket guides take some beating
Streetwise, pennywise, Insight supplies the smarter guys
Helpful features, small and large, makes every trip a bon voyage
Uptown and downtown it never lets me down
It's small but perfectly in-formed
Without them I'd be a stranger in Paradise
Information first rate – the globetrotter's best mate

They're pocket size and wordly wise
I'm all dressed up and know-where to go
They save the task of having to ask
I'm a sight worse off without them
Travelling with the pros, avoids the cons
Travel's a breeze with their expert-ease
They put the knowing into going
In my case they're the best book forward
Extensive knowledge, handy advice, pictures attractive, format concise
When you've gotta go, you've gotta know
Hong Kong to Bahamas, they're my Judith Chalmers

POPULAR

▶ **I think Capital Radio is the best POPULAR radio station in London because...**

PRODUCT: Radio broadcasting station

It brings a smile to everyone's dial

▶ **Picture shows one cheese saying to another cheese 'Why are we so POPULAR?'... for which entrants had to devise a slogan**

PRODUCT: Dutch cheeses
COMPETITION: Edam and Gouda Dutch cheeses

They can slice us, cube us, grate us, grill us – even scoop us out and fill us
After trying my red and your amber, they know where to go for the tastiest cheese
We're from the low countries – low price, low fat, low calories
We're a colourful pair crammed full of flavour, less fattening but nice with a taste that folks savour
For losing pounds or saving pence, double Dutch makes more sense
Once people taste so Goud-a cheese, they don't give Edam for anything else
Like Dutch tulips we're colourful, cut beautifully, are ideal for parties and cheer up slimmers
We try to please everybody, as the actress said to the bishop
Once bitten twice buy, the simple explanation why

POWER

▶ **Ribena, Lucozade and Horlicks means fitness, health and energy because...**

PRODUCT: *Fruit drink, glucose drink and malt drink*

They give triple satisfaction and energy in action
They keep my body working right, alert by day, relaxed by night
I always sip into something tasteful after a hard day
You get a clean bill of health at the checkout
Ribena ready, Horlicks steady, Lucozade – Go!

▶ Daz adds power to my wash because...

PRODUCT: *Washing powder*

It adds ohm to the foam, lowering watt grime resistance remains

▶ I buy Varta batteries at Asda because...

PRODUCT: *Batteries*

Varta batteries boldly glow, where none have ever shone before
Asda powers the pockets, for Varta to make all systems go
The Varta triangle means space age power at down-to-earth prices
Asda and Varta create low price encounters of the most powerful kind
They beam you up and never let you down
Asda – one small price for man – Varta, one giant bargain for mankind
Even NASA can't surpass a Varta power pack at Asda price
Their power's astronomical, the price in Asda – nominal
They get a superstore of power at a down-to-earth price
Varta are to power what Asda is to savings
Like solaras, Asda and Varta are the perfect chargers
Shopping at Asda they're obviously smarter, so naturally they buy Varta
Asda shoppers are always smarter for value volts they veer to Varta
No other battery, no other store, pocket the difference, who wants more
Varta and Asda are a team with one theme – power to save

▶ I buy Varta batteries at International stores because...

PRODUCT: *Batteries*

For power so bright, Varta's right, International shoppers have seen the light
Varta make light of being International champions
Varta is an International source of power
Many enlightened shoppers carry a torch for International – Varta powered of
    course
International shoppers expect the best, Varta batteries outlast, outshine,
    outclass the rest
They maximise the count-down change when lifting off the Varta range
Batteries without Varta power – like a shuttle launch without zero hour
Varta the wide world over, pack the power of a super nova
I like being smarter with long lasting Varta
I spot star value – that means Varta
I know those blue and yellow packs means Var-ta-lot of reliability

▶ **I buy Varta batteries at the Co-op because...**

PRODUCT: Batteries

With Varta-powered toys the only pit stop is bedtime
Batteries without Varta power are like a shuttle launch without zero hour
A node is as good as a wink with Varta
Ohm or away, 'mais oui' suggest, Co-op and Varta are currently best

▶ **Shopping at Superdrug is electrifying because...**

PRODUCT: Superstore goods

They are switched on to powerful bargains
The prices won't give you any nasty shocks
The sizzling low prices make your hair stand on end
It's gratifying not getting a shock each time you shop
I appreciate supercharged quality at undercharged prices
You switch to a most economical concept in shopping
They're light on price – 'amp'le choice, offers you can't refuse
Their 'current' prices are shockingly low
Prices are down to earth and quality worth a plug
I'm not too dim to spot their light charges
It's alive with bargains at shockingly low prices
They socket to you baby
They throw a little light on the subject of savings
Their sparkling reputation needs no plug
Ample choice, watt a store, prices shock, who wants more
All bright sparks save there, they've seen the light
Their prices generate sparks of joy to switched-on shoppers
The bargains are powerful, the prices are static
Watts high in potential is low on charge

▶ **I use Memorex rechargeable batteries because they...**

PRODUCT: Rechargeable batteries

Are by far the best at outlasting the rest
Are charging ahead in the power race
Are price shattering – their rivals have taken a battering
Are the 'current' hit
Are providers for all ages, giving lost power to wages

▶ **I buy Osram light bulbs because...**

PRODUCT: Electric light bulbs

It's a shining example of watts being saved
Their light charges make us beam
They're just watts needed when daylight's receded
There's no flicker of a doubt they're last to go out

They ensure my money 'glows' further
They are full of bright ideas
You would be left in the dark without them
Osram's chosen by all the nation as the leading light in illumination
With Osram there's never a dull moment
Darkness wanes when Osram reigns
In my view, fitting Osram is the best light exercise for you
Osram have the light approach
Sunlight, starlight, nowt's so bright as Osram light
They are cheap and bright to give 'Extralite'
Edison's idea was bright, now Osram are the leading light
The Osram brilliance leaves other bulbs hanging dimly in the shade
When other lamps whimper, flicker and sigh, Osram lamps refuse to die
Dim is watt I used to be until Osram enlightened me

Batteries

They go flat out when other batteries are out flat
One's fully powered longer, the other's powerfully stronger
I don't like being caught with my batteries down
Their sounds are crisper from a roar to a whisper
They are the big noise in the corridors of power
They take the snap and crackle out of 'pop'
The performance makes Rocky Sharpe, Gary Glitter and James Last
I get encores after the others have played their finale
Good listening is amplified, good value is satisfied
They give a marathon run in aid of clarity
They put more watts in every OHM
They know watts what
It's the best way of playing for extra time
They prefer service and satisfaction rather than the old hard cell
They are part of RAC's super cell-action

Lighting

They've brought to perfection Swan and Edison's invention
Always reliable, always bright, a power of vision day or night
Shining bright or soft, they reign supreme aloft
When put to the test they're the brightest and best
For power so bright I have seen the light
They are full of bright ideas
In the lighting game there's no brighter name
You get a good sight more than those you've had before
Sufficient light means efficient sight
The quality of British bulbs shines clear ahead
They're a shining example of British technology
Made to last, priced just right, they brighten Britain every night
Their longer lasting illumination makes them No. 1 throughout the nation

Their superiority shines brighter and casts shadows over their rivals
Clearly streets ahead, others don't come up to scratch
They have a brilliant flare for keeping obscure brands in the dark
When the switch is flicked, they have the opposition licked
They use the light of their own experience to outshine all competition
On reflection, they're perfection
They are leading lights in the corridors of power
Their peerless performance, perpetually bright, makes them leaders of the lamp
   elite
Their name in lights has reached great heights
They are a shining example of light engineering
Blazing a trail, outshining the rest, needs the safest and the best
They are a top line design with a superfine shine
Light-wise they're streets ahead
They made light of any illumination problem
When potential is assessed they're currently the best
Safety and efficiency are the essential 'elements' of a brighter future
Without a shadow of a doubt they're light years ahead
They have more power, no matter watt
It's so little to pay to turn night into day
It ensures that my money 'glows' further
They're tops for pockets as well as sockets
The outlook's brighter and the bills are lighter
Money stretches like elastic when you fit the light fantastic
They shine so bright on a moonlit night
No-one is left in the dark by their brilliance
Their superior criteria make my interior cheerier
They give glowing assurance of ongoing endurance
Wherever I go I notice the glow
When the glowing gets rough the tough keep glowing
There's no flicker of doubt, they're the last to go out

PREFER

▶ **I PREFER to buy Carlton Marco Polo products because...**

PRODUCT: Men's toiletries

Specialists select them, perfectionists select them

▶ **I PREFER the taste of Douwe Egberts because...**

PRODUCT: Coffee

It adds the touch that makes dinner a winner
Second to none it reigns when it pours

It is by far and away the finest ever to filter through
It's pure, full-bodied, rich and fine, smells delicious, tastes divine
I can sip luxury without having to swallow bitterness
Dinner Over Unanimously We Enjoy Every Grain Because Egberts Really
    Tastes Supreme *(DOUWE EGBERTS = ACROSTIC)*
It's the cream of the coffees and I'm not milked
It gives me no grounds for complaint
They filter the best, discarding the rest
It puts eloquence in any after-dinner speaker
Its blend and roast is first choice for the perfect host
In a world of imitations Douwe Egberts gets my seal of approval
Its worldwide popular flavour grinds the rest into the ground
It's the flavour I can bank on without losing my balance
Everybody knows you'd be a mug to drink anything else
It 'perks' me up so much, I can't 'stir' without it
Every succulent sip is great. Douwe Egberts is my coffee mate
They boast the roast I like most
Dutch Originality Utilising Worldly Experience Ensures Great Blends,
    Exquisitely Refreshing To Savour *(DOUWE EGBERTS = ACROSTIC)*
With aroma and flavour intact – perfection's assured and freshness a fact
Four countries in my cup give me international co-offee-ration at its best
Driving it's reviving, working it's perking, resting it's zesting
It keeps me perked up and full of beans

▶ I PREFER dairy ice cream because...

PRODUCT: Ice cream
FIRST PRIZE: Family holiday to Euro Disney

Low-fat, no-fat, always be wary, don't trust the taste, unless it's dairy

RUNNERS-UP: Cool bags

My 'Sundae' best, scooped in a glass, gives my guests, a taste of class
Whatever occasion, whatever time, its taste sensation is simply sublime
Be it cones, wafers, nuts or sauces, it's really tops for our last courses
Delicious, nutritious, it tastes supersonic, and the range of flavours is
    astronomic
Milk and cream, the perfect pair, no other ice cream can compare
Its creamy taste is well renowned, and disappears at the speed of sound
Like the best creations made Disney supreme, the best ingredients make dairy
    ice cream
Flight of fancy ain't no dream, with every taste of dairy ice cream
Dairy ice cream on my menu, flying Concorde to Euro venue
Dairy ice cream is in its prime, a frozen asset every time
Real country flavour, tasting supreme, you can't match the taste of dairy ice
    cream
Delicious taste and texture supreme, are only found in dairy ice cream
Iced temptation perfectly concorded – sweet inspiration that's easily afforded

Tasty temptation, free from inflation – and imagine the sensation, a Concorde vacation

For the taste supreme, every mouthful a dream, I choose dairy ice cream

The taste of the dairy is beyond compare, frozen for convenience, quel savoir faire

Dairy ice cream is my rule, when I'm hot, it keeps me cool!

It's a star on the Milky Way

Smooth, delicious, la crème de la crème, each 'scoop-a-tonic' – a dairy gem!

I always dream of dairy ice cream, on a Concorde flight, it would be supreme

It's the perfect pleasure for those I treasure

It's refreshing, delicious, really divine, takes my taste buds to cloud nine

Smooth and creamy flavours unite, every lick a sheer delight

Other coolers don't come close, dairy ice cream we love the most

There's goodness and bounce in every ounce

Its extra richness – c'est magnifique, with versatility so unique

Pure, creamy, like its name, a taste of the good life, on a 'higher plane'

Mary! I scream, to my wife, dairy ice cream, love of my life

It is my all-time favourite topping, with a chance to go Euro-hopping

Wickedly tempting, tastes like a dream, nothing can top, dairy ice cream

Its velvety texture tastes so nice, smooth and creamy, my favourite ice

For an ice-cream sensation, milk and cream give the best combination

Pure and natural, it tastes a dream, refreshingly creamy, dairy ice cream

For simpler tastes or haute cuisine, the queen of ices reigns supreme

That fairy tale taste always has a happy blending

Universally adored, like Disney and Concorde, dairy ice cream is a luxury I can afford

In a dish or in a trifle, dairy ice cream's quite an 'Eiffel'

It is smooth, creamy, cold and nice, the taste of the country, frozen in ice

Luxurious taste, must be unique, cool sensation, fantastique

That old-fashioned flavour brings back memories to savour

It's a rich, creamy, delicious treat, nature's best that none can beat

Traditional ingredients ensure perfection, in this creamy, fruity, delicious confection

In the summer heat, it's sheer delight, that dairy taste remembered with every bite

Cool and creamy, rich and dreamy, perfectly concorded, delicious, nutritious and easily afforded

Quality taste second to none, dairy ice cream is number one

Taste buds tired, need a tonic, dairy ice cream – supersonic

Delicious ingredients, tasting supreme, only the n'icest in dairy ice cream

For the supreme confection it's the obvious selection

A connoisseur I love to savour, dairy ice cream's supersonic flavour

Pleasant to taste and sweet to savour, you cannot beat the creamy flavour

 Asda shoppers PREFER Varta batteries because...

PRODUCT: Batteries

They come from a power-packed team where longer life shines supreme
For brighter bulb or mighty motor, Asda's value, I'm a voter
Like Asda, they give excellent bright service at a very economical price
Like Varta, be smarter, join the Asda's conquest of prices
Varta power and Asda's prices – 'watt' everyone needs in the 'current' crisis
Asda and Varta have power in store
Asda's buying power plus Varta battery power means more power per pence
High performance and quality range always ensures a pocket full of change

▶ **I PREFER Duplo toys for my child because...**

PRODUCT: Toys
COMPETITION: Duplo toy box

They turn leisure into pleasure for my little treasure
They make learning child's play
Duplo toys provide the thrills and help him master basic skills
They educate my little son – while he just thinks he's having fun
Play value designed with safety combined, they are strong and colourful with
   progress in mind
With no sharp edges and bright colour bands, they're ideal for little hands
I've auditioned the rest and Duplo are magically the best
Then he can learn to play to learn
I feel no other toys can touch 'em
Duplo's fun way makes learning child's play

▶ **I PREFER the wines of Bordeaux and Bordeaux Superior because...**

PRODUCT: French wines
FIRST PRIZE: Trip for two to Bordeaux

They are Beautiful, Original, Robust yet Delicate, Exceptionally Aromatic,
   Usually Xceptional, Sometimes Unusual but Perfectly Elegant, Rarely
   Improvable, Otherwise Remarkable *(BORDEAUX SUPERIOR =
   ACROSTIC)*

RUNNERS-UP: Wines, glasses and decanters

They are subtle and fine with an elegant flavour, a delicate bouquet with a taste
   I can savour
It solves all problems, answers all questions and meets all challenges

PREMIUM

▶ **You will always find PREMIUM quality at Unwins because...**

PRODUCT: Food store foods

They make life richer for the pourer

QUALITY

▶ **I prefer the QUALITY of BASF tapes because...**

PRODUCT: Audio/Video tapes
PRIZES: Holidays in Turkey

Bought enough to last for years, if I don't win I'll be in tears

They're the latest 'tech' for the smallest cheque

Beautiful sounds, delightful sensations, evoking thoughts of exotic locations

Pavarotti's quavers never waver, Madonna's shrieks are never weak, BASF
    sounds unique

It grew to fame by being a trusted name

Their magnetic attraction guarantees satisfaction superbly recording the
    dynamic action

They are the only repeats worth watching

They are clear and precise at a remarkable price

Documentaries, sockumentaries, comedies for the big fight, BASF has the copy
    right

Great picture, sound, say no more – he should have taped Channel 4

BASF are winners, giving expert results for pros and beginners

Flying on a magic carpet, none can beat them on the market

Pop, classical, quality abounds, jazz, rock, just listen to 'dem' sounds

Other tapes soon fade and blur, with BASF this won't occur

What better reason could there be, than tape recording trouble free

We get a perfect picture, perfect sound – better value pound for pound

Sound and vision reign supreme, with this brand in my video machine

Reflections are clear, colours are bright, watching the vid is sheer delight

Watching Cilla, or rocking to Queen, BASF tapes sound like a dream

Music's clearly heard not slurred, films are always seen, not blurred

I'm so choosy – they make funk more funky, and blues more bluesy

While other tapes may quickly fade, BASF will last another decade

For spoken word and musical note, BASF gets my vote

Their sound sleek and unsurpassed, they are unique and not 'tapecast'

From faintest whisper to loudest roar, BASF tapes clearly catch more

The sound and vision generated makes other tapes look second rated

Every recording gives visual perfection, pity all viewing's the boring election

Whilst lightly browning in the sun, all my recordings are well done

They're in perfect harmony with my needs, crystal clear sounds guaranteed

After the wedding, and without exception, they guarantee the finest reception

Walkman, hi-fi or car, BASF tapes are the best by far

BASF – built to last and perfectly preserve the past

Clear results can't be slighted, with your product I'm delighted

Brand is grand, price is right, I would love your Turkish delight

Quality tapes, clarity of sound, recording perfection, worldwide renowned

Clarity begins with chrome

To ensure my memories stick fast, I need a product to last

Football, rugby, tennis or cricket, whichever sport I won't miss it
Video set to Turkey I roam, perfect recordings when I get home
The colour is stunningly bright, miraculously – my set's black and white
Unlike Andrex, they're strong, long and re-usable
Tried other brands, pretty tragic, switched to BASF – viewing magic
High standard quality and pictures so bright, BASF is my Turkish delight
With quality sound and superb vision, even home movies have Spielberg
    precision
The image is clear, projection ideal, in capturing life reel to reel
For sound and vision with German precision, BASF is the logical decision
With BASF quality I'm besot, recorded for posterity my Turkey trot
To stint on the pound will result in poor sound
Less distortion at higher volume, drowns out brother in the next bedroom

▶ **The QUALITY and flavour of '99' tea is unchanging because....**

PRODUCT: Co-op tea
COMPETITION: Co-op/Leo's/'99' tea

Day in, day out, the perfect brew pours from the spout
The best of its kind helped generations unwind
So skilled was the original blending, it's never required amending
Bought at Leo's, it's a roaring success
It's a good blend from the first to the last bag
Serious tea drinkers 'disc'over this compact package revives all systems
Even mad hatters know consisten-TEA matters
Like 147 in snooker, 180 in darts, '99' is unbea-TEA-ble
Its qualiTEA and quantiTEA has reached its extremiTEA
When you're under par it's a great cuppa char
The Co-op reasoning is 'sound' such 'disc'erning palates are around
As mother always stressed, you can't buy better
The Co-op have got their blend to a 't'
Only the finest tea leaves the pot
It's the housewives favourite with the inbuilt guaranTEA
It's the every day pleasure, for each family to treasure
No fancy gimmicks, passing trends, just finest teas, perfect blends
Why milk the flavour of exper-TEAS?

QUICK

▶ **Nothing else is QUICK enough because...**

PRODUCT: Make-up remover pads
COMPETITION: Quickies/Nothing else is quick enough

For a take-off slick and zippy, nothing can outstrip a quickie

RACE ON

▶ **I want to RACE ON a Raleigh for Robinsons at Tesco because...**

PRODUCT: Fruit juices
COMPETITION: Robinsons/Tesco Raleigh
PRIZES: Raleigh bicycles

I'd look a real wally, sitting on mum's Tesco trolley
Robinsons run a radical race and Tesco are totally extreme!
I'm cool, I'm hip, I'll be the championship bike rider from Tesco
Raleigh, Tesco and Robinsons 'R' best, so I'd be streets ahead of the rest
A racing Robinsons Raleigh goes faster when powered by Robinsons juice
Working up a wicked thirst, with this team I must be first
Being a credible dude with crucial character, I could Raleigh to any extreme
     with Robinsons
I want to be the faster shopper in town
All three are real bad crucial dudes who lead in the fast lane
The wheels are great and I'd never be late
I am mummy's little horror, I want it NOW – NOT tomorrow
At Tesco my inner tubes never tyre of Robinsons carton drinks
I'm small but I'd feel quite tall on a Raleigh
I would zoom and zip and enjoy the trip
Mummy keeps riding my skateboard
With crucial bike and favourite thirst quencher, finding chickens with Dudley
     would be an adventure
It's the best way of 'carton' it home
Ride and slurp and giggle and burp with the Robinsons gang at Tesco
It's more cool than school
I think your advert on TV is really cool, it's the best I've ever seen
I'd look pretty mean on my Raleigh machine
Mummy won't let me race with the trolleys
I will be first past the checkout flag
I want to be part of a winning team
This young dude gets thirsty
With a team like that we'd be unbeatable

RECOMMEND

▶ **Hoover Logic 1200 RECOMMEND Ariel for all their washing machines because...**

PRODUCT: Washing powder
PRIZES: Hoover Logic washing machines

Whatever the challenge, whatever the grime, sparkling results every time

Ariel washes all aglow soft and clean without bio
Reputable, reliable and caring – they're programmed for perfect pairing
It is simply the best quality washing powder around
Wash n' Dry in one go thanks to Ariel auto
When washing day is hell, this combination casts a spell
Hoover Logic, the names's the best, whilst Ariel washed with success
Hot or cold, programmes vary, for every wash, trust Ariel
Launderers automatically win, when Ariel gets Hoover Logic into a spin
Washing's a breeze with names like these
Energy saving – energy giving, join them together for happy living
They're each designed with the other in mind
Ariel gets down to nitty-gritty, Hoover Logic washes – while I sit pretty
Brilliant performance is a must, Ariel kindness they can trust
Ariel always washes right, colours are colourful and whites white
While Hoover Logic takes the strain – Ariel takes the stain
They go together like strawberries and cream
Ariel's power plus Hoover's wand, makes every stubborn stain abscond
For removing grease and grime, Ariel's best – every time
Any program, regardless of grime, Ariel cleans perfectly every time
Stronger colours, whites so white, Ariel first for cleaning might
Hoover Logic's choice is totally logical, Ariel's the finest non-biological
Ariel magic makes stains disappear, without spoiling your favourite gear
With the good Fairy all your dreams come true

REFRESHING

▶ **Sun country wine is the most REFRESHING alternative
because...**

PRODUCT: Wine

It's the most refreshing sensation to sweep the nation
After 10 green bottles you'll accidentally fall
It's a thirst class blend
It's not only a thirst quencher, but also an exciting taste adventure
It's summer sun, mountain air, bottled, priced beyond compare
It's thirst come, thirst served

▶ **When I shop at Kwik Save, Princes fruit juices are a
REFRESHING sight because...**

*PRODUCT: Fruit juices
COMPETITION: Kwik Save/Princes fruit juices
PRIZE: Nova Carlton car*

Princes packs always hearten when 'gaspin' for a Nova Carlton

Where else can three litres turn into a four seater
The number plates you see are Kwik Save – 63P
They're always guaranteed to 'win-Nova' your taste buds
Princes at Kwik Save are a sight for more buys
I am highly 'motor-vated' by the flavours they're created
Princes juices reign supreme: is the Nova just a dream?
They're the greatest reviver for a thirsty driver
Three packs minus seals equals brand new set of wheels
They are the greatest revivers for thirsty trolley drivers
Offering luscious appetisers, there's Nova a nonsense with breathalysers
Kwik Save 'loaded trolley drivers' need Princes juices as revivers
Princes stand out like a 'Nova' brilliant star performer
For finest juice without inflation Kwik Save is an inNOVAtion
Princes juices – thirst choice – Kwik Save prices – first choice
My taste buds come alive spinning me into overdrive
I'm on the right road for the good bodywork code
Quality - Princes rule of thumb renders me a NOVAjoyed mum
Princes juice brings satisfaction replacing thirst with five speed action
When I thirst for the best I drive away refreshed
On a long distance shop it's my pit stop
Such cool juices, no 'Novalty', always trust in Princes quality
Quality seal, price appeal, gives Kwik Save shoppers twice the deal
Their 'thirst' gear sends my trolley into 'Nova-drive'
Their many varied flavours are the starters for Kwik Savers

REGULAR

▶ **I like to make Coca-Cola a REGULAR part of my shopping list because...**

PRODUCT: *Soft drink*
COMPETITION: *Tates/Coca-Cola*

Shopping early, shopping late, Coca-Cola tastes just great
Like Tates, Coke is great to open all hours
Being a Tate shopper, it's my favourite party popper

REMEMBER

▶ **Having breakfast with the characters at the Euro Disney resort would be a meal to REMEMBER because...**

PRODUCT: *Supermarket foods*
PRIZES: *Family trips to Euro Disney*

I hear Donald Duck serves a good egg
Dining with dragons, ducks and dalmations is hardly your everyday standard
vacation
With Mickey so charming, Minnie so sweet, croissants and coffee, oh what a
treat

▶ **My most romantic moment to REMEMBER forever would be...**

PRIZE: Weekend for two in Florence

The magic of Florence, shared by two, treasured FOREVER, a dream come
true

REMINDS

▶ **Drinking Labatt's lager REMINDS me of Canada because...**

PRODUCT: Lager
COMPETITION: Sainsbury's/Labatt's Toronto
FIRST PRIZE: Holiday for two in Canada

It's Canada's finest brew (something Malcolm always knew)

RUNNERS-UP: Baseball jackets

Like Niagara Falls, it goes down famously
It's Cool And Neat And Downs A treat *(CANADA = ACROSTIC)*
The crisp clean taste's sure unique, like Rockies mountain peaks
Any other lager would make me grizzly, unbearable and pine!
Both are chilled, often with ice, thanks Malcolm – So Nice!
Superior taste, refreshing and strong, even the French cannot say 'non'
Of Clough and Mansell, clean, cool, yet refreshingly abrasive
The Blue Jay calls, when Labatt's, like Niagara Falls
The 'True Blue Brew' that grew up with Canada
Refreshing, strong, golden brew, Labatt's can add dimension new
When a can's opened cold, I strike Klondike gold
It's the big taste from the big country
Perfect brew, nothing lacking, sets you up for lumberjacking
Its refreshing power lifts me up higher than the CN Tower
Labatt's lager is unsurpassed, Labatt's Blue Jays are never out-classed
A Drinker Always Needs A Can *(CANADA = ACROSTIC)*
Snow capped mountains, crystal streams, ice cold Labatt's, stuff of dreams
Labatt's answers when thirst calls, with power like Niagara Falls
Every 'can' leads to an 'ada' one
Prairies, lakes, Rocky Mountains, Labatt's flows like crystal fountains
Both excite me, both delight me, both please invite me
Blazing sunshine or freezing cold, always an experience to behold
It's in the can, like Mounties getting their man

Without a Labatt's four-pack, I'm a lumber-jack
Refreshing taste, crisp as snow, laughter, excitement and Labatt's glow
It puts the 'Can' in Canada
First rate taste, spruce presentation, is their 'province' and 'dominion'
Labatt's in hand, skydome glory, every 'pitcher' tells a story
It's the smoothest way to take a rocky trip
Keen like a 'booted Mountie', kicks like a 'bootie'
I CAN-A-DA think of drinking anything else
After downing mine, I can see 'tree fellers'
From Toronto to Vancouver, Labatt's is Canada's thirst remover
Every 'pitcher' tells a story, Canadians love Labatt's 'striking' glory
It's the fresh taste of the wild country
Labatt's ringpulls, like Niagara Falls, are my favourite watering holes
I'm a Can-a-day man, Blue Jay fan
Thinking of maples, mounties and lakes, thinking of Labatt's Canadian greats

RESULTS

▶ **You can look forward to better RESULTS where you see the
Kodak monitoring service sign because...**

PRODUCT: Photographic processing service

Kodak keeps the tabs on the labs
It means Kodak makes sure the focus is on quality
It points the path to perfect prints
The Kodak seal means a quality that's real
It ensures a clear winner at the photo finish
It guarantees expert fingers on your prints
It's a hallmark of consistent and high processing standards
Kodak's careful inspection produces prints of perfection
They add science to the art of bringing back memories
The quality's assured after the suspense you've endured
If you count on quality it's where quality counts
Only the best will pass the test
Kodak filter out the poor developers
The labs they test surpass the rest
Kodak keep laboratories on their toes
They don't need second chances to make good first impressions
You get the best back when it's checked by Kodak
It is the symbol of quality, reliability and complete satisfaction
Kodak's eye view ensure the colour's true
Kodak oversee what I saw overseas

RIDING & CYCLING

 I want to RIDE on a Raleigh Extreme bike because...

PRODUCT: Fruit juices
COMPETITION: Sainsbury's/Robinsons
PRIZES: Raleigh Extreme bicycles

My bike got pinched and I am not getting another one
Raleigh bicycles go where other vehicles fear to place their tread
It gives cycle encounters of the preferred kind
I would be hop, hop, happy on a Raleigh
To Raleigh down the alley, skedaddle on a saddle, would be 'extreme'ly fun for
    a Robin'son
I'd win every rally with a Raleigh
I rate it great!
My dream is to drive a mean machine that is ozone clean
It's better than riding in the back of my mum's Skoda
I would feel like I'm rocketing into space
The girls won't be able to catch me
Smart wheels for short legs
I could drive it 'round the bend' instead of my daddy
It's healthy, trendy, environmentally friendly and makes my friends 'green' with
    envy
I'd look daft carrying it
Dear Mister, I want to catch up with my sister
They are very snazzy
I'd love a new bike for my new school

▶ **Yeoman is really fit for the family because...**

PRODUCT: Dried mashed potato
PRIZES: Bicycles and back packs

It's a natural link in the nutrition chain
For great taste at high speeds it's geared to our needs
It boosts the figure – but not the vigour
Ride through the nineties with convenience and ease, healthy family, appetites
    pleased
It's passed the family proficiency test
We race to finish first to get seconds
It keeps them in top gear all year
Four-star fuel for family fill-ups
When the going gets touch, Yeoman is 'wheelie' fun-tastic stuff
After our cycling trips it's healthier than chips
It's instant nutrition for our inner tubes
Its benefits are clear, it keeps everyone in top gear
Its track record is second to none, always my number one

It's so quick you don't need to wait training
High fibre, energy, vitamin C – means no couch potato family
Other instant mash potatoes just don't work out
It is rich in fibre and value for Yeo-money
It never takes us for a ride but makes us warm inside
Most nutritious product of the pack gives the dream all others lack
They wouldn't be saddled with anything else
It's an instant success we never tyre of
It's what active families like, showing great minds think abike
Wherever you wheel and deal, Yeoman puts you on the right track
It's the goodness from within that keeps my family trim
It's good for the diet and prolongs the life-cycle
High fibre and low calories mean no spare tyres
For speedy spuds it's the finest handle bar none
Seven days without it makes one weak
Yeo Man! It's cool for instantly recycling energy
It ain't heavy and it's no bother

▶ **If I win first prize, I would RIDE my bicycle to ... (Place)
because...**

PRODUCT: Newsagents goods
COMPETITION: Forbuoys Newsagents/Raleigh
PRIZES: Raleigh bicycles

Bottle banks ... I like to get things re-cycled
Health farm ... no more spare tyres for this bicycle belle
Ben Nevis ... I want my fitness to reach a peak
Cycling proficiency classes ... who dares loses – who cares wins
Speakers' corner, Hyde Park ... it's the best place to hold a Raleigh
Bank Manager ... it would prove I can balance
Really swish restaurant ... at sixteen I can't handle bars
Amsterdam ... my solitaire needs perfect setting
A seance ... where flagging white spirits would start to Raleigh
The highest safety standards ... I want a long life cycle
The Stock Exchange ... I want to be a big wheel in the City
Smithfield Market ... everyone would want a butchers at my bike
'Ackney ... it's my favourite spot
Looe ... I need to get there quickly
Plymouth ... Sir Walter's ghost would enjoy bowling along a Raleigh
Thailand ... I'm no globe trotter, just think Siam (*I am)
Liverpool ... it's the town that made four boys famous (*Forbuoys)
Norway ... it's the only way I can 'a-fjord' to travel
Fitness ... I'm tyred of having my frame spoken about

▶ **CYCLING is a good form of transport because...**

PRODUCT: Bicycles
PRIZES: Raleigh bicycles

Never mind the four wheel drive, two wheels keep your heart alive
Avoids motorway melee, city crawl, ideal for families, and fun for all
It's good clean fun for everyone from great-grandad to great-grandson
Everyone can 'Raleigh' around, whether it's pleasure, work or Tesco bound
It's trendy and trustworthy and terrific in traffic
It keeps you well on the road to a healthy life-cycle
It's a right healthy 'old knees up'
Any spokesperson would agree, fun and fitness are the key
A new frame transforms old masters into pictures of health
It's reliable when traffic's perverse, stretching your muscles but not your purse
In the Tour de Shops it comes out tops
Saddling your trusty steed beats the bus and train stampede
Happiness is bike shaped
Any time I like, I can ride off into the sunset
Discovering the countryside takes my breadth away
Surely 10 million Chinese can't be Wong
It's the link in the chain that gets you places
It still costs less than a penny farthing a mile

▶ **I RIDE in style with Club because...**

> *PRODUCT: Chocolate biscuits*
> *COMPETITION: Wm Low/Jacob's Club biscuit multi-packs 'Ride in Style'*
> *PRIZES: Raleigh bicycles*

My inner tubes never tyre of them
On the hills – on the street, real thick chocolate, hard to beat
Plain milk, orange or fruit, keeps me going to finish the route
Like my puncture outfit, it's compact and effectively fills a hole
You can't beat a man with a Club
Handy for my saddle bag, boosts me when I start to flag
Club can 'Raleigh' and revive, keeping pedal power alive
Crossing hills or moorland track, Jacob's are the ones I pack
You're biking the right track when biting the right snack
It's the exclusive Club with low membership fees
When I brake for a bite, a Club feels just right
With supplies of Club in pockets, Raleigh bikes will go like rockets
They 'Raleigh' my 'low' spirits when I need a break
Club Lessens Uphill Blues *(CLUB = ACROSTIC)*
One bite of these chocolate bars, I'm Evil Knievel jumping cars
Trendy bike smart and new with Jacob's Club my dream come true
First in flavour, full of energy, Club should wear the yellow jersey
You are streets ahead with chocolate biscuits that are miles better
Tour de France, the race supreme, Raleigh and Club the unbeatable team
They put wings on my heels and whizz in my wheels

Washday CYCLES and CYCLING

A cycle a day washes the blues away

You will never get your Ariel pinched
The only pump needed is one for the tyres
It makes life richer for the tourer
Like Ariel it allows me to get clean away in top gear
A good spin keeps you white on to the end of the load
While cars that queue remain quite static, your 'Ariel' view is automatic

RIGHT

▶ **I find Johnson's RIGHT for my baby because...**

PRODUCT: Baby care

They keep her fresh and healthy, even though I am not wealthy
For skin so tender, loving care they render
She was heaven-sent, and Johnson's keeps her heaven-scented
They're perfectly pure and purely perfect
Although a fine seventeen, she's fair as she's ever been
They're the best that mummy can buy
For a gentle touch, no one can touch Johnson's
They keep my little treasure in mint condition
For keeping him clean and content it's money well spent
She's the smoothest babe in Devon – a sleek 36-24-37
They're the finest fare in baby ware
Their high degree of care is way beyond compare

▶ **Vileda are just RIGHT for the modern kitchen because...**

PRODUCT: Cleaning cloths

With uses so extensive they are far from expensive

ROAD

▶ **Robinsons fruit juice keeps you on the road because...**

PRODUCT: Fruit juices
COMPETITION: Tesco/'Robinsons Keeps you on the Road'
PRIZES: Miniature Robinsons vans

A refreshing container of Robinsons with me, I'm happy trucking my HGV
For dryness and thirst it's the one I'd choose first
Motorways or moorland track, Robinsons is the one I pack
It's the one bottle-neck I enjoy getting stuck in
Like the A.A., if you break down, you're soon recovered

Their orange, lemon, grapefruit or lime, keeps me alert and fresh all the time

Geared for kids it's on the right track

From Scotland to England everyone says 'Tarmac'

That real fruit flavour is a real life saver

It's four star unleaded, keeps the driver level headed

With motorways slow and bottle-necks worse, it cools your temper while quenching a thirst

Its power of revival promotes your safe arrival

Drinking Robinsons night and day, keeps me trucking all the way

It's refreshingly different, surprisingly nice, three different flavours, reasonable price

It's the perfect 'break' fluid

With every drop I get a lift

It turns a hot cross tourist into a real cool driver

With Robinsons for company you won't need a hard shoulder to cry on

You 'juice' keep rolling along

It's a million times better than a 'Jug-a-nought'

It's a recovery service next to none – gives inner strength to carry on

Coming and going, to-ing and fro-ing, your taste buds will savour the rich fruity flavour

The 'juice' in the bottle keeps your foot on the throttle

Being 'loaded' with energy and 'stacked' with fruit

Safe driving's guaranteed whatever the route

For long journeys or small, it's the best drink of all

Splendid drink on which I thrive, also I can drink and drive

It helps you to function to Spaghetti Junction, and keeps you alive on the M25

Their famous juice is right on course, for miles of smiles, the driving force

It's your personal 5-star fuel solution, in various colours and no pollution

Its fruity taste is so reviving, the perfect companion for long distance driving

On a long distance haul, it's the juice to beat all

Need a brake? Engage thirst gear, pick-up and tilt for fruitful cheer

They go together, whatever the weather: a great British reviver, and a driver's survivor

I always boost my personal throttle, can't go wrong with a Robinsons bottle

Robinsons keeps you in the driving seat with a formula one can't beat

With Robinsons at your side you'll be in over-drive

When drivers Robinsons imbibe, they go from thirst gear to overdrive

With Robinsons you come alive, out of thirst into four wheel drive

Wheels in motion, your mind on the road, drinking Robinsons the best Highway Code

Brain is alert, tiredness kept at bay, when drinking and driving the Robinsons way

Whatever your route or general direction, Robinsons give you fruitful perfection

Robinsons is the route to the real taste of fruit

For the drink that's miles better, be a Robinsons go-getter

Robinsons is wonderfuel

In this world of automation, Robinsons provides the most refreshing lubrication
When the going gets tough, it's refreshing stuff
You are well in front when you've left your thirst behind
Squashed up in a mini you still arrive looking 'Porsche'
It's a recovery service next to none, gives inner strength to carry on
It's a first class reviver for the long distance driver
With Robinsons' fruity refreshing blend, I'm in top gear to the journey's end

ROBBERY & CRIME

▶ **I would like to commit a daylight robbery because...**

PRODUCT: *Supermarket foods*

A smash in grub raid would steal my family's hunger away
I could escape with the cake and miss the pay-off

▶ **You can't forge a Guinness because...**

PRODUCT: *Beer*

The wrong hops wouldn't leave you a keg to stand on

▶ **I would like to investigate a mysterious murder with Kestrel and McEwan's Export because...**

PRODUCT: *Lagers*

Elementary, my dear Watson – I always detect when something's brewing
Having tackled my first case, I could murder another
With murderous intent my thirst is well spent
My wife would kill me if I bought another brand of beer
They're taste thrillers and thirst killers
These two brews provide the clues to beat those murderous mystery blues
Even Poirot's intellect couldn't detect company more select or more refreshing
It's thirsty work being a super sleuth

▶ **The real secret of an R. Whites Lemonade drinker is...**

PRODUCT: *Lemonade*

A hidden cache, a quick look round, a sparkling glass, contentment found

Blue Riband biscuits competition

PRODUCT: *Chocolate biscuits*

Blue Riband has lined up Britain's richest wafers and got them well covered
When anyone asks 'who wants Blue Riband' it's always 'hands up'

Drink with a prison theme

Alcatraz a famous 'clink', imprisoned with my favourite drink

Supermarkets

The 'coppers' I save there help 'arrest' the rising cost of living

Travelling on the Orient Express with a 'Who dun it?' theme

PRODUCT: Train travel

I'd love to swap my pinny for a trip with Albert Finney

History, mystery, a hint of romance, background to murder? I'd take the chance

'On the track' of a boredom killer, I'd be 'carried away' by this armchair thriller

To travel in luxury, comfort and style, would carry me spellbound, mile after mile

Being the scene of Agatha's 'Who Dun it', a dream would 'Christie-lize' if I won it

I'd love to travel with a hint of mystery to a city with a mint of history

Chosen by Christie, Fleming and Green, the first-class Pullman with first-class cuisine

ROCK

▶ **Red Rock cider competition**

PRODUCT: Cider

When the scene is particularly thrilling and the atmosphere somewhat spine-chilling, pour out a jar, of this Somerset star, which definitely deserves top billing

Rock and Roll is here to stay, it's much too good to fade away, it kept the fifties on the map, and bridged the generation gap

Rock and roll is here to stay, I've got no time to lose, I have to pass my jiving test, and clean my blue suede shoes

Rock and Roll is here to stay, because the rockers still rock, the jivers still jive as music for pleasure keeps it alive

Once you've tasted Red Rock, all the rest are out-ciders

It grapples with my inhibitions, and thrills me to the core

It's liquid bliss at a premi-yum, knocking socks off tippling tedium

Well Red drinkers need no persuasion to make each glass a great rockasion

Red Rock cider 'boulder-ly' goes where no cider taste has gone before

With applevescence alive and kicking, this scrumptious cider takes some licking

Smack your chops, lick your lips, even Spanish ladies do the splits

It's the apple alliance of science

It has Oscar winning flavour for which fans clamour
It's a topless bottle stripped for action, Red Rock's 'fizzique' has a 'pressing'
    action

ROMANCE

▶ **Les Romantiques/L'Oréal adds ROMANCE to my hair because...**

PRODUCT: Hair care
COMPETITION: Les Romantiques/L'Oréal

They make hair soft as a lover's whisper
L'Oréal is the perfect key to all shining locks
They hold the golden key to beautiful hair
It gives my hair the soft appeal of moonlight
L'Oréal wakes up the sleeping beauty of my hair

▶ **Eating a Cadbury's Flake in Florence is very ROMANTIC because...**

PRODUCT: Confectionery

Sweet sensations, Florentine charms, no wonder we melt in each other's arms

▶ **Pretty Polly styles are ideal for a ROMANTIC night out because...**

PRODUCT: Tights

These glamorous foundations gently enhance, guaranteeing many an admiring
    glance
Legs look longer and slimmer when Pretty Polly softly shimmer
Colours, sizes, quality wear, never a hitch, always a stare
Silky soft, delightfully sheer, makes him happy, having you near
A special evening surely begs for perfect Pretty Polly legs
Luxurious and ultra light, elegantly dressy for that special night
Romantic dinner with fantastic fella, thanks to Pretty Polly – Signed Cinderella
The range is extensive and far from expensive
When style and sensuality really matter, Pretty Polly always flatter
Affordable prices, luxury feel, created for maximum appeal

▶ **What makes your ROMANTIC man so special that you would like to visit Rome with him as the weekend guests of Mills & Boon?**

PRODUCT: Books

COMPETITION: *Mills & Boon Romantic Partner*
PRIZES: *Weekends for two in Italy*

Paul buys me perfume, cards and flowers, loves good wine and happy hours
Italian panache, good looks to match, with Mills & Boon, he's my winning catch
He shares, is always there, he'd make this second honeymon a perfect affair

► **Weddings and Mateus Rosé are the perfect match because...**

PRODUCT: *Wine*

It's for richer, for pourer, for better, for thirst
Bridegroom sparkling with pride, rosé for the bridesmaids, white for the bride
Of the pearl bottle, the gold label and the diamond sparkle

SAFE

► **I feel SAFE with Safeway because...**

PRODUCT: *Supermarket foods*

Safeway's prices don't hit the roof and are safe as houses
The quality of their produce is the Safeway to fine living
I'm secure in the knowledge that poor quality is barred
It would be criminal to shop anywhere else
It holds the key to successful shopping
There's no risk of getting anything but the best
It's the store where my purse never gets mugged
My 'counter attack' beats their 'shelf defence'
They lock quality in and high prices out
They are always open when I need them for choice and value

► **Huggy Bear helps me to play with my toys SAFELY because...**

PRODUCT: *Safety Regulations*
COMPETITION: *Huggy Bear/Safety in the Home*
FIRST PRIZE: *Family holiday to Legoland plus £500 cash*

What to keep? Which to buy? He educates my parents and I

RUNNERS-UP: *Huggy Bear teddy bears*

Children know when Huggy has spoken, tidy the toys, trash the broken
Hospital's not the place for me, home is where I'd rather be
Mummy teaches me to share, Huggy teaches me to care
He makes my mummy think
He shows mummy what is best. As I play, her mind's at rest
Everyday before I play, I remember what he had to say

He helps me see how things can be dangerous to me
Cuts and falls are never nice, so I always follow Huggy's advice
In his fun way he makes learning child's play
Huggy says don't clown around, keep those feet safe on the ground
Without a doubt he knows how to keep trouble out
Only fools ignore Huggy's rules
Where children are concerned, he's a real care bear
Huggy thrives on saving lives
His safety first turns leisure into pleasure for my little treasure
Know Huggy – Know Fun. No Huggy – No Fun
Huggy Bear is really brill, he teaches us home-safety drill
He's just the ticket for a safe 'trip'
Huggy Bear's rules are common sense and they stop me causing accidents
His tips are tops for tiny tots
If Huggy says O.K. I know it's safe to play
Huggy's tips – no hospital trips
If I play safe today I'll enjoy tomorrow
Made in the right mode he knows his safety code
He gives me advice on keeping toys nice
He has the best tips on his fingers, sorry I mean paws
Huggy's 'ABC' is special with toys – 'Always Be Careful'
Huggy teaches ABC, always be careful is his plea
His balloons tell everyone, how to play safe and have fun
His woolly head, wise and kind, gives my mummy piece of mind
Making me aware of danger, makes disaster a stranger
He reminds me tears of joy are the only ones wanted from a toy

 Volvo cars are among the SAFEST on the road because...

   PRODUCT: Car

Volvo really care about its VIPs – Very Important Passengers
They start with safety and stop with style
Volvo determine the risks and avoid them for you
The prime consideration from conception to production is passenger safety

Road SAFETY and safety in general

It's better to get it dead right than be dead, right?
Be alert today and still alive tomorrow
It could be your funeral if you're not careful
Taking care with simple checks, saves so many precious necks
Use your head today, don't be a headline tomorrow
I want to go fishing without going missing
Being careless in (around) water could make your life shorter
They are on the right road
They know their highway code, steering clear of cavities in the road
They're no fools, they stick to the rules

They take lots of care to make accidents rare
Make your goal speed control
Here lies a driver, gone at last, passed on because he wouldn't be passed
Reckless driving makes angels out of fools
Drivers who think first, last
Fast drivers serve more time than they save
Ease-up when there's a freeze-up
A good turn has prevented many a bad accident

Toothpaste SAFETY theme

PRODUCT: Toothpaste

They brush up each day to show a faultless display
It's smile and be seen, start fresh and stay keen
While confident smiles make all aware, their dental care is beyond compare
The operative word is prevention to see that teeth get regular attention
They know it's better to prevent than lament
They brush with care and not with danger
They give risks the brush-off
They recognise dangers on life's highway, whether from traffic or tooth decay
They're alert to dangers dental and risks environmental
They brush away the risk of acci-dental damage
They take care on their way and avoid tooth decay
They think ahead, avoid neglect, follow the code, brush to protect
Remembering the drill – they're keenly aware, looking ahead with routine care
They've put the brakes on tooth decay, by regular brushing every day
They take that extra bit of care in looking after their 'choppers'
Signalling dental hygiene's right of way, back-pedalling paths in tooth decay
With minds Aqua-fresh and smiles Aqua-bright
Aquafresh fluoriders, safe and sound, brush up, brush down and all around
Aquafresh fluoriders you can trust they know careful action is a must
Whatever their route or general direction, Aqua fluoriders gain protection
Fluoriders concentrate on safety, while 'A1' teeth pass filling stations
Beechams teecham fluoride proficiency, 'Fluo-riding' with Aqua

SAILING

► **Asda makes shopping plain sailing because...**

PRODUCT: Supermarket foods

Each store is loaded with goods but the prices are still docked
They know the ropes which enable them to sail ahead
My cash flow is only a trickle but Asda lets me splash out a bit

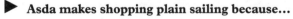

▶ **You can taste the good life with Longboat butter because…**

PRODUCT: Butter

Its natural flavour is tops and sails ahead of others

▶ **I would like to get together with my family and the Fidelity Telecentre because…**

PRODUCT: Electrical goods
PRIZES: Family cruises aboard the Canberra

Looked at from any angle it sounds like a good idea
It's a superb example of family planning
It's four for one and one for all
One 'can berra' night in together with such a choice in quality entertainment
Fidelity's capacity for quality means clarity begins at home
For once we'd all be on the same wavelengh
That might turn land-lubbers green but they'd still enjoy Fidelity's spatial scene
As a 'crew' we all agree, it's the ultimate in entertainment from Fidelity
For harmonious relations nothing's remotely as switched on
I could control them all at the touch of a button
They are both a loyal unit

▶ **Bisto makes all the difference because…**

PRODUCT: Gravy browning

When the boat comes in, it's full of flavour
When the boat comes in it's 'shore' to please
Bisto gets everyone's vote, nobody wants to miss the boat
Bisto tops off meat a treat
The taste and flavour do the meal a favour
It's made with ease and sure to please
Rich, dark and inviting, it makes meals exciting
From simple meal to festive treat, Bisto complements the meat
It's the dishy addition that's now a tradition
Smoothly blended, piping hot, Bisto flavours top the lot
It makes any meal m-AHH-vellous

▶ **Splashing out with Old Spice means…**

PRODUCT: Aftershave

Riding on the crest of a wave from pre-electric to after-shave

Biscuits and crackers with a boating theme

You're a cracker, let's be mates, spreading happiness on the nation's plates
Everyone loves to spread it about with a tasty little cracker
They're delicious, nutritious, tastefully light, in every way exactly right

Best kept under 'lock' and 'quay' to 'bridge' the gap 'tween lunch and tea
As a 'crew' we all agree, wat-er-way to finish our tea

Captain Morgan rum and a pirates theme

PRODUCT: Rum

In spirit Henry Morgan is still the Governor
This is no pirate, it's genuine
This Captain's treasure 'sales' ahead of all rum runners
Every sale is a voyage of discovery
It supplies the main bracer
It's a case of Caribbean delights
It's the only good black mark around
It's the only tot that's got the lot
It gives you that rum feeling
It stands out, tall, dark and handsome
Captain Morgan's rum is always my first port of call
With Captain Morgan breaking the ice, each schooner led to paradise
They have oceans of appeal with the Captain Morgan's seal
Now I have something to declare at customs
I went overboard for Captain Morgan's winning spirit

Cruising

It's the perfect way to fathom out the secret of the bottle
They sailed smoothly down the hatch with flavours unmatched
The message in the bottle is refreshingly new
It's a great destination for a quenching sensation
A great base gave me a perfect lift off to a sparkling splash down
I enjoy them because of their distinctive taste, which ensured they were sunk
    without trace
They have the taste that launched a thousand sips
'High' spirits from the land of quality have me floating on CTC
Sinking a few buoyed me up and I cruised through the day
They are voyages of discovery in the best possible spirit
They have obviously gone overboard to ensure a smooth passage
They subtly capture the rapture of life on the ocean wave
The extra golden touch put me on the crest of a wave
They harbour that special pleasure, which increases the enjoyment of leisure
Like the Titanic they went down well, with a 'little ice'
You can sip and dip at any time of your trip
'I'm riding along on the crest of a wave'
They extend the horizons without worrying about the berth rate
Always arriving at ports of call wearing clothes which contain no creases at all
Peace and privacy if desired, with fun and company when required

Wet Ones baby wipes

PRODUCT: *Moist tissues*

They're the 'castaways' that always come to the rescue

SATELLITE

▶ **When we buy Princes we zoom into orbit because...**

PRODUCT: *Canned fish*
COMPETITION: *Kwik Save/Princes*
PRIZES: *Satellite installations*

We go to Ma's for tea
Waistline friendly, little bread Princes Kwik Save 'light' years ahead
Kwik Save empire strikes back, blasting prices off every pack
A 'star' buy from Kwik Save's aisles, 'dishy' Princes satellite smiles
Princes dishes without exception, always get a great reception
Together they proffer an Unbeatable Family Offer *(UFO = ACROSTIC)*
It's a capsule of health from a store saving wealth
We know we'll come down to earth tuna or later
Princes tuna to our choppers, Kwikies programmed to save coppers
In a galaxy of tins, Princes always wins
Kwik, cheap, no waste satellite your sense of taste
They're light years ahead in the store wars
Princes tuna kwik and zippy, healthier than a Martian chippy
Sky's the limit, great selection, 'dishing up' Princes sheer perfection
No alien fish will we receive on our dish
Armstrong first on lunar lands, Princes first for tuna brands
It's Princes network transmitted by Kwik Save received by shoppers
Kwik Save's Princes tuna dish'll taste heavenly – that's O-fish-all
Princes tuna tasty dish Kwik Save prices, every woman's wish
Such Fishical pleasure in store even Patrick asks for Moore!

▶ **Why do you consider that Sky TV is out of this world?**

PRODUCT: *Shampoo*
COMPETITION: *Kwik Save/Vosene shampoo*
PRIZES: *Sky satellite systems plus installation*

Sky's the limit! pure perfection 'dishing up' greater viewing selection
Because it beams the best and beats the rest
And I've 'Disc'-overed Sky TV has 'Set-a-lot-a-lite' entertainment
Be smart says Bart, don't sigh watch sky
It's astromically inspired, highly desired, with all the programmes required
It's proved it's worth – it's the greatest show off earth

A 'galaxy' of entertaining fun, it's 'universally' second to none

Because 'Sky by day' 'Sky by night' means viewer's delight

For star programmes, Sky has the best I've eVosene

Because Sky and Vosene are the brightest things on air

This Universal Focusing Object Systematically Keeps You in the picture *(UFO SKY = ACROSTIC)*

With Sky your viewing's 'Set-a-lite', morning, afternoon, evening and night

Nobody else can match Sky TV's 'high' standards

Watching it puts me into orbit

Everyone will have one, lunar or later

I no longer think what on earth I can watch

Because Sky always dish out my favourite programmes

Because this enterprise will have stars treking onto your screen

Some know your Viewing Of Satellite Entertainment Never Ends *(VOSENE = ACROSTIC)*

There's a choice with a dish, not just Michael Fish

Because, like Vosene, it makes your H(air) waves gleam

S for superb, K for Keenness, Y need you ask, do dishes lie? *(SKY = ACROSTIC)*

Because it SATURNly is MARSvellous

It's a universal Tele-scoop

As my own 'dish' has disappeared into thin hair

Like Vosene, Sky is always on the right wavelength

It's the 'medium' that raised the spirits

Because it makes other TV stations look up to it

It's the heavenly way to watch the stars of today

Because it is the perfect dish on the menu

Because when you switch on you're turning on the world

Because it keeps inferior entertainment out of my H'air

It's the brightest lumin'hair'y I've eVosene

It's the only dish to 'setallite' the H-airwaves

Because like Vosene shampoo, it's 'Dish'-tinctive too

Up above the world so high, endless entertainment – that's Sky

Because I spend more time 'Saturn' my backside

It's high time the viewer got a better reception

It's miles above the rest, so it is the best

Because it's so 'Astra'nomical

With Sky installation, viewing is orbital inspiration

Because the whole family will be over the moon

Boldly going where no other television company has gone before

Number one in the race it beams from outer space

So when you've got it you're off like a rocket

It's a super channel with knockout shows all year round

Because you can't keep a really good station down

A system that will 'setallite' your viewing choice

▶ **Maryland Cookies make my day because...**

PRODUCT: *Biscuits*
PRIZES: *Satellite dishes with TV*

From toddlers to OAPs, Maryland Cookies always please
I always find 'space' for that Satel-'lite' crisp taste
My senses are 'Set-allite' after only one bite
Morning, noon and night, my taste buds are 'satellite'

▶ **I drink Tetley Bitter because...**

PRODUCT: *Beer*
COMPETITION: *Tetley/Sky TV*

Born in Leeds, raised in glasses, praised in the skys
It's top of the hops in pubs and shops
Other bitters fade and die, Tetley's head remains sky high
It sparkles and glitters, the star of the bitters
Thanks to Tetley's brewing craft, canned perfection tastes like draught
Tetley's reception never fails in England, Ireland, Scotland or Wales
I reach for the Sky and end up in Tetley's heaven

▶ **The Sky's the limit with Braun at Asda because...**

PRODUCT: *Electrical goods*
COMPETITION: *Asda/Braun*
PRIZES: *Sony satellite kits*

Seeking to reach the discerning buyer, Asda features Braun – quality couldn't
   be higher
Braun offers a galaxy of quality devices and Asda's switched on to lower prices
They dish up a galaxy of selection, but Braun gets the best reception
Braun 'channel' their new devices, to Asda's 'low-zone' friendly prices
Quality, value and five-star care, make Braun and Asda a higher-flyer pair
Braun products I conceal between groceries with skill – hubby happily paying
   my bill
Down to earth, that's Asda price, while Braun on reflection, twice as nice
Asda value, Braun precision, both could bring me heavenly vision

SAUCES

▶ **Colman's make cooking a touch better because...**

PRODUCT: *Sauces in boxes*
COMPETITION: *Colman's Home Style Cook in Sauces*

With Colman's I can ring the changes without circling the world

They've put a world of new ideas at my fingertips
Everyone will spot the difference at my next Home Style meal
You'll find a welcome home to Colman's
What's sauce for the goose is always worth a gander
The only additive is pure genius
Colman's are a cook's best blend
With simple instructions from packet to pot, this galloping gourmet can slow to
    a trot
Added to my favourite dinner, it makes the dish an instant winner
It turns boring dinners into tasty winners
Behind suburban kitchen doors, mums simmer with pride when Colman's
    pours
Tasty tricks are worked by each magic mix
Quick, efficient and tasty and the family spot the difference

▶ Colman's Home Style sauces suit my life style because...

PRODUCT: Sauces in boxes

Around the world they're turning stock into a liquid asset
They halve the labour and double the flavour
Once I guessed the time and measure, now I've time for guests and leisure
Cooking a meal with Colman's means you'll never Reckitt
Even hasty days are tasty days
I prefer to ride the range, not slave over it
Why pore over recipes when you can pour over Home Style?
They are an investment with inbuilt stocks for family shares
They're natural sauces of inspiration, for meals of tasteful innovation
Whilst maximum latitude of taste, they minimise longtitude of preparation

▶ I catch the gravy train at Hillards because...

PRODUCT: Stock cube
COMPETITION: Oxo/Hillards

It's better than going by cube

▶ Oxo is one of life's little treasures because...

PRODUCT: Stock cube

X marks the spot on the every single packet

▶ I buy Knorr at Woolworths because...

PRODUCT: Sauces in packets

The flavour is right and the change is left
Knorr's range, pot or pack, provides the cooking skill I lack
There is less haste, no waste and great taste

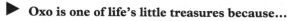

Bisto gravy

It's the difference between BEEFore and AHHfter
They have got gravy making down to a fine AHH-t
When the boat comes in it's full of flavour
For flavour and aroma it wins the diploma

SAVING & INVESTING

▶ **The Co-operative Bank Top Tier High Interest Savings Account is second to none because...**

PRODUCT: Savings Account

Its rates are good, instructions clear and deserves the name TOP TIER

▶ **I have checked out the Leeds Travel Money Service because...**

PRODUCT: Holiday services

The service provided sounds simply divine. Your currency, cheques and a useful helpline

▶ **I would like to save in a Midshires Tessa because...**

PRODUCT: Savings Account

The effort's so small, although the extra savings seem amazing

▶ **Prestige Lifetime cookwear is a good investment because...**

PRODUCT: Pans
COMPETITION: Prestige Pans/Abbey National Building Society

The Prestige smile and the Abbey habit both last a lifetime

▶ **I'm choosing a Halifax Tessa because...**

PRODUCT: Savings Account

TESSA means relax, interest free of tax, bonus on maturity, Halifax security

Banks

The pounds in my account keep my balance in great shape
It doesn't tax my interest or interest my tax man

Saving with Building Societies

PRODUCT: Savings Accounts

I look forward to a present in the future
I want to feather my nest with a little down
From the moment savings start, your best interests are at heart
There's no need to speculate, merely appreciate
Pennies placed permanently in a proper place prosper into pounds
In this galaxy they are best, their interest rate eclipses the rest
The best kid's club around has the best deals and offers to astound
I want to have security when I reach maturity
Top Savers know the truth, Anglia invest in youth
My little bits of silver will someday 'Leed' to gold (*Leeds B.S.)
Pocket money comes and goes, a little with the Leeds soon grows
I'm following my 'Leeder' to a golden future

Thorn Mazda Power Saver competition...

PRODUCT: Electric light bulbs

It lightens the bill as well as the room
On a light bill cheaper, off it looks much neater
It's a shining example of watts being saved
The price is right but the light's still bright
Little light lost, big savings on cost

Tesco stores saving you money

PRODUCT: Supermarket foods

For my money Tesco's the one to 'bank on'
The check-out at Tesco means a cheque in your bank
As money gets shorter, Tesco makes it last longer
Kitchen sinking or armchair drinking, budget stretching means Tesco thinking
For someone with expensive taste, Tesco is my saving grace
Others make profuse promises, Tesco keeps them
Only Tesco can make the best better

SCHOOL

Ashe & Nephew Armchair Skolar competition

PRODUCT: Lager

When it's cold outside, then it's SKOL inside
In every town and every city, armchair Skolars are sitting pretty
They qualify for thirst glass honours
Skolar's homework, it's understood, is Sofa, so good
Educated armchair drinkers are dedicated Skol sinkers
It's general knowledge that they 'pass' on other lagers
They're at home with the top of the glass
For a 'degree of pleasure' they sit drinking Skol at leisure
Their insatiable thirst for knowledge is quenched by Skol – not college
They get the greatest, no queuing, savings accruing, bottoms up – great
    brewing
They gain a high degree of satisfaction in their own study
Whilst enjoying modern leisure, drinking Skol is their pleasure

SHEEP

Australian whisky competition

PRODUCT: Sheep Dip whisky

Bo Peep got the sack on the day, that all of her sheep went astray, that's a
    lesson for you... (Competitors had to complete the limerick)
With the poll tax now due, she'll be back on 'eweth' (*youth) training today
So take care what you d'ewe', or end up fleeced without any pay
Take a trip to Peru and let social security pay
Let your flock learn Kung Fu, in case they should meet a gourmet
Dreams only come true when all of the rules you obey
For 'shear' carelessness too, you get sacked, that's a fact, with no pay
You just can't trust a ewe, unless Sheep Dip's prescribed, they won't stay
Not to play with Boy Blue, and think life is no work and all play
Keep yer eyes open, Blue, or your sheep dip'll go the same way
I'm the man from the Pru, you lost 'em, you find 'em – Okay
Take more care of each ewe, or the rams will steal them away
So whatever you do, don't let your sheep dip run away
Don't mess with Boy Blue, while the sun shines you musn't make hay
Don't join the dole queue, get a dog to make sure that they stay
Said a militant ewe, we'll come back for a fair day's play
She was dancing it's true, now her flock has lambada-ed away

SHINES

▶ **Mighty Ajax SHINES pans better because...**

PRODUCT: Pan scourers

Ajax moves in ever degreasing circles

SHOES

▶ **It is important for the family to wear good shoes because...**

PRODUCT: Shoes

They lead the way to success through all walks of life

▶ **I use Kiwi shoe products to care for my shoes because...**

PRODUCT: Shoe polish

The Kiwi shine stands supreme, setting standards seldom seen
For children's wear and Gucci pair, Kiwi features polished flair
Kiwi products are superior for reviving shoes that look inferior
Scruffy shoes never please for Kiwi cleans with 'expert-ease'
Kiwi is the all weather leather protector
Simply selected, easy to use, Kiwi products protect my shoes
Old shoes, new shoes, Kiwi shoes stand out in queues
I feel fine with the Kiwi shine
Dirty shoe, muddy boot, Kiwi cleans and saves you loot
Step into a Kiwi shine, feel terrific, look divine
From baby's shoe to soldier's boot, Kiwi products always suit
Every 'shoe' can 'sport' a gleam, using Kiwi's protection team
Kiwi enhances my chances of getting admiring glances
Having tried all the rest, I find Kiwi the best
When protection is the watchword, Kiwi is the 'buy' word
Scuffs and scrapes everyday, soon put right the Kiwi way
That Kiwi gleam makes me beam
Kiwi's shine is the reflection of longer-lasting shoe protection
Minimum fuss, minimum mess, Kiwi's Kwick always the best

Tesco and Kiwi in partnership

PRODUCT: Shoe polish

Tesco and Kiwi together they shine, they're feets ahead when they combine

Shopping at the Co-op

PRODUCT: Supermarket foods

Stop and shop at the Co-op – the store that's stamped its reputation
   throughout Britain (*Dividend Stamps)

SHOP & SHOPPING

▶ **I SHOP at Tesco because...**

PRODUCT: Supermarket foods

Beauty care to Home n' Wear, Tesco is beyond compare
Their price 'pegging' means value on every 'line'
All we need top to bottom, guaranteed Tesco's got 'em
Forget about the falling pound, Tesco prices hold their ground
Tesco products clean and healthy, Tesco prices keep me wealthy
Of the goods, good choice, good prices and good service
Tesco makes the pound go round
Value is always underlined, but quality is never undermined
Wide bargains, bargains galore, why change superstore?

▶ **I SHOP at Wm Low because...**

PRODUCT: Soft drink
COMPETITION: Wm Low/Coca-Cola
PRIZES: Christmas hampers

Still or FIZZY, the price won't make you DIZZY
It offers low prices, exceptional variety, outstanding value and satisfaction
The only things watered down are the prices
Lots of choice, easy to park, open every day – super
No fuss, no flap, just bargains on tap
The prices are right for my pocket
For value, service and quality, Wm Low tops my Christmas tree
Quality, value, low prices I find, naturally spring to mind
With Wm Low's selection it puts spring into shopping
Non-stop service, tip-top value, down-dropped prices – what a trio
I economise without compromise
Service sparkles, bargains stream, natural products from the Wm Low's team
With quality, value and service in store, who needs more?
Favourable prices, favourite brands (still in bottles – not in cans)
Quality's excellent, prices right, choice extensive, service bright
Wm Low keep their prices still, without watering down sparkling quality
Originality, not much to spend, unbeaten quality, Wm Low's my friend

▶ **I like to make Coca-Cola a regular part of my SHOPPING list because...**

PRODUCT: *Soft drink*
COMPETITION: *Tates/Coca-Cola*

Shopping early, shopping late, Coca-Cola tastes just great
Like Tates, coke is great to open all hours
Being a Tate shopper, it's my favourite party popper

▶ **I make Coca-Cola a regular part of my SHOPPING because...**

PRODUCT: *Soft drink*
COMPETITION: *Sainsbury's/Coca-Cola*
PRIZES: *Trips to Disneyland*

Original, diet, caffeine free, I can't choose so I buy all three
Coke's got the taste beyond compare, leave Sainsbury's without it? I wouldn't dare

▶ **I prefer SHOPPING at Presto because...**

PRODUCT: *Soft drink*
COMPETITION: *Presto/Coca-Cola*

I tried pushing a rival's trolley, but couldn't 'budget'
Tried the others, shopping's tragic, went to Presto, utter magic
Whenever Presto pops the question, Coca-Cola's my thirst suggestion

▶ **The fresh look of Lyons original will always be on my SHOPPING list at Tesco because...**

PRODUCT: *Coffee*
COMPETITION: *Tesco/Lyons coffee*

It's blended with care, then vended with flair
The eyecatching packs of unequalled flavour are another Tesco money saver
The green and gold vacuum pack captures flavours others lack
Superior taste, distinctive pack, Tesco value, draws me back
Light, dark or medium, it helps to beat the tea-dium
When flavour is the main attraction, Lyons gives sealed satisfaction

▶ **SHOPPING at the Co-op means...**

PRODUCT: *Supermarket foods*

Shares in high living at a low cost
Buying today and saving for tomorrow
More than you'd bargained for at less than you'd expect
They paper our precious little 'persons' at precious little cost
The one thing never sold is you ... down the river
There's a satisfying choice at a gratifying price

Their interest ensures my saving
It's such a friendly store, also the gift bought elsewhere could cost more
The customer is treated like a princess

SHOPPING *theme*

The quality is right, the change is left
Parking's free, savings whopping, super selection, one stop shopping
They keep a welcome at the till-side
I won't pass out at the check-out
Their supermarkets reign supreme, where services and choice are a shopper's
    dream
They make record cuts in the cost of my Chopin Liszt
They know the ropes which enables them to sail ahead
The 'coppers' I save there help 'arrest' the rising cost of living
My modest cheque in, means a most generous check-out
Balancing my budget's easy now, I think I'll teach Sir Geoffrey Howe
It gives me and my purse buy-onic power
Asda is the four letter word discerning shoppers swear by
Good sound service beyond compare, makes Asda top of the shops, everywhere
My cash flow is only a trickle but Asda lets me splash out a bit

SHOWER

▶ **I would like to SHOWER with OZ because...**

PRODUCT: *Limescale cleaner*
PRIZES: *Miralec electric showers*

I could clean up more cheaply by scaling down my electricity bills
The healthiest way to start the day is p-OZ-itively the Miralec way
I'd have the whole spray and nothing but the spray, so help me OZ
I'd be showered with MIRAculous gifts
Cleanliness is next to OZ-liness
C'OZ a Mira, Mira on the wall, is definitely the fairest of them all
Over the rainbow is where I'd be, if OZ showered this prize on me
Miralec Is Refreshing And Leaves Everyone Clean, Oz Zaps That Evil Scale
    Clean Off *(MIRALEC OZ TESCO = ACROSTIC)*

SIGN & SIGHT

▶ **The Co-op sign is a sure sign of...**

PRODUCT: *Supermarket foods*

The caring sharing store that saves me so much more
Quality fare, staff who care and profit to share

▶ **I'm a sight better off with Swiss Cheese at Safeway store because...**

PRODUCT: Swiss cheeses

Whatever the venue, Swiss cheese fits the menu
Rival products can't compare, Swiss cheeses are unique
Cheese Has Essential Elements Specially Emmenthal from Switzerland
    (CHEESE = ACROSTIC)
Pure ingredients and traditional care make Emmenthal and Gruyère
They are tasty, nutritious and simply delicious
Alpine meadows with clean fresh breeze produce a fuller flavoured cheese
Quality food, standards high, from Safeway, the best place to buy
Flavour outstanding, dinners are divine, Suisse on the label, the pleasure is
    mine
The Swiss symbol stands supreme and Safeway sets standards seldom seen
For taste and flavour no cheese can compare with nutty Emmenthal and
    matured Gruyère
As a mature student who enjoys delicious cheeses, Swiss are a Safeway of
    guaranteeing satisfaction
My palate is hard to please, I only eat the finest cheese
It's the Safeway to guarantee quality
I've tried the rest and I know what's best
They're a GRATE idea for any occasion, from fondue supper to a family
    invasion
For lunchtime temptation or evening treat, tasty Swiss cheeses are hard to beat
Cheese is only bliss when it's real Swiss
It's irreswisstibly the taste for me
I like to savour the flavour of an alpine fondue
My mother Swiss, a childhood treat, a cheese fondue, the memory sweet
Their taste is a mountainous experience, like a yodel in fresh air
They're always at the peak of perfection
A connoisseur I love to savour, their unique and distinctive flavour
It has the flavour my tastebuds love to savour
Mountainous flavours, outstanding to eat, standard never wavers, a fresh alpine
    treat
They have wonderful taste, superb textures and are so versatile
Emmenthal has 'hole'some flavour, Gruyère – spicy taste to savour – delicious
    'two' in a Swiss fondue
They taste so delightful, meals are divine, Suisse on the label, the pleasure is
    mine
Eaten alone or with bread or wine, Swiss cheese are great, there's none so fine
I know that the alpine horn blower on the label means satisfaction around the
    table

▶ **When I shop at Kwik Save, Princes fruit juices are a refreshing sight because...**

PRODUCT: *Fruit juices*
COMPETITION: *Kwik Save/Princes fruit juices*
PRIZE: *Nova Carlton car*

Princes packs always hearten when 'gaspin' for a Nova Carlton
Where else can three litres turn into a four seater
The number plates you see are Kwik Save – 63P
They're always guaranteed to 'win-Nova' your taste buds
Princes at Kwik Save are a sight for more buys
I am highly 'motor-vated' by the flavours they've created
Princes juices reign supreme: is the Nova just a dream?
They're the greatest reviver for a thirsty driver
Three packs minus seals equals brand new set of wheels
They are the greatest revivers for thirsty trolley drivers
Offering luscious appetisers, there's Nova a nonsense with breathalysers
Kwik Save 'loaded trolley drivers' need Princes juices as revivers
Princes stand out like a 'Nova' brilliant star performer
For finest juice without inflation Kwik Save is an inNOVAtion
Princes juices – thirst choice – Kwik Save prices – first choice
My taste buds come alive spinning me into overdrive
I'm on the right road for the good bodywork code
Quality – Princes rule of thumb renders me a NOVAjoyed mum
Princes juice brings satisfaction replacing thirst with five speed action
When I thirst for the best I drive away refreshed
On a long distance shop it's my pit stop
Such cool juices, no 'Novalty', always trust in Princes quality
Quality seal, price appeal, gives Kwik Save shoppers twice the deal
Their 'thirst' gear sends my trolley into 'Nova-drive'
Their many varied flavours are the starters for Kwik Savers

SIMPLE

▶ **The Dolmio range makes cooking SIMPLE because...**

PRODUCT: *Pasta sauce*

Dolmio quality guarantees perfect results with expert ease
It helps my culinary prowess when I wish to impress
You're sure of perfection whatever your selection
They're made in a trice, those meals that entice
Dolmio sets me free to watch my favourite TV
Unlock jar, release sauce, freedom from any cookery course
Authentic expertise, makes superb meals a thing of ease

Authentic ingredients ready to savour, just open up Italian flavour
With a family to impress Dolmio 'cannelloni' be a success
Simply delicious and quickly done, TV dinners are such fun

SING

▶ **Coca-Cola and Schweppes always give me something to SING about at Tesco's because...**

PRODUCT: Soft drinks
COMPETITION: Tesco/Coca-Cola/Schweppes Christmas carol

While Shepherds watch 'you know who' is stocking up
Slimline Schweppes or Diet Coke brand lead Tesco's healthy keep fit band
They are a classical pair and harmonise with other fare
Every be-bopping bubble bounces to the beat
Mix and mingle or straight and single, they make me swingle
I saw three Schweppes coke sailing by, tonic, coke and ginger dry
Coke and Schweppes keep me young, and like Cliff, Tesco's number one
They're a cracking Christmas double, loadsa savings, loadsa bubble
Whenever people gather and mingle, Tesco and Schweppes provide the jingle
Party time is tickety-boo with Tesco, Coke and Sch... 'You know who'

SIZZLING

▶ **British sausages make a SIZZLING good idea because...**

PRODUCT: Sausages
COMPETITION: Tesco/Wall's
PRIZES: Store vouchers

They're a gastronomic thrill without an astronomic bill
Barbecued, grilled or fried, they leave everyone satisfied
Links or slice – taste ever so nice, always
Big and meaty, Tesco delights – Wall's sausages satisfy appetites
Mouth watering can't wait, meaty Wall's never late
British is best for a Tesco buy
Gastronomic sausages are fine, they fulfil my wishes with economical dishes
Tesco quality, Tesco price, makes meals twice as nice
British sausages being 'gristle less', provide a tastier 'sizzleness'
Yummy tastebud satisfaction, superb and savoury meal attraction
Sausages make a Tesco start to a British breakfast
Tasty bangers and mash, Tesco value for cash
Frying and grilling they are so tasty and filling

Quality, taste and nutrition, link Tesco food to tradition
Bangers and mash is good value for cash
Action packed, full of taste Tesco means no waste
Savoury And Unadulterated Sausages Are Great Economical Satisfiers
    (SAUSAGES = ACROSTIC)
In these days of recession, their nutrition banishes depression

SLIMMING

▶ **I enjoy Findus Calorie Counters because...**

PRODUCT: *Low calorie frozen meals*

They make slimming a piece of cake

▶ **I buy Rye-King crispbread because...**

PRODUCT: *Low calorie crispbread*

It's the crisp answer to everyone's figure problems

▶ **I enjoy Diet 7 Up as part of my calorie-controlled diet because...**

PRODUCT: *Diet drink*

Tastes a treat, makes end meet, in the pocket, around the seat
It quenches thirst throughout the day, in a tasty calorie-controlled way
Its light refreshing taste helps take inches off my waist

Health farms

Before your very eyes it slims your hips and thighs
A massage a day keeps the cellulite at bay
They make me thinner – they're a real winner
Beneath the bulge there's a curve just waiting to emerge
Champney's would turn 'goodness' into 'gracious' me

Low calorie salad dressings

Waistline is the answer to wishful shrinking
Over salad, fish or meat, any meal becomes a treat
Starters, salad, cold or not, Hellmann's dressing tops the lot

Slimming theme in general

Nothing added, always pure, calories counted, diet sure
Long-lasting, convenient, low in fat too; recipes become lighter, and so do you
It enhances slim chances
Once tried, 'weight' and see, it improves all dishes, including me

It shapes you up to make your presence svelte (*felt)
It's the answer to a long svelte want
It's a lifeline for sinking slimmers
It's a wonderful aid to girth control
Formerly frumpish, fat and forty, now I frolic in fashions quite naughty
It provides for those wishing to keep in touch with their toes
Deflation figures make good headlines
It's filled the need in me
Low calorie fitness, low price at till, One-Cal and Asda fit the bill
It's the goodness from within that keeps a family trim
It's naturally nature's way to keep slim
Their slimmers find a pleasant way, enjoying fibre every day
They provide healthy solutions to figure problems

SMILE

▶ **Heinz and Gateway make me SMILE because...**

PRODUCT: Supermarket foods
PRIZE: Sony camcorder

Heinz 57 is the Gateway to heaven

▶ **Dolmio pasta sauce and Co-op tea make me SMILE because...**

PRODUCT: Pasta sauce
COMPETITION: Co-op/Dolmio

Perfect flavours, cheerful smiles, super value, Co-op style
'Pasta' my best, I've 'urn'ed a rest
A Dolmio 'tea leaves' others standing
Jars inverted, bag inserted, taste buds alerted, doldrums deserted
Both take pride in the pleasure they provide
Dolmio-drenched pasta brings happiness faster
It's a constant sauce of satisfaction
The aroma goes from my head to-ma-toes
I don't mince words – it's simply superb
I just grin and prepare it

▶ **I always put the Dolmio SMILE on my face when...**

PRODUCT: Pasta sauce
COMPETITION: Tesco/Dolmio 'Win a trip to Disney'

Dolmio, Tesco and lady luck, could lead me straight to Donald Duck

SNACKS

▶ **Tellybags are lush because...**

PRODUCT: TV snacks

On the sofa, TV loafer, Tellybags I always go for
Taste and quality are abundant, little snacks become redundant
They satisfy a snack attack whilst I'm watching 'Bergerac'
They are yummy, scrummy and great in my tummy
They give watching the telly a whole lot more welly

KP mini chips – Computer theme

PRODUCT: Potato mini chips

For small fry they're a big buy
Insert digits into mini chips, the finest snack to pass your lips
They are perfect 'pressed-digit-taters'
No other 'joy sticks' put a beam on my 'screen'
They're the experimental prototype (protato) chippy of tomorrow
Basically, it's no 'silli-con', they're crisp and crunchy with salt on

Snacks in general

When it comes to the crunch they are snacks with a punch
The crunch comes in the packet, not in the pocket
The choice, tremendous, the crunch stupendous
Crunch for crunch they're the perfect munch
They've got the reputation for the crunchiest sensations
It's the mouth-watering snack in the eye-catching pack
A man struck by the nibbles has a one-snack mind
By taking goodness from a jacket they put pleasure in a packet
Smiths make biting exciting
For quality, value and nutrition, Smiths is a great British tradition
Every morsel is ready to savour, from ready salted to cheesy flavour
The are perfect space invaders

SNOOKERED

▶ **The Co-op leaves other biscuits SNOOKERED because...**

PRODUCT: Biscuits
COMPETITION: Co-op '99' tea/Tennent's lager

Co-op's atTENNENTion to biscuit cravings, crumble inflation with
    CHAMPION savings

They're the best TENNENT'S in my LADA
For the perfect break they DAVIState the opposition
They have the biscuit to suit every type of break
Every bicky they bake is my lucky break
'99' pots and Co-op bakes are incomparable super breaks
Even hurricane slows to savour Co-op's century breaking flavour
You don't need Dennis Taylor glasses to see quality
Their biscuit mix knocks them for six
You can improve any break with biscuits the Co-op make
The Co-op give the break the rest cannot make
They make champion breaks while the opposition crumbles
Co-op cushion prices and leave you in the pink
During a break they disappear at hurricane speed
They're the RAY of sunshine I've been REARDON
From packet to pocket there's safety assured and members applaud
For good value eatin' they just can't be beaten
Their six winning hot shots have cornered the angles
One crisp break and I am ready for a clearance
Their CUEnique taste is worthy of any break
For a nominal stake – the perfect winning break
They're so good everybody is going potty over them
Co-op scrumptious bakes makes many maxi-mmm breaks

SOPHISTICATION

▶ **Melitta, the real name for coffee, brings SOPHISTICATION to every occasion...**

PRODUCT: Filter coffee
COMPETITION: Asda/Royal Doulton
PRIZES: Royal Doulton coffee sets

Now there are four ways to be seduced by a smooth dark sensation
Freshly brewed, piping hot, aroma, flavour, it's got the lot!
Tastefully enticed by rich aromas to savour, you always re-'fined' the real coffee flavour
Day or night, connoisseurs select and sophisticates prefer Melitta
Coffee mug and cup of bone china, when filled with Melitta, there's nothing finer
Served in Royal Doulton after dinner, Melitta completes the course – the outright winner
Serving Melitta will always impress, providing the 'grounds' for social success
The filtering taste of fine roast coffee, is perfect enjoyment, right down to the grounds
In chunky mug or fine bone china, this real coffee's flavour could not be finer
Fine fresh flavour, Doulton coffee cup, hostess me, fills a little one up

It gives me confidence to serve, fine coffee that guests deserve

Melitta's reputation well deserved, guarantees that fresh ground flavour, enhanced and preserved

Smooth taste and pleasing aroma, are awarded the coffee Diploma

For quality, charm or perfect style, Melitta coffee stands out a mile

Melitta knows what is proper and tasteful, the rich aroma gives grounds to be grateful

Whether best china, tin mug or Irish in a glass, Melitta always adds undeniable class

These elegant blends impress my friends and call for recognition

Whether mug on the rug or finer china, good taste filters through

Full bodied, smooth tasting, coffee supreme, served with Royal Doulton, what a team

Melitta's irresistible aroma, perfect brew, adds class to any 'bit of a do'

Even the pourer can enjoy the richness of Melitta coffee

I never spill the beans when it comes to haute cuisine

Melitta Original distinctive and classically blended, ensures all occasions are perfectly ended

That classic pure coffee taste makes Melitta elite-a

This super aromatic blending, ensures a satisfying ending

SOUNDS

▶ **My SOUND advice is always shop at Asda because...**

PRODUCT: Supermarket foods

They're 'leader of the brands' and I'm keenest of their fans

No beating about the 'Bush' they take the 'Sting' out of inflation

Their compact prices beat the blues – superb quality with rave reviews

That's where your notes score the biggest hit

They're in tune with everything on my Chopin Liszt

They make record cuts

Asda's system clearly makes the notes last longer

Wherever the rest go, you're better off at Asda

Their track record is second to none, I've discovered they are number one

You'll find classical goods at popular prices

You can 'Coll-ins'Kate around, pick your 'Phil' and still be 'Rich'ard

My money and I part with a song in my heart

Record price beyond compare from fruit 'n' veg to home 'n' wear

My automatic choice is biological and Asda is 'buyer logical'

Record cuts on shopping bills are music to customers at the tills

I save a 'tenor' every time I 'pop' in for my 'Chopin'

You can get your Phil without a Sting in the bill

The prices are compact but the prices are sound

Their prices are soh low but always save me doh
Record breaker, 'Hit' maker, bargains galore at my number one store

▶ Value Stores mean SOUND shopping because...

PRODUCT: Food store foods

They tune in well to low prices and excellent quality
We 'harmonise', the reason is 'sound' – 'reception' and value's the best around
For the record they are 'top of the shops'
Good sound service beyond compare, makes Asda top of the shops everywhere

▶ I would like to win the Superdrug SOUNDS spectacular because...

PRODUCT: Superstore goods

It would sound spectacular to me if I won
I'd enjoy the sights and sounds both centres offer
Spectacular prize for spectacular buys – so I can't lose
Having never won before, this would be a record

▶ Soft & Gentle SOUNDS fantastic at Boots because...

PRODUCT: Ladies' deodorant
COMPETITION: Boots/Soft & Gentle 'Sounds Fantastic'
PRIZES: Sanyo music equipment

There's never 'Tears for Fears' and 'Relax' it doesn't 'Sting'
If I 'roll' then 'rock' I'm fresh around the clock
Nobody does it better – the spray who loved me
Rock n' roll-on or aero-soul keeps you swinging without stinging
It re-45s the parts other deodorants can't reach
Sting should be heard and not felt
Disco dancers need no inspiring, 'C-P' products prevent their perspiring
Switch off your set – great sounds, no sweat
Their prices start me singing, their products stop me 'humming'
'Scent'sationally packaged 'disc'tinctively fine, this 'note'worthy team's a 'hit'
        every time
Roll-on or spray, you're fragrantly dry all day
This number one pair record freshness beyond compare
It's a gentle, effective way to keep odours at bay
The product makes scents and the price makes sense
Clever girls get protection from Soft and Gentle's hit selection
It beats any other 'air'o'soul
One 'hiss' is just so – no risk of B.O.
Boots are known for selection, Soft and Gentle for protection
Dancing, aerobics, skating about, keeps me dry without a doubt
Mild on skin, strong on action, beats others for satisfaction
Right price, smells nice, chart topper from head to Boots

It's the soothing sensation that stops perspiration
Roll-on or spray saves a little 'doh' each day
It makes many a charmer keen to penetrate my armour
It's my natural selection for lasting protection
When refrains are inspiring you'll refrain from perspiring
You'll hear no anguished crying whether buying or applying
Turned-on product, tune-in price, makes selection doubly nice
Soft and Gentle for activity, no objection to close proximity
This rock and roll-on is going for a song
Dance, tap your feet – Soft and Gentle beats the heat
From morning till late they keep fresh this old '78
You can get in the swing, without the sting
Beatles – shout, Bowie – sighs, Barry – swoons, Band-Aid – live
This 'Message in a Bottle' works without 'Sting'
Perfect harmony in both, you find value and quality combined
Priced at low doh, who is 'hunting high and low'?
Price is right, perfume light, feel confident, day and night
Top value, less debt, no sting, no sweat
They're sound performers who never 'hit' your pocket
Tuned into competitive prices gives value that always entices
It's the spray that says 'no' to B.O.
It's the kinda spray that works all day
Value is always of 'note' – freshness will never 'B Sharp'
They give the protection I desire, the selection I require
You always find sound value without breaking the price barriers
If you're armed with this you're fresh in the pits
The value is unmatched for day-long protection; no stings attached
Boots win the odour war, putting Soft and Gentle 'under arms'
A non-sting roll-on will be my number one
For just the right price you can smell quite nice
You can jive all night and still smell alright
For a mere 59 pence I have complete confidence
There's freshness made to last for music slow or fast
Unlike Police, neither needs Sting to get to Number 1
I can be like 'Goldilocks' and easily 'bear' the price
It sells for a song and eliminates pong
Its gentle lasting perfumed spray gives confidence throughout the day
Its number one collection giving fans the finest protection
It inspires a pleasant call to arms
Rock, jitterbug, twist or jive, body freshness stays alive
Roll-on or canned, a confident performance is on hand
For lasting protection they're the natural selection
Better 'tell her about it' because it's for 'Uptown Girls'
Their record is beyond compare, number one for body care
You can feel the beat and beat the heat
With them, wherever I am, I'm home and dry
It's the single release deodorant, giving long-playing protection

The leader of the brands protects from over-active glands
After trying the rest, this combination is still best
They're an all-round sensation from a sound location
Their protection 'racket' doesn't cost a packet
They vouch for no ouch whether spraying or paying
It's a perfect solution to underarm pollution
Whether hot, cold or warm, it just keeps rolling on
No Sting in the spray, music like his every day
Deodorants purchased, bathing done, dancing to Sanyo, 'Real Cool' fun
It gives Miss Jones more Grace and Stevie more Wonder
Work or leisure, you get 'tuned in' for sensational pleasure
Though picked up for a song, it stops me 'humming'
For a painless price you can smell very nice
Ever 'miss' is a 'hit' at the 'top of the shops'
One provides complete protection, the other offers more selection
The reason is sound, best quality and value around
Its refreshing performance is top of the armp(h)it parade
With no Sting to risk, enjoy 'Sting' on a disc
Every 'new release' of this fantastic spray, protects with a magnificent bouquet
'Synthesising' this combination makes my 'Sound of Music'
'Sing'ular value – reassuring them in you're home n' dry with this team
In harmony, they're number one, 'Good Vibrations' being their song
Soft and Gentle sounds supreme, fantastic, pleasant, keeps you clean
The artists are first rate, Soft and Gentle is great
Shake, spray n' roll, gives a body more soul
Boots shoots today's spray straight to No. 1
Mildly perfumed, effective and strong, increases confidence all day long
It's a heart-stopping, chart-topping body sensation
Sanyo, the art of Soft and Gentle listening
For protection round the clock, price is at bottom – rock
Whilst I beat B.O. I could win a Sanyo
Whether roll-on or spray you're in tune all day
Stereo sound, music galore, delicate perfume, protects you for sure
Boots shoppers seek perfection, Soft and Gentle ensures protection
Soft and Gentle second to none, delicately perfumed for everyone
They're a girl's best friends, 'in tune' with present trends

Racasan SOUND theme

PRODUCT: Air fresheners

The freshness that they 'transmit' forces all evil smells to submit
When tuned into 'air space' they 'tone' up the place
With them in the air my 'channels' are never blocked
It's all stations go with care 'broadcasting' freshness everywhere
They have got the special flair for working on 'air'
For cleaner air and fresher pan you can't 'beat' Racasan
Pleasing purse, scent and sight, Racasan's wavelengths are right

Record shops

They smash the 'track' price in any record race
All tracks end up at the best music centre in town
It's the best music centre in town
Turning the table in inflation, brings music and laughter to the nation
They are the only 'music centre' to 'turn the tables' on inflation
They have turned the tables on the opposition in the LP revolution
You can take your sleeves out without emptying your pockets
It's the joint with the best disc-location
For fantastic choice and marvellous disc-ounts
It's a store of disc-tinction
They know what their disc-iples want
They roar into top gear with smash hits all year
For number one they have knack, always on the right track
They sell chart hits at the speed of sound
They always make a killing with their 'hit list'
You can hold a note longer while singing their praises
They offer more music for less notes
Their prices speak volumes, they're music to the public ear
You won't slip a disc looking for great choice and value
With speed selection, they're the 'hi-fiers' of the music business
Their drive for the best outspins the rest
With so many good titles they could fill the House of Lords
They 'Handel' everything from hot chocolate to American pie
Beatles or Beethoven, Lulu or Liszt, Woolies prices are truly 'blitzed'
Woolworths wins gold in the 'Discathlon'
The Woolworths trail 'blazer' has great 'sleeves' and keeps us in 'pocket'
A record is an achievement and Woolworths try to achieve the best
You can CD difference
C-Ductively speaking
It's no Coin-CD-ence
They're an all 'round' sensation
They do not have a one track mind
They make a little 'doh' go so 'fah'
With such star qualities you're transported to another sphere
They've got that super sound when you rev them up
They've lapped the field in track events
When it comes to reproduction, rabbits have nothing on them
They're all in the best possible 'base'
You give yourself finest 'airs' by putting on the 'stylus'
Up to date, able to prove, their selection is in the groove
They select brilliant cuts for your diamond
Every spin is a smooth joy ride
Its discs move in the best circles
Their discs get the needle when the others get the elbow
Their discs revolve around all popular tastes

Disc for disc they give other competitors the needle
Their albums love to be taken out for a spin
Their sleeves and jackets are tailored to suit every pocket
They're no desert island when it comes to discs
They are a sound investment and winners in the field of play
You are on the right track for sound investment
They're a revolving world of pleasure for every child to treasure
Tuned to my needs they always give me a good reception
It brings a smile to everyone's dial
Clarity begins at home
You can hold a 'note' longer while singing their praises
For quality and value they're on the same wavelength
We get great reception, wide selection, price perfection

SOUND in general

High performance and quality range always ensures a pocket full of change
They're in tune with every need – satisfaction guaranteed
They are in tune in putting their customers number one
They are, without exception, 'turned on' for the best 'reception'
They're tuned up and ready to give long running pleasure
For quality and value they're on the same wavelength
Good taste is satisfied when value is amplified
Always rotating in the best circles, their success is no 'spin-off'
The tills are alive with the sound of music
Their prices ring a sweet melody while shopping in high fidelity
Competitors are left in a spin by their track record
Who needs quadrophonic to realise their value's supersonic?
Super 'range', 'record' change, the 'frequency' of my trips explained
This famous 'duet' hold the 'key' to good value
Throughout the years they have always had quality taped

Yamaha electric organs

PRODUCT: Musical organs

The leader of the band
Open the door to musical pleasure – Yamaha have the key
Brahms, Bach or Kenny Ball, the Yamaha Electrone plays them all
Yamaha organs are easy to play because of their 'teacher features'
Nip-pon your Yamaha organ and kick start to a new world

SPECIAL

▶ **Elsenham conserves are SPECIAL because...**

PRODUCT: *Conserves*
FIRST PRIZE: *Round-the-world trip for two*
RUNNERS-UP: *Dover/Calais crossings*

They are the fruits of refusing to compromise
They are the passport to a world of exciting tastes
Just one spoonful (to investigate) made my tastebuds circumnavigate
They put all other preserves into the reserves
They have plenty 'a-peel' and flavours so real
With extra fruit and extra care, extra flavour always there
From darkest Africa to remotest Cheltenham, discerning connoisseurs demand
    Elsenham
Synonymous with taste – together with tea, my everyday global necessity
From Adelaide to Amsterdam, no marmalade matches Elsenham
Only the pick of the crops is found under Elsenham tops
It's Elsenham by name, it's excellent by nature
They are the jewelled memories of summer's generous bounty
They offer a jam-boree of tasteful sensations
You taste the whole fruit and nothing but the fruit
Exploding with fruity zest, they are the berry best
From Jamaica to China, there's no jam-maker finer
Superb quality sets tastebuds ablaze, extra richness earns 'tum'ultuous taste
'Berried' treasure, well preserved, Elsenhams, so spread the word
Hand prepared in copper pans, the finest jams are Elsenhams
With Elsenham on the label, distinction on the table
They guarantee a morning booty, well preserved and very fruity

▶ **Quality approved Scottish salmon makes Christmas SPECIAL because...**
   PRODUCT: *Fish*

Scottish salmon, the quality fish, makes the perfect Xmas family dish

▶ **Wall's Viennetta and Moët & Chandon make that celebration SPECIAL because...**
   PRODUCT: *Viennetta ice cream dessert and Moët & Chandon champagne*
   COMPETITION: *Safeway/Wall's Viennetta & Moët & Chandon*
   PRIZES: *Bottle of Moët & Chandon*

Both are in a glass of their own
Two teasing temptations, champagne vintage sensations of revelations
They complement each special date, bet Terry found them worth the 'Waite'
They're the height of 'fizzical' delight
When excellence is required, they're the taste that's admired
They're perfect for a 'bit of a do'
Aristocrats of labels grace the most discerning tables
They are always top of their class
Any table would be 'graced' by their label

Guests know you care when you serve this special pair

Who could resist the delicious sensation of succumbing to a sparkling sensation

Their cool sophistication makes it impossible to resist temptation

Superior products of high esteem, grace the table for a celebration supreme

Alluring, delicious, beguiling – the perfect pair to keep you smiling

Both are cool, smooth and chic and quite unique

The 'course' of true love runs 'sweet'

What an entertaining pair, here's to their gastronomic fare

They set the scene for 'haute cuisine'

Luxurious taste, bubbles that explode, everyone's in the celebration mode

They're a great combination for a taste sensation

Such a delectable double make any party bubble

They make 'grape' minds think alike

With luxury beyond compare, I'd feel like a millionaire

Champagne excellence, Viennetta's flair, like Bonington's Everest, beyond compare

Scrumptious slice, sparkling glass, to any repast, brings a 'taste of class'

Deliciously iced and served in glasses, jubilation to anniversaries or university passes

They have sparkle and style, making the occasion worthwhile

Bubbles pop, taste buds flow, you feel that extra special glow

Moët & Chandon and Wall's Viennetta, make celebration days truly 'Red Letter'

Delicious, refreshing, taste beguiling, they add fizz to parties, keep guests smiling

This ice cool combination with warm congratulations will crown the jubilation

'Sin'tillating Viennetta, Moët & Chandon zing, makes a celebration a very classy fling

One pops the cork, the other tops the fork

One provides the starter, the other the ultimate finish

Both rich and cool and ostentatious, they make any celebration outrageous

With Viennetta and bubbly, any party's doubly lubbly

For that special date – they're the nicest way to celebrate

Moët & Chandon tickles my nose and Wall's Viennetta tickles my fancy

Composed by Wall's, this suite is best accompanied by the finest flute

They taste wickedly expensive but are wonderfully affordable

They're both designed with good times in mind

You cannot beat this 'bubble and sweet'

They are the connoisseur's dream of richness supreme

This perfectly blended pair adds cherished moments to any romantic affair

Whether cosy liaisons or family invasions their unsurpassed taste complements all occasions

Rich and sparkling, they're merry making and so cool they're brrr-eathtaking

They're a marriage of equals – for richer and pourer

The unashamed luxury without the scandalous price

They make a cool party go with a bang

A tasteful twosome oozing class has all the grandeur none can surpass

They're supercalawallsfantastic extra bubbles - oh shucks!
You can bank on the interest they create
They're made by the makers of happy ever afters
Wall's Viennetta is the bizz, Moët & Chandon has the fizz
A wickedly rich ice queen and bubbly French aristocrat always sparkle together
The celestial combination is hellishly rapturous

▶ **John Player Special is even more SPECIAL in Asda because…**

> PRODUCT: *Cigarettes*
> COMPETITION: *Asda/John Player Special*

Give black an inch and they'll take a smile

SPICE

▶ **Heinz and Schwartz SPICE up my life because…**

> PRODUCT: *Spices in jars*
> PRIZE: *Caribbean holiday for two plus £500*

The sensual smells and 'souper' spice, send me to paradise

▶ **Ginger loaf adds SPICE to life because…**

> PRODUCT: *Cake*

This hot favourite is a certain tea-time winner

SPIRITS & DRINKS

▶ **I think that San Miguel is a gold medal winning premium lager because…**

> PRODUCT: *Lager*
> PRIZES: *Trips to Olympic Games at Barcelona*

Like all winners it has a strong clean finish
Unlike the Olympics, no-one should have to wait four years for another
Every 'Opening Ceremony' is followed by a lap of honour
To Cat-a-lan story short, in the race for perfection it can't be caught
They haven't made a platinum medal yet
It's sharp as a javelin, smooth as a rink, a winner in Spain and our favourite
 drink

▶ **I prefer Tia Maria over ice because...**

PRODUCT: *Coffee liqueur*

Taste In Action Makes A Really Inviting Attraction *(TIA MARIA = ACROSTIC)*

▶ **When choosing fine port I always select Graham's because...**

PRODUCT: *Port*

Bottled late it's worth the wait

▶ **I would nominate ... (Person) to share my Sandeman port because...**

PRODUCT: *Port*

Chay Blythe: he is reserved, has seen many ports in a storm, but never flounders

Sandy Lyle: this swinging 'Sandeman' would 'open' the conversation and prove perfect to a tee

▶ **Glenmorangie whisky is my favourite purchase from Victoria Wine because...**

PRODUCT: *Whisky*

Tain refrain from casks fae Spain, and let it soak – in oak

With pleasure in every measure, Glenmorangie is Victoria's gold liquid measure

It's the supreme malt from the shop without a fault

It's the 'Monarch O' the Glen' for all whisky drinking men

It's highland dew, Ross-shire air – bottled and priced beyond compare

The highlands beckon take me forth, to Glenmorangie 'spirit' of the North

I've tried the rest and like Glenmorangie the best

The supreme malt from highest still, is supreme value from lowest till

Good service, without fault, serves me the best malt

From Tarlogie springs, pleasure it brings, unique and fulfilling, the Scotchman's Darjeeling

After years of trying the rest, Glenmorangie is still the best

The taste is luxurious, my wallet's victorious

What the sixteen men of Tain perfect, I at Victoria Wine select

Glenmorangie is a malt beyond measure, smooth, distinctive and always a pleasure

From a range inspired, its taste once acquired is forever desired

Fresh and fragrant delicately flavoured, Glenmorangie is made to be savoured

Delicate and distinctive, king of malts, my favourite drink from Victoria's vaults

For me, the taste is premier with Glenmorangie 'The Malt the Merrier'

I can't fault Glenmorangie malt, from Victoria's extensive vault

▶ My advertising slogan is...

PRODUCT: Whisky
COMPETITION: Famous Grouse Scotch whisky

The Famous Grouse, it's class in a glass
Blended with past skills to meet present tastes
An old master in a modern world
From a great past they have created a great present
Upholding famous traditions
For those who appreciate the best
Scotch the birdie
Give any old whisky the bird, buy a Grouse
GAMEbird – SET apart – MATCHless whisky
Don't beat about the bush, ask for a Grouse
An elusive bird? an exclusive whisky
Ensure the bird in your hand is a Famous Grouse
From the best 'still' and still the best
The Scotch not to be mist
Up with the lark but to bed with a Grouse
The blend of a perfect day
Measure for measure a real Scotch treasure
Di'still'inguished
Aim for the Famous Grouse
Set your sights on the Famous Grouse
Dram-atic
Try the high flier – the Famous Grouse
Grouse puts other whiskies to flight
Scotsmen perfect it – Scotchmen select it
Grouse from the hills and liquid gold from the stills
A well-made choice for a choice well made
A taste of heaven doesn't cost the earth
Stock and share the Famous Grouse
Still the best
Be game – grin and share it
Great Scot – great Scotch
A little bird told me about the Famous Grouse
The moor grouse the better
Grouse season – 12th August to 11th August
Famous to the last drop
Discover the spirit of the wild
Every measure is a pleasure
The Highland Spirit
Born in Scotland, raised worldwide

▶ It's neat to mix it with Cockspur because...

PRODUCT: Rum

Cocktails cockspurred win praise, shaken or stirred
This message in a bottle mixes harmoniously with a 'sting'
Mixed or neat it tastes a treat
Shaken or stirred, it is always preferred
It's the record breaker mixer shaker
Specialists perfect it, connoisseurs select it
Every Judy falls for this Punch
Ice likes it, lemon adores it and sodas everyone else
An exotic potion sets the chemistry in motion
Like the Titanic it goes down well with ice
It beats the Sch.... out of you know who
It's the perfect combination for taste and presentation
Everyone makes passes at Cockspur filled glasses

▶ **The Famous Grouse Scotch whisky and the RSPB can work together to protect British birds by...**
PRODUCT: Whisky

Both keeping the pecker up
Using the water of life to promote the spirit of conservation
Saying cheers for every swallow as donations fly in
Making a dram a-vert a crisis
Proving that, quite frankly my dear they do give a dram

▶ **What I most enjoy about Californian wine is...**
PRODUCT: Californian wine

It pampers the palate, mellows the mood, and complements almost any food
Party, lunch, formal dinner, rich smooth taste, certain winner
One swallow makes a summer
The taste of liquid sunshine in every glass
It makes every occasion a celebration
It tastes nice and sunny and is 'grape' value for money
It's a wine that entices at irresistible prices
It's born in California and raised elsewhere

▶ **Dixons camera shops and Cinzano combined means...**
PRODUCT: Vermouth

They are the top of the optics
For sparkling eyes and sparkling buys they're the pair that harmonise
Cinzano's liquid assets perfectly match Dixons' many facets
One's nice on ice, the other's nice on price
They break the ice with a splash, recording happiness in a flash
They focus attention, add dimension, record the accord of that special occasion
They combine the pleasures of electronics with the most pleasing tonics
Cinzano taste is aromatic, Dixons' value is dramatic, the combination is
    charismatic

▶ **I drink Lucozade after sports because...**

PRODUCT: Glucose drink

Once tasted, soon gone, but the benefits linger on
Every can gives bottle, every bottle says you can
Instant energy is put back, countering an energy deficit attack
After a gruelling session on the track, Lucozade puts energy back
When your vital go has gone, Lucozade helps you carry on
When your body's stamina is under attack, Lucozade puts the energy back
Nothing's a test when your fuelled by the best
Whether it's cycling, sailing, running or swimming, Lucozade ensures my
    energy's brimming
A hectic day full of strife, Lucozade adds that sparkle of life
It turns fed up and slow into get up and go
When your sparkle begins to fade, put it back with Lucozade
Aces, athletes and amateurs agree, Lucozade works to a T

▶ **I prefer Diamond White because...**

PRODUCT: White cider

You don't have to take the rough with this smooth cider
Brilliance and sparkle both combine to make a cider none can outshine
Its subtle style makes taste buds roar – cider was not like this before
It's a clear cut gem of class, liquid crystal in a glass
Its strength and extra bite make it 'all white' on the night
It's light, it's white, it's dynamite
When other bottles are discarded, Diamond White is closely guarded
Strong, smooth, dry and white, Diamond White sparkles day or night
Refreshing by day, exciting by night, the extra strength of Diamond White
Whiter appearance, stronger taste, it's a sparkling gem, amid the paste
Same old spirits, boring beer, distinctly delicious, Diamond White has no peer

▶ **Smirnoff Vodka and Schweppes Russchian competition**

PRODUCT: Vodka
PRODUCT: Schweppes Russchian – Mixer for vodka

Without Smirnoff I'll Bette Bogart never Maed his Marx
Smirnoff has a secret that only a Russian can reveal
They reign when they're poured
They're in a glass of their own
Whether a liberal or conservative drinker, they provide the heart of any party
It's a case of East coming West and winning the best – a great match
With Smirnoff the sire, Russian the mother, blend them together, 'rush off' for
    another
It's man's best blend
Too good, it's elementary, their qualities are complementary

One has spirit, the other has sparkle, they compliment each other and
    complement your taste
Together they paint your party red
Tumbling roubles and roulette – you've joined the daring Russian set

▶ **Mateus Rosé Gourmet competition**
PRODUCT: Wine

Whether first or fifth course, even with discourse it's the ideal companion
Goes well with any meal and is reasonably priced
It's a capital wine for a capital meal
By itself or with a meal, this palace wine has drink appeal
Being the champagne of rosés, it complements every dish

Assorted drinks and stores

It's a man's best blend
They qualify for thirst glass honours
Experts perfect it, connoisseurs select it
They're in a 'glass' of their own
The best has a pale complexion, the rest have a ruddy cheek (*Sherry)
When put to the taste it goes down a treat
It's thirst come, thirst served
It's kept in bars and sold in ounces
It was born in (*country of origin) and it's raised in glasses everywhere
They raise your spirits without spiriting away your raises
It's class in a glass
Every measure is such a pleasure
One swallow does make a summer
Sharing quantity and quality make the pourer richer
It's made to perfection for the finest selection
It's chosen with flair by people who care
It's always offered with confidence and accepted with pleasure
Vintage Variety, Splendid Selection, Obliging Options, Purse-fitting Prices are
    as Victoria said 'most gratifying' *(VVSSOOPP = DOUBLE ACROSTIC)*
    (*VSOP Courvoisier Cognac)
Asda quenches my thirst without drying my purse
It's the drink that has the most flavour
Asda squashes price rises

Assorted soft drinks, squashes and stores

It has the big heart that's more than cordial
It's got style, it's got class, it's good health in a glass
Picked with care, bottled at peak, the selective flavour is quite unique
There is nothing to peel and your orange is real
They turn any old day into a Sun-day
As Nell Gwyn cried with zest – 'It's more fruity than the rest'
It's easily bought, easily poured, easily best, easily stored

Where have all the bottles gone, long time emptied
Juicy Britvic, Antiguan sun, what a cocktail to be won
Kia-Ora – Maori for good health, Asda English for good value
Kia-Ora's range is sweet temptation, Asda's change defeats inflation
Pulling the ring unleashes the zing, completing the sparkle of a Caribbean fling
Alcatraz, a famous 'clink', imprisoned with my favourite drink
Refreshingly fruity, delicious on ice, big bottle value, small bottle price

Assorted wines and stores

I've heard of nothing better on the grapevine
It graces discerning tables, the aristocrat of labels
By itself or with a meal, this pleasing wink has drink appeal
Nobody puts up a better case for affordable wine enjoyment
It adds a touch of French polish to my table
France puts their accent on great wines, Morrisons translates them into great value
They are cooling fiestas after my sunny siestas
Peseta or pound they are the best value around
My favourite's there in store – Corrido vino 'pour' favor

Cider makers and ciders

PRODUCT: Ciders

I like my apple a day this way
It's the happy apple
It reaches the core of my thirst
It's so de-cider-dly good
It makes me a pitcher of happiness when I get the pip
When boy meets girl, where sand meets sea, it's great beside 'er with cider, see
When paradise is hot and boring, contentment comes from cider-pouring
Be it Blackthorn or Gold, it's the best cider sold
Gold blond, bubbly with laughter, Taunton has the body I'm after
Sun makes you sunburnt, sea makes you wet, but Taunton make cider you'll never forget
Taunton cider is the sea cider, a drink that has no 'pier'
Woodpecker singles out what the long playing public thirst for

Colt 45 lager

As the sun gets up, Colt goes down
No drink pack kicks like a cold Colt can can
Colt – just the play for arms and the man?
Cool combination on the costa del Colt
Colt – a bigger draw than a small bikini
The only thing he would ever notice topless is Colt
Let's share a Colt and see what we can trigger off

Drink my Colt and my racket will leave an impression
Your tennis always suffers if double Colt's are served
It's so rewarding it ought to be on a wanted poster

Cyprus sherry

I've tried it, compared it, declared it a 'sip-riot', superb

Drinks in general

Specialists create it, connoisseurs nominate it
It's made to perfection from the finest selection
It's thirst come, thirst served
They qualify for thirst glass honours
Straight from the best still and still the best straight

Dry Fly sherry

It has a delicate flavour but a strong appeal I know I've hooked the best catch
    in sherries

Henry Morgan rum

Captain's treasure 'sales' ahead of all rum runners
There is no pirate, it's genuine
In spirit Henry Morgan is still the governor

Off licences

Their enormous vaults have made them the nation's best cellars
It brings the right spirit into the high street
The outcome suits my income
With their competitive spirit we're in for a rosé future
They win the price race by saving your silver and bronze
It's the store from which bargains pour
By bottling and boxing clever, competition is outglassed forever
They 'box' the world's greats for 'knock-out' 'cut' rates
A better class of spirit is present at this haunt
Of their cross country competitiveness and superiority in the vaults
Every line is cheaper by the dozen, just in case
They start as winners hands down and bottoms up
Their Christmas wine list reads like a best cellar
Their price fighters can't be beaten
You have a 'barrel' of laughs Co-oping up your savings
Everything is there, lock, stock and three barrels
Where quality, choice and service combine, there's only one answer – Victoria
    Wine
Victoria vaults to victory
Victoria Wine always keeps its 'nose' in front
Victoria Wine have the adVINtage over their competitors' 'pour' performance
For someone with expensive taste Victoria Wine's my saving grace
Cutting everything but the corners 'Grants' them success

Perrier mineral water

A home is just a 'hm' without its 'o'
Which eaunly geaus to sheau... that many eaus add up to eauceons of Perrier

Schweppes drinks mixers and mineral water

PRODUCT: Soft drinks

I don't give a Sch.... for you know who
Bottled sunshine, less to pay, worries have been schwepped away
At the hiss of a top off, life's pressures drop off
There is no query and no guessing – everyone is schweppervescing

Soft drinks

Thirst and foremost in the nation, what a perfect combination
It's two great names 'squashed' into one great store
It's a fruitful partnership for crushing the cost
It's full fruit flavour from the store of the saver
Both please when they squeeze the fruit and price
They put the brakes on prices in thirst gear
They even dilute the price to taste
It's the refreshing transaction that brings financial satisfaction
When put to the test, this combination refreshes you best
One panders to the plate, the other to the purse
One's cool with ice, the other's hot on price
It quenches a thirst of buying quality first

Sunquick fruit squash

PRODUCT: Concentrated fruit squash

It's easily bought, easily poured, easily best, easily stored
Less to carry, less to store, less to pay, more to pour
It's a deuce of a juice, ace of a price
The price is 'squashed'
It's a combination certain to bring refreshing savings
One squashes thirst, the other squashes inflation
The sun shines when it pours
It's the little bottle with the big taste
Lighter to carry, true orange taste, Sunquick's delicious, straight or laced
Though others taste like flavoured water, Sunquick tastes like fruit drinks
    oughter
Sunquick's tangy, does you good, Sunquick tastes as fruit drinks should
It's nice to start the working day fully refreshed the Sunquick way
Preferring to pay for juice, not water, makes me a Sunquick supporter
I'm bewitched by its 'Sun'-sational spell, wish I had a Sunquick well
Six pints don't need a lot of bottle

Whiteways fruit wine competition

PRODUCT: Wine

Their high quality keeps them in the best cellars
I like my fruit stoned
It's British, it's smooth, it's the taste I approve
Each tempts me to try another – a case of quality bearing fruit

Whyte & Mackay whisky brand

PRODUCT: Whisky

With Whyte & Mackay breaking the ice, each schooner led to paradise
I trip the light fantastic when I try the real Mackay
Those two lions in each measure brought loud roars of double pleasure

Wine boxes

You're in charge of opening and closing times
It's like having a wine waiter in a box

SPORT

► **I give Jacob's and Hovis cream crackers more than a sporting chance because...**

PRODUCT: Crackers
COMPETITION: Jacob's and Hovis/Sporting Chance

Whatever the venue they appear on my menu
Their track record is second to none, always be my number one
Eaten plain or with topping, once started there's no stopping
They consistently make first class 'breaks'
For me they're just the ticket to enjoy whilst watching the cricket
Snap! They're a dead eat at the winning post
When packing school dinners they're cracking good winners
They're more than a match for any biscuit
They make 'grandstand' thrillers for 'hole in tum' fillers
Every sportsman worth his salt savours their taste for hunger assault

► **The average smoker uses Swan Vestas because...**

PRODUCT: Boxed matches
COMPETITION: Swan Vestas Matches/Cricket

He finds the matchless quality of quality matches – striking
He knows the pleasure of striking cleanly every match
When it's his strike he can always depend on the light

Bad light never threatens match play
When it comes to the test, it outmatches the rest
Of Shastri, Willis, Amarnath, Nafrez, Verity, Emburey, Sakinda, Thomas,
    Amiss, Sarfraz – OK *(SWAN VESTAS = ACROSTIC)*
He knows that it will be a good match with Swan
It would bowl my friends over, stump my critics and be a nice run out
Without the will, he won't
Without the will to win, you're beaten before you begin

▶ **Boots sports preparations are ideal for me because...**

    PRODUCT: *Sports preparations*
    COMPETITION: *Boots the Chemists/Sports*

Keeping fit meant strain and grief before Boots worked out pain relief
Out of form in distress, Boots have a formula for success
When pain stops play, Boots save the day
Champion I'll never be, but Boots keeps me pain free
When every muscle feels aflame, Boots restores me to my game

Sports shops

For sportswear that's really ace, they always set the pace
Offering sportsmen so much more, Olympus is the best 'run' store

Victoria Wine shops with a sports theme

By bottling and boxing clever, competition is outglassed forever
They 'box' the world's greats for 'knock-out' 'cut' rates
Of their cross country competitiveness and superiority in the vaults
They start as winners hands down and bottoms up
Their price fighters can't be beaten
Victoria vaults to victory
Victoria Wine always keeps its 'nose' in front
Victoria Wine have the adVINtage over their competitors' 'pour' performance

SPREADS

▶ **Marmite yeast extract is tasty anywhere in the world because...**

    PRODUCT: *Savoury spread*

There isn't a more delicious spread, within the four corners of my bread
When the menu's exotic, Marmite's patriotic
A familiar treat in an exotic location, sets the seal on a perfect vacation
Sushi's tasty, squid's alright, when in Rome make mine Marmite

The flavour that delighted Gran, still tastes great to a globe-trotting man
It can be enjoyed anywhere on the earth's crust
Capricorn to Cancer, wherever I roam, Marmite reminds me of tea and toast at
    home
World scenes and climates alter, but Marmite's quality doesn't falter
It's the message in a bottle understood by every tongue
Wherever you are, whatever you do, one little jar will fortify you
It's available, it's instant and its taste is out of this world
That rich wholesome flavour for gravy or spread, a true family favourite
    wherever you tread
The earth's crust never goes to waste, spread with Marmite's tempting taste
Buttered bread, wherever eaten, spread with Marmite can't be beaten
Frogs legs? Birds nest? Do me a favour, Marmite's flavour is the one to savour
Its flavour spreads from coast to coast, to every corner of my toast
Over the Channel, Atlantic or Med, Marmite's the healthiest tastiest spread
A loaf of bread, a Marmite jar, brings instant happiness near or far
From Blackpool beach to Ivory Coast, Marmite goodness gets my toast
Jars of Marmite small and large, make every trip a 'bon voyage'
Wherever I suffer a hunger attack, it's a healthy convenient anytime snack
Rio or Sydney, wherever you are, home is in the Marmite jar
Flavour from the little brown jar, appeals to folk both near and far
Going through customs I must declare, it's a seasoned traveller welcomed
    everywhere
When battles over, meals begin, Marmite soldiers always win
It spreads a smile on your soldier's face, so spread the word, spread the taste

► **When I shop at Kwik Save, Princes are my favourite spreads
because...**

    PRODUCT: Meat and fish pastes
    COMPETITION: Kwik Save/Princes spreads
    PRIZES: Kwik Save shopping vouchers

No waste, super taste, makes sense, saves pence
They have the best selection of the Princes collection
Kwik save the price saver, Princes has perfect flavour
They're the top of my pots and don't cost me lots
For perfect taste, a royal munch, with pennies saved, it packs punch
I get Kwik service, Kwik flavours and Kwik savers
They help me make ends 'meat'
Lunches, picnics, snacks, dinners, with Kwik Save they are 'breadwinners'
It's value shopping, family fed, provides quality, princely spread
Lower priced, super tasting, they give rivals a proper pasting
The round pot's petite, the variety's very elite
Buying Princes at Kwik Save really spreads your bread
Competition, there is none, lower prices, best brands for everyone
Sealed in their pot, Princes beats the lot
Salmon, beef, pâté, paste bought with confidence, spread with taste

For old, young or teens, they're great for go-betweens
Bread becomes haute cuisine with Princes as the go-between
I want the tastiest topping and lowest priced shopping
Once opened, soonest eaten, Princes spreads just can't be beaten
Kwik Save is my money saver, Princes offer perfect flavour
Largest choice, lowest price, nothing else half as nice
Watching movies late a night, Princes makes the perfect bite
The best dressed bread wears Princes spread
A Princes spreader makes a better 'Gorge' than Cheddar
More choice in my trolley, pots more for my lolly
Chuffed to bits, my sarnies are fit for the Ritz
I'm completely besotted, with every spread potted
Bargain buys, big brand name, other spreads are not the same
Princes provide tasty bites, Kwik Saves me check-out frights
With tastebuds teased and pockets pleased, excellent value is guaranteed
The humble loaf becomes well-bred, decorated with Princes spread
Tired of scampi, caviare, squid, answer lies under Princes lid
Princes is 'kwik' to spread satisfaction

▶ I buy Robertson's Silver Shred because...

PRODUCT: Conserve
COMPETITION: Tesco/Robertson's

It's as fresh as the day the lemons were picked
There's no better investment than in family silver
They guarantee a morning booty – well preserved and very fruity
Robertson's is number one, first for flavour, second to none
Without a shred of doubt, Robertson's is the tastiest out
Buy Golly! It's good. Tastes like marmalade should
It brings Mediterranean sunshine to my breakfast table
Golly's tangy Sicilian slices – twice as nice at Tesco prices
It has the hallmark of perfection for my breakfast selection
I get tasty toast topping and super saver shopping
Her Majesty and me enjoy it with our morning tea
Sicilian silver gives a golden start to the greyest day
They've captured sunlight to make my breakfast bright
Nicer peel and price appeal conjure up a magic deal
The golly symbol reigns supreme, setting standards rarely seen
Cram-jam full of sunshine – it puts others 'in the shade'
Every jar has a silver lining
I don't buy lemons – I buy Robertson's in-shred

STANDARD

▶ **For the highest STANDARD in coffee I buy Melitta from Tesco because...**

PRODUCT: Coffee
COMPETITION: Tesco/Melitta

I save an awful lot of coppers in ze-bill
I can quaff like a toff without selling the Van Gogh
When spirits flag they turn Blue Peters into Jolly Rogers
Its strength is my weakness
Both have changed me from an 'instant' housewife into a 'real' hostess
Taste temptation free from inclination and imagine the sensation – a Rio
    vacation
From mountain top, from ship to shop, Melitta/Tesco crown the crop
It's a pricey taste at a tasty price
Backing winners makes good sense, this classic double saves the pence
No fancy gimmicks, passing trends, just finest beans, perfected blends
Tesco's a girl's best friend while Melitta's a man's best blend
They both give their competitors a good roasting
Traditional cup or cappuccino, Tesco prices leave cash for the vino
It's like Wembley, easily the finest ground for success in the cup
Always it gives elevenses out of ten
Melitta from Tesco – a nice penthouse taste at a basement price

STAR

▶ **You're always assured of STAR value at Presto because...**

PRODUCT: Washing powder
PRIZES: Trips to Disneyland

They point the way to economical shopping, leaving me change for Florida
    hopping
They care, they share, they're fair, they're there
Staff never Grumpy, stores clean and bright, they're B-Levers in treating
    customers right
Chancellors are 'Laws-on' to themselves, Presto balances my budget every
    week
Presto's awash with best buys of all – poor Cinderellas have a ball
They make your average 'trouble n' strife', feel more like a Hollywood wife

▶ **Danish quality foods from my Bob Store gives my meals STAR appeal because...**

COMPETITION: Bob Stores/Danish Foods

These bobby dazzlers make my eyes pop, prices drop, quality tip top

▶ Dolmio is the STAR ingredient in my kitchen because...

PRODUCT: Pasta sauce
COMPETITION: Safeway/Dolmio

Forget Hoffman, Cruise and Swayze – Dolmio drives my tastebuds crazy
Dolmio is the only Safeway to have a saucy Italian
It is simply SupermovapastarrificexpertDolmiocious
Natural ingredients, guaranteed to please, Italian cuisine without any E's
No 'Casualty' for 'Fools and Sauces', it 'Masterminds' 'Blockbuster' courses
Its appeal is 'Universal' and its taste 'Paramount'
'Super' smashin' 'simply great' – bullseye scored on every plate
Like Pisa – it's always on the list
A prize performer in cuisine, Dolmio always steals the scene
Produce Dolmio – 'pan meat' – 'zoom' to table – 'action' – eat

▶ Kayser tights and stockings are my STAR choice because...

PRODUCT: Tights and stockings

I've auditioned the rest but Kayser are sheerly the best

▶ Video screen STARS eat Princes spreadables because...

PRODUCT: Spreads in jars
COMPETITION: Tesco/Princes Spreads Video
PRIZES: Personal video recorders

It's paste Jim – but not as we know it
They know how to make knife-edge thrillers
Even E.T. 'tis said, phoned home for his spread

▶ Coca-Cola always STARS in my Wm Low shopping trolley because...

PRODUCT: Soft drink
COMPETITION: Wm Low/Coca-Cola
PRIZES: Trips to Disneyland

When Coke's on the 'bill' at Wm Low, its sparkling performance steals the
    show
With Disney in the air, you can't beat the feeling of shopping there
It's the best drink 'in the can' and always a permanent feature
Never in my wildest flight of fantasia would I forget Coke – what could be
    crazier?
Coke is the best soft drink I know and I always shop at Wm Low

▶ **I would like to take the TV challenge with Benson & Hedges because...**

PRODUCT: *Cigarettes*
COMPETITION: *B & H/Hillards take the TV Challenge*

I'd have action, attraction and King Size satisfaction
In everyway golden opportunities make my day
Whoever you are, with Benson and Hillards you're the 'Star'

START

▶ **Heinz and Kwik Save START me off best...**

PRODUCT: *Supermarket foods*
COMPETITION: *Kwik Save/Heinz sports prizes*
FIRST PRIZES: *Raleigh mountain bikes*

Their economic shopping deals show rivals a clean pair of wheels
Heinz and Kwik Save never skive, they know how many beans make five
Kwik Save value cannot be surpassed, fine food from Heinz never outclassed
With beans for breakfast, who's countin'? Kwik Heinz send a mountain
With fitness and health in body and wealth

RUNNERS-UP: *Sports towels*

Heinz Raleigh satisfied mountainous appetites Kwik smart
On terms desired, nutrition required, fibre tips wholly inspired
With quality and value that passes the proficiency test
They just keep me jogging along
On the school run they are best in the long run
Because in the race to please, they win with ease
Heinz buyers Raleigh round, because Kwik Save keeps prices down
With their three R's – reliable quality, real value and reduced costs
Tummies full and uniform pressed, variety awaits as I leave the rest
Because they're one step ahead but leave prices behind
I've bean to others but yours pass the test
Educating me with expert tuition, in the arts of housekeeping and nutrition

STAYING

▶ **I believe Araldite has STAYING power because...**

PRODUCT: *Adhesive in sticks and tubes*
COMPETITION: *Araldite Staying Power*

FIRST PRIZES: *Home gym kits*

Hopeless housewife, accident prone, swears by Araldite around the home
With guide puppy loose, Araldite's in daily use
It has stuck with me longer than two previous husbands
Stick around, this is gripping stuff
Unlike B.R., it always keeps its connections

SECOND PRIZES: *Fitness kits*

Two sticks, stick better than one
Great traction, strong action, pure reaction, total satisfaction
Lasting results with only two squeezes, Araldite's performance always pleases
Top performer second to none, a handyman's number one
Their's the power, mine's the glory
Araldite has the muscle without the cramp
Araldite is your lifetime property bond, stick with it
For 40 days and 40 nights, Noah's secret was Araldite
I'm Miss Moneypenny and I'm keen on Bond-age
My wife still doesn't know it's been broken!

THIRD PRIZES: *Sports bags*

Connery, Moore, Dalton went overnight, the permanent Bond is Araldite
Whatever the surface, ceiling or floor, Araldite sticks for evermore
I'm a 'keep-fixed' fanatic
It's on my permanent fixture list
It's the one you choose first – to last
Its strength and durability never lets us 'dum-bells' down
One tiny touch maintains so much
Super strength, spot by spot, Araldite has got the lot
Epoxy resin is unsurpassed, for lasting long and holding fast
It binds, holds, locks, works, even when subjected to physical jerks
It's the master of the gluniverse
Araldite is supremely sure, the finest 'Bond' since Roger Moore
You just need a pinch for a permanent clinch
It you want it done right, do it with Araldite
A small deposit secures any article
It's a product with strength that never loses its grip

STICK & STUCK

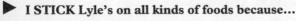 **I STICK Lyle's on all kinds of foods because...**

PRODUCT: *Golden Syrup*

I'm brain washed you see, by that catchy jingle on TV
Syrup was on ration when I was a tot, now I indulge my passion and Golden
top the lot

My kids get stuck into everything with Lyle's Golden Syrup

▶ **I love to get STUCK into Lyle's because...**

PRODUCT: Golden Syrup

Dipping in the tin puts my taste buds in a spin
Lyle's sticky treats I adore, so I dash to Gateway for some more
Ordinary foods become a treat, Lyle's helps to make life sweet
It's a delicious sweet topping I don't mind swapping
For breakfast, dinner, tea and pud, I'm stuck on Lyle's cos it's so good

▶ **I love pancakes with Lyle's because...**

PRODUCT: Golden Syrup

Yummy, nutritious, sticky and sweet, Lyle's on pancakes is our regular treat

▶ **I buy Lyle's at Gateway stores because...**

PRODUCT: Golden Syrup

Their golden value which I treasure, transforms a chore into a pleasure
Syrup for breakfast, lunch or tea, fills the family with glee
Thunder and lightning this Cornishman's dream, bread and syrup topped with cream
I can fulfil my family's wishes with my tempting syrupy dishes
With golden goodness, through and through, it's tempting, tasty and nutritious too
'Purse-nelly' they save me coppers, for value they're golden toppers
Golden oldies take some beating, proof of pudding's in the eating
It closes the generation gap, a golden oldie at prices way back
Golden offers for refined tastes, mean approving smiles and empty plates
They have the strength – I have the weakness
I once used it syruptitiously, now I'm pudding it on everything
It's versatile on the one hand and 'amberdextrose' on the other
Sweetest syrup, favourite store, this is the team that always score
It's got what it takes for great puddings and cakes
Mother nature never made a purer, sweeter cooking aid
Smooth, good, naturally sweet, it transforms my plain pud into a treat
Pancakes flip, puddings steam and never fail to taste supreme
It makes golden crêpes quite unique, the discerning say 'C'est Magnifique'
It's the perfect pour-on topping from the perfect store for shopping
Both always easily impress, truly a story of sweet success
Since these two wed, every pancake I toss is thoroughbred
The syrup that bears the Royal crest obviously sweetens the very best
Quality and value beyond compare, I make a bee-line for the lion's share
Everyone's favourite, young and old, is a lion's share of Lyle's gold
There's gold in them there 'aisles' when you go 'prospecting' for Lyle's

For home baking they love so much, Lyle's adds the Midas touch
Lyle's make puddings, hot or cold, adding sparkle with their liquid gold
In the art of sweet confection, Lyle's Golden Syrup has achieved perfection
Lyles's at Gateway is tradition for golden value and nutrition
Gateway and Lyle's, a perfect pair, make my pudding a unique affair
With Lyle's in the Gateway trolley, it's golden days and puddings jolly
The Gateway to my husband's heart is Lyle's treacle tart
For beautiful teas, shopping with ease, Lyle's Golden Syrup and Gateway
   please
Gateway sells the golden goods relied upon for perfect puds
For traditional taste at old-fashioned prices, Lyle's at Gateway always entices
That sweet taste, distinctive tin, Gateway value draws me in
Nostalgia beams from Gateway's aisles, old-fashioned prices, sweetest smiles
For golden value, thickly spread, choose Lyle's and Gateway for your bread
Lyle's is number one, first for flavour, second to none
Puddings without Lyle's – unthinkable, shopping without Gateway –
   unprintable
For syrup'ed pancakes, crisply eaten – Gateway's ingredients can't be beaten
A Gateway and Lyle's affair is love at first bite
Pancake flat prices, flipping good flair, make Gateway and Lyle's beyond
   compare
My flapjacks have Lyle's luscious appeal, with Gateway's lovely golden deal

STORES

Stores in general

It's the group with the number one record
Each counter attacks inflation
Service is slick and turnover quick, with guaranteed value whatever I pick
Their price pegging means more value on every line
Popular prices, super display, guaranteed quality and a cheerful good-day
In spite of inflation they're still a sensation
The price is right, it offers me more, and fills my trolley with bargains galore
Perfect harmony in both you'll find, value and quality combined
There's savings all round giving power to my pound
Step away with less to pay
They make the penny drop
Legend says the bargain seeker, dashes in and shouts 'Eureka'
More quality to start with, less money to part with
They offer friendly service and good advice plus quality products at a
   competitive price
Masters of their trade deserve the highest accolade
One stop shopping, massive range, buy more, spend less, lots of change
It's hand in glove with cash in hand
For feeding the nation it's the best filling station

When I've a trolley that's full to the top, it's the most economical place to shop
Though not a detective, I'm super selective
In any poll they win at the gallup
Goodwill, a good-fill and a smaller bill
A double dose of saving graces, lines our pockets not our faces
The outcome suits my income
They're heaven scent opportunities for shoppers with a nose for bargains
They ensure you won't have to be shopping and changing
They stock a stack at prices that stick
It has a reputation for value and values its reputation
They mind their P's and Q's – price and quality
They are plum goods to be picked from every branch, and all at pruned prices
Whatever their needs, all ages know, Asda is the place to go
Their prices don't go ding-dong merrily up-high
You can bet it's where Santa does his stocking up
My cash flow is only trickle, Asda lets me splash out a bit
It makes sense where there's less expense and Asda's choice is so immense
Asda's magic can turn a cross section of the public into satisfied customers
Hair raising prices crimp my style, Morrisons fringe benefits make me smile
There's more money left at the end of my week instead of more week left at the
    end of my money

STYLE, LIFESTYLE & IMAGE

▶ **I enjoy putting on the STYLE with Gancia because...**

PRODUCT: Sparkling wine

It fires my sparking plugs

▶ **Tesco and Kellogg's are just my STYLE because...**

PRODUCT: Breakfast cereals

Tesco crunches prices, Kellogg's crunch is nicest
Tesco's prices lead the way, helping Kellogg's start my day
Kellogg's fuel this human machine, whilst Tesco helps to keep me lean
In the good value race, they always take first place
They give me a 'bran' new feeling at an old fashioned price

▶ **Colman's Home Style sauces suit my LIFESTYLE because...**

PRODUCT: Sauces in boxes

Around the world they're turning stock into a liquid asset
They halve the labour and double the flavour
Once I guessed the time and measure, now I've time for guests and leisure
Cooking a meal with Colman's means you'll never Reckitt

Even hasty days are tasty days
I prefer to ride the range, not slave over it
Why pour over recipes when you can pour over Home Style?
They are an investment with inbuilt stocks for family shares
They're natural sauces of inspiration, for meals of tasteful innovation
Whilst maximum latitude of taste, they minimise longtitude of preparation

▶ **I trust Fuji film to capture any IMAGE because...**

PRODUCT: Camera film

I can't picture life without it
Family memories fade too fast, Fuji film ensures they last

▶ **Agfa and BMW create the perfect IMAGE because...**

PRODUCT: Camera film
PRIZE: BMW car

You cannot escape their quality control, mile after mile, roll after roll

▶ **My IMAGE is complete with Drakkoir Noir because...**

PRODUCT: Aftershave

Though visually sound, I need Drakkoir Noir for close-ups
It's the signature that attracts admiring glances and closer inspection
Experts perfect it – connoisseurs select it
Handsome, not I, but its fragrance is a graphic equaliser
Pleasant aroma, expertly blended, the finishing touches that Laroche intended
We co-star in close-ups
It brings me sharply into focus
The situation 'lens' itself to zooming on good grooming
It announces my arrival and delays my departure
It has a sharp focus on style
It turned a demanding man into a man in demand
It's the finishing touch that brings everything into focus
Now she loves to share my close-ups
One touch programmes the extra-sensory reception
Drakkoir Noir develops it from negative reflection to positive projection

SUITS

▶ **Citrice SUITS me because...**

PRODUCT: Sparkling drink
PRIZE: Two nights in London plus £500

Opening the bottle unleashes the zing, lemony sparkle, capital fling

SUN & SUNSHINE

▶ **I would like to drink Perrize in the sun because...**

PRODUCT: *Sparkling drink*

Golden days of leisure deserve golden pleasure
Whether restful or zestful my Perrize glass is best full
Paradise is – lying on a sun drenched beach – refreshing Perrize within reach
It is the cool toast of the warm coast
It's the taste sensation for every location
On the beach I'd rather have a little squirt, than come across a physical jerk

▶ **My family and I would have fun under the sun with Morning Fresh this winter because...**

PRODUCT: *Washing-up liquid*

Gleams really do come true, when Morning Fresh washes up for you
We'd holiday on the Corinth Canal with Cussons – both cut through Greece
Providing Morning Fresh fulfils our wishes and all will enjoy those foreign
  dishes
With Co-op travel care, our Cussons guarantee Morning Fresh air
With warming sun and gentle breezes – we'd forget our coughs and sneezes
Sun, sand and family treat – like Cussons' shine it's hard to beat
Morning Fresh makes dishes and wishes come shining through

▶ **When I taste the sunshine in Haven premium dried fruit I want to...**

PRODUCT: *Dried fruit*
PRIZE: *Holiday to Crete*

Savour the flavour, treasure the treat, capture the rapture of 'sunsational' Crete

Shopping in the sun

As the temperatures soar, you'll find bargains galore
Bermuda or back garden bound, every requirement is easily found

SWEETS

▶ **If I won a car I'd drive to...**

PRODUCT: *Confectionery*
COMPETITION: *Cadbury's Double Decker*

Piccadilly Circus – I heard a little Wispa it's crawling with Double Deckers

▶ **I choose Mars and Marathon chocolate bars because...**

PRODUCT: Confectionery
COMPETITION: Mars/Marathon

Both win by finishing last. These nourishing bars are unsurpassed
They're ready to eat, steady for price, give you go and they're Oh so nice
Of our long running relationship

▶ **I enjoy eating Nuttall's Soft Mints because...**

PRODUCT: Mints

These melting, crumbling, cool creations give monumental taste sensations
They're the mintiest sensation without a doubt, softness bursts from inside out
They are cool, minty, sweet and light, in every way exactly right
They don't stint on the mint or overdo the chew
A cool refreshing minty flavour gives that icy taste to savour
Soft mints are hard to beat, crisp and cool a real treat
They are smooth, minty, quite unique, in my opinion 'C'est magnifique'
I don't need to own the royal mint to enjoy a packet
They are heavenly mints at a down-to-earth price
Crumbling, delicious, they're cool perfection – a pure white melting mint
    perfection

Bassett's Liquorice Allsorts with a Christmas theme

A sweet yule enjoy at a price that will sleigh you
A Santapplause selection
All together sweeter holly days
A sweeter Christmas 'stock in' with fewer hang ups
Tills ringing – ding dong merrily on low with Allsorts to show
A stocking full of goodies and Allsorts of prices
Allsorts of altogether excellent ways to wish goodwill to all men
An enterprising Bertie Bassett making his presents felt
A tasty stocking filler from Bert, a bargain at Asda for cert
Bassett's make a frown turn upside down
'Francly' speaking, Bluebell Follies mix so well with Bassett's dollies
Both have excellent qualities to satisfy 'All Sorts' of people
They provide the best trolley mixtures

Dime Bar slogans

PRODUCT: Confectionery

It's a Dime-a-Nite bar
Secret wish – to wear a diamond that cost me a dime
They are devastating dime after dime
It's a little cracker of a bar
It explodes with flavour right in your Andes

Maltesers chocolates

> PRODUCT: Confectionery
> COMPETITION: Maltesers travel

They pack a treat for any occasion
There's nothing to declare but satisfaction

Pop bubble gum

It's fruitful bang
A fruitful explosion rocks the hop
Disco over, a great sound, catch-a-chew-chew
Beboppers have the last waltz with chew
New records are created, groovy flavours are inflated
There's more bubbly music at the hop

Ritter Sport chocolate bars

When the Germans say 'wunderbar' they're talking about Ritter Sport

Wrigley's chewing gum with a train theme

This 'chew-chew' has a flavour that never runs out of steam
That's another fine chew-chew I'd like to get into
To see wonders from carriage pane on the most historic chew-chew train
For excitement and travel at its best, I'd chew-chew from Paris to Bucharest
I often dream of chew-chews past, with memories 'by gum' that will last
With its chewing and fro-ing it's the best way of going
Chewing it over with deliberation, this train's definitely above my station
It's more refreshing than going by chew-b
If I could chewse a dream trip I'd chewse the Orient Express, wouldn't chew?
The Orient Express, what a thrilling idea, something I've chewed over year
    after year
What other 'choo-choo' has the gumption to make luxury travel its mainline
    function?
I could murder a taste of excitement – couldn't chew?
By gum! It's the 'chuff' that dreams are made of
I think I might look really cute pronouncing the French for juicy fruit
Wrigley has stood the taste of time
Though in French I'm not articulate, going sight-seeing with Wrigley's I'd
    gesticulate
While Wrigley's wraps a cheeky chew-chew, the Orient Express the choicest
    choo-choo
The best, by gum, beyond compare, flavours to savour, anywhere
To chew it is to love it
Minty sensation you cannot beat, every chew becomes a treat
Minty, fruity, sugarless too, the flavour lasts throughout the chew
You can chew, bubble or smile, all in style

I can chew-man, think-man and walk-man
I'll give you a clue, it's the chosen chew
Refreshing and invigorating, it helps me when I'm concentrating
It freshens the palate when smoking's a habit
Super flavours, second to none, longer lasting, my number one
They are small in size but big in flavour
Refreshing! Keep your teeth sound – be friendly, pass some round
This multi-saver, multi-stacks, multi-flavour in multi-packs
Tangy fruit or mint fresh, Wrigley's flavour stays the best
In a tizz? Under pressure? Wrigley's is the great refresher
Switched on product, tuned in price, Wrigley's selection, double nice

Sweet products in general

They are sweet encounters of the preferred kind
Taste and value you can lick but never beat
I always 'chew-s' the best
They're a sweet sensation for every generation
Price perfection and choice confection
A super sweet that's twice as nice at half the price
You can lick 'em but you won't beat 'em
They're a very sweet deal
In the confectionary market it's the bar-gain buyers' target
A jingle in your pocket and a tingle on your tongue
They are the easy to handle bars

SWITCHED ON

▶ **We've SWITCHED ON to Trex at Kwik Save because...**

PRODUCT: Cooking fat
COMPETITION: Kwik Save/Trex with the best
PRIZES: TVs with teletext

I paged the Oracle, it Kwikly replied, FasTrex' pleases nationwide
My hubby's motive one suspects, he wants set with TeleTrex
Charging less, tasting grand, they make sure we're programmed
Little Trexperts all agree, peak chewing time – chips for tea
Perfect blending, perfect store, tuned in customers need no more
Everything will be all-light, even the price is right
Fry or bake Trex n' Kwik saves apiece 'a' cake
Trex is Flex-ible to use – Kwik Save values we can't re-fuse
Beautiful baking, fabulous fry, flexible Trex is an excellent buy
Tre'experts perfect 'em, connoisseurs select 'em, thieves Nic'am
We've tuned into a double feature well worth repeating
Leaving out Trex and Kwik Save – omission impossible

We oilways cook on the light side of life
Kwik save bargains make me richer, Trex value completes the picture
Trex inspires gourmet thrills, Kwik Save reduces shopping bills
Making pastry, frying light, come on down, price is right
Trex the best 'flour arranger' is a masterpiece in oils
Fast Trex keeps us up to date with 'currant' events
For healthy tasty meals – Kwik Save presents pure Trex appeal
A good cook knows the Trex of the trade

TASTE

▶ **Dolmio gives me a TASTE for travel because...**

PRODUCT: Pasta sauce

Italian food is unsurpassed, thanks Dolmio, I'm packing fast
It 'Romes' on my tongue with a cosmopolitang!
I was born under a wandering jar
Pasta perfection in every direction, simply means catching the 'Dolmio
    connection'
Bags of fun, smiles galore, action packed – more, more, more
These perfect sauces I adore, a world of culinary taste to explore
'Packed' with flavour, quality 'label' – destination deliciousness on my table
The distinctive taste, the supreme sensation, transports me to an Italian
    destination
With less time on kitchen chores, more time on foreign shores
In London, Paris or Rome, with Dolmio I'm right at home

▶ **Tesco and Hilton give you a TASTE of the good life because...**

PRODUCT: Supermarket foods
COMPETITION: Tesco/Hilton hotels
PRIZES: Luxury breaks in London Hilton hotel or weekend breaks in Britain

Champagne, smoked salmon and Stilton, bought at Tesco, eaten at the Hilton
Their superb quality, cleanliness and style, means every visit produces a smile
Careful attention to customer needs, means satisfaction and pleasure are
    guaranteed
High Street or Park Lane, their quality is the same
Dedication to excellence knows no bounds, at Tesco and Hilton – paradise
    found
However Important Luxury, Taste Or Needs, Their Excellent Service Creates
    Outstanding Satisfaction *(HILTON TESCOS = ACROSTIC)*
Both richly deserve EGGceptional praise – Hilton for style, Tesco for
    mayonnaise
Each with own brand of care, add quality to life beyond compare
Luxury put Hilton on the map, Tesco's put luxury on your lap

Each deserves a standing ovation, for giving elevated prices a welcome vacation
Five star value, five star praise, plus crème de la crème mayonnaise
Tesco and Hilton are streets ahead, tasteful quality from A-Z
Luxurious quality with prices right, a traveller's dream, a shopper's delight
Forget 'Onassis' yacht in Med – try Tesco champagne in Hilton bed
Tesco's mayo – best taste around, Hilton's hospitality – world renowned

▶ **I enjoy the TASTE of Scottish Cheddar because...**

PRODUCT: Cheese
PRIZES: Weekend breaks to Gleneagles

Great cold, great hot, great flavour, great Scot!
Never buy your cheese in haste, choose Scottish Cheddar for its taste

▶ **Shippams pastes and spreads are the TASTIEST because...**

PRODUCT: Meat and fish pastes

Each recipe's designed with full flavour in mind

TEA

▶ **The fresh look of Lyons Original will always be on my shopping list at Tesco because...**

PRODUCT: Tea
COMPETITION: Tesco/Lyons tea

It's blended with care, then vended with flair
The eyecatching packs of unequalled flavour are another Tesco money saver
The green and gold vacuum pack captures flavours others lack
Superior taste, distinctive pack, Tesco value, draws me back
Light, dark or medium, it helps to beat the tea-dium
When flavour is the main attraction, Lyons gives sealed satisfaction

▶ **The quality and flavour of '99' tea is unchanging because...**

PRODUCT: Co-op tea
COMPETITION: Co-op Leo's/'99' tea

Day in, day out, the perfect brew pours from the spout
The best of its kind helped generations unwind
So skilled was the original blending, it's never required amending
Bought at Leo's, it's a roaring success
It's a good blend from the first to the last bag
Serious tea drinkers 'disc'over this compact package revives all systems
Even mad hatters know consisten-TEA matters

Like 147 in snooker, 180 in darts, '99' is unbea-TEA-ble
Its qualiTEA and quantiTEA has reached its extremiTEA
When you're under par it's a great cuppa char
The Co-op reasoning is 'sound' such 'disc'erning palates are around
As mother always stressed, you can't buy better
The Co-op have got their blend to a 't'
Only the finest tea leaves the pot
It's the housewives' favourite with the inbuilt guaranTEA
It's the every day pleasure for each family to treasure
No fancy gimmicks, passing trends, just finest teas, perfect blends
Why milk the flavour of exper-TEAS?

▶ **Co-op '99' is my most treasured of teas because...**

   PRODUCT: Tea

Other teas velly sloshy, make tea that is wishee woshy
The best from the chest is brought out under water
One drink and I'm no longer a sunken wreck
The swag's in the bag
There's nothing finer to cure a Mao-Tse tongue
Any other brand would make a mandarin duck
It's a thirst quencher and also an oriental taste adventure
It's collected with care to give a flavour that's rare
You get a precious lot for precious little
You can stir it but you won't beat it
Richer, poorer, sickness, health, with '99' who needs wealth?
Richness flavour every sup, with fortunes found inside every cup
Steve Davis couldn't make a better pot
Stock markets crash but '99' slips down gracefully
Such a tea beyond compare, makes me feel like a millionaire
A great tasting tea is enough riches for me
Its secret's in the bag
Its flavour is priceless and priced less
You never get a short measure with this tea treasure
Its great wall of flavour is a real life saver
'99' tea velly nice, velly good tea, velly good plice
After one cup its competitor's junk is sunk without trace
After peeking in the packet I can taste the tang
I can have liquid gold without spending all my brass
I discovered '99' after a long voyage through uncharted teas
In tin or ming it's just the thing
It puts heirlooms in yer chest
Of the lodes of flavour for a little cache
It blends Britain's traditional drink with timeless eastern finesse
It blends so tastefully with my char ming china
It's a teafarer's haven in a sea of pirates
Being the caddylac of brews it complements my rolls nicely

Each bag is a little sunken treasure
Exploring from Britain to China couldn't unearth anything finer
Exquisite, distinctive, truly auspicious, even Confucius say 'dericious'

▶ **Choicest Blend tea is the tea of distinction because...**

PRODUCT: Tea

Thirsting for the best leaves me dramatically refreshed
Passing trends quickly go, perfect blends steal the show
Outstanding selection and brewing technique, guarantees flavour truly unique
Distinct refreshing morning cuppa – lifts at luncheon, soothes at supper
Its good taste is never left to pot luck
With finest leaves expertly blended, choicest blend tastes absolutely splendid

TEAM

▶ **Asda and Wilkinson Sword are a winning TEAM because...**

PRODUCT: Blades and razors
COMPETITION: Asda/Wilkinson Sword

With inflation to hedge they both have the edge

▶ **The microwave and freezer make a perfect TEAM because...**

PRODUCT: Electrical goods

From ice to steam, the meal is a dream
They're the technological treat which takes the 'wait' of your 'feat'
Cook or thaw, they always score

▶ **Hoover and Ariel are the winning TEAM because...**

PRODUCT: Washing powder
COMPETITION: Tesco/Hoover/Ariel Cleaning partners
PRIZES: Hoover washing machines

One turns the problem over, the other provides the solution
The perfect combination turns my frown upside down
They are the prima donnas of the soap opera
They're each designed with the other in mind
They make all clothes bright and beautiful for all people great and small
Whatever the challenge, whatever the grime, they're perfect finishes every time
They're the leading 'union' of white collar workers
In the mixed doubles, they are game, set and match
One is biological, the other is buyer logical
Reports from any 'test match' confirm that make the cleanest catch

Hoover technology, Ariel biology – that's too much brain for the stain
Their whites really bowl a maiden over
I use their expertise to wash with expert ease
Hoover without Ariel would be folly, just like Stanley without Olly
Their power makes them number one, for a super finish, second to none
Washday problems go away, with Hoover and Ariel the match of the day

TEMPTED

▶ **I am TEMPTED to buy biscuits at the Co-op when...**

PRODUCT: Biscuits

I fancy a price-less nibble with never a fancy price quibble
Whenever my biscuit barrel needs reloading

TENNIS

▶ **Clairol products help me to make a love match because...**

PRODUCT: Hair care
COMPETITION: Clairol/Win tickets to Wimbledon

No other 'set points' excite such 'colourful' finals
I'm all set to make a smash hit with Clairol
Being Bjorn blond like Borg, it's game and set match Clairol
Beautiful hair singles you out for a doubles match
Clairol means that love can still win at forty
Mixed doubles can still be a ball when lofted so colourfully

▶ **I need Dextrosol's extra energy because...**

PRODUCT: Glucose tablets
COMPETITION: Boots the Chemists/Dextrosol short tennis
PRIZES: Short tennis sets

Playing tennis without it would be courting disaster
Always game for anything, Dextrosol gives me that extra spring
Outmanoeuvring friend and foe necessitates the speed of Coe
I've got too few 'amps' in my pants
Tennis racket, really whack it, not without a Dextro-packet
Over 40 I need all the advantages I can get
It gives me the advantage that nets the prize
It gives me the zip to fasten onto sport
Mum has to be good at 'serving' and rallying around

Whenever I reach 'break point', Dextrosol gives me the advantage
After going all out, I'm often all in
When playing basketball, I soon lose my bounce
Watching sports is my game, taking part is my aim
Being ambidextrous, I need Dextrosol for my extra dexterity

▶ Robinsons Barley Water is the champion refreshment because...

PRODUCT: Fruit juices
COMPETITION: Tesco/Robinsons/Wimbledon
PRIZES: Collections of tennis accessories

Singles, doubles, indoor or out, Robinsons wins without a doubt!
Robinsons tasty fruity zing, gives my racquet extra swing
Smashing taste, cool on court, Robinsons is ace for sport
Robinsons in my trolley, helps me serve, lob and volley
Robinsons is seeded number one, for people everywhere having fun
Wimbledon without Robinsons? You cannot be serious!
McEnroe shouts, umpires overrule, but Robinsons keeps everyone cool
Robinsons seeded number one, bottles opened and it's gone
Whatever sport, whichever star, Robinsons made 'em what they are
Feeling refreshed, playing great, Robinsons is your best team-mate
Playing tennis with all accessories, Robinsons' one of the necessities
Every serving down the line, Robinsons' aces win every time
There is nothing bigger than Robinsons' liquid vigour
Being unknown or seeded, Robinsons Barley Water is always needed
Tennis champions come and go, Robinsons keeps the status quo
Robinsons serve a refreshing ace, quenching thirst at sparkling pace
For Wimbledon, or just for fun, Robinsons is No. 1
Robinsons and tennis a team, traditional as strawberries and cream
When parched with thirst, champions reach for Robinsons first
For seasoned pro, or a beginner, Robinsons' an instant winner
When Seles grunts, Agassi gasps, they down a Robinsons glass
When thirst is under attack, Robinsons wins game set and match
A Wimbledon champion continuously hears, Robinsons groupies raising cheers
Full flavour takes the tennis seed, Robinsons is No. 1 seed!
Robinsons on the label, means trophies on the table
Robinsons serve the perfect deuce, the ace winning liquid juice
When McEnroe's temper feels aflame, Robinsons restores a peaceful game
Whether rally, return or ace, Robinsons refreshes whatever the pace
Like Borg and Connors, Robinsons have earned the highest honours
What Wimbledon is to tennis, Robinsons is to squash
Monica grunts, Agassi grins, but Robinsons' taste always wins
Every player tells the story, of Robinsons their best accessory
To play or just observe, Robinsons' the best to serve
Even McEnroe agrees, refreshing Robinsons never fails to please
Prize ingredients in every glass, Robinsons Barley is world class

Super taste, refreshingly mysterious, no Robinsons you cannot be serious
On merit, Robinsons seeded first, faultless service when quenching thirst
British finalist may be rare, but Robinsons is always there
Players come, players go, Tesco and Robinsons continue the show
Players of the highest grade, love their Robinsons thirst aid
With Robinsons great drinks, even the opposition clutches at straws!
'A gassi' drink is no competition, compared to Robinsons' great tradition
Robinsons has the finest flavours, Wimbledon tennis the greatest players
Steffi grins, Agassi may run, but Robinsons stays number one
In singles or mixed fours, success reigns when Robinsons pours
Robinsons is on the ball, serving aces to us all
Back garden or centre court, Robinsons rewards games well fought
For Agassi or mere beginner, Robinsons always serves a winner
Victory signs up all around, means Robinsons is being downed
Robinsons always win the thirst serve!

TERROR

▶ **Take the TERROR out of tiling with Unibond because...**

PRODUCT: Adhesive
COMPETITION: Death Becomes Her with Unibond
PRIZE: Seven-day trip to Hollywood for two

A fearsome task becomes fiendishly simple with Unibond

THINK

▶ **I THINK of Presto for food because...**

PRODUCT: Supermarket foods

I can choose with ease at a price to please
They're the perfect partners for prime provisions

TICKET

▶ **Lil-lets are just the TICKET because...**

PRODUCT: Tampons
COMPETITION: Lil-lets Win a ticket to freedom

Never mind the passport to freedom – just send me the ticket

They allow her personal freedom and an easy mind
They give 'independence' to a Liberty Belle
They help a modern miss escape the tyranny of time
They give a 'go anywhere' confidence with absolute comfort
They help women's liberation

▶ Tampax are just the TICKET because...

PRODUCT: Tampons
COMPETITION: Tampax/Win tickets to freedom

No more 'sorry I can't come', Tampax freedom has begun
With Tampax to choose, there's no time to lose

▶ I think Journey Club Membership will add value to my annual season TICKET because...

PRODUCT: Season ticket for travel

It gives greater pleasure to leisure
There's more chance to break away, with so much less to pay
I can afford free time travel without going off the rails
We get double the pleasure at half the cost
Bargains in fares so low, mean further afield we can go
It makes it 'just the ticket' for the family
The whole family can gain from the train

▶ Just the TICKET at bathtime

It's just the ticket, first class fayre, for bathtime euphoria and express skin-care

TIGHTS & STOCKINGS

▶ Scholl Lite Legs keep hard working legs feeling fit and looking good because...

PRODUCT: Support tights and stockings

They stand the pace with elegance and grace
Hard-working women need all the support they can get
Stylish, comfortable and ultra-light – perfect support day and night

▶ I always buy Aristoc tights because...

PRODUCT: Tights

Others are sheer today, but gone tomorrow
Styled to suit, price to please, they fit the leg with sheerfit ease

▶ **Pretty Polly styles are ideal for a romantic night out because...**

PRODUCT: Tights

These glamorous foundations gently enhance, guaranteeing many an admiring glance
Legs look longer and slimmer when Pretty Polly softly shimmer
Colours, sizes, quality wear, never a hitch, always a stare
Silky soft, delightfully sheer, makes him happy, having you near
A special evening surely begs for perfect Pretty Polly legs
Luxurious and ultra light, elegantly dressy for that special night
Romantic dinner with fantastic fella, thanks to Pretty Polly – signed Cinderella
The range is extensive and far from expensive
When style and sensuality really matter, Pretty Polly always flatter
Affordable prices, luxury feel, created for maximum appeal

▶ **Kayser tights and stockings are my star choice because...**

PRODUCT: Tights and stockings

I've auditioned the rest but Kayser are sheerly the best

▶ **I wear Kayser because...**

PRODUCT: Tights

For two pins – what else?

TIME & DATES

▶ **TIME is well spent at Asda because...**

PRODUCT: Supermarket foods

Their prices are cut at every stroke
The prices are under close watch every second of the day
It's got the stock to make you tick
Their prices stand still while time marches on
They put back the clock with their prices
You clock in for variety and clock out with value

▶ **Timex watches give you the TIME of your life because...**

PRODUCT: Watches
COMPETITION: Argos catalogue/Timex
PRIZE: Florida holiday for two

Whatever your age, the time, the place, Timex has the perfect 'face'
A slip in time and Mickey's mine

Reliable, attractive, durable too, Timex for me, how about you?
They are all things bright and beautiful, on faces great and small
Handsome face, a fashion must, more precisely, a name to trust
One timely purchase from Argos and four could be shaking Mickey's hand
Whilst others simply tick along, a Timex watch keeps going strong

▶ We always find TIME to wear Piz Buin on the beach because...

PRODUCT: Sun tan lotion
COMPETITION: Piz Buin/Timex watches

We would have style on the one hand and time on the other, to clock up super
    Piz Buin tans
Like Piz Buin products, they 'watch' over bodies with care every 'second' so
    that one is in the swim for a fantastic time
Back from our holiday all Piz Buin brown, we'd be 'tick'-led pink and the 'tock'
    of the town

▶ It's always TIME for '99' tea because...

PRODUCT: Co-op tea
PRIZES: Holidays in Switzerland

When it's time for a perfect brew, only '99' will do
It's second to none at a price that won't alarm
I clock in for a good brew and clock out for value
The prices are under close watch every second of the day
Thirst come, thirst served, '99' is the brew preferred
Expert blenders perfect it, connoisseurs select it
At any time of day I like brewing what comes naturally
When it's hands up for choice, '99' wins hands down
It's all it's clocked up to be – simply fantastic... tic... tic
A Swiss holiday, courtesy of '99', would be just the tick-et

▶ I always keep a Jarrold calendar on the wall because...

PRODUCT: Calendars
COMPETITION: Jarrold calendars Pick-a-DATE

This is one 'hang-up' I don't mind having
I'd not find a better one in a month of Sundays
Then I have a room with a view
There's no better way to view the day

▶ Metamec clocks make ideal presents because...

PRODUCT: Clocks

They have style on the one hand, precision on the other
When it's 'Hands Up' for choice they win 'Hands Down'
Hard working hands guarantee Metamec is not just a pretty face

They're all they're clocked up to be
The gift of the moment goes on for a lifetime
There's no present like the time

▶ The quality and flavour of '99' tea is unchanging because...

PRODUCT: Co-op tea
COMPETITION: Co-op Leo's/'99' tea

Day in, day out the perfect brew pours from the spout
The best of its kind helped generations unwind
So skilled was the original blending it's never required amending
Bought at Leo's it's a roaring success
It's a good blend from the first to the last bag
Serious tea drinkers 'disc'over this compact package revives all systems
Even mad hatters know consisten-TEA matters
Like 147 in snooker, 180 in darts, '99' is unbea-TEA-ble
Its qualiTEA and quantiTEA has reached its extremiTEA
When you're under par it's a great cuppa char
The Co-op reasoning is 'sound' such 'disc'erning palates are around
As mother always stressed, you can't buy better
The Co-op have got their blend to a 't'
Only the finest tea leaves the pot
It's the housewives' favourite with the inbuilt guaranTEA
It's the everyday pleasure for each family to treasure
No fancy gimmicks, passing trends, just finest teas, perfect blends
Why milk the flavour of exper-TEAS?

TO...

▶ If I were to win I would look forward TO...

PRODUCT: Cocktail mixer
COMPETITION: Dubonnet best of red holiday

A Red Square – with a twist of Lenin
Red-letter day, escape UK, postcard reads 'Shalom Dubonnet'
Meeting Indians, Redwood bred, although not a-'patche' on Dubonnet Red
Reds, blues beyond belief, Dubonnet cocktails on the Barrier Reef

TOBACCO

▶ **I would like to re-name San Francisco...**

PRODUCT: Cigarettes
COMPETITION: Benson & Hedges cigarettes

King Sighs: Midas touched this golden state, millions filter through its gate
(*Golden Gate Bridge)

▶ **At which of six locations would you choose to have your dream and why?**

PRODUCT: Cigarettes
COMPETITION: Martin & Lavells newsagents/Silk Cut cigarettes

Sicily ... Silk Cut duty free, only Etna could outsmoke me
Cyprus is the one for me, a silken cut in azure sea
Crete ... because I enjoy the unknown and Crete's all Greek to me
Ibiza ... what more could a Silk Cut nut bask for?
Cyprus ... to drink all their sherry and end up Silk Cut
Smoking Silk Cut in Crete would be one Hel-i-os of a treat
Sicily ... 'godmother' because I'm 'branded' for life and can't leave the 'pack'
I've a S'Silly notion to see Mount Etna smoking
Seven days, seven nights, off comes the silks and cut the lights
Crete ... Greek men trip the light fantastic, I'll light the tip, fantastic
I'd cut loose for a week, live like Zorba the Greek
Sicily ... in the hope that my wife would be kidnapped
I'd dress in Silk and Cut a dash in Ibiza
Egypt ... after all, Cleopatra found it very ASPiring
China ... where I'd cocoon myself in Silk Cut from the roll
Malta Hilton ... if you want to do it, do it in style
Canary Islands ... I've always been one for the birds

▶ **I would take my deck chair to...**

PRODUCT: Cigars
COMPETITION: Henri Wintermans cigars

The Caribbean, because dat's de place to be in the Winterman
Bondi Beach, because whenever I open a deckchair it's upside down

▶ **As an MGT owner I would continue to smoke Old Dutch because...**

PRODUCT: Pipe tobacco

No other brand Matches Great Tasting Old Dutch *(MGT = ACROSTIC)*
Wind in hair, double declutch, always there, my Old Dutch
I'm ecstatic in a classic with a pipe of aromatic

Old Dutch's aroma, MGT's flair, together they make a classic pair
With Old Dutch in my pocket, I'd go like a rocket
I'd gracefully manoeuvre the bends, whilst savouring tobacco's best blend
Tobacco connoisseurs agree, it's as individual as MGT
Rich in aromatic style, match the MGT mile after mile
They double your pleasure when enjoyed together

Benson & Hedges King Size cigarettes

It has gone to great lengths in allowing us extra time to share together
With B & H you discover gold because ... Assay So!

John Player Special cigarettes

Give black and inch and they'll make a smile

Marlboro cigarettes

In Marlboro country where the men walk tall, this lonesome squaw would have a ball
No horizon is too broad for the Marlboro man

Silk Cut cigarettes

Every pack has twenty tips on good taste
Fortune on me must surely have smiled – thanks to my duty-free Silk Cut mild

On the beach with Silk Cut cigarettes

With sand like silk, but off by the sea, my dreams would become reality

TOGETHER

▶ **Mastercard and Thomas Cook go TOGETHER well because...**

PRODUCT: Credit card
PRIZES: Trips to New York to see the film 'Hook'

With minimum fuss, maximum speed, this global alliance is all I need
Perfect planning, pay with plastic, together they trip the flight fantastic
When travel requirements must be met, they make the best combination yet
Together they give a travel style, without hook, hitch or crocodile

▶ **Hale Trent cakes and Presto stores combined TOGETHER give...**

PRODUCT: Cakes

COMPETITION: Presto/Hale Trent cakes

Quality cakes without a doubt and shoppers with something to yodel about
'Hey' Presto, 'Hail' Trent, tasty cakes, I came, they went
A chance for this lass to enjoy a Swiss pass
Chances to climb mountains if you come in and take your pick
We have a cracker of a jamboree when they Club together
People have always associated the Co-op with the best in biscuits
They provide a delectable destination for my economy drive

▶ **Paris and Girobank go well TOGETHER because...**

PRODUCT: Bank services
FIRST PRIZE: Trip for two to Paris

Toulouse yourself in Paris is worth Lautrec there and back

▶ **White Horse Scotch whisky and racing go TOGETHER like...**

PRODUCT: Whisky
PRIZES: Shares in a racehorse

Derby and June
Champion Chasers
A Classic Double
Spirit and Dash

▶ **Christmas and Hillards go TOGETHER because...**

PRODUCT: Supermarket foods

Christmas 'spirit' down every aisle, prices to make Scrooge smile
'Stable' prices with 'Star' value make Hillards the 'Inn' place
You can bet it's where Santa does his stocking up
Their prices don't go ding dong merrily up high
Stock up there with extra special purse-nal flair
For the festive good cheer, Hillards won't 'reign dear'
You celebrate at Hillards' till, enjoying season of 'good fill'

▶ **The Famous Grouse Scotch whisky and the RSPB can work TOGETHER to protect British birds by...**

PRODUCT: Whisky
COMPETITION: RSPB/Famous Grouse Scotch whisky
PRIZES: Olympus cameras

A nip of Grouse supped twice daily, will help protect the Capercaillie
Combining the true spirit of distinction in fighting bird extinction
Famous Grouse feathering the nest, so RSPB can do the rest
Inviting Grouse lovers to RSPB means a vital donation to RSPB
Making the Grouse in your glass help the Grouse in the grass
A Grouse a day helps the birds work, rest and play

A drop in the house provides home for the Grouse
An extra Grouse enjoyed at night helps wildlife win their worthwhile fight
Both giving pleasure, one to drink, the other to treasure
Making Grouse sales roar to give the RSPB more
Moors and wildlife go together, can't have Grouse without the heather
This promotion makes us buy and in turn helps more birds fly
Watching them with stealth and drinking to their health
Encouraging whisky drinkers of distinction to save wildlife habitats from extinction
Helping them sing sweeter by donating £1 a litre
Linking Scotland's most prestigious dram with Britain's wildlife survival programme
Making a dram avert a crisis
Offering a dram of distinction to help keep birds from extinction
Providing havens for ravens, cover for plover and houses for Grouses
Converting grain from grain into safe houses for Grouses
FGSW + 1PND = SOS (RSPB) = SLR 4 ME?
Insisting Grouse be drunk and savoured, not shot, cooked and flavoured

▶ Campari and Grand Prix motor racing go well TOGETHER because...

PRODUCT: Vermouth

Grand Prix has chicane: for Campari the chic aim
They are smooth, fast and gone in a flash
Campari leads in its class – a formula one cannot surpass
Both are hot on the tracks of good living
Panache is combined with a dash
Both drivers and drinks are best ice cool
Great starters, they overtake tyred favourites all the way
Campari's secret recipe blends the winning formula
One's chilled to thrill, the other has thrills that chill
Lorraine likes a tipple and I like a chase

▶ Campari and Carnivals go TOGETHER because...

PRODUCT: Vermouth

Campari's the drink that never goes in disguise
One is well asked for, the other is well masked for
Distinctive taste, definite hue, even masked the fun comes through
Campari is in full employment wherever there's enjoyment
Campari in St. Marks could lead to fun and larks

▶ I choose Kodak film from Dixons camera shops because...

PRODUCT: Photographic goods
COMPETITION: Kodak/Dixons together

Together they keep you in the picture

They are both continually developing better ways of keeping you in the picture

Both have long experience in supplying quality products but keeping value in focus

Together they offer an unrivalled team which caters for all your photographic needs

They are positively the best double act in films for miles around

These two together are surely tops, Kodak films and Dixons shops

Kodak's quality provides a perfect image, Dixons' image is to provide perfect quality

Dixons price snips match Kodak's prize snaps

Kodak's products are the tops, and Dixons sell them in all the shops

With Kodak's productions and Dixons' directions, my pictures steal all the limelight without casting reflections

If you rifle through Dixons, you'll shoot a winner with Kodak

Whatever your budget, whoever you are, with Kodak and Dixons you're the star

They're growing and developing with current technology

For sparkling eyes and sparkling buys, they're the pair that harmonise

Kodak's quality provides a perfect image, Dixons image is to provide perfect quality

These two together are surely tops, Kodak films and Dixons shops

TOGETHERNESS

Tesco and Kiwi together they shine, they're feets ahead when they combine

Just like Dud and Pete a winning combination, quick to 'Cook' and 'Moore' to eat

So quick to heat and eat, such delicious combinations that you'll find them hard to beat

Come pre-paired for us that's neat

Paired up to perfection to make any meal complete

For sheer elegance and chic their combination, c'est magnifique

One selects superior stock, one arrests my hunger clock

For choice, value and nutrition, both surpass all competition

Both look after your interest and give value for money

It's a reliable combination which gives good service

When two greats meet, their fame is hard to beat

TOILETRIES

▶ **Oxy Clean can blitz those zitz because...**

PRODUCT: Medicated facial wash
COMPETITION: Woolworths/Oxy Clean blitz those zits

PRIZE: Hi-fi system

By removing grease and grime it kills spots in 'record' time

▶ **Life can be rough without Wilkinson Sword because...**

PRODUCT: Blades and razors
COMPETITION: Woolworths/Wilkinson Sword

Wilkinson's swordmanship is the finest defence against roughnecks and cut-throats
It's the soothing answer to a burning problem
When there's ground work to be done, Wilkinson's the one
They combine good quality with fair prices
Shaving whiskers off prices, they're a cut above the rest
Shaving prices, the edge against inflation
They are on my 'side', low transfer fees for the 'velvet glide'
At home or away, it's worth a replay
The sun will never set on their 'dual' success
They both have the edge for taking the rough with the smooth
One never cuts when you shave, the other cuts so you save
They give succour to savers and liberate shavers
A good save is as satisfying as a good shave
Let's face it, they never rip us off
Quality products can never be 'swordid'

▶ **I would like to win Ultrabrite's Midi Magic because...**

PRODUCT: Toothpaste
PRIZE: Midi hi-fi system

It gives other sounds the 'brush off'

▶ **The Silvikrin range at Boots keeps hair one step ahead because...**

PRODUCT: Hair care
COMPETITION: Boots the Chemists/Silvikrin

This 'hair traffic controller' ensures perfect 'take off' every time
They are a step in the right direction towards hair care perfection
It gives you the style that drives other gels wild
Shampoo, conditioner, mousse or spray, Silvikrin fixes hair the modern way

▶ **It's fun to be blonde with Clairol because...**

PRODUCT: Hair colourant
COMPETITION: Clairol fun to be blonde

In any setting Clairol's attention getting
When it's so easy you just can't keep it bottled up

It shows in a crowd and makes you feel proud
Blondes succeed where others concede
Clairol gives a fair deal
It turns plain into pearl
Clairol perfects them so gentlemen select them
You're streaks ahead
Girls who use flashlights soon discover they have a winning streak
Clairol's blonding range is like champagne, it makes you bubbly and
    lightheaded
It's the ideal tonic when you want to curl up and dye
It's attention getting whatever the setting
Wolf whistles abound, heads turn around and my ego is crowned
I feel on a par with a Hollywood star
You become the main attraction, driving men to sheer distraction
Blondes make more Bonds
Flaxen, tawny, ash or highlighted, gentlemen prefer us, we are delighted
Formerly mousy, frumpish and forty, now I frolic as a blonde quite naughty

▶ **I take Band Aid on holiday with me because...**

PRODUCT: Plasters

You can master your disaster with a Band Aid plaster
It's the name that sticks
You know we stick together in every crisis

▶ **Nair makes my life trouble and stubble free because...**

PRODUCT: Depilatory cream

Life's too short to rant 'n' shave, go bare with Nair and life's a rave

▶ **I think Lypsyl is ideal for lips because...**

PRODUCT: Lip salve

It's the obvious selection for your lips' protection
The protection required comes with the look that's admired

▶ **Shaving with Wilkinson Sword is a classic experience because...**

PRODUCT: Blades and razors

There would be no trouble with stubble at the Hofmeister double
There are no 'hairs and graces' – just velvety smooth faces

▶ **Savlon Dry is the holiday treatment because...**

PRODUCT: Antiseptic cream

Handy Savlon easy to use, quickly applied protects and soothes
Grazes, scratches, insect stings, Savlon eases all these things

▶ **Why is Fenjal an essential part of a skin care routine?**

PRODUCT: Swiss bath oil

Carefully balanced, expertly blended, keeps skin soft, as nature intended
Fenjal Swiss body care keeps skin as fresh as mountain air
Luxuriate in the Fenjal collection, they moisturise giving skin perfection
Fenjal helps keep moisture in, the vital part of healthy skin
It turns a demanding woman into a woman in demand
This is the key to soft scented skin, used daily locks the moisture in
Like Switzerland, it creates a fresh feeling and a breathtaking view
Fragrant Fenjal cossets skin, brings back its bloom, seals softness in
Clear and fresh as alpine air, that's your skin with Fenjal care

▶ **I use Ambre Solaire because...**

PRODUCT: Sun tan lotion

Holidays without Ambre Solaire – like Ginger Rogers without Fred Astaire
It's the soothing answer to a burning problem

▶ **I use Cossack because...**

PRODUCT: Hair grooming

It's the first 'steppe' to perfect grooming
It keeps my hair down better than the Cossacks kept down the peasants

▶ **Pierre Cardin Pour Monsieur out-performs the rest because...**

PRODUCT: Aftershave

Who wears wins
It's a winner on all Sir-faces
It's a formula one fragrance

▶ **Optrex is perfect for contact lens wearers because...**

PRODUCT: Eye wash

You've taken off the glasses, they've taken out the specks
Stunning colours, ultra fine, perfectly safe, it looks divine
It is safe and easy to apply with special regard to the sensitive eye

Aftershaves

In the pits or in the Ritz – Brut fits
Something 'old', something 'new', the 'Spice of Life' for you know who
Nothing would be nicer than putting life into this old spicer

Baby care products

Prevention is better than 'sore'

They clean baby's creases and his other bits and pieces
The 'bare' facts are simple – they protect fold and dimple
They gently cleanse messy faces and other dirty little places
To ignore their dri-way code would be a rash decision
Happy babies, kindly mums, bubbly baths and powdered bums
Happy faces with clean little places
They are specially designed with babies in mind
They're special tissues for special issues

Bath time and shaving

It's just the ticket, first class fayre, for bathtime euphoria and express skin-care
Its creamy texture and delicate perfume, creates magic in everyone's bathroom
Pamper and care for necessities bare
Pamper and pander to make me feel grander
It's worth getting into hot water for
It makes even the children 'dive' for the bathroom
It pays to be choosy in bath, shower or Jacuzzi

Boots the Chemists

They have the prescription – products with the Boots quality inscription
I trust their guarantee to care for me and mine
Boots shave the price
Boots help stretch my money because it cuts the cost of caring
Holiday cruise or summer sun, Boots have something for everyone
Quality, value, choice is wide, Boots catalogue makes a handy guide
My tip for the top is to buy records and toiletries from Boots

Cussons Imperial Leather dream theme

PRODUCT: Toilet soap

Its value impresses me, its lather caresses me, and its fragrance un-stresses me
It soothes away my cares and troubles, doesn't burst my South Sea bubbles
It creates a bathroom transformation, creamiest, dreamiest soap in the nation
With its luxurious scent and lather like cream, it's surely soap fit for a dream
It has the feel and quality of a luxury soap at a wide-a-wake price
Cussons soap makes dreams come true, leaving skin like morning dew
Cussons will reign supreme, an affordable luxury is everyone's dream
Luxurious bubbles as light as a feather, transport me to cloud nine with
    Imperial Leather
Jacuzzi or tin bath tub, Imperial Leather's the luxury rub
A dream lasts forever with Imperial Leather
The lather of Imperial Leather keeps me soft and clean, an altogether pleasant
    imperialistic dream
Imperial Leather creates magical mornings, dreamy days and shining knights
Imperial Leather's everyone's dream, lets you spend like a pauper but bathe
    like a queen

Deodorants

I make meetings with confidence and partings with ease
At work or at play, a splash or a spray, keeps me fragrant all day
They give the protection I desire, the selection I require and the reflection I
    admire

Foster Grants with an adventure theme

PRODUCT: Sunglasses

With style and flare they cut the glare
Wherever you go, whatever you do, quality, performance and style go too
When the outlook's too bright, they're the best thing in sight
Whatever hazards are endured, style and safety are still assured
The action is laid bare as they strip away the glare
They get reflections deflected, while you get the action perfected
The pair without glare add flair to the dare
You can set your sights on any challenge
Further, faster, higher, daring, they'll always stop the sun from glaring
They are the anti-glare reaction in every field of action
High on action, low on glare, they're essential adventure action-wear
Foster Grant are a good sight better, for the adventurous go-getter
Foster Grant quality, it's supreme, but teamed with adventure – what a dream
Foster Grant has the solution to optical confusion
Foster Grant the designer name that puts you in the frame

Hairsprays and shampoos

It's the No. 1 hair traffic controller
In any 'setting' it's attention getting
It's the perfect key to all shining locks
A spray a day makes my hair obey
From Piccadilly thru' Times Square, my guys and dolls want healthy hair
It wakes up the sleeping beauty of my hair
It's the confidence trick that keeps me ahead
I would feel improperly tressed without it
Looking good means going places
It gives me a brilliant head start and a perfect finish
They transform lifeless weak ends into lively weekends
When it comes to hair care I'm not prepared to go second class

Kleenex holiday competition

PRODUCT: Travel tissues

Although a cold's incurable, with Kleenex it's endurable
They are the handy package deal everyone wants
A tissue does for faces what sunshine does for places
A-tissue, A-tissue, they never let me down

Whatever your emotional state they leave you feeling great
Summer sun or icy blast, useful, handy and they last
They keep right on to the end of a cold
Biting wind or winter snow it always softens the blow
Made for faces going places they polish off unwanted traces
Spill, sneeze, smudge or cry, tissues wipe it dry
They'll wipe a smile on your dial

Medicare at Boots the Chemists

PRODUCT: Shampoo

Low prices show at Boots, Medicare's hallmark is shining hair
Boots prices, Medicare's care, go to make a winning pair
Medicare's results are really 'ace' – Boots 'service' takes first place
Medicare's value at Boots means fresher skin and healthy hair

Medicines

It's the best minister of health and economy in my cabinet
Finest ingredients, value too, they pick me up and pull me through
It would perk me up, calm me down and take away that worried frown
It's the only natural course to take
It gives me a voice to sing its praises
It's the tastiest tickle tackler on their shelves

Men's toiletries

It helps me keep my cool after a close shave
With other fragrances comes the chore of picking up girls after they hit the floor
It scores a hit with every miss – but your best reference is my girl's preference
One's confidence grows, since everyone knows, it serves all the aces for men
    going places
Within this life of toil and sin, your head gets bald but not your chin
I'd have no hair raising problems, only close shaves
I can now boast of 'receiving' more 'backhand' compliments

Radox bath salts

Radox makes a refreshingly perfect end of a perfect day
Radox at night, bodies delight, Radox at morning, nobody yawning
Feeling weary, worn and sad, Radox quickly makes you glad

Skin care

Face to face confrontation can be sheer degradation
It's the perfect base for a lovely face
Beautiful skin and shining hair are hallmarks of their expert care
The amazing dual action gives me lasting satisfaction

Spot removers

The good buy spot for goodbye spots
It knocks the spots off other toiletries

Toilet paper

They are a pretty important roll behind the scenes
Sheet for sheet they can't be beat

Virgin Airlines and Durex contraceptives

They make a good thing 'inconceivably' better
I fly Virgin, the best carrier and carry Durex, the best barrier
With the Durex brand the future's well planned

Wet Ones baby wipes

They mop up the opposition with sweet scented flair
They're special tissues for special issues
They're the castaways that always come to the rescue
They treat and care for baby's wet ones

Wilkinson Sword razors and Suzuki motorbikes

PRODUCT: Blades and razors
COMPETITION: Wilkinson/Suzuki

Retracters move whiskers, Suzuki whisk movers
I'll show riders behind a clean pair of cheeks
I get razor sharp handling even round the trickiest curves

TOP

▶ **Clair air fresheners are TOP of my Gateway shopping because...**

PRODUCT: Room fresheners
COMPETITION: Gateway/Clair air fresheners

For fresher rooms and brighter smiles, Clair and Gateway win by miles

▶ **Robinsons drinks are TOP of the pops because...**

PRODUCT: Fruit juices
PRIZES: CD players

I often give silver discs in exchange for these compact drinks
They've got style, taste and fun, they go straight to number one
They're family favourites and they go in record time
I get taste perfection from their hit collection

▶ **Jacob's savoury snacks are TOPS on taste because...**

PRODUCT: Savoury snacks
COMPETITION: Tesco/Jacob's Savoury Snacks
PRIZES: Mountain bikes

Each bite brings delight (often with knobs on)
'Yum Yum' thrillers provide 'Hole in Tum' fillers
A.T.B. – All Tastebuds Benefit *(ATB = ACROSTIC)*
Neat to eat, every bag's a treat
The crunch keeps me going 'til lunch
Their crispy crunch makes a mountaineer's lunch
'Mountainous' appetites are suppressed – Jacob's also taste best
Your tastebuds tingle as they savour the flavour
I've twigged how gorgeously moreish they are

TOP SCORE

▶ **The Uncle Ben's range gets a TOP SCORE from me because...**

PRODUCT: Stir-fry sauces and rice
COMPETITION: Asda/Uncle Ben's Olympic Games
PRIZES: Amstrad double-decker video recorders

Exotic spice, perfect rice, twice as nice, at Asda price
Uncle Ben's a medal winner, 'Asda' make a perfect dinner
Family taste buds record delight, demanding replays every night
Gold medal lunches, perfect dinners – essential ingredients for Olympic
   winners
'Doubly' delicious, 'Doubly' good, tastes like gold medal winners should

TRADITION

▶ **Parlour Maid is my choice for a taste of TRADITION because...**

PRODUCT: Ice cream
COMPETITION: Gateway/Parlour Maid ice cream

Custom made to be the best, Parlour Maid out scoops the rest
It's well worth handing over my lolly for
Parlour Maid always leaves me happy ever afters
Old fashioned value, fresh creamy taste, perfect for this cool mum, with no
   time to waste
Once tasted, always eaten, as for value – never beaten
It's the Gateway to supreme ice cream cuisine

Times change and vary but good taste always stays the same
It combines excellent choice and perfect quality with delicious refreshing taste
The taste's a delight at a price that's right
There is no nicer way to end a meal than with a cool classic dessert
It's a delicious handy sweet, inexpensive and a treat to eat
From Lord of the Manor to simple maid, it puts other ice cream in the shade
It's the hot favourite of this cool customer
They're all c-oldies but goodies
Its delicious creamy taste takes me back to bygone days
When put to the test they freeze out the rest
A freezer without Parlour Maid is like the North Pole without any snow
Rich and creamy with a taste that's dreamy
They hold the key to unlock the Gateway to pleasure
It's the ice that entices at irresistible prices
By tasting best it beats the rest
Top of the ice cream hit parade, Parlour Maid
Simple sweet or party confection, Parlour Maid ensures perfection
It's a vintage ice cream that tastes like a dream
It's a Gateway to the future with a taste of the past
Party time or Sunday teas, every flavour made to please
Cool and delicious they're instant temptations to cook up excuses for special
    occasions
What the butler saw was the best sweet on the dumb waiter
I've backed a winner with Parlour Maid for dinner
It has a creaminess I feared had quite disappeared
Upstairs, downstairs all rejoice, for Parlour Maid's a gorgeous choice
I thoroughly enjoy all its frozen assets
When guests call round I've always found the perfect treat for the sweet is Maid
Eaten after dinner or in your deckchair, that cool dreamy taste is always there
It's a delicious sweet, always a treat, everyone's wish for another dish
It gives you delicious tempting flavours, prices are nice too
It tastes so angelic, it could be maid in heaven
The choice of a winner, the price right too, so off to Gateway all of you
It complements any meal, no-one can refuse a lovely ice cream
Cool classic, a touch of ice, make Parlour Maid a fact of life
It offers variety for family friends and value for money
With so many Parlour Maids who needs a chef?
It's maid in that cold-fashioned way

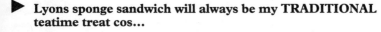 **Lyons sponge sandwich will always be my TRADITIONAL
teatime treat cos...**

PRODUCT: Cake

Like Madam, I'm adamant that only the best is served

TRAIL & TRACK

▶ **I would like to take the wine trail with Berkeley Superkings because...**

PRODUCT: Cigarettes

Like great wine producers, Berkeley go to great lengths to ensure perfection

▶ **Campari and Grand Prix motor racing go well together because...**

PRODUCT: Vermouth

Grand Prix has chicane: for Campari the chic aim
They are smooth, fast and gone in a flash
Campari leads in its class – a formula one cannot surpass
Both are hot on the tracks of good living
Panache is combined with a dash
Both drivers and drinks are best ice cool
Great starters, they overtake tyred favourites all the way
Campari's secret recipe blends the winning formula
One's chilled to thrill, the other has thrills that chill
Lorraine likes a tipple and I like a chase

TRAVEL

▶ **Dolmio gives me a taste for TRAVEL because...**

PRODUCT: Pasta sauce
COMPETITION: Kwik Save/Dolmio
PRIZES: Sets of matching luggage

It sends my tastebuds on migration – Italy their destination
Packed with flavour, I become a rambling trailblazer
Dolmio 'hold-all' the aces – 'bags' of flavour in all 'cases'
My taste buds take flight, transported to Italy with every bite
Dolmio's delicious taste sensation invites more adventurous explorations
It's the 'case' that Dolmio 'hold-all' the answers
Dolmio's rich Italian fare, leaves me wishing I was there
Good sauces travel fast and Dolmio is unsurpassed
It captures the flavour of times 'Rome-ing' and 'Turin' Italy
With a 'quick' stir, Dolmio gives pasta 'bags' of flavour
Italian food is unsurpassed, thanks Dolmio, I'm packing fast
It 'Romes' on my tongue with a cosmopolitang!

I was born under a wandering jar

Pasta perfection in every direction, simply means catching the 'Dolmio connection'

Bags of fun, smiles galore, action packed more more more

These perfect sauces I adore, a world of culinary taste to explore

'Packed' with flavour, quality 'label' – destination deliciousness on my table

The distinctive taste, the supreme sensation, transports me to an Italian destination

With less time on kitchen chores, more time on foreign shores

In London, Paris or Rome, with Dolmio I'm right at home

▶ **My best friend when I TRAVEL is an Insight pocket guide because...**

PRODUCT: Pocket guide

It puts a friendly face on a foreign place

▶ **I would like to TRAVEL on the Orient Express with Wrigley's because...**

PRODUCT: Chewing gum
COMPETITION: Wrigley's/Orient Express

Because of its luxury style and fame, just like Wrigley's a well known name

With its 'chewing' and fro-ing, it's the best way of going

My train of thought is decidedly one track, longing for the excitement, courtesy of 'four pack'?

This 'chew-chew' has a flavour that never runs out of steam

That's another fine chew-chew I'd like to get into

To see wonders from carriage pane on the most historic chew-chew train

For excitement and travel at its best, I'd chew-chew from Paris to Bucharest

I often dream of chew-chews past, with memories 'by gum' that will last

Chewing it over with deliberation, this train's definitely above my station

It's more refreshing than going by chew-b

If I could chews a dream trip I'd chews the Orient Express, wouldn't chew?

The Orient Express, what a thrilling idea, something I've chewed over year after year

What other 'choo-choo' has the gumption to make luxury travel its mainline function

I could murder a taste of excitement – couldn't chew?

By gum! It's the 'chuff' that dreams are made of

I think I might look really cute pronouncing the French for juicy fruit

Wrigley's has stood the taste of time

Though in French I'm not articulate, going sight-seeing with Wrigley's I'd gesticulate

While Wrigley's wraps a cheeky chew-chew, the Orient Express has the choicest choo-choo

▶ **I would like to TRAVEL in style with Hush Puppies because...**

PRODUCT: Shoes
PRIZE: Travel on Concorde to Paris and back on the Orient Express

Comfort and style make travel worthwhile

▶ **I always TRAVEL with Berlitz because...**

PRODUCT: Language courses
PRIZES: £1,000 cash

'Yen' for travelling? 'Mark' my word, 'cheque-ing' out others is 'franc-ly'
    absurd!
Experience shows wherever one's going, what's not in Berlitz really isn't worth
    knowing
Pocket-sized with facts abundant, makes every other guide redundant
There's nothing that Berlitz overlook, wherever I'm going, I go 'buy' the book

▶ **I TRAVEL with Jacob's Club biscuits because...**

PRODUCT: Chocolate biscuits
PRIZES: £1,000 travel bonds

Chocolate covering so sublime, filling absolutely divine, delicious to eat
    anytime
When I yen a choccy bicket, Club is just the ticket
Chunky chocolate, biscuit light, it was inevitable, love at first bite
They're thick, chocolatey, sweet and light, in every way exactly right
They have chocolate outers, scrumptious inners, treatsize, neatsize, certain
winners

RUNNERS-UP: Burberry luggage

I've fallen for a thickie, Club is my favourite bickie
The name invites, the flavour excites and the taste delights
I fell for that thick chocolate. It's a love 'ate relationship
Wherever I travel or roam, with Club I always feel at home
Weekdays, birthdays, fun days, everydays, Sundays, happy days, always Club
    days
Thick chocolate, fillings supreme, find them together, Oh what a dream
To the last crumb ... succumb
Full of zest, packed with zeal, they do down best! Mmm! ideal!
When it comes to the crunch it makes the ideal choice for lunch

▶ **Butt Knit co-ordinates are perfect for TRAVELLING because...**

PRODUCT: Knitwear

Whatever the local custom, it's your duty to declare complete satisfaction

▶ **I would most like … (Personality) as an ideal TRAVELLING partner because…**

Marcel Marceau … with him there would be no language problems, anywhere
Captain James T Kirk … we could boldly go where no man has gone before
Anyone other than Jonathan Ross … he would be 'The Last Resort'
Secret Agent 007 … travelwise and wordly, this reliable 'Bond' is licensed to thrill
Madonna … I'm 'Mad on her'
Jeffrey Archer … he entertains me in a novel way
Margaret Thatcher … every picture sells a Tory
Leslie Grantham … I'm no Joan Collins in suspenders, more like Angie in Eastenders
Nigel Mansell … I'd show him a woman is Le Mans best friend
Christopher Reeve … airports would not apply – I believe this man can fly
Kate Adie … conversation should be interesting as we shared a climatic hot spot
Chay Blyth … he's seen many ports in a storm but never flounders
Mark Thatcher … when lost, no effort would be spared to find us
Dumbo … he'd remember the passports and save my air fares
Paul Daniels … he'd ensure that every location was a magical experience

▶ **I think Imperial Leather Classic is the ideal TRAVELLING companion because…**

PRODUCT: Toilet soap
PRIZES: Foreign holidays

When I use Imperial Leather, I never come Acropolis
It makes a good impression with our foreign 'Cussons'

▶ **Thomas Cook TRAVELLERS' Cheques and Girobank are streaks ahead at the Post Office because…**

PRODUCT: Travellers' cheques

Together they have the formula to lap the world
Their track record leaves other competitors behind in the starting grid
There's no racing about to put you in a spin
They get your holiday off to a racing start
They're twinned for speed and reliability
No queues, no wait, first to the airport gate
They are today's financial facilities for tomorrow's travellers
They have the number one formula to beat their rivals by hours
Their high-speed trouble-free performance covers any distance with ease
Banking on this recipe steers you through trouble-free
Monies safe when ready to spend, won't be driven round the bend
Going abroad, gotta hurry, this winning team saves me worry
Down the straight, through the chicane, Cooks and Girobank win again

Faster service close at hand, is formula one for travel planned
Countrywide, coast to coast, you're always near the winning post

▶ **I book with Thomas Cook because...**

PRODUCT: Package holidays

I get a heavenly holiday at a down-to-earth price

▶ **I can really go places with Uncle Ben's because...**

PRODUCT: Stir-fry sauces

Travel is easy, just need my wok, Thai Curry Sauce – Hello Bangkok!

▶ **I would like to take a Wings holiday because...**

PRODUCT: Horticultural seeds
COMPETITION: Co-op/Bees seeds

Once my flowers disappear, there's nothing left to keep me here
While Bees guarantees my gardening plan, Wings looks after my holiday tan
They are obviously the 'package' tops with both Bees and Co-ops

Train TRAVEL on the Orient Express

Britain's heritage, the Orient expresses it
In the age of the train, the Orient Express is the train of the age
Anyone for Venice?
'Ee by gum' a Queen I'd reign, travelling posh in t'fancy train
Posh and pampered all the way, a first class start to my holiday
Coast to coast it offers the most, superlative comfort, perfect host
The lure of luxury travel appeals, it's the ultimate graceful living on wheels
Whatever the weather, wherever the stop, 5-star luxury's what you've got
Buzzing along on this rolling Ritz is my idea of being thrilled to bits
From today's commutings, push and shove, to yesterday's elegant calm I'd love
This glamorous train so full of mystique is a step back in time luxurious,
    unique
Travelling in luxury, eating in style, such VIP treatment would make me smile
The splendour, the service, the champagne, the style, fabulous scenery and
    smiles every mile
The first class luxury line would combine good taste with an old fashioned
    flavour
I'd like to journey into the elegant past, on flanged wheels revolving fast
A romantic journey by first class rail would be a real life fairy tale
It's a thrilling journey which blazes the trail, for gracious living on a high-speed
    rail
A living legend, built to last, lives on eternally from the past
To escape the nineties' furious pace, and travel in a world of satin and lace
Entering a world of charm and sophistication, I'd leave reality at the station

Conceived by the perfect marriage of engineering ability and luxuriously
    elegant interior comfort
A train of the ages, in historical pages, an incredible feat, while travelling elite
Spinning wheels threading their way through yesterday
To go down memory lane on that nostalgic train
Wherever you alight it's a transport of delight
It's a journey with the gentry and the best of the century
It's mile after mile of elegance and style

TRAVELLING on the Orient Express Victorian train

PRODUCT: Train travel
COMPETITION: Orient Express 'Who Dun It?'

I'd love to swap my pinny for a trip with Albert Finney
History, mystery, a hint of romance, background to murder? I'd take the
    chance
'On the track' of a boredom killer, I'd be 'carried away' by this armchair thriller
To travel in luxury, comfort and style, would carry me spellbound, mile after
    mile
Being the scene of Agatha's 'Who Dun it', a dream would 'Christie-lize' if I
    won it
A trip to Venice on any other train would be murder
This luxury venture on wheels has an air of intrigue that appeals
Murders, spies, romances, such intriguing tales, a golden opportunity to 'go off
    the rails'
Murder and mystery, legend and lore, luxury travel, who could want more?
Murder on the Orient Express is better than 'killed in the rush at Paddington'
It's no mystery, it would be a thriller
I would enjoy the NOVELty from start to FINney
Seen the film, read the book, now I'd like to take a look
Age of steam, expressed in a dream, caught in times, like an Agatha Christie
    crime
Romance and adventure from Agatha's page, plus the luxurious elegance of a
    bygone age
It's a mystery tour I'd be chuffed to take, a lifetime's journey for Agatha's sake
After my long in the 'Housetrap' I could murder a good holiday
I've seen the scene on the screen, living the dream would be supreme
I'd love to travel with a hint of mystery to a city with a mint of history
Chosen by Christie, Fleming and Green, the first class Pullman with first class
    cuisine
It would be a novel experience
A novel experience a 'rail' life adventure, Victorian luxury, memories to
    treasure

TREASURE

▶ **Treasure hunters eat Club and Trio as their favourite chocolate biscuits because...**

PRODUCT: Chocolate biscuits

Real thick chocolate '4T'fies, those who hunt for better buys
Chocolate so rich, fillings supreme; to find them together is a prospector's dream
Pirates searching the seven seas, never found booty as good as these
Like Christopher Columbus they open up a new world of delight
Even Tutankhamen would come alive, could he taste this pack of five
As Tutankhamen said to mummy, 'Jacob's are so very scrummy'
Every bite is 18 carat, quite a change from eating parrot
Chocolate Lovers Uncover Bargains, They Really Insist On Jacobs *(CLUB TRIO = ACROSTIC)*
You can't beat a man with a Club
With a different flavour every day, who needs treasure anyway?
Specialists perfect them, perfectionists select them
In their quest for the best, real thick chocolate passed the test

▶ **Everyone strikes it rich at Numark because...**

PRODUCT: Chemist goods

To share in Numark's golden bonanza, customers just take their 'pick'

TUNED

▶ **We're TUNED into Princes tuna because...**

PRODUCT: Canned fish
COMPETITION: Kwik Save/Tune in with Princes tuna
PRIZES: Sound equipment

It re-45's the charts other tuna's cannot reach
Rock, jitterbug, twist or jive, Princes tuna brings meals alive
Princes piscatorial delights, jazz up our canned kareoke nights
It's humanely caught with quality and thought
The best tunas come from the leader of the brand
Number one with summer salads, taste buds sing delightful ballads
Brilliant butties, perfect pizza, turn to tuna for a 'feasta'
Sound value, perfection canned, like a piano, it's grand
It makes a lovely 'pizzacato' with cheese, olives and tomato
They're in tuna with everything on my Chopin Liszt

▶ **When we buy Princes spreadables at Co-op Leo's we get TUNED into the beat because...**

PRODUCT: *Meat and fish spreads in jars*
COMPETITION: *Co-op Leo's/Princes Tune into the Beat*
PRIZES: *Panasonic sound equipment*

They rave at every tasting and give others a pasting
The compact jars beat the blues, delicious taste, rave reviews
Value and taste are amplified, if Princes and Leo's coincide
Tasty topping, thrifty shopping, always gets our tastebuds bopping
Rock, jitterbug, twist or jive, Princes spreads bring sarnies alive
'Topo' the pots for eating, Leo's prices take some beating
Pop into Leo's, Princes paste holds major key to taste
Princes spreadables are the rave, with Leo's select-n-save
They're spreadable, they're edible, they're just incredible
Pots of taste at Leo's rates, no dire straights
Rock, boogie, twist or jive, this duet brings bread alive
We're getting D major spreads at D minor prices
Brown, white bread, crispy crackers, Princes spreads make happy snackers
To all tastes rock, folk, jazz, Princes spreadables add pazazz
Perfect Princes, perfect store, tuned in customers need no more
Leo's always gets my vote, Princes spreadables hit the note
Good music delights, as Leo's value invites, Princes flavour excites
Leo's prices beat the rest, serenading tastebuds with Princes best
We'll be knock knock knocking on Leo's door for more
High note, low note, they both get our vote
With Leo's sound co-operation, Princes spreads some good vibrations
Princes leader of the band always on my Chopin Liszt
We trip the bite fantastic
For snacks gastronomic, they're as sound as Panasonic
Superb taste, prices potty, and as essential as Pavarotti
Prices rock, service is smart, Princes certainly top my chart
For taste, they're the Temptations, for quality the Supremes
I take no rap when I plaster the bap
Princes classics are Leo's pride, for everyone's tastes are satisfied

UNBEATABLE

▶ **Thick liquid Vigor is UNBEATABLE because...**

PRODUCT: *Cleaner*

Used sparsely it speedily spurns greasy dirt, leaving spectacular sparkle

UNDERWEAR

▶ **Playtex bras and girdles are great playtime garments because...**

PRODUCT: Ladies's lingerie

They're great supporters for swinging ladies

▶ **I buy Playtex at House of Fraser because...**

PRODUCT: Ladies' lingerie
PRIZES: Travel vouchers

An uplifting experience is born, keeping abreast of fashion form
I support them – they support me
Their range is extensive, but never expensive
Best choice, quality – provisions for family – 'exercise' control for me
On Playtex quality I'm insistent, but dislike 'hovering' assistants
I can rely on the store for giving me more
They're fashionable and appeal to me – and support comfortably
For sheer appeal, there's evidence Playtex is ideal, makes common sense
My housekeeping can pay for luxuries – don't tell hubby
I get rising inflation without going bust
House of Fraser, Playtex price nominal, flattery and fit phenomenal
Both 'shape' up to provide – goods sold with pride
In comfort and style, I stand out a mile
Pretty or sporty, perfectly pleasing, lacy or naughty, tantalisingly teasing
Less time spent shopping, more time spent al fresco
My 'cups' runneth over with savings
Their great prices and styles 'support' my hubby's smiles
House of Fraser cut prices as attractively as Playtex cut bras
Cheques are not the only things that don't bounce
Playtex new collection excitingly unique, stunningly attractive, comfortable yet
    chic
Their supporting role leaves me in control
House of Fraser's Playtex collection entices with beautiful bras at affordable
    prices
For a wonderful lift, from this superstore it's a gift
Concealed between groceries with skill, hubby happily pays the bill
When put to the test, they figure best

Briefs

It adds a little bit of cheek with a shape of surprise
Sartorially perfect, comfortably free, far better briefed than any QC

USE

▶ **I USE Clearasil lotion because...**

PRODUCT: Spot medication

It leaves my complexion a spotless perfection

▶ **I always USE Racasan products because....**

PRODUCT: Toilet cleaners and air fresheners

Freshening the air, cleaning the pan, nothing can beat Racasan
They clean discreetly and freshen completely
Placed in cistern and pan, toilets are fresher with Racasan
Toilets clean, germs kept at bay, Racasan's the easy way
Freshness abounds when Racasan's around
For such freshness and scent, every penny's well spent
They have won the first test in a clean bowled toilet

▶ **I always USE 1001 because...**

PRODUCT: Liquid carpet cleaner

It lightens labour and lessens expense, using it makes common sense

▶ **I always USE Sucron in preference to sugar in cooking because...**

PRODUCT: Sugar substitute
COMPETITION: Sucron 'Win a kitchen'
PRIZE: £7,500 kitchen

Sucron helps this lucky lassie, preserve a rather classy chassis

▶ **I USE Nulon because...**

PRODUCT: Hand cream
COMPETITION: Nulon/Take your body in hand
PRIZES: Health farm weekends for two

Nulon brings richness to the pore
In a show of hands, it's a winner every time
It takes time off my hands
Fragrant, gentle, cruelty-free, Nulon's caring formula pampers me
I know my investment is in good hands

▶ **I USE Ever Ready Power Plus batteries because...**

PRODUCT: Batteries

They're the greatest things for torches since darkness
Their force out-cells the others
They're Ever Ready, Ever Steady, Ever Go!
For light, sight or sound, no better can be found
In the reliability stakes they always make the 'running'
They're the long distance runners in canned energy
They're better and they're stronger – they're Ever Ready longer
In the long run they leave the rest standing
It's a power station you can afford
Put to the test, they beat the rest

▶ **I like USING Wolf tools because...**

PRODUCT: D.I.Y. tools

Whatever the task, Wolf tools are winners, giving expert results for pros and
beginners

VALUE

▶ **Today's Tesco adds new values to VALUE because...**

PRODUCT: Supermarket foods

At Tesco you feel they value you
Best price shopping, spotless stores, cheerful service, who needs more?
They always cut the cost but never the quality
In every section, every tab is the bright direction
You get the world's choicest produce without paying the earth
Quality, price go hand in glove – perfect marriage shoppers love
Tesco offers the worthwhile price, household goods for the pennywise
It's the best value anywhere around
Kitchen sinking or armchair drinking, budget stretching means Tesco thinking
A heart of gold and a silver soul minds the brass
Others make profuse promises, Tesco keeps them
They know families thrive on the benefits derived
Tesco produces today's greatest variety on the smallest bills
They give high priority to superiority
Dealing out value with zeal, shoppers enjoy a great deal
They have made it their cause to merit public applause
Stores are bright, staff polite, with prices always right
There's quality plus value second to none – something for everyone
Economy and convenience, together ensure shopping expedience
With prices no worse they are kind to the purse
The check-out at Tesco means a cheque in your bank
Bargains invite the eye, excite the purse, delight the family

Fashions with built-in flair, I'll take home 'n' wear
It cuts prices without cutting corners
Canny shoppers can drink to the choicest offers
As money gets shorter, Tesco makes it last longer
Only Tesco can make the best better
They have the highest quality plus lowest take-away prices
They know which new lines are worth knowing
For my money Tesco's the one to bank on
It's all the best at the best of all prices
They are a great deal better at giving a better deal
They value the values of the housewife
It cuts down on slaving and encourages saving
Tesco is adept at adapting to customers adopting every convenience
Value is worth and Tesco is worth every penny

▶ **My chosen item from Boots offers the best VALUE for money because..**

PRODUCT: Chemist goods
COMPETITION: Boots/Old Spice aftershave

Old Spice increases the comfort – Boots shaves the prices

▶ **Spar foods are good VALUE because...**

PRODUCT: Food store foods

Their down-to-earth prices are out of this world
Each shop's a showcase, inviting inspection – quality economy a masterly
    selection

Stores and VALUE in general

Value is always underlined but quality is never undermined
Their price pegging means value on every line
They make the pound go round
It's hand in glove with cash in hand
The quality is superb but the prices don't perturb
They stock a stack of prices that stick
Total satisfaction is a dead cert with Asda's starting prices
With Asda's trolleys I look for the best deals on wheels
All we need top to bottom, guaranteed Tesco's got-em
Beauty care to home n' wear, Tesco is beyond compare
Tesco product clean and healthy, Tesco prices keep me wealthy
Prices, grooming, tooth decay, all are controlled the Tesco way
Forget about the falling pound, Tesco prices hold their ground

VEGETABLES

▶ **Sainsbury's new potatoes are the best because...**

PRODUCT: Potatoes
PRIZES: Holiday to Egypt

With tasty tubers to grace your meal, Sainsbury's offers a Pharaoh deal

▶ **I buy Cirio tinned tomatoes because...**

PRODUCT: Canned tomatoes

They are pasta masters of the Italian School
Like Pisa, it's always on the list
They bring southern Italian sunshine into my kitchen
The flavour goes from my head to-ma-toes
Their products have taste like Alfa has style
They put sunshine into winter casseroles

▶ **I buy Bird's Eye frozen peas because...**

PRODUCT: Peas

Those past their peak are just OAPeas
They all get the VIPea treatment
Only the best singles are chosen from the LPeas
They are all Euro-PEA-n champions
They're the PEA-st de resistance
They are a perfect PEA-ce offering
They have the power of the PEA-ple behind them

Frozen and fresh vegetables

A little simmer brings out summer all the year round
They keep cropping up in all the shops
They are harvested and packed at exactly the ripe moment
They hit the right flavour note
Only the chosen few are picked
They don't grow too big for their roots
They lead the field by leaving it first
Everything is beautiful in it's gr-own way
I'm never a melan-cauli baby
They 'kick' out more than any 'can can'
I'll give 'em their 'dew', they're fresh enough
There's no business like grow business
Supercoolervegalisticfreshpeacarrototious
Nothing 'soils' their reputation
There's never mushroom for has-beans

They are picked to be in tune with every fork
They beat all pulses
They have 'em 'bagged' while others are still 'stalking' theirs
Baggers can be choosers
The best are chosen and bagged while the rest are 'sacked'

VIEW

▶ **Bargains are always on VIEW at Presto because...**

PRODUCT: Supermarket foods

Their price cut show is a continuous performance

VISIT

▶ **I would like to VISIT New York with Michelob because....**

PRODUCT: Beer
COMPETITION: Gateway/Michelob
PRIZE: Trip to New York

Though Gateway stock my favourite buyline, I prefer the New York skyline

▶ **I would like to VISIT Canada because...**

PRODUCT: Canadian holidays

An Irresistible Rendezvous, Canada Affords Natural And Delightful Attractions
(AIR CANADA = ACROSTIC)

▶ **I should like to VISIT ... (Place)...**

The Bank of England ... I have always wanted to meet the loan arranger and
    silver
San Francisco ... I would like to try out my bullet proof vest
San Francisco ... I'd have a taste of the exotic out of someone's else's pocket

▶ **I want to VISIT Father Christmas because...**

PRODUCT: Chain store goods
COMPETITION: House of Fraser/Lapland
PRIZES: Trips to Lapland

Like visiting House of Fraser, it would be bliss, a Santastic trip, I hope I don't
    miss
He gives everyone so much pleasure it would be nice to thank him personally

My children's glowing faces, glimpsing magical scenes, Santa, snow and
    reindeer, please fulfil their dreams
A Frasercard buys you time to pay, for the gifts you send from Santa's sleigh
The spirit of Christmas is giving, so I hope he gives me first prize
Skidoo through the snow, where's Santa? Let's go, what a delight, let's win that
    flight
My little 'deer' with starry gaze, asks every year, where Santa stays
I want to put the Fraser logo above the entrance to Santa's grotto
Childhood fantasies only come true, for the House of Fraser fortunate few
He is childhood's most magical and enchanting memory
I'd sit on the lap of that wonderful chap and give him gifts to unwrap
He travels fast just like a laser, he is quick like the House of Fraser
He'll then see me in the land of lap and not in the land of nod
With reindeer ready, his sleigh full of toys, Santa brings happiness to girls and
    boys
Searching for Santa at the end of the year, beats sitting at home in the reindeer
    (*rain, dear)
Visiting Santa on skidoo, beats travelling by coach on the M62
We could skedadal in a skidoo and see Father Christmas in an igloo
Now we've got a gas fire he won't be coming down our chimney

▶ I would like to VISIT Henlow Grange because...

PRODUCT: Beauty care
COMPETITION: Cystemme/Henlow Grange Health Farm
PRIZES: Weekends for two

I'd keep the blues at bay, cosseted the Henlow way
It's every woman's dream to be pampered

▶ My favourite place to eat Buitoni Pasta would be...

PRODUCT: Pasta

Nowhere exotic, just at home, reliving the pleasures of dining in Rome
In Jules Verne's time machine – perfect pasta deserves future projection
La Scala Opera House and sing praises accompanied by 'Strings and Bows'
Gazing into gondolier's eyes, dark handsome looks to bridge my sighs
St. Marks Square because Buitoni pasta always makes time with loving care

WATCH

▶ I WATCH for Loctite because...
PRODUCT: Adhesive

Its vertical hold is visibly superior
Loctite 'screen' every product, then 'stick' with the best
I'm glued to their set
You get a good 'sight' more for a good sight less
They look after our image with vision
It brings a smile to everyone's dial

WEAR

▶ **I WEAR Alexon clothing because...**

PRODUCT: Designer wear

Specialists perfect it, perfectionists select it

▶ **I WEAR Alexander business and daywear clothing because...**

PRODUCT: Clothing

Whatever the Season or time of day, Alexander suits me in every way
A busy business woman with no time to spare, relying on Alexander which
    takes time to care
Any occasion morning till night, Alexander clothes are always right
I wouldn't be 'with it' without it

WEIGHT

▶ **I buy Weight Watchers from Heinz products from Safeway
because...**

PRODUCT: Low calorie foods
COMPETITION: Safeway/Weight Watchers from Heinz
PRIZES: Hanson electronic scales

Overweight and very fat, Weight Watchers can change all that
Safeway's prices are money spinners and Heinz Weight Watchers make
    successful slimmers
It's the safest way to slim, fewer calories in every tin
They keep me slim at prices terrific, unlike rivals grim and cal-horrific
Heinz and Safeway, what a team, save the pounds and look supreme
Counting every ounce and pound, they tip the balance I have found
The waist is whittled but the taste isn't skittled
They restore me as nature intended, with strength and vitality well blended
I've tried the rest and now stick with the best
This priceless combination, counter-balances inflation

The family's favourite low-cal brand, is sensibly priced and temptingly canned
They're planned for healthy eating and Safeway prices are worth repeating
Watching my weight whilst saving pence, that's good old Safeway common sense
Great taste, cost a cinch, slim waist, lost an inch
On the scale of one to ten, both score maximum once again
A harassed housewife under stress, Heinz from Safeway slim me best
Friendly service, good advice, Weight Watchers products at a reasonable price
It's the Safeway to indulge while beating the bulge
Saving money, losing weight, my purse and I are feeling great
More to eat, less to weigh, greater choice and less to pay
Nice lean prices, calories few, more in your pocket, less on you
Super savings and terrific tastes, pile pounds in pockets, not around waists
This grocery go-getter thinks they're weigh weigh better
I choose Heinz for healthy eating and Safeway prices take some beating
Men don't like the bulge when women indulge
With slimmer hips and trimmer middle, I'm beautifully fit without the fiddle
Heinz make it easy to slim, Safeway keeps the budget in trim
They are less expense, saving money and less expansive for my tummy
Safeway always fits my meanz, Heinz meanz fitting my jeans
With Safeway savings less to pay, Weight Watchers keep the pounds a-weigh
Delicious food I love to scoff, both ensure I'm pounds better off
Penny-wise holds Safeway supreme, pound-foolish need Weight Watchers regime
They provide the best proposal, for helping with my waist disposal
Losing weight, price appeal, gives Safeway shoppers twice the deal
Weight Watchers' goodness keeps me healthy, Safeway prices keep me wealthy
They save pounds and help me look more Hanson
Safeway prices seduce me, Heinz Weight Watchers reduce me
Heinz at Safeway perfect taste, more in purse less on waist
Low in calories, lose the flab, buy in Safeway, choice is fab
When I shop for my shape, Heinz and Safeway beat the tape
Low in calories, low in fat, low in price too - fancy that
Heinz quality and Safeway care, make them a winning pair
They assist my reduction without much deduction
For shopping at Safeway figure wise, Heinz scale problems down to size
Safeway's dieters shopping venue, puts cheaper Weight Watchers on their menu
I keep myself slender with less money to tender
Heinz stops those pounds from mounting, cuts down on calorie counting
In price and value Safeway win, Heinz Weight Watchers keep me trim
With help from Heinz and Hanson, I'll soon be slim and handsome
Great taste, low price, thin waist, that's nice
For removing that inch you can pinch, they're a cinch
Tastes are great, my weight is less, Heinz and Safeway spell success
Super product, super store, super savings, weight no more
They keep me sweet while I stay petite

Heinz from Safeway just my taste, keep me trim around the waist
Weight Watchers scale the heights of taste, adding nothing to the waist

WICKED

▶ **I think Holsten Pils is a pure beer in a WICKED world because...**

PRODUCT: Beer

Exacting German purity laws, suit 'Herr' outside and her indoors
When angels fear to tread Holsten Export stays cool, keeps its head
With Holsten Export, heaven is only a ring-pull away

▶ **Cycling gives me a WICKED appetite for New York Burgers because...**

PRODUCT: Meat burgers
COMPETITION: Safeway/New York Burgers
PRIZES: Peugeot bicycles

It's great, it's yummy, it satisfies my tummy
My hunger's a-bun-dant, making other burgers redundant
Speeding About Fast Enthusiastically Wheely Affects You *(SAFEWAY = ACROSTIC)*
'Open Sesame' to build my ana-tummy
After huffin and puffin I need stuffin
They are Perfectly Exquisite Unbeatable Great Extraordinary Original and Terrific *(PEUGEOT = ACROSTIC)*
Its chain reaction makes me go weak at the knees
Weather tyre or need a break, they're the gear appropriate
To be really specific, they taste 'wheely' terrific
It's a tasty fulfilling snack with energy that's a fact

▶ **I think the taste of Sunquick is WICKED because...**

PRODUCT: Fruit squash

I'm bewitched by its sunsational spell, wish I had a Sunquick well

WILD WEST

▶ **I would like to capture the spirit of the American Wild West by...**

PRODUCT: *Wild West holidays*

Feeling the history, breathing the air, exploring traditions beyond compare

▶ **I enjoyed the American adventure experience because...**

PRODUCT: *American holidays*

America's finest and all it entails, bring terrific adventures to Derbyshire Dales

▶ **I would like to experience the Wild West with Marlboro because...**

PRODUCT: *Cigarettes*

No horizon is too broad for the Marlboro man
In Marlboro country, where the men walk tall, this lonesome squaw would
    have a ball
Travel broadens the mind, especially if the land matches the brand
In a rugged country where men are tough, Marlboro's rich taste gives strength
    enough
Watching wild mustang stampede, is just the fillip I need

▶ **I prefer the taste of Colt 45 because...**

PRODUCT: *Lager*

A hot little number deserves a cool 45
The pulling power of Colt 45 is amazing
Let's share a Colt and see what we can trigger off
Drink more Colt and your filly will nag
Colt 45 has the body I'm after
Cool combination on the costa del Colt
At the seaside I don't think redskins used Colt 45's
The water's fine but 'I-CY' Colt is better

WIN

▶ **I always WIN with Mars because...**

PRODUCT: *Confectionery*
COMPETITION: *Mars 'Win a trip to the Olympic Games'*

A handful of bronze buys a gold medal snack

▶ **I always WIN with Uncle Ben's range of products because...**

PRODUCT: *Rice, sauces, stir-fry sauces*
COMPETITION: *Kwik Save/Uncle Ben's Olympics/Dolmio*

PRIZES: Uncle Ben's sports bags

'Opening Ceremony', to 'prize presentation', every 'event' an 'unrivalled'
   sensation
Akabusi hurdles, Christie flies, but Dolmio takes first prize
Being first in the 'taste games' gives Dolmio eternal F(l)ame
It's in the number one position, having out-riced the opposition
Uncle Ben's the one, Olympians 'relay' on
Uncle Ben's means no stress or mess, just guaranteed success
For high speed dinners, they're gold medal winners
Like Spanish sun Olympic roars, Uncle Ben's always scores
Having an 'old flame' to dinner, guarantees I serve a winner
In my race for perfection, Dolmio was my selection
Dolmio sets the pace, winning tastes from every race
Super meals soon unfold with Dolmio for 'Gold'
They win more medals than I've had hot dinners
My 'Daley' 'Rush' for gold is 'Crammed' in 'Evert'y packet
It's quick, tasty, good nutrition, easily outruns the opposition
Light candles, set date, Dolmio means she's never late
I get a head start, fast finish and perfect results
Mexican, Chinese, savoury, sweet, these creations are always a treat
Their track record reigns supreme, like any Olympic team
Meat or fish, hot or cold, Dolmio strikes for gold
Rich in quality, reasonable price, super buy – sauce for rice
I always go for gold, imitations leave me cold
'Eddery' (*every) serve 'Cram'med with Entyson (*enticing) F-lavers
   (*flavours) 'Gibbs' (*gives) 'Becker' (*better) 'Cash' value
Mealtime hurdles cleared with ease, thanks to Dolmio's expertise
Experience and expertise means Dolmio will always please
Straight from the starting gun, Dolmio is number one
Flowing rice, teamed with sauce, guarantees a winning course
First for taste, no waste, money spinner – all round winner
They're hot winners, wholesome, supreme – like our Barcelona team
Dolmio sauces and rice give my meals extra spice
Romantic dinner or family invasion – top performer for every occasion
Sprinting about, chasing perfection, Dolmio was the obvious selection
No other product can compare, for promoting gold standards everywhere
Fluffy rice, sauce treat, Dolmio can't be beat
Inviting Dolmio to dinner, everybody's a winner
My family team is biased – It's always 'bias' Dolmio
On the rostrum stand supreme, Dolmio's unbeatable team
Delicious ingredients costing less, make my meals an unrivalled success
When the meal's completed, hunger is 'defeated'
It's a golden winning relay – me, Dolmio and Kwik Save
Meals inspired by Dolmio always score a perfect 10
They're delicious to eat and impossible to beat

▶ **I always WIN with Uncle Ben's at Asda because...**

PRODUCT: Rice, sauces, stir-fry sauces
COMPETITION: Asda/Uncle Ben's Olympics/Dolmio

Fluffy rice, spicy sauce, worth a medal, gold of course
Dinner times I serve an ace, Dolmio takes first place
Their track record's second to none, always my number one
Always first across the line 'perfect results every time'
For taste and quality they just can't be beaten
Good ingredients, tasty and light, Dolmio's my mister right
Dolmio's winning combinations set the pace whatever the race
Fluffy rice and Texas aroma, Asda win gold in Barcelona
Their reputation reigns supreme, I'm always on the winning team
Their boxes invite, their jars excite, and the memories delight
Olympic standards on every table, Dolmio's the only label
My 'team' sprint home excitedly and 'lap' them up delightedly
From mild to extra hot, Dolmio's got the lot
In the shopping race Dolmio takes first place
Their winning lines in tasty dishes, satisfies my family's wishes
With Dolmio's Olympic name, 'everyjuan' (*everyone) can 'rice' to fame
So expertly perfected, it 'Asda' be that I'm selected
They're always top of the table
Meals that are delicious and fast are no 'marathon' task
Their reputation wins every test, guaranteeing always a personal best
When everyone loves a winner, there's never anything for seconds
They help me cross the 'fine-dish' line
This sauce of inspiration always receives a standing ovation
With Olympics we agree, nutritional balance is the key
They are a runaway success with results that impress
I am never a loser being a Dolmio user
It provides a flying start, I just add the finish
They sponsor perfection in taste and conception

WINNER

▶ **Milk's a WINNER because...**

PRODUCT: Milk

It's nutritionally foremost and first past the door post

▶ **Moët & Chandon, Britain's best selling champagne is a WINNER because...**

PRODUCT: Champagne

PRIZES: Day at the races with a champagne lunch

It 'reigns' when it pours
It pops your cork when you drink it
It's the thoroughbred that leads the field

▶ **Heinz and Wm Low are a WINNER for family shopping because...**

PRODUCT: Supermarket foods

Both are 'parent' companies, going 'father' for mother, sister and brother
Of the wide variety of Wm Low and other products, cleanliness and friendly staff
They've found the formula to succeed, more 'per pound' is guaranteed
Healthy taste – budget price, together make the spice of life

▶ **Pierre Cardin Pour Monsieur out-performs the rest because...**

PRODUCT: Aftershave

Who wears wins
It's a winner on all Sir-faces
It's a formula one fragrance

WINNING

▶ **HP is my WINNING sauce because...**

PRODUCT: Brown sauce
PRIZES: Tickets to British sporting events of winner's choice

'Eddery' (*every) bottle is 'Cram'med with En'tyson' (*enticing) flavours and 'Becker' (*better) cash value
For added punch, let's be frank, it's HP sauce on which Eubank (*you bank)
Chicken, pork, beef or veal, it adds punch to every meal
On micro 'chip' or mega 'byte', HP sauce is pure delight
It's the only minister of taste in the cabinet
Although Frank Bruno packs punches, it needs HP to enhance my lunches
This rich smooth sauce reigns supreme, turning humdrum dinners into haute cuisine
Food is hoarse when its raised voice says champion the wonder sauce
Meals go with a swing, HP has that extra zing
It keeps pace, in the race, for the perfect taste
My partner could eat a horse, but not without HP sauce
The leader of the brands and I'm the keenest of fans

Eubank may strut, Bruno packs clout, but HP's punch knocks me out
It's tall, slim, dark and good cooking
Ideal for stews, burgers and pies, the spicy flavour takes first prize
It holds all the answers to a question of sauce
No doubt about it, can't eat my meal without it
It's tasty and delicious, I love it on all my dishes
I'd rather back a losing horse, than go without my favourite sauce
No other can ketchup without it – know what I mean?
After one try I was converted
I'm on to a winner, with HP for dinner
Saucy habit – I can't lick it – HP is just the ticket
Food raw or cooked, hot or cold, HP sauce wins the 'gold'
I'm always on course with this champion sauce
HP's the only sauce of income worth having
It's thick, dark and weighty, and also over eighty (like me!)
Breakfast, lunch or dinner, HP makes my meal a winner
It reigns when it pours
Meals not quite at tastebud peak, are transformed with HP's technique
Faldo drives, Mansell flies, HP sauce takes first prize
Whatever the venue, it's first on my menu
HP adds instant appeal, from simple snack to family appeal
HP sauce makes food taste scrum-my, it converts the bland to yummy
Dark, saucy packs a punch, Frank and I love it for lunch
I have excellent taste, but no money to waste
When the chips are down, HP fits the frown
I can say without doubt, it's the best sauce about
It packs a punch that beats the bunch
Seekers of the rare and prized, need their tastebuds tantalised
In the race to please, it wins with ease
David Coleman may be 'mustard', but HP has all the answers, Harry!
HP sauce, hey brother! Packs a punch like no other
HP sauce? A bottle I'd wolf, just to see the open golf
Whether breakfast, dinner, tea or lunch, HP delivers meals with a punch
It knocks spots off other brands, deliciously spicy, thrills the fans
With bacon, burgers, pies and chops, HP sauce is always tops
It adds extra spice to meals every morning, noon and night
It adds a little spice to my life

▶ **Ariel and Food Giant are a WINNING team because...**

PRODUCT: Washing powder
COMPETITION: Food Giant/Ariel Olympics
PRIZES: Seat Marbella cars

Ariel knocks out stains – makes colours brighter, Food Giant's the champion
    prize fighter
Ariel's excellence, Food Giant's flair – together they make a perfect pair
I get whiter whites and blacker blacks – colours bright and value packs

▶ **Weight Watchers from Heinz and Kwik Save are my WINNING team because...**

PRODUCT: Low calorie foods
COMPETITION: Kwik Save/Weight Watchers from Heinz
FIRST PRIZE: Holiday for four in Florida

With their money-spinner dinner, I'm a thinner winner

RUNNERS-UP: £10 food vouchers

They make shopping bliss, quality never hit and miss
Heinz quality and Kwik Save price – a dieter's dream and shopper's paradise
Their price rises, I've found, are thin on the ground
Weight Watchers lost me pounds and Kwik Save saves me pounds
Kwik Save value, Heinz taste, their triumphs never go to waist
I can budget for good health with help from these friends
There's always more pounds in my purse and less on my person
Heinz/Kwik Save lead the way, keeping weight and wait at bay
Quality wins the price race – saves my silver and bronze
They're the heavyweight answer to a lightweight dream
Without their help you'll end up in the losing team
Heinz save my figure and Kwik Save my purse
Heinz, Weight Watchers, Kwik Save tills, means lower weight and lower bills
The pounds that are lost are not to my cost
They meet the challenge with vigour, good as gold for my figure
Kwik Save's value, Heinz calorie care, combine to make my perfect pair
Heinz and Kwik Save meanz much more varietiez to pleaze
They give so much and add so little
The pounds you lose with Weight Watchers can be quickly saved at Kwik Save
Eating well, keeping slim, saving pounds, I'm bound to win
In the battle of the bulge they allow me to indulge
Gold medal performance is their tradition, first for taste, first for nutrition
Shedding pounds whilst saving pence, scores double points for common sense
They help stretch the salaries, by reducing the calories
They're the Kwik-est savings in town – they never let you down
Counting calories, counting pence, Weight Watchers from Kwik Save make
        common sense
Their superb variety, value and flavour, tip the scales in my favour
Champions both to challenge either, rivals are loath
I've lost weight, saved money, now I'd like to go somewhere sunny
I can reduce my shopping to go Florida hopping
Every inch selection of pleasure, they have things taped beyond all measure
Lean in calories, low on cost, a combination that has never lost
Together they feed the nation and reduce inflation
With such a good combination I will soon reach my goal weight
Reducing costs as I grow thinner, makes this pair a certain winner
For these table toppers there is no substitute
They make sure I don't waste my money

I can buy more for less but still fit in my dress
Together we save pounds, without favourite foods being out of bounds
Both simplify a good buy
Wholesome variety, Weight Watchers goodies, worthwhile rations, healthy
    buddies
I am on a salary-reduced diet
They're star performers all round, reducing waist and saving pounds
Just perfect in every 'weigh', I can enjoy them every day
They're the tasty answer to wishful shrinking

▶ Rowenta and Currys make a gold WINNING team because...

PRODUCT: Electrical goods

Together they are joint firsts in product popularity and professional
    presentation
For quality and service they are both front runners
Their 24 carat gold reputation is never tarnished
The elegant technology and shining prices provide the most glittering of prizes
With every purchase a glittering prize they cut ironing down to size
Experts perfect them connoisseurs select them
Rowenta steam past the rest and Currys only choose the best
Top performer second to none, Rowenta and Currys show how it's done
Names of such 'esteem' together reign supreme

▶ I think Tesco and Hoover make a WINNING combination because...

PRODUCT: Washing machines
COMPETITION: Tesco/Hoover
PRIZES: Hoover washing machines

They wave the wand while I read James Bond
Both use technology as an aid to economy
They are a legend in their own grime
Economically and ecologically washloads are easily overcome
They are both value for money
Their clear action beings clean satisfaction
They're both fast and efficient
Green plus green adds up to a laundry bright white
Tesco keeps the prices right, while Hoover gets the whites bright
Together they are a mean cleaning machine

▶ Asda and Wilkinson Sword are a WINNING team because...

PRODUCT: Blades and razors
COMPETITION: Asda/Wilkinson Sword

With inflation to hedge they both have the edge

▶ **Heinz and the Co-op are a WINNING combination because...**

PRODUCT: *Supermarket foods*

Heinz flare and Co-op care, together make a winning pair

▶ **Heinz and Kwik Save are a WINNING combination because...**

PRODUCT: *Supermarket foods*
COMPETITION: *Kwik Save/Heinz 'Win a trip to Florida'*
PRIZES: *Trips to Florida*

Of the price on the tin and the goodness within
They squeeze prices like Miami vices
The odds are in their flavour, quality brands from a money saver

▶ **Heinz and Nisa are a WINNING formula because...**

PRODUCT: *Food store foods*

Top quality products and value for money go hand in hand

▶ **Rothmans and Honda make a WINNING team because...**

PRODUCT: *Cigarettes*
PRIZE: *Honda car*

They're in the lead for quality

▶ **A Dolmio meal is always a WINNING production because...**

PRODUCT: *Pasta sauce*

Action packed, full of taste, Dolmio meals mean no waste
Classic meals I make in only one take
It stars a red hot saucy Italian who'll never get canned
The family cheers when it appears

WINTER

▶ **It will be a warmer winter at today's Tesco because...**

PRODUCT: *Supermarket foods*

Their lower prices will let us stock up on food and fuel
To beat the cold they've got things wrapped up
My hot tip is, they save you a packet
More money stays in your pocket after the weekly shop
At yesterday's prices I can afford to store more
For the food with the inner heat, Tesco is hard to beat

They ignite value that never puts you out
They've plenty of fuel to fill you up
Insulation instigation lowers bills and cuts down chills
With their prices turned down low, all the bargains glow
Tesco is hot on the best foods
You can take off your hat to RHM foods
Hot foot you will depart with many bargains that warm your heart
They sell all the food I seek – centrally eating – so to speak
They insulate the housekeeping against snowballing prices
Their foods are burning with energy at prices well insulated against inflation

▶ **I can beat the winter with Unichem...**

PRODUCT: Chemist goods
COMPETITION: Unichem Healthy times
PRIZES: Holiday vouchers: £2,000, £1,000 & £500

Cold gone, feeling fab, now needing a visa and jab
Autumn, winter, all year through, Unichem products look after you
Accessibility – no sweat, affordability – no debt, reliability – best yet

WITHOUT

▶ **A cupboard WITHOUT Uncle Ben's products is like...**

PRODUCT: Rices, sauces, stir-fry sauces
COMPETITION: Tesco/Uncle Ben's Olympic shell suit
PRIZES: Olympic shell suits

Chilli-con-carne without rice, uninteresting and not very nice
An athlete without dedication, both of these lack inspiration
Curry without rice, Torvill without Dean and strawberries without cream
Olympic Games without British gold – both leave me completely cold
Chilli sauce without a bean, an optimist without a dream
Pole vault without a pole, or stir-fry without bowl
Olympic contests without the flame – enjoyable, but not the same
The 'tabloids' without the 'Royals' – empty
A politician – full of promise, but no substance
A chilli con
Olympics without a track – 'Sprint' to Tesco then 'rice' back
A Greek Olympian who came Acropolis
Sprinting without Linford's power, or the sweet without the sour
Italy without pasta – a total disaster
A hostess who's off her trolley
Gold medals without any winners – plates without any mouth-watering dinners
The Olympics without medals or Chris Boardman's bike without pedals
Raleigh without Queen Bess or Nessie without Loch Ness

Olympics without gold – unbelievable; Tesco without Uncle Ben's – inconceivable
Wishing good cheer in pub with no beer
Winning a trip to the Olympics and losing your tickets
An extremely unpromising larder, making cooking success so much harder
Champagne without ice – curry without rice – a fool's paradise
An empty space – with 'Ben' unplaced, leaves a 'chilli' aftertaste
A week without the weekend – no 'stir-fri'day feeling
A wok without spice, Olympics without rice
An Olympic athlete without speed – Uncle Ben's he should feed
An Uncle Ben's shell suit without me in it
Unforgivable I say, off to Tesco straight away
A banquet without the guest of honour
Wimbledon without any strawberries
Mother Hubbard's kitchen space – off to Tesco I must race
Olympic torch without the flame, or pantomime without a dame
En'grain'ed with boredom, lacking spice, won't cook up anything nice
Lacking ingredients for a meal, with that 'Gold Medal' appeal
The Olympics without the gold or Tesco being undersold
England winning gold medals – they're both unlikely
Linford without his medal or Boardman without a pedal
Games without winners, pools without swimmers and plates without dinners
A dog without a bone or mum without a phone
An untrained athlete – fit for nothing
A gin and tonic without a gin
Spaghetti Bolognese without the meat, not as tasty and incomplete
Boardmans without his new bike – better go on hunger strike
A beanless chilli, utter despair, rice without curry, totally bare
A face without a smile
The Olympic Games without the flame, thoughtless, tasteless and mundane
A meal without its spice, something filling yet nothing nice
Racing without Sally Gunnell – a hurdle to a winning table

▶ **My breakfast would not be the same WITHOUT Marmite Yeast Extract or Frank Cooper's marmalade because...**

PRODUCT: Savoury spread and conserve
COMPETITION: Marmite Yeast Extract/Waldorf Hotel
PRIZES: Breakfast at the Waldorf Hotel

Grandpa loved 'em, so did dad, my breakfast favourites since I was a lad
It's the only breakfast that's worthwhile, combining taste, tradition, quality, and style
Without Cooper's or Marmite in the morning, breakfast should carry a low taste warning
Traditionally more British than most, they add the bite to my morning toast

RUNNERS-UP: Tefal four-slice toasters

I like to start my every day, in a top rate, first class, Waldorf way

For breakfast pleasure, use your loaf, indulge yourself, include them both

A few 'rounds' with them makes me feel champion

They have the taste I relish most, with early tea and slice of toast

My favourite spreads, tasting supreme, nutritious, delicious – a great breakfast team

Frank Cooper's is super, Marmite just right, perfection on toast to the very last bite

Frank Cooper's and Marmite we're agreed, makes a successful breakfast guaranteed

Marvellous 'my mate' and fruity Frank Cooper's, upgrade my breakfasts from so-so to super!

My family would throw daily dramatics, if breakfast didn't include these wonderful winning classics

No savoury goodness, no citrus zing? I may as well ignore the alarm clock's ring

Getting my gang moving is my mission, these two are my ammunition

Doubly delicious, doubly good, they start the day like breakfast should

These traditional accompaniments to buttered toast, are those that remind me of childhood the most

I've no desire to cruise the Med, I crave Marmite soldiers in a Waldorf bed!

Toast all golden or well done, with the best bit missing is not much fun!

An English breakfast is best, Frank Cooper's and Marmite have stood the test

This winning team grew to fame by putting quality behind their name

Tangy, tasty, money well spent, familiarity spreads content

Who needs awakening with a kiss, with a tangy twosome treat like this

WOMAN

▶ **The woman I admire the most is my mother because...**

PRODUCT: Woman

She may not have Jane Fonda's credentials but my loving mum's got all the essentials

She lovingly caters, she tenderly cares, she'd fill every box in celebrity squares

Good times, bad times, wrong or right, she's always loving, cheerful and bright

She puts heart and sole into her supporting role

As my close friend, my dearest chum, she's the greatest, she's my mum

She's the best Minister of Home Affairs

She's exciting to take out but nice to come home to

▶ **The woman we admire the most is our mother because...**

PRODUCT: Woman

Our fraternity think her maternity should be recognised from here to eternity
Her family comes first, this is quite clear, on duty 365 days of the year
She is a mini-mum with a maxi-mum of love
Home is just a house without her
She's my father's old china but our masterpiece
She's been in the 'Housetrap' for 24 years, such long running dedication
     deserves grateful cheers
She's gravy stirrer, tear repairer, Jill of all trades and master carer

WONDERLAND

▶ **Safeway is my shopping WONDERLAND because...**

PRODUCT: Supermarket foods

What Disney did for the silver screen, Safeway have done for the shopping
     scene
Off with their heads is Safeway's cry, if prices rise too high
It's the theme park that never takes me for a ride
Even Grumpy would grin at the treasures within
Even Alice wouldn't shrink at their prices
They always leave me cash in hand, not lost in Never Never Land
Tried other shops, pretty tragic, but Safeway value is really magic
Safeway value and Lady Luck, could lead me straight to Donald Duck
Only the Mad Hatter would shop anywhere else

WORLD

▶ **Avon is a WORLD beater because...**

PRODUCT: Avon cosmetics company
COMPETITION: Avon/Globeshoppers World Beaters
PRIZES: Trips to New York, Paris and London

Whether it's dollar, franc, or pound, there's no better value to be found
From North to South, East to West, Avon products are simply the best
Quality products is the name of the game, bringing 'global warming' to Avon's
     name
In New York, Paris, London or home, Avon cosmetics are a class on their own
Across the globe and to my door, it brings good value and ideas galore
Their message is one the world can share, quality, value and promise to care
There's lots of variety, plenty of choice, in worldwide matters, Avon has a voice
It speaks the international language of beauty whilst to the environment
     fulfilling its duty
Avon is the passport to the best, for quality goods that beat the rest

▶ **Asda shoppers think Ever Ready are out of this WORLD because...**

PRODUCT: Batteries

One looks for value when money is tight
They amaze the connoisseur, while their prices will attract the entrepreneur
Their prices are low and their staff rating is high

▶ **Marmite yeast extract is tasty anywhere in the WORLD because...**

PRODUCT: Savoury spread

There isn't a more delicious spread, within the four corners of my bread
When the menu's exotic, Marmite's patriotic
A familiar treat in an exotic location, sets the seal on a perfect vacation
Sushi's tasty, squid's alright, when in Rome make mine Marmite
The flavour that delighted Gran, still tastes great to a globe-trotting man
It can be enjoyed anywhere on the earth's crust
World scenes and climates alter, but Marmite's quality doesn't falter
It's the message in a bottle understood by every tongue
Wherever you are, whatever you do, one little jar will fortify you
It's available, it's instant and its taste is out of this world
That rich wholesome flavour for gravy or spread, a true family favourite
     wherever you tread
The earth's crust never goes to waste, spread with Marmite's tempting taste
Buttered bread, wherever eaten, spread with Marmite can't be beaten
Frogs legs? Birds nest? Do me a favour, Marmite's flavour is the one to savour
Its flavour spreads from coast to coast, to every corner of my toast
Over the Channel, Atlantic or Med, Marmite's the healthiest tastiest spread
A loaf of bread, a Marmite jar, brings instant happiness near or far
From Blackpool beach to Ivory Coast, Marmite goodness gets my toast
Jars of Marmite small and large, make every trip a 'bon voyage'
Wherever I suffer a hunger attack, it's a healthy convenient any time snack
Rio or Sydney, wherever you are, home is in the Marmite jar
Flavour from the little brown jar, appeals to folk both near and far
When battle's over, meals begin, Marmite soldiers always win
It spreads a smile on your soldier's face, so spread the word, spread the taste

ZEALOUS

▶ **ZEALOUS customers flock to the Co-op because...**

PRODUCT: Beds
COMPETITION: Co-op/Slumberland beds

They know they can feather their nest with a little down

BRAND NAMES, SHOPS AND STORES

A

AA (Automobile Association)
Abbey National (Building Society)
Abbey National (Instant Saver Account)
Access (Credit card)
Aero (Confectionery)
Agfa (Camera film)
Airwick (Air freshener)
Ajax (Cleaners, pan scourers)
Alcan Snappies (Cling film)
Alexander (Clothing)
Alexon (Designer wear)
Ambre Solaire (Sun tan lotion)
Ambrosia (Desserts)
American Express (Credit card, travellers' cheques)
Amstrad (Video recorders)
Anchor Half Fat (Low fat butter)
Andrex (Toilet rolls)
Anglia (Building Society)
Apt & Village (Food store)
Aquafresh (Toothpaste)
Aquamaster (Electric carpet cleaner)
Arai (Motor bike wear)
Araldite (Adhesive in sticks and tubes)
Argos (Catalogue, showrooms)
Ariel (Washing powder)
Aristoc (Tights)
Armitage (Dog cereal in bags)
Asda (Supermarket)
Asda Biological (Washing powder)
Asda Bunny Bags (Plastic bin bags)
Ashe & Nephew (Wine store)
Associated (Biscuits manufacturer)
Austin (Car)
Avon (Cosmetics company)

B

Babe (Perfume)
Band Aid (Plasters)
Barclaycard (Credit card)
BASF (Audio/video tapes)
BP (Garages, engine oil, service stations)
Bassett's (Liquorice Allsorts, sweets)
Batchelors (Food company)
Baxter's (French pâté)
Beanfeast (Packet meals)
Bees (Horticultural seeds)
Bejam (Supermarket)
Bell's (Whisky)
Belstaff (Specialist clothing shops)
Benson & Hedges (Cigarettes)
Berkeley (Cigarettes)
Berlitz (Language courses)
Bernard Matthews (Meats)
Berni Inn (Restaurant)
Biactol (Facial spot cleanser)
Bird's (Frozen food company)
Bisto (Gravy browning)
Blue Riband (Chocolate biscuit)
Blue Stratos (Aftershave, men's toiletries)
BMW (Car)
Bold (Washing powder)
Bols (Liqueur)
Bob (Food store)
Bonus (Dog food)
Boots (Chemist goods, holiday accessories, sports preparations)
Bordeaux/Bordeaux Superior (French wines)
Bosch (Spark plugs, electrical appliances)
Bowyers (Sausages)
BR (British Rail)

Braun (Electrical goods)
Breakaway (Chocolate biscuit)
British Airways (Airline)
British Leyland (Car manufacturer)
British Telecom (Communications)
Britvic (Fruit juices)
Brut (Aftershave)
Bubblicious (Bubble gum)
Budgens (Supermarket)
Budweiser (Beer)
Buitoni (Pasta)
Bunny Bags (Asda brand of plastic bags)
Burberry (Luggage)
Burnez Frères (Brandy)
Burniston (Caravans)
Butt Knit (Knitwear)

C

Cabana Blanca (Rum)
Cadbury's (Confectionery)
Campari (Vermouth)
Canberra (Cruise Ship)
Capital Radio (Radio broadcasting station)
Captain Morgan (Rum)
Carling Black Label (Lager)
Carlton Marco Polo (Men's toiletries)
Carpet Fresh (Dry carpet cleaner)
Carrefour (Supermarket)
Castlemaine XXXX (Lager)
Champney's (Health farm)
Charlie (Perfume)
Cheddar (English cheese)
Choicest Blend (Tea)
Cinzano (Vermouth)
Cirio (Canned tomatoes)
Citrice (Sparkling drink)
Clair (Air freshener)
Clairol (Hair care, hair colourant)
Claridges (Chain store)
Classic MGB Roadster (Car)
Clearasil (Medicated lotion, spot medication)
Climatube (Tube lighting)
Club (Chocolate biscuit)
Coalite (Coal)
Coca-Cola (Soft drink)
Cockspur (Rum)
Colman's (Sauces in boxes, wines in boxes)
Colt 45 (Lager)
Comet (Electrical store)
Commodore Amiga (Computer)
Co-op (Supermarket)
Co-op Bank (Top Tier High Interest Access Savings Account)
Co-op Leo's (Supermarket)
Co-op '99' (Tea)
Concorde (Aeroplane)
Concorde (Gardening books)
Corrido (Wine)
Cossack (Hair grooming)
Countryman (Bread)
Cover Girl (Cosmetics)
Cow & Gate (Baby food manufacturer)
Crown (Paint in tins)
Crunchie (Confectionery)
Cunard (Shipping line)
Currys (Electrical store)
Cussons Imperial Leather (Soap)
Cussons Pearl (Soap)
Cuthbert (Horticultural seeds)
Cystemme (Beauty care)

D

Daler-Rowney (Artists' materials)

Danish (Bacon)
Daz (Washing powder)
Decca (Electrical appliances)
Del Monte (Canned fruit)
Dentyne (Chewing gum)
DER/Lufthansa (Airline)
Dettol (Disinfectant)
Dewhurst (Master butchers)
Dextrosol (Glucose tablets)
Diamond (Walnuts)
Diamond Blush (Pink cider)
Diamond White (White cider)
Diet Coke (Soft drink)
Diet 7 Up (Diet drink)
Dime Bar (Confectionery)
Discount for Beauty (Beauty shop goods)
Dixons Ltd (Electrical and photographic goods)
Dole (Dried fruit)
Dolmio (Pasta sauce)
Double Decker (Confectionery)
Douwe Egberts (Filter coffee, coffee filters)
Drakkoir Noire (Aftershave)
Dream Topping (Synthetic cream for desserts)
Dry Fly (Sherry)
Dry Magic (Dry carpet cleaner)
Dubonnet (Cocktail mixer)
Duplo (Toys)
Dutch Royal Crest (Bacon)
Durex (Contraceptives)

E

Easy-On (Spray starch)
Eclairs (Confectionery)
Edam (Dutch cheese)
Eden Vale (Dairy products manufacturer)
Electrolux (Electric carpet cleaner)
Elizabeth Shaw (Confectionery)
Emmenthal (Swiss cheese)
Eurocheques (Travellers' cheques)
Ever Ready (Batteries)
Expert (Books)

F

Fairy (Washing-up liquid)
Famous Grouse (Whisky)
Farmhouse (Sausages)
Fenjal (Swiss bath oil)
Fiat (Car)
Fidelity Telecentre (Electrical goods)
Fiesta (Paper towels)
Filetti (Swiss washing powder)
Findus (Findus Calorie Counters: Low calorie frozen meals, Findus Double Deckers: Potato/meat fritters)
Fine Fare (Supermarket)
Fisons (Garden soil in bags)
Flake (Confectionery)
Flash (Cleaner)
Food Giant (Supermarket)
Forbuoys (Newsagents goods)
Ford (Car manufacturer)
Ford Sierra (Car)
Foster Grant (Sunglasses)
Foster's (Lager)
Frank Cooper's (Marmalade)
Freshtex (Moist Tissues)
Frosties (Breakfast cereal)
Fry's Cream Bar (Confectionery)
Fuji (Camera film)
Fundador (Brandy)

G

Galaxy (Confectionery)

Gancia (Sparkling wine)
Gateway (Supermarket)
Gaymer's Norfolk (Cider)
Gaz (Camping Equipment)
GEC (General Electric Company)
Ginger Loaf (Cake)
Girobank (Bank)
Glade (Air freshener)
Gleneagles (Golf club)
Glenmorangie (Whisky)
Gloucester (English cheese)
Goldbergs (Chemist goods)
Golden Wonder (Snacks)
Gouda (Dutch cheese)
Grandways (Supermarket)
Graham and Brown (D.I.Y. materials)
Graham's (Port)
Great Mills (D.I.Y. store)
Greenup (Lawn feed)
Gruyère (Swiss cheese)
Guinness (Beer)

H

Hale Trent (Cakes manufacturer)
Halifax (Building Society)
Halifax TESSA (Savings account)
Hamilton (D.I.Y. materials)
Harpic (Disinfectant, toilet cleaner)
Harvest (Bread)
Harvest Bran (Breakfast cereal)
Haven (Dried fruit)
Haze (Air freshener)
Healthcraft (Vitamin tablets)
Heinz (Food company)
Hellmann's (Mayonnaise)
Henlow Grange (Health farm)
Henri Wintermans (Cigars)
Henry Morgan (Rum)
High Definition (Foundation make-up)
Hillards (Supermarket)
Hilton (Hotel chain)
Holsten Pils (Beer)
Honda (Car)
Honeywell (Plumbing materials)
Horlicks (Malt drink)
Hot Cross Buns (Bread buns)
Hotpoint (Electrical appliances)
Hoover (Electrical appliances)
Hoover Logic 1200 (Washing machine)
House of Frazer (Chain store)
Hovis (Bread, crackers, cream crackers)
HP (Brown sauce)
Huggy Bear (Safety regulations)
Huntley & Palmer (Biscuits manufacturer)
Hush Puppies (Shoes)
Hyatt (Hotel chain)
Hyundai (Car)

I

Imperial Leather Classic (Toilet soap)
Impulse (Perfumed body spray)
Index (Catalogue, showrooms)
Insight (Pocket guide)
Intense (Perfume)
International Stores (Supermarket)

J

J Cloth (Cleaning cloth)
Jacob's (Biscuits, crackers, Club biscuits, savoury snacks)
Jaeger (Knitwear)
Jarrold (Wall calendars)
Jet (Toilet cleaner)
Jet Ski (Watercraft)
Jeyes (Cleaners, disinfectant)
Jeyes Bloo (Cleaner, toilet freshener)
John Menzies (Newsagents goods)
John Player Special (Cigarettes)
John West (Canned fish)
Johnsons Glade (Air freshener)
Johnson Pledge (Furniture polish)
Johnsons Sparkle (Cleaner)
Johnson's (Baby care)
Johnston's (French cookery courses)
Journey (Aftershave)

Journey Club (Season ticket for travel)
JVC (Video tapes)

K

Karrimore (Jackets)
Kayser (Stockings, tights)
Kellogg's (Breakfast cereals)
Kenco (Coffee, filter coffee)
Kerrygold (Butter)
Kestrel (Lager)
Kew Farm Fresh (Food store)
Kia-Ora (Fruit squash)
KiteKat (Cat food)
Kiwi (Shoe polish)
Kleenex (Travel tissues)
Knorr (Sauces in packets, packet soups)
Kodak (Camera film)
Kodak colour check (Photographic processing service)
Kosset (Carpet company)
KP (Crisps, mini chips, nuts)
Kraft (Processed cheese slices)
Krona (Margarine)
Kwik Save (Supermarket)

L

Labatt's (Lager)
Ladbrokes (Betting shops)
Ladycare (Ladies' vitamins)
Lancers (Wine)
Lancôme (Skin care)
Landmark (Cash & Carry warehouses)
Lee (Denim jeans)
Leeds Permanent (Building Society, Travel Money Service)
Leicester (English cheese)
Lennons (Food store)
Levi's (Denim jeans)
Lil-lets (Tampons)
Lilt (Soft drink)
Little Chef (Motorway restaurant)
Littlewoods (Chain store)
Loctite (Adhesive)
Loloball (Toy ball)
Longboat (Butter)
L'Oréal (Hair care)
Lucozade (Glucose drink)
Lyle's (Golden Syrup)
Lynx (Men's toiletries)
Lyons (Cake, coffee, tea)
Lypsyl (Lip salve)

M

Macleans (Toothpaste)
Maestro (Car)
Maltesers (Confectionery)
Marathon (Confectionery)
Mardi Gras (Cocktail drink)
Marigold (Household gloves)
Marlboro (Cigarettes)
Marmite (Savoury spread)
Mars (Confectionery, ice cream)
Martin Lavells (Newsagents goods)
Martini (Vermouth)
Marvel (Low fat dried milk)
Maryland Cookies (Biscuits)
Mastercard (Credit card)
Mateus Rosé (Wine)
Mayfair (Cigarettes)
Mazda (Electric light bulbs)
Mazda Softglow (Electric light bulbs)
MB (Board games manufacturer)
Maclaren (Baby buggies)
McDougalls (Flour)
McEwan's (Lager)
McVities (Biscuit manufacturer)
Medicare (Shampoo)
Melitta (Coffee filters, Filter coffee)
Metamec (Clocks)
MFP (Records)
Memorex (Rechargeable batteries)
Mercury (Communications)
Metro (Car)
MGT (Car)
Michelob (Beer)

Midshires (Building Society)
Midshires TESSA (Savings account)
Miele (Electrical appliances)
Mills & Boon (Books)
Milupa (Baby foods)
Minima Bodyform (Sanitary towels)
Mini Mayfair (Car)
Mini Metro (Car)
Mini Sprite (Car)
Miralec (Electric showers)
Moët & Chandon (Champagne)
Moffatt (Cookers)
Monergy (Energy-saving scheme)
Morning Fresh (Washing-up liquid)
Morrisons (Supermarket)
Moulinex (Electrical appliances, microwave ovens)
Mr Bassett's (Confectionery)
Mr Kipling (Cakes)
Mr Sheen (Cleaner)
Mrs Peeks (Christmas puddings)
Mum Solid (Ladies' deodorant)
Murco (Service station)

N

NASA (National Aeronautics and Space Administration)
Nabisco (Biscuits manufacturer)
Nair (Depilatory cream)
Napolina (Pasta)
National Trust (British Heritage Trust)
Neighbours (Australian TV soap opera)
Neville Johnson (Kitchen units)
Nevins (Food store)
New York (Burgers)
New Zealand Lamb (Meat)
Nik Naks (Snacks)
'99' (Co-op tea)
Nisa (Food store)
Norfolk (Cider)
Norwest Co-op (Supermarket)
Nova Carlton (Car)
Nulon (Hand cream)
Numark (Chemist goods)
Nuttall's (Mints)

O

Oakland (Men's clothing)
Obo Seals (Plumbing accessories)
Ocean Spray (Cranberry sauce)
Old Dutch (Pipe tobacco)
Old Spice (Aftershave)
1001 (Liquid carpet cleaner)
Optrex (Eye wash)
Orchid (Travel Agents)
Orient Express (Victorian train)
Osram (Electric light bulbs)
Oxo (Stock cube)
Oxy Clean (Medicated facial cleanser)
Oz (Limescale cleaner)

P

Palmolive (Skin care)
Pampers Phases (Disposable nappies)
Panasonic (Electrical goods)
Panda (Car)
Paramount (Film studio)
Parlour Maid (Ice cream)
Pedigree Chum (Dog food)
Pepsi Cola (Soft drink)
Percy Daltons (Monkey nuts)
Perrier (Mineral water)
Perrize (Sparkling drink)
Persil (Washing powder)
Peter Dominic (Wine store)
Peugeot (Bicycles)
Pez Candy (Sweets)
Philips (Electrical goods, hairdryers, shavers)
Philishave (Shaver)
Pickfords (Removal firm)
Pierre Cardin Pour Monsieur (Aftershave)
Piz Buin (Sun tan lotion)
Planters (Peanuts)
Playtex (Ladies' lingerie)
Pledge (Furniture polish)

Plumrose (Canned meats)
Pomagne (Sparkling wine)
Pommy (Frozen chips)
Pop (Bubble gum)
Porkinson (Sausages)
Porsche (Car)
Post Office (Aerogrammes)
Preedy (Newsagents goods)
Prestige (Pans)
Presto (Supermarket)
Pretty Polly (Stockings, tights)
Princes (Canned fish, canned vegetables, fish
       pastes, fruit, fruit juices, meats, meat
       pastes, pâtés, sandwich spreads)
Proton (Car)
Pure & Simple (Cleansing lotions and soap)
Pye (Hi-fi equipment)

Q

Quaker Oats (Harvest Crunch, porridge)
Quality Street (Confectionery)
Quickies (Make-up remover pads)
Quorum (Aftershave)

R

RAC (Royal Automobile Club)
Racasan (Air freshener, toilet cleaner)
Radox (Bath salts)
Ragdale Hall (Health farm)
Ragu (Pasta sauce)
Raleigh (Bicycles)
Ready Brek (Porridge)
Reala (Camera film)
Reckitt & Colman (Cleaning products, sauces)
Red Rock (Cider)
Renault 5 (Car)
Revlon (Cosmetics)
Rexel (Wall planners)
Ribena (Fruit juices)
Ridder (Norwegian cheese)
Ritter Sport (Confectionery)
Ritz (Hotel chain)
Ritz Crackers (Wheat crackers)
Robertson's (Conserves)
Robinsons (Fruit juices)
RoC (Skin care)
Rolls Royce (British car company)
Ronseal (Wood stains, wood varnishes)
Roses (Confectionery)
Rothmans (Cigarettes)
Rover Metro (Car)
Rowenta (Cordless vacuum cleaners, irons)
Rowntree's Nestlé (Confectionery)
RSPB (Royal Society for the Protection of
       Birds)
R. Whites (Lemonade)
Royal Doulton (Fine china)
Rumbelows (Electrical store)
Rye-King (Crispbread)

S

Sadolin (Wood preservative)
Safeway (Supermarket)
Sainsbury's (Supermarket)
Salter (Digital weighing scales)
Sandeman (Port)
San Miguel (Lager)
Sanyo (Music equipment)
Sassoon, Vidal (Hair care)
Savlon Dry (Antiseptic cream)
Savoury & Moore (Supermarket)
Savoy (Hotel chain)
Scatch (Board game)
Scholl (Pedicure items, support tights,
       stockings)
Schwartz (Spices)
Schweppes (Soft drinks)

Schweppes Russchian (Mixer for Vodka)
Scottish Salmon (Fish)
Seat Marbella (Car)
Selfridges (Chain store)
Sergio Tacchini (Aftershave)
Sharp (Hi-fi equipment)
Sharwood's (Chutneys and spices)
Sheep Dip (Whisky)
Shield (Soap)
Shippams (Fish and meat pastes)
Shredded Wheat (Breakfast cereal)
Shreddies (Breakfast cereal)
Sikkens Masterstroke (Wood varnishes, wood
       sealant, varnishes)
Silk Cut (Cigarettes)
Silkience (Shampoo)
Silvikrin (Shampoo)
Skol (Lager)
Sky (Satellite TV)
Slumberland (Beds)
Smirnoff (Vodka)
Snappies (Cling film)
Snickers Bar (Confectionery)
Soft & Gentle (Ladies' deodorant)
Sony (Audio/video tapes, camcorders, music
       accessories, Watchman pocket TVs)
Soreen (Fruit malt loaf)
Spar (Food store)
Sparkle (Cleaner)
Spillers (Dog food manufacturer)
Stag (Furniture)
Stanley (D.I.Y tools)
Stick-Up (Air freshener)
Stilton (Cheese)
Strollers (Confectionery)
Sucron (Sugar substitute)
Sudmilch (Desserts)
Sugar Puffs (Breakfast cereal)
Sun Country (Wine)
Sun Maid (Dried fruit)
Sunlight (Washing-up liquid)
Sunquick (Fruit squash)
Superdrug (Superstore)
Sutherlands (Fish and meat pastes)
Suzuki (Motor bikes)
Swan Vestas (Boxed matches)
Swish (Curtain tracks)

T

Tampax (Tampons)
Tates (Food store)
Teatime (Biscuits)
Tefal (Electrical goods, heated trays, non-stick
       surfaces)
Tellybags (TV snacks)
Tennent's (Lager)
Tesco (Supermarket)
Tesco British (Meat pies)
Tetley (Bitter)
Tetley (Tea)
Texas Homecare (D.I.Y. store)
Thomas Cook (Travel Agents, travellers'
       cheques)
Thorntons (Confectionery, toffee)
3M (Spray adhesive)
Tia Maria (Coffee liqueur)
Tiffany (Bathroom suites)
Timex (Watches)
Toffifee (Confectionery)
Toilet Duck (Toilet cleaner)
Tom Caxton (Home brewing kits)
Tommee Tippee (Toys)
Toys 'R' Us (Superstore)
Trex (Cooking fat)
Trill (Bird seed)
Trio (Chocolate biscuit)
Trust House Forte (Hotel chain)

Tru-tile (Tiling grout)
Twist 'n' Squeeze (Fruit drinks)
Twix (Confectionery)
2CV6 (Car)

U

Ultrabrite (Toothpaste)
Uncle Ben's (Rice, sauces, stir-fry sauces)
Unibond (Adhesive, wood sealant)
Unichem (Chemist goods)
Unipart (Car parts)
Universal (Film studio)
Unwins (Food store)
Unwins (Horticultural seeds)

V

Value Stores (Food store)
Van Den Berghs (Food manufacturer)
Vanish (Cleaner)
Van Nelle (Filter coffee)
Varta (Batteries)
VDQS (Wine store)
Vendona (Coffee)
VG (Food store)
Vichy (Skin care products)
Victoria (Wine store)
Vidor (Batteries)
Vigor (Cleaner)
Vileda (Cleaning cloths)
Virgin Atlantic (Airline)
Visco 2000 (Engine oil)
Viscount (Chocolate biscuits)
Vitbe (Bread)
Volvo (Car)
Vosene (Shampoo)

W

Waistline (Low calorie salad cream)
Waldorf (Hotel chain)
Wall's (Meat pies, microwave sausages,
       sausages)
Wall's Viennetta (Ice cream dessert)
Wavy Line (Food store)
Weetabix (Breakfast cereal)
Weight Watchers (Low calorie foods)
Wet Ones (Moist tissues)
White Horse (Whisky)
Whiteways (Wine store)
Whites, R. (Lemonade)
Whitworths (Dried fruit)
Whyte & Mackay (Whisky)
Wilkinson Sword (Blades and razors)
Wm Low (Supermarket)
Willow (Butter)
Wilton (Carpets)
Windolene (Cleaner)
Wintermans (Cigars)
Wintermans, Henri (Cigars)
Wispa (Confectionery)
Wolf (D.I.Y. tools)
Woolworths (Chain store)
Wrigley's (Chewing gum)

X

XR3 (Car)
XR3i (Car)
XR4i (Car)

Y

Yamaha (Musical organs)
Yeoman (Dried mashed potato)
Yorkie (Confectionery)

Z

Zamoyski Warsawthis (Polish vodka)
Zanussi (Electrical appliances)

GENERAL INDEX

HERE'S YOUR CHANCE TO PUT YOUR "COMPING" SKILLS TO THE TEST WITH THE OPPORTUNITY TO WIN A FREE COPY OF EVERY BOOK PUBLISHED BY GUINNESS IN 1994 – A PRIZE WORTH OVER £600! THERE ARE 10 RUNNERS-UP PRIZES OF THE 1995 GUINNESS BOOK OF RECORDS, EACH PERSONALLY SIGNED BY NORRIS McWHIRTER.

YOUR

PERSONAL

LIBRARY

FROM

GUINNESS

To enter, simply answer a, b or c with your completed tie-breaker on the form below and send it to:-

Slogan Competition
Guinness Publishing
33 London Road
Enfield
Middlesex EN2 6DJ.

1 According to the Guinness Book of Records, which is the tallest building in the world?
 a Empire State Building
 b Sears Tower
 c World Trade Centre

2 Which racquet sport is featured on the cover of this book?
 a Squash
 b Badminton
 c Tennis

3 Which artist spent the most consecutive weeks at No. 1 in the UK charts?
 a Bryan Adams
 b Whitney Houston
 c Bing Crosby

Answers to above: *(tick correct box)* **Q.1** a ☐ b ☐ c ☐ **Q.2** a ☐ b ☐ c ☐ **Q.3** a ☐ b ☐ c ☐

Tie-Breaker: (complete in fifteen words or less) I'm always a winner with Guinness Books because:

....

....

Name: ....

Address: ....

....

Postcode: .... Date: ....

Closing date for entries are: 30th September 1994 & 31st January 1995

As this book will be available throughout the year, the organisers feel that two slogan competitions should be held, therefore all entries received after the 30th September 1994 will be automatically entered into the second competition.

rules

AND

CONDITIONS

1 Entries on this application form only

2 Only one entry per person

3 Entries from persons under 18 must be accompanied with a signature from a parent or guardian

4 Closing date is **30th September 1994** for the first competition and **31st January 1995** for the second

5 The entrant who correctly answers the three questions and completes the tie-breaker in the most original way, in the opinion of the judges, will be the winner

6 Winners will be notified and/or prizes despatched in October 1994 for the first competition and February 1995 for the second

7 Value of first prize is £650 approximately

8 Value of Runners-up prize £14.99

9 A list of winners names and addresses will be available from the competition organisers from October 1994 and February 1995

10 **The decision of the Panel of Judges (which will contain at least one independent member) will be final.** Correspondence will be entered into only at the absolute discretion of Guinness Publishing Limited

11 Limited to UK residents. Competition not open to employees of Guinness plc, associated companies or their families

12 Entries altered, illegible or insufficiently completed will be disqualified

13 There is no cash alternative

14 Proof of posting is not accepted as proof of delivery

15 Copyright in winning tie-breakers will become the property of Guinness Publishing Limited who reserve the right to publish them

MEDIEVAL ENGLISH ROMANCE IN CONTEXT

Edinburgh University Library

Books may be recalled for return earlier than due date:

Texts and Contexts
Series Editors: Gail Ashton and Fiona McCulloch

Texts and Contexts is a series of clear, concise and accessible introductions to key literary fields and concepts. The series provides the literary, critical, historical context for texts and authors in a specific literary area in a way that introduces a range of work in the field and enables further independent study and reading.

Other titles available in the series:
Postcolonial Literatures in Context, Julie Mullaney
The Victorian Novel in Context, Grace Moore